Contextualizing Angela Davis

Bloomsbury Introductions to World Philosophies

Series Editor:
Monika Kirloskar-Steinbach

Assistant Series Editor:
Leah Kalmanson

Regional Editors:
Nader El-Bizri, James Madaio, Ann A. Pang-White, Takeshi Morisato, Pascah
Mungwini, Mickaella Perina, Omar Rivera and Georgina Stewart

Bloomsbury Introductions to World Philosophies delivers primers reflecting
exciting new developments in the trajectory of world philosophies. Instead of
privileging a single philosophical approach as the basis of comparison, the series
provides a platform for diverse philosophical perspectives to accommodate the
different dimensions of cross-cultural philosophizing. While introducing thinkers,
texts and themes emanating from different world philosophies, each book, in an
imaginative and path-breaking way, makes clear how it departs from a conventional
treatment of the subject matter.

Titles in the Series:
A Practical Guide to World Philosophies, by Monika Kirloskar-Steinbach and
Leah Kalmanson
Daya Krishna and Twentieth-Century Indian Philosophy, by Daniel Raveh
Māori Philosophy, by Georgina Tuari Stewart
Philosophy of Science and the Kyoto School, by Dean Anthony Brink
Tanabe Hajime and the Kyoto School, by Takeshi Morisato
African Philosophy, by Pascah Mungwini
The Zen Buddhist Philosophy of D. T. Suzuki, by Rossa Ó Muireartaigh
Sikh Philosophy, by Arvind-Pal Singh Mandair
The Philosophy of the Brahma-sūtra, by Aleksandar Uskokov
The Philosophy of the Yogasūtra, by Karen O'Brien-Kop
The Life and Thought of H. Odera Oruka, by Gail M. Presbey
Mexican Philosophy for the 21st Century, by Carlos Alberto Sánchez
Buddhist Ethics and the Bodhisattva Path, by Stephen Harris
Intercultural Phenomenology, by Yuko Ishihara and Steven A. Tainer

Contextualizing Angela Davis

The Agency and Identity of an Icon

Joy James

BLOOMSBURY ACADEMIC
LONDON • NEW YORK • OXFORD • NEW DELHI • SYDNEY

BLOOMSBURY ACADEMIC
Bloomsbury Publishing Plc
50 Bedford Square, London, WC1B 3DP, UK
1385 Broadway, New York, NY 10018, USA
29 Earlsfort Terrace, Dublin 2, Ireland

BLOOMSBURY, BLOOMSBURY ACADEMIC and the Diana logo
are trademarks of Bloomsbury Publishing Plc

First published in Great Britain 2024

Series design by Louise Dugdale
Cover image © AZBIDSGNX / Adobe Stock

A catalogue record for this book is available from the British Library.

A catalog record for this book is available from the Library of Congress.

ISBN: HB: 978-1-3503-6862-0
         PB: 978-1-3503-6863-7
       ePDF: 978-1-3503-6864-4
      eBook: 978-1-3503-6865-1

Series: Bloomsbury Introductions to World Philosophies

Typeset by Integra Software Services Pvt. Ltd.
Printed and bound in Great Britain

To find out more about our authors and books visit www.bloomsbury.com
and sign up for our newsletters.

Contents

Series Editor Preface

The introductions we include in the World Philosophies series take a single thinker, theme, or text and provide a close reading of them. What defines the series is that these are likely to be people or traditions that you have not yet encountered in your study of philosophy. By choosing to include them you broaden your understanding of ideas about the self, knowledge, and the world around us. Each book presents unexplored pathways into the study of world philosophies. Instead of privileging a single philosophical approach as the basis of comparison, each book accommodates the many different dimensions of cross-cultural philosophizing. While the choice of terms used by the individual volumes may indeed carry a local inflection, they encourage critical thinking about philosophical plurality. Each book strikes a balance between locality and globality.

Contextualizing Angela Davis interprets the biography of Angela Y. Davis in the light of transformative moments in contemporary US-American and world history. The volume offers a unique multilayered analysis of the life and theory of this icon within this framing. Furthermore, it brings its interpretation of this history to bear on the present. These ruminations consider how the collective losses of the recent past can be rendered meaningful such that more tangible gains in freedom and justice can be secured moving forward.

Preface

Cold War as Context

An Introduction to Angela Davis

I was introduced to Angela Davis during the Cold War. The introduction was made at a Manhattan women's conference by the leadership of WREE—Women for Racial & Economic Equality. A doctoral student—studying political philosophy in New York City and writing on Hannah Arendt—I organized in my spare time against racism, sexism, homophobia, police/state violence, and militarism. I worked with various groups, from Black internationalist radicals to feminist formations, womxn dojos and WREE. Then, there were three worlds—some struggling for autonomy, others for continued conquest. After 1991, there would be only one world, that of US hegemony. $\rightarrow$ *fall of Soviet Union* We would be forced to shape our political imaginations into one "pragmatic" construct or context. I met Davis while engaged in political organizing in NYC, Nairobi, Moscow, and Alabama in a march and vigil for Johnny Imani Harris, who was on death row.[1]

The Soviet Union, or Union of Soviet Socialist Republics (USSR), dissolved during the Reagan administration, which funded terrorist "contras" and death squads to crush Third World socialist, trade unionist, and liberation movements. Visiting refugee camps for Salvadorian resisters introduced me to the low-intensity warfare championed by Henry Kissinger, Zbigniew Brzezinski, and others,[2] and funded by US taxpayers. The deaths and carnage were highly intense. Within the interlocking tiers of First, Second, and Third Worlds—before drone strikes became the weapon of choice—I learned from Black and white communist women in the Communist Party USA (CPUSA) and Black internationalists how to think strategically and contextually.

The world in which I met Davis was one of nuclear proliferation, close scrutiny of facts, and face-to-face meetings with resisters with bold platforms and crisp acronyms: PLO, SWAPO, ANC, FMLN—all supported by Cuba, and thus all supported by the Soviet Union, which played a significant role in elevating Angela Davis to the global public. WREE was an affiliate of the CPUSA and a branch of the Eastern European-based Women's International Democratic Federation (WIDF). In a high school auditorium in Manhattan, I sat in a cramped seat at the WREE conference to listen to the keynote speaker, Professor Angela Davis, give her address. WREE also introduced me to Charlene Mitchell, who mentored Davis and invited her to join the CPUSA through the Che-Lumumba Club. Mitchell lived in Harlem, and we occasionally met in NYC; we would also meet a few times in California when I had a Ford Foundation postdoc to study with Davis at UC Santa Cruz in the 1990s.

PLO – Palestine Liberation Organization
ANC – African National Congress → SA Anti-Apartheid group
SWAPO – South West Africa Peoples' Organisation (Namibia independence party)
FMLN – Farabundo Marti National Liberation Front (Salvadorian rebel group)

I had also worked as a WREE delegate with Davis at the 1985 UN Conference on Women in Nairobi, Kenya.[3] Our delegation gathered signatures for a petition against poverty, nuclear weapons, and military budgets, and for a women's and children's bill of rights. Staying at the WIDF compound during the 1985 conference on the UN Decade of Women, Davis and I greeted armed Kenyan guards with assault weapons as we entered and exited the compound of high-profile women who were intel and guerrilla fighters battling fascists in the Second World War, and later countering contras, mercenaries, and occupations. Female leadership from the organizations largely criminalized by the United States included representatives from the ANC, SWAPO, FMLN, and PLO. We were housed in the same quarters as diplomats, human rights advocates of the First, Second, and Third Worlds, and the freedom movements against contras or apartheid mercenaries in the present day. I remember organizing a memorial at a building of a UN NGO for Dulcie September, the anti-apartheid activist assassinated in Paris, France, in 1988. The WIDF hosted an international peace conference that same year in Moscow; I sat in the cavernous hall and watched Davis sit in an upper tier seat on stage. I imagined that Mikhail Gorbachev's growing alliance with President Ronald Reagan would mean that she would not speak at the microphone (Davis and Reagan had been antagonists since 1969, when he had had the Regents fire her from teaching at UCLA; then, most egregiously, in 1971, Reagan sought for her to receive the death penalty for the August 7, 1970, Marin County Courthouse tragedies). In the 1990s, my postdoc—Ford Foundation was influenced and funded by the Central Intelligence Agency (CIA) during the Cold War—enabled me not only to spend a year with Professor Davis at the History of Consciousness Program but also to later collect papers to edit into *The Angela Y. Davis Reader,* which would be published in 1998.

Three World Wars

Karl Marx's philosophy was repurposed by intellectual V. I. Lenin following the 1917 Russian Revolution, sparked by traumatized, disgruntled, and defeated soldiers returning home from the First World War, as well as peasant and laboring women unable to feed their children; their uprisings brought Lenin back from exile. Lenin founded the Communist Party of the Soviet Union (CPSU); he died from a blood disease in 1924. Marx and Engels's theories were disfigured by the dictator Josef Stalin, who ruled the USSR from 1929 to 1953. The Third Reich invaded the Soviet Union, violating a non-aggression pact the Soviets had signed in order to stave off an invasion.[4] Without the support of the Allies—Winston Churchill of Britain and Franklin D. Roosevelt of the United States—the Soviets went to war and would lose some 20 million lives but defeat Hitler's armies. The day after the Nazi invasion into the USSR, Mao Tse-tung offered solidarity; he wrote the June 23, 1941, directive for the Central Committee of the Communist Party of China, "On the International United Front against Fascism":

> [T]he fascist rulers of Germany attacked the Soviet Union. This is a perfidious crime of aggression not only against the Soviet Union but against the freedom and

independence of all nations. The Soviet Union's sacred war of resistance against fascist aggression is being waged not only in its own defence but in defence of all the nations struggling to liberate themselves from fascist enslavement.

For Communists throughout the world the task now is to mobilize the people of all countries and organize an international united front to fight fascism and defend the Soviet Union, defend China, and defend the freedom and independence of all nations. In the present period, every effort must be concentrated on combating fascist enslavement.[5]

For Mao, the Chinese Communist Party had three tasks: use its National United Front against Japan to aid the Soviets and "drive the Japanese imperialists out of China"; battle "anti-Soviet and anti-Communist activities of the reactionaries among the big bourgeoisie"; and "unite against the common foe" with Britain, the United States, and other countries determined to defeat the Axis powers—fascistic Germany, Italy, and Japan.[6] The Allies defeated the Axis powers; in 1945, the United States dropped atomic bombs on Japan's Hiroshima and Nagasaki and declared the end of the Second World War. That is, the formal war had ended.

In 1953, Khrushchev promoted the concept of peaceful coexistence to defuse escalation between the Soviet Union and the United States, the only nation with the atomic bomb. By 1956, peaceful coexistence was the basis of Soviet foreign policy even as it funded Third World liberation struggles against colonialism and racism. The CPSU pragmatically held to "peaceful coexistence"[7] as the United States and NATO waged brutal counterrevolutionary wars against Third World freedom struggles.

The context for understanding the politicization of leftists of that student era is warfare. In the post–Second World War era, anti-colonial struggles destabilized the old order of European hegemony. There were three worlds: the First World of Western European nations and the United States, and their allies; the Second World of the communist bloc of the Soviet Union; and the Third World of racially denigrated and exploited territories and nations, the so-called non-whites in Africa, Asia, the Middle East, and the Americas. Military domination, extraction of indigenous wealth and labor, and oppression through financial strangulation and manipulated markets had been the rule for colonization. But rule over colonies created by Western Europeans fell apart. As the premier capitalist nation, the United States would assert itself as the domineering empire, taking over from Great Britain. The USSR manifested as the antithesis to the United States. The Soviet Union presented and postured in Eastern Europe as an alternative to capitalism and imperialism. Internationally, it provided educational training and material support to formerly colonized nations seeking to break the repressive holds of colonial regimes from the United States and Western Europe. The North Atlantic Treaty Organization (NATO) was formed to hinder anti-colonial struggles and Soviet influence and to stabilize racial capitalism, which expanded through slavery and genocide. Communists believed that they had the political will and capacity to unseat a racially-fashioned empire. They organized in political units and in familial units.

Before the United States entered the Second World War, the Western capitalist countries refused to form an alliance with the Soviet Union against the Nazis, forcing Stalin to sign the Molotov-Soviet Pact of nonaggression.[8] Communists were anti-capitalists. Nazis as pro-capitalists studied the US systems of racial subjugation of Indigenous and Black people. "Sympathetic" to Nazis and fascism and hostile to communists before the Third Reich invaded them, Western nations, the FBI, and the CIA monitored communications and intellectual connections between US Black activists and Third World anti-colonial movements. Radicals—and military/police intelligence officers—were reading Marx and Engels's *The Communist Manifesto*; *Collected Works of Lenin*; Lenin's *What Is to Be Done?*; *The Selected Works of Mao Tse-tung*; *Malcolm X Speaks*; *The Autobiography of Malcolm X*; and Frantz Fanon's *The Wretched of the Earth*.

Third World Liberation movements were linked to, but also distinct from, Soviet struggles in Eastern Europe. Antagonists against racial colonization opposed capitalism but grappled with imperialism throughout the three "worlds." Also in struggle were/are Indigenous and enslaved or ostracized populations within these sectors. The internal colony of the United States would have been the Black and Indigenous and Puerto Rican populations—hence the formations, respectively, of the Black Panther Party, American Indian Movement, and the Young Lords and Chicano Movement.

CPSU/CPUSA

The CPSU/CPUSA embraced Lenin's 1913 *Critical Remarks on the National Question*, theorizing Black Americans as an "internal colony" until the 1930s. The CPUSA then was becoming one of the rare US organizations in the twentieth century where Blacks, whites, and "people of color" could socially intermingle as they organized against labor exploitation, racism, and war. The CPUSA became an imperfect, but stable, surrogate "political family" for besieged Black Americans who desired to work within a multiracial formation with international networks. The CPUSA made significant contributions in labor organizing, legal defense for persecuted communities, and human rights advocacy. Persecuted for decades since its founding in 1919, two years after the Bolshevik Revolution in Russia, the CPUSA would steer millions into human rights advocacy, through labor activism, and creating or supporting organizations linked to the CPUSA and sometimes distanced from its communist profile.[9] During the first decades of the twentieth century, in its heyday of hundreds of thousands of fellow travelers and party members, the CPUSA worked to address political repression and police brutality. US communist activists and unionists "lived, worked, and sometimes died with miners in Appalachia, farm workers in California, steel workers in Pittsburgh."[10] The CPUSA built financial, ideological, and educational networks with the International Workers Order, the National Negro Congress, and Unemployment Councils. As a "dues-paying member of the Comintern (the International Communist organization run from Moscow)," the CPUSA also prioritized Moscow's domestic and foreign policies.[11] That did not deter pragmatic

Black activists from forming alliances with or joining the CPUSA to fight against legacies of enslavement and Confederate power. Having for decades weathered the "red scare" and McCarthyism, CPUSA survived COINTELPRO; its membership suffered loss of employment, imprisonment, social isolation through anti-communist hysteria. The CPSU, though, offered funding and haven if needed and stabilized the party. Peaceful coexistence would also help.

In 1956, what conservatives and anti-communists had alleged became accepted "fact" in the Second World and throughout the left in the First and Third Worlds: Stalin's atrocities against humanity were confirmed by the CPSU. CPUSA membership plummeted. The CPUSA had been an apologist for Stalin ever since he rose to power after the death of Lenin. Nikita Khrushchev's "secret speech" to the Soviet Party Congress in 1956 denounced Stalin's crimes; and the USSR invaded Hungary.

The CIA Shapes the Cold War

The FBI and CIA had infiltrated and influenced the CPUSA. for decades. The CPUSA also had financial and political backing from the USSR for decades. The CIA allegedly secretly funded the communist organizations it infiltrated. From the 1950s to the 1980s, the KGB delivered millions of dollars to FBI double agents, brothers Jack and Morris Childs.[12] In the 1950s, the CIA also heavily funded cultural organizations such as the Ford Foundation, which rarely publicly opposed US foreign policy positions. CPUSA leadership, which received material support and asylum from the USSR, never criticized the CPSU. The party, as would be the Black Panther Party, was infiltrated and funded by US police forces and CIA agents and assets. The CPUSA survived as a pragmatic party advancing workers' rights and human rights, but it was damaged and its reputation as deeply committed to the masses was flawed.

When Alexandr Solzhenitsyn, former Soviet prisoner and author of the *Gulag Archipelago*, received the Nobel Prize on October 8, 1970—Angela Davis as an FBI fugitive was arrested on the 13th of that month—he was allowed to immigrate into the United States. Several years later, Solzhenitsyn would attack Davis for not denouncing CPSU repression against political dissidents in the Soviet Union; anti-communist leaders of the American Federation of Labor and Congress of Industrial Organizations (AFL-CIO) and ex-communists Irving Brown and Jay Lovestone supported him. Large trade unions, receiving CIA funding, would target smaller, militant trade unions supporting Davis as a member of the CPUSA. According to James Petras, the AFL-CIO "poured millions of dollars into subverting militant trade unions and breaking strikes through the funding of social democratic unions" in Europe. In post-war Europe, the CIA worked with the Mafia to decimate radical labor unions—a mainstay of communist and socialist parties' rank-and-file discussed in the "Family Jewels" report.[13] When the CIA supported a "Democratic Left" for cultural and "ideological warfare," it created a unit "to circumvent right-wing Congressional objections" and also to combat the *radical* left. That is, the agency sought to drive down the middle lane and stabilize society and democracy, or so its supporters said. The "left-wing" of the CIA was comprised of intellectuals "rewarded with prestige, public recognition, and research funds precisely for operating within the ideological blinders" established by an agency that created "some of the biggest names in philosophy, political ethics, sociology, and art." Those who brought up the role of the CIA in nonprofit and corporate funding were castigated as "conspiracy theorists" by liberals and by those who resisted analyses of police forces. (With the death of J. Edgar Hoover in 1972, it was easier to castigate the use of lethal force as the immorality of an individual "rogue cop.")

After Stalin's repression was denounced in 1957, the *Daily Worker* stopped being printed due to lost membership. From 1958 to 1968, the newspaper was republished in a reduced format. CIA agent Philip Agee argues that CIA subscriptions kept it afloat. In 1968, the CPUSA republished the paper in New York as *The Daily World,* merging with California's *People's World*, a more independent paper of the CPSU. Published from 1987 to 1991, the years of Glasnost and the emergent deterioration of the Soviet Union, the *People's Daily World* recorded some of the CPUSA discord and USSR dissolution that led to Angela Davis's marginalization in the party, along with several hundred other CPUSA leaders who sought internal reforms in the CPUSA and resisted Gus Hall and party stalwarts who sought to support the Stalinists within the CPSU.

The New Left

From the 1960s to the 1970s, the New Left attempted to revise and modernize radical formations. It was a coalition of anti-war activists, anti-racists, unions, socialists, communists, feminists, and environmentalists. When Davis and other reformers left or were pushed out of the CPUSA in 1991, they subsequently formed the socialist-leaning "Committees of Correspondence" (CoC). Named after provisional governments in the thirteen American colonies prior to the Revolutionary War against Britain, the CoC was progressive but increasingly would align with the Democratic Party.

Black Panthers were communists—not all, but there were a notable number in leadership. Their spoken word and community caretaking were powerful, as was their newspaper with the art work of Emory Douglass, which made them increasingly popular and a font for analysis and education. Black Panther-turned-anarchist Lorenzo Komboa Ervin notes:

> Radical organizations garnered wide support based on their ability to address the material needs and aspirations, as well as ideals, of their communities. For example, reservation, barrio, or urban youths were (and are) disaffected by and overwhelmed with frustration at dead-end jobs, poverty, inferior and disciplinary schooling, and police violence. It is logical then that the Black Panther Party, Brown Berets, Young Lords, Young Patriots, and American Indian Movement would have mass appeal among the young. While the majority media focused on the armed aspect of such groups, it was their free breakfast programs, free medical clinics, freedom schools, and social services that elicited wide support. They offered an

alternative to the state; and by their massive appeal in oppressed communities, they presented the government with the real threat of popular insurrection built by revolutionaries.[14]

Ervin's 1979 *Anarchism and Black Revolution*[15] asserts that "three major forms of socialism—Libertarian Socialism (Anarchism), Authoritarian Socialism (Marxist Communism), and Democratic Socialism (electoral social democracy)"—were in conflict and that the non-Anarchist Left and the bourgeoisie dismiss "[a]narchism as an ideology of chaos and lunacy."

Acknowledgments

My thanks to Janine Jones, Nicole Yokum, Suiyi Tang, Selamawit Terrefe, IB, Ayami Hatanaka, Claudia Forrester, Kim Holder, A. Shan, JB, M. A. Kirloskar-Steinbach, Mickaella Perina, and the many others who supported this endeavor.

Figure 1 Angela Davis and Kendra Alexander, members of the Che-Lumumba Club of the Communist Party USA, enter UCLA's Royce Hall October 7, 1969. © George Louis, 1969. Reproduced under a Creative Commons Attribution 3.0 Unported license via Wikimedia Commons.

Introduction

In 2020, *TIME* honored Angela Davis as one of their hundred most influential persons.[1] Also in 2020, Angela Davis was inducted into the National Women's Hall of Fame on the hundredth anniversary year of the 1920 ratification of (white) women's right to vote.[2] The last year of President Donald Trump's administration and residency in the White House saw the rise of neofascists, white supremacists, misogynists, and climate-change deniers; such factions in democracy fueled the January 6, 2021, siege on the US Capitol in an insurrection attempting to nullify certification of the election of President Joe Biden and Vice President Kamala Harris—through the disappearance or assassination of another arch-conservative white man, Vice President Mike Pence.[3] As a 2020 National Hall of Fame ambassador, Davis introduced six Black women and women of color who made significant contributions to culture and social justice as inductees, stating that when "Black Lives Matter all lives will finally matter." The inductees were "Queen of Soul" artist Aretha Franklin; NAACP co-founder Mary Church Terrell; Henrietta Lacks, whose cancer cells are the source of the HeLa cells; Barbara Hillary, the first Black woman to reach the north and south poles; civil rights activist Barbara Rose Johns; and novelist Toni Morrison.[4] In 1951, when Davis was in elementary school, at the age of sixteen, Barbara Rose Johns—the niece of Vernon Johns—organized a high school strike against segregated, underfunded Black schools, which led to the only student-initiated legal case, *Davis v. Prince Edward County*, being cited in the 1954 US Supreme Court *Brown v. Board of Education* ruling against segregated public schools (discussed in Chapter 3).

The educational and cultural contributions of the six women as stellar figures in US history worked within integrationist settings that do not easily align with the radical origins of Angela Davis emerging as a public persona, first through her defiance as an open member of the Communist Party USA, in 1969, while becoming the first Black philosopher to teach in the University of California system and later by becoming an ally to Black revolutionaries. Davis's roles in that era of Black rebellion against racism, capitalism, and imperialism have become popular through cultural memory, which does not always reflect objective history. *TIME* and other mainstream sectors celebrate the twenty-first-century Angela Davis, who is aligned with progressivism; in the twentieth century, during the cold war, corporate media were wary of a leading member of the Communist Party USA (CPUSA), who was also an important ally to Black radicals and the Black Panther Party.

Davis joined the CPUSA in 1968 through the Che-Lumumba Club; she remained a loyal member and leader of the CPUSA until 1991 (the Che-Lumumba Club essentially folded when she went underground in August 1970). White nationalists and anti-communists made constant death threats against her once she publicly acknowledged that she was a member of the communist party while teaching philosophy at UCLA in 1969. Exercising her Second Amendment rights she regularly trained in the California hills with members of the Che-Lumumba Club—an all-Black CPUSA organization—the gun training, mandatory for the Black Panther Party (for Self-Defense), was likely prohibited by the CPUSA. Davis's ties to Black revolutionaries were predominantly linked to George Jackson and his younger brother Jonathan Jackson, who became Davis's bodyguard and used her weapons in the ill-fated attempt to free Black prisoners from California's Marin County Courthouse on August 7, 1970. During the courthouse raid, prison guards shot into an idling van that held the Black fugitives and white hostages.[5] Their injuries and death turned "Angela Davis" into a household name once she fled the state. An FBI hunt ensued; she was captured that October, returned to California, and jailed in the Marin County Courthouse. Her campaign for freedom, her trial, and her June 1972 acquittal expanded her public profile. Davis focused on human rights, writing her autobiography with Toni Morrison and re-entering academia.

After the acquittal, she turned down an offer from UCLA to return to teaching in the philosophy department.[6] Instead of immediately returning full time to academia, Davis taught as a visiting professor at Claremont College, San Francisco State, Stanford, and UC Santa Cruz. She would be tenured as a full professor in the UCSC History of Consciousness program and later named a distinguished university president chair before retirement.

Fifty years ago, the activism and alliances that created Angela Davis as an international icon were central to dissent for social justice and liberation movements. Today, those signifiers and symbols continue to register across generations, but the meanings of radicalism and Black liberation have shifted. Mass protests led by Black militants seeking to evolve beyond the legacies of mass enslavement, mass rape, and mass exploitation and disappearance would be funded in the rise of "Black Lives Matter" through nonprofits or corporations and reform movements. Davis would mentor some of the most prominent figures who also became globally known and political celebrities. The militant movement cultures of the 1960s and early 1970s cannot be regained. Yet, today, those movements are interpreted through the life and lens of an excellent student studying European philosophy while disengaged in Black political struggles until she returned to the United States to become a UC doctoral student and an ally of Black militants. That radicalism from which she had been sheltered for most of her life, she would seek to lead in part with her academic skills and training. Academic-trained Black elites from white universities and organizations merged with Black cadres embedded in revolutionary struggles where local police and the FBI forced them to choose between being war casualties and war resisters. This leads to a fragile alliance, particularly if the assimilating elites view their relationship with US democracy as conflict, not antagonism.

Book Structure

Contextualizing Angela Davis begins in Alabama, with Davis's birth and childhood in segregated Birmingham. It ends in California, in August 1970, with her surrogate political family, comprised of imprisoned militant George Jackson and his younger brother Jonathan Jackson. Jonathan organized the raid on Marin County Courthouse in order to free Black prisoners; he used Angela Davis's weapons in that tragedy. *Contextualizing Angela Davis* focuses on her childhood and student years from high school through graduate school and adjunct university teaching. It incorporates political philosophy, history, sociology, and feminist and abolitionist theory to decipher agency and identify key actors in turbulent organizing and targeted Black liberation movements.

Part I, "Socialization and Education," begins with Chapter 1, "Sweet Home Alabama," which discusses the legacy of the confederacy in Davis's home state, which created southern Jim Crow segregation, Ku Klux Klan (Klan/KKK) terrorism, and Black resistance to racist violence. Black Alabamans fought the violence from government and civilians as the first Black Panther parties emerged in Alabama as self-defense committees and protectors of voting rights organizers. These organizations would inspire the formation of Panther parties in California in 1966–7. Chapter 2, "Sallye Davis's Red-Diaper Babies," focuses on the mother of Angela Davis, Mrs. Sallye Bell Davis, who had organized with the Communist Party USA (CPUSA) for decades; children of US communists were often labeled as "red-diaper babies." Mrs. Davis was instrumental as a strategist when her eldest child, Angela, became a fugitive, prisoner, and exonerated defendant from 1970–2. Chapter 3, "Student Assimilationists and Rebels," examines Davis's pre-high school education, shaped by segregation, by juxtaposing her experiences with those of Freeman Hrabowski, a Birmingham student taught by Sallye Davis, who, unlike the Davis children, became active in the civil rights movement before leaving the south to integrate northern private schools. Chapter 4, "From 'Bombingham' to the Big Apple," focuses on fifteen-year-old Angela Davis's departure from Birmingham's Klan-police violence, and entry into Manhattan's exclusive leftist Elizabeth Irwin School, created by affluent Jewish parents hounded by 1950s McCarthyism and the House Un-American Activities Committee (HUAC). Chapter 5, "Traumatic Awakenings in Devastated Children," examines 1960s university life for Davis as an undergraduate student in Massachusetts, physically distanced from but psychologically impacted by racist violence. In particular, the September 1963 murders of four Black girl activists in Birmingham became an emotional-political touchstone in Davis's narratives about civil rights activism and segregationist violence.

Part II, "University," begins with Chapter 6, "Undergrad," which outlines the political environment within Brandeis University in Walden, Massachusetts, where Davis met philosopher and professor Herbert Marcuse, engaged in international student festivals, and met the graduate student from Germany who would accompany her to Frankfurt. Chapter 7, "Marcuse's 'Most Famous Student,'" discusses the impact on her studies and trajectory through the famous leftist theorist. Chapter 8, "1967 Entry Points," centers on Davis's departure from Europe and her return to California to begin doctoral studies in California with Marcuse at the University of California San Diego; Davis also returns in order to join the radical movements for Black liberation. "Philosophy Professor and Communist Target," Chapter 9, examines Davis as a doctoral student teaching philosophy at UCLA; being "outed" as a member of the CPUSA; organizing with UC San Diego students; and the context of Marcuse being harassed by white conservatives and nationalists at UC San Diego. Her membership and growing leadership in the CPUSA, through the Che-Lumumba Club, enabled her to visit Cuba in the summer of 1969 and, as a graduate student, meet with Fidel Castro. That fall, hired as the first Black instructor in philosophy at the University of California Los Angeles, Davis would be "attacked" as a member of the CPUSA; Governor Reagan and the UC Regents would threaten her employment.

Part III, "Political Activism," begins with Chapter 10, "Not Your Mother's CPUSA: The Che-Lumumba Club," which examines how the all-Black CPUSA club mentored Angela Davis as an important ally for the BPP and leading spokesperson for the Soledad Brothers Defense Committee. Chapter 11, "Doppelganger Panther Women: Roberta Alexander, Fania Davis Jordan, Angela Davis," contextualizes Panther women who were students attending elite institutions when they came out as political actors. The three women explored in this chapter had different entries into radicalism and diverse alliances to the BPP, as well as diverse experiences with police/military violence used against activists. Chapter 12, "Queering Radicalism: On Tour with Oakland Panthers and Jean Genet," focuses on Davis's role as a translator for the French intellectual who volunteered to raise funds for imprisoned Panthers by speaking at university campuses. "Crucibles," Chapter 13, explores the varied formations and conflicts among and within the Black Panther Party and the Student Nonviolent Coordinating Committee (SNCC), and Angela Davis's relationships with each formation.

"Conclusion: Context and Democracy" analyzes Angela Davis's 2019 interview at her alma mater Brandeis University's fiftieth anniversary of Black Studies and her vision of past, current, and future civil/human rights based on electoral politics, feminism, and abolition.

A Tribute to Mentor Charlene Mitchell

The most influential communist in the life of Davis was not Marx, and perhaps not even her impactful mother, but the singular Black woman strategist and theoretician Charlene Mitchell. Mitchell joined the CPUSA at age sixteen, in 1946; Davis was two years old. In 1968, Mitchell would recruit and mentor a young Black woman who would become in the twentieth century the most prominent CPUSA member in the United States: Angela Davis. Mitchell passed in 2022. On December 19, 2022, *Portside* republished the December 14, 2022 Mitchell family statement—"Charlene Mitchell, Leader of the Campaign to Free Angela Davis"—on the transition of Charlene (Alexander) Mitchell on December 14, 2022, at the age of ninety-two in NYC. Born Charlene Alexander in 1930 in Cincinnati, Ohio, the second of eight children, Mitchell as a teen modeled her working-class activist parents and herself became an activist; when the family moved to Chicago, she joined the CPUSA. She founded and led the Los Angeles branch of the CPUSA, the Che-Lumumba club. Mitchell recruited Davis; other members included her brother Franklin Alexander and his wife Kendra Alexander (who appears in the photograph of Angela Davis and UC students), and her younger brother Deacon (who briefly dated Angela Davis). The family statement describes her as a "key leader of the movement in the early 1970s to free imprisoned activist Angela Davis." That movement led to Mitchell becoming a central founder and co-leader of the National Alliance Against Racist and Political Repression (NAARPR), which worked on behalf of Joan Little and the Wilmington 10. Angela Davis is quoted in the family statement:

> Having known Charlene Mitchell through political victories and defeats, through personal tragedies and triumphs, I can say with confidence that she is the person to whom I am most grateful for showing me a life path.
>
> What I have most appreciated over these years is her amazing ability to discover ethical connections between the political and the personal, the global and the local. I don't think I have ever known someone as consistent in her values, as collective in her outlook on life, as firm in her trajectory as a freedom fighter.[7]

In 1991, when Davis and Alexander, along with 200 other members of the CPUSA, were barred from voting by Gus Hall, Mitchell "was elected leader of the Committees of Correspondence for Democracy and Socialism, a Marxist organization," which was based in New York City; its membership included Manning Marable and Angela Davis. I was fortunate enough to be briefly mentored by Charlene Mitchell.

Charlene Mitchell is remembered as a brilliant strategist for the CPUSA and civil and human rights. She was the first Black woman to run for the presidency of the United States, in 1968, on the Communist Party USA ticket. Ms. Mitchell instructed me to go to the Schomburg Library in Harlem to study W. E. B. DuBois's memoirs and his rejection of Black educated elites. Thus, Charlene Mitchell was the catalyst for my publishing *Transcending the Talented Tenth*, which explores the erasure of Black women's agency and analyzes DuBois's borrowed concept of elite Black leadership managing the Black mass; that concept was designed by white philanthropists to ensure that Blacks rejected armed rebellion against white supremacist terror (and government indifference) in the postbellum era and sought to "rise" through assimilation into Black colleges and universities. DuBois learned through painful personal experience that the talented tenth of Black elites, which he promoted in the 1903 *Souls of Black Folk*, would betray and abandon radicals in order to appease and rise within the ranks of repressive government and a racist social order.[8]

Charlene Mitchell, a CPUSA and anti-racist union activist from the age of sixteen, mentored young communists and their allies. Perhaps the most productive mentors are those who, rather than trying to lead or control progressive youths, function as midwives—coaching but not directing painful labor that delivers security and builds strength to combat predatory states and practices. If I had joined in the late 1980s when asked to do so, I would have left the CPUSA with Davis and Mitchell and others in 1991, when they were barred from electing more progressive leadership. Joining or refusing to join a party you have worked with for months or years can be a difficult choice. Being pushed out of a party you helped to build—which is what happened to Mitchell and Davis in 1991—is painful. Yet I consider the history of Miss Ella Baker, a key mentor to the student shock troops fighting in the southern civil rights movement, the Student Nonviolent Coordinating Committee. Following the Montgomery Bus Boycott, Miss Baker had left NYC to organize with the southern movement. A member of the small organization In Friendship, along with Bayard Rustin, and Jewish attorney Stanley Levison, Baker counseled Rev. Martin Luther King, Jr. The formal and iconic leadership of Black male clergy formed the Southern Christian Leadership Conference (SCLC). When SCLC requested that she steer young activists into an organization built and controlled by reverends such as King and other middle-class integrationists, she refused. Miss Baker warned students not to become the youth wing of the SCLC; she urged SNCC *not* to bring their passion and risk-taking love for freedom into an established organization that they could never lead until they became replicants of their more conservative elders. With the aid of a brilliant midwife, the most transformative entity in the southern civil rights movement, SNCC, was born, and from SNCC's demise, the emergence of the Black Panthers became a magnetic political formation for Angela Davis.

Part I

Socialization and Education

1

"Sweet Home Alabama"

Angela Davis: An Autobiography was published in 1974, the same year that the white male Floridian rock band Lynyrd Skynyrd hit the top ten charts with *Sweet Home Alabama*. That homage to a segregationist state (where the band did not reside) was a response to Canadian singer Neil Young who wrote several songs, including *Southern Man*, condemning whites lynching southern Blacks. (Young also wrote *Four Dead in Ohio* following the National Guard's killing of students at Kent State during a protest against racism and the war in Vietnam.) Using Black women as backup singers, *Sweet Home Alabama*'s album cover featured a white male face imprinted with a postage stamp–size confederate flag below the mouth. The band's lyrics celebrated arch-segregationist and former Alabama Governor George Wallace.[1] Alabama, where law, police, and Klan enforced Jim Crow segregation, was a "sweet" state for white nationalists and racists who celebrated statues and memorabilia for the "lost cause" amidst confidence that "the south will rise again." Racial hatred structured the social order within which Angela Davis spent her early childhood. Understanding that there was little sweet about the white supremacist state, Davis's parents resisted Jim Crow terror in order to create a family with more options. They deployed the routines of everyday life within battles against the resurrected Confederacy; in many ways, using class, education, and connections with progressive connected whites, they managed to defeat the confederates in respect to their individual family.

Alabama Terrors

The National Association for the Advancement of Colored People (NAACP) was founded in 1909 to counter anti-Black lynching and Jim Crow terrorism.[2] A decade later, in 1919, the CPUSA was formed to counter worker exploitation; later, it would address the oppression of Blacks. The NAACP that DuBois embraced—until it jettisoned him when he began to advocate for economic rights for the working class and laborers—was engaged in civil rights activism that was also anti-communist.

Alabama was historically prominent in the Southern Confederacy, a bedrock for its white supremacist politics and Jim Crow terrorism. In 1861, the Confederacy chose Montgomery, Alabama, as the site for its emergency conference to forge a constitution for slave states seceding from the Union. Nearly a century later, Montgomery became a test site for civil rights as Rosa Parks refused to relinquish her segregated bus seat, and Martin Luther King, Jr., agreed to become the titular head of the Montgomery Improvement Association that spearheaded the bus boycott, which would be studied around the world. Some 200,000 Blacks fought to ensure the north's victory over the south and the realization of emancipation.[3] When the federal government and President Rutherford B. Hayes betrayed Reconstruction and withdrew troops protecting emancipation, the south kept its promise to rise again. Slave codes became Black codes. Black codes became Jim Crow. It was under the yoke of Jim Crow, as a war zone, that Angela Davis would spend most of her childhood in the south. Respite or sanctuary for the Davis children from that war zone meant summers in NYC, and high school boarding in northern elite white schools. Their parents had the connections with white privileged northerners to counter white supremacist southerners. Black parents secured the lives of and opportunities for their children not only with nightly gun patrols against the Klan but also with academic outmigration. While in Alabama, and for those who could not or would not leave, organizing was essential for survival.

A. Philip Randolph was the socialist leader of the African Blood Brotherhood and the first president of the National Negro Congress (NNC).[4] The NNC was the parent organization of the Southern Negro Youth Congress (SNYC). Formed in 1935 at Howard University, the NCC eventually boasted 11,000 members across ten states. As it focused on Black voter registration and desegregating unions, the NNC grew to 3 million members. Its 1936 Chicago convention hosted 800 delegates and 551 organizations. As part of the CPUSA's "popular front coalition," these organizations attracted largely lesser-known or local Negro leaders such as Sallye Bell Davis. They also attracted Black luminaries: Mary McCloud Bethune, Paul Robeson, Charlotte Hawkins Brown, A. Philip Randolph, Horace Mann Bond, and W. E. B. DuBois. (As a high school student, Angela Davis would meet DuBois at the Manhattan home of her schoolmate Bettina Aptheker.) Sallye Davis was a member of the SNYC. She worked with Horace Mann Bond, the father of SNCC leader Julian Bond (a close aide to Martin Luther King, Jr.) and father-in-law of Howard Moore, Jr. who would later become Angela Davis's lead defense attorney. Bond and SNCC would advocate for Davis during her political trials.[5] Sallye Davis co-organized the largest SNYC conference held in Birmingham in 1939; some 650 delegates represented high school and college students, rural laborers, educators, and progressive whites gathered to fight joblessness and job segregation.[6] Along with League of Young Southerners (LYS), SNYC "became the radical movement in Birmingham."[7] The Davises were close to the Burnham family; parents Dorothy and Louis Burnham, CPUSA leaders, hosted the Davises after the Burnhams were forced out of Alabama and moved to New York. (Their daughter Margaret, Angela's childhood friend, later became one of her defense attorneys.) Louis Burnham led Black students toward socialist or communist demands to remedy economic deprivation and racism during the Depression and New Deal era.

A central regulatory site to promote white supremacy, Alabama deployed violence in racial-sexual assaults. As a child, Angela Davis would hear firsthand, or through grown-ups speaking at organizing meetings at her family's home, of the violence rained upon Black women and girls, and Black men and boys. The impact would engender not only fear but also outrage and a political will to resist and, if necessary, rebel. Black activism emerged in response to white supremacist terror and rape. In 1944, the year that Angela Davis was born, the NAACP—concerned about the unprosecuted interracial sexual assaults against Black women and girls by white males—sent civil rights icon Rosa Parks into the south as their lead investigator against racially-fashioned sex crimes and assaults. In Abbeville, Alabama, Parks gathered evidence against white men, including a local sheriff, who had abducted and gang-raped Recy Taylor, a young Black married mother of two, who also worked sharecropping. The crime was not unusual for Alabama or the deep south. Still, the formidable political network of Black women and church and community leaders built by Parks and other anti-rape activists became the foundation for the 1955 Montgomery bus boycott and the Montgomery Improvement Association.

In 1945, Angela Davis had her first birthday and her brother Ben was born. That spring, President Roosevelt, who led New Deal progressivism, swayed southern congressmen and senators to support New Deal legislation by permitting them to exclude Blacks from relief roles in southern states. The next month, Germany surrendered, on May 7, after Hitler committed suicide. In June, the United Nations Charter and the International Court of Justice (World Court) were established. On August 3, President Harry Truman authorized the use of atomic bombs on the Japanese cities Hiroshima and Nagasaki. The end of a world war and the creation of international law and judicial bodies did not stop white supremacist terrorism in the United States. Returning white veterans, militarized and conditioned to killing, appeared to increase assaults on Blacks, whose family members had also fought with distinction against fascism, and who now increasingly demanded their civil rights.

In the 1950s phenomena of mass marches, protests, and desegregation strikes that followed the Second World War, the 1955 Montgomery bus boycott became the dominant symbol of civil rights with Rev. Martin Luther King, Jr., as the public figurehead. From 1948 to 1955, King had attended Crozer Theological Seminary in Pennsylvania, obtained his PhD in systematic theology at Boston University, and enrolled in philosophy courses at Harvard.[8] As noted in the Introduction, the greater public preferred young, well-educated intellectuals as emergent figureheads and leaders; the names of poor sharecroppers, with the exception of Fannie Lou Hamer, are rarely cited or remembered in civil rights narratives. Rev. King, following the Johnson Administration's request, betrayed Miss Hamer and the Mississippi Freedom Democratic Party (MFDP). Miss Fannie Lou Hamer had endured brutal beatings, and subsequent lifelong injuries, while campaigning for voter registration drives. While jailed in Mississippi for civil rights organizing, white jailers forced Black male prisoners to beat her back and legs with a black jack saying that if they did not it would be used on them. White jailers also hiked up her dress. Hamer was left partially crippled. Years prior Miss Hamer had been sterilized without her knowledge or permission; she referred to the medical violence as a "Mississippi appendectomy," as white physicians engaged in eugenics.

King and Davis, fifteen years apart in age, shared identity markers as Black "middle class" achievers who attended white universities in the north (later, for Davis, in Europe and California). As members of the talented tenth, they were student models of Black equality—which is distinct from Black liberation. Davis avoided the southern movement led by SNCC students (Black and white students left universities to battle for freedoms in the south); King was made titular head of the Montgomery bus boycott and gradually became radicalized. Non-elite Black Alabamans were critical to organizing. Alabama's impoverished Black agricultural laborers understood by proximity that a white person could kill them with impunity on whim or for refusal to relinquish their land, labor, or bodies to be appropriated by whites. Without formal education, rural organizers were forcing Alabama, the bellwether state for segregation, to transition from a nineteenth-century Confederacy stronghold into a springboard for twentieth-century civil rights for Negroes and all Americans. The more Alabama oppressed Blacks, the more oppressed Blacks organized and rebelled.[9]

The Davis family and their children would live through southern civil rights history largely without what SNCC called "direct action," which was juxtaposed as an alternative to "voter registration" until the students realized that there was no difference between the two. Voter registration was seen as direct action or rebellion, and one could lose limbs or their lives if they engaged in either. The impoverished and the working class, joined by university, college, and high school students, were the focal point of the movement. Sallye Davis was on the right side of ethics and history; however, *An Autobiography* offers no clear description of the Davis children engaging in direct action or joining any organization to break the backbone of Jim Crow segregation. In their youth, the primary goal was for them to receive an excellent education outside of segregation. The objective was to obtain the same quality of education that affluent whites were given in the north. Sallye Davis remained active in social change and connected to the CPUSA. She would stay in the south as her four children came of age as teens and were channeled up north for educational privileges that should have been rights for all children. An escape from the Jim Crow south to the Jim Crow north (Malcolm X called the north "Up South") in the quest for mobility and stability that mitigate racism also revealed schisms between elites and non-elites, the well-connected and the poor. The Black rural militants in Alabama who stayed on the land and used force as self-defense against violence by the state and its terrorist militias would become the new "professors" for the students migrating from California and the north and south to be part of the movement. Those who did not travel to become a part of the southern movement watched it from afar through newspapers and television. That scrutiny, another form of tutelage, inspired varied Black Panther parties.

Alabama's Black Panthers—a Variation on Your Parents' Protections

Angela Davis understood the Oakland Panthers, founded in 1966, as having a lineage in Black southern resistance to white supremacist terror and policing. She would critique Panther mythology that erased the civil rights and self-defense legacy of Black communities besieged in the Jim Crow south: "I saw Black people resisting. There is this myth that Black people did not resist until what? Until Malcolm or the Black Panther party? It's just not true."[10] Alabama had preceded California's Black militancy, and the iconic formation of its political party named after that Black cat that reportedly only attacked in self-defense. The California Panthers were familiar to Davis, who recognized their prototype, and ethics, as a legacy from Black communities in her home state.

Alabama and California, the two repressive anti-Black states that shaped Angela Davis's growing radicalism, created their own respective "Black Panther" parties (Alabama did so several years before the California parties formed) while Davis was studying in Frankfurt. Davis would become familiar with the leaders of both Panther parties: Stokely Carmichael, in Alabama's Lowndes County, and Huey P. Newton, in Oakland, CA. Carmichael was active with the Lowndes County Freedom Organization (LCFO), also known as the "Black Panther Party." In 1967, government reports identified the LCFO as the progenitor of the Bay Area Black Panther Party— the most militant among "civil rights" organizations. Eventually, the "Panther Party" that she would build an alliance with would be the one in Oakland, headed by Newton, Seale, Hilliard, and Brown. Despite the controversial vagaries of the Oakland Black Panther leadership, Angela Davis found the pragmatic contributions of the Panthers familiar given their antecedents: "The first thing that the Black Panther party did of course in Oakland was to patrol the community, to set up an armed patrol in order to ensure that Black people were not harassed and intimidated by the local police department. But that had been done in the South. It was done in Birmingham."[11] Lowndes County, Alabama, had been the inspiration for the Oakland founders Huey P. Newton and Bobby Seale. In 1966, national broadcasts flashed, across household television screens, the Lowndes County Freedom Party's Black Panther logo. Footage of a singular protest was aired, showing Rev. Martin Luther King, Jr., haplessly standing nearby as SNCC's Stokely Carmichael, recently released from jail and traumatized by accumulations of police beatings, galvanized the gathering to chant for "Black Power!" The symbol of the panther captured the political imagination of Black youths. Assassinated in 1965, Malcolm X's calls for self-defense had been in the air for a decade. The terrain for political dissent was shifting from the deep south into northern and urban centers.

To better understand the Panthers of Lowndes County requires an examination of their roots in Jim Crow segregation and violence. During SNCC's first voter registration meeting in Lowndes County, Alabama, Black farmers appeared with guns and proceeded to instruct the young nonviolent organization and its members that they would need armed self-defense to survive their attempt to expand the franchise to Black voters. White supremacists had recently murdered white civil rights activist Viola Liuzzo,[12] a Michigan white mother of five, and white seminarian activist Jonathan Daniels, in Lowndes County. The distraught community was determined not to let another tragedy unfold.

Alabama's Lowndes County was 80 percent Black. Half of the county lived below the poverty line. Blacks could register to vote in the county to determine taxes, budgets, schooling, and police enforcement.[13] In 1966, LCFO candidates unsuccessfully (largely due to voter suppression) ran for office with the slogan "Black Power." Low literacy rates mandated symbols alongside the titles of Alabama political parties. LCFO's snarling black panther (some say the image came from the African Methodist Episcopal Church school Clark College, founded after the Civil War[14]) was accompanied by slogans of "Black Power!" and "All Power to the People!" The political imaginations of politicized, poor, rural Alabamans became the imaginary of the (inter)national militants. In the West Coast radicals, Black America recognized aspects of itself in an oppressed Black southern rural county.[15]

The Lowndes County Black Panther Political Party in Alabama was a catalyst for the formation of the Black Panther Party *for Self-Defense* (author's emphasis) in Oakland, California. Watching events unfold in Lowndes County from Oakland, Huey P. Newton and Bobby Seale asked and received permission to use the LCFO Black Panther emblem and slogan.[16] Their 1966 formation of the Black Panther Party for Self-Defense (BPPSD) customized and disseminated Black Alabaman symbols and slogans throughout the Bay Area. The Alabama Communist Party, formed in response to capitalism and police violence, remained independent thinkers[17] (it would later rally to support comrade Davis during her incarceration and trial).[18] Angela Davis understood that the concept of self-defense and the construct of the Black Panther originated in the deep south, where the vast majority of African Americans faced enslavement, Black Codes, Jim Crow, white supremacist terror, labor exploitation, and poverty.

Stark differences existed in Alabama between the Lowndes County Panthers and the Birmingham self-defense clubs that Davis knew from her childhood neighborhood. The Alabama Panthers were largely rural laborers and working class, organizers securing their rights to decent wages and dignified lives through political participation in US democracy. The Birmingham self-defense clubs that Davis's father participated in also sought full civic participation in democracy; however, the Davis parents were not poor and did not work for whites, in their homes or in their fields. They were integrationists and whites resented their assets and abilities to move into white middle-class neighborhoods and purchase homes. The class differences were distinct but never fully addressed in *An Autobiography*.

Sallye Davis's Red-Diaper Babies

Precarity, extreme stress, and exhaustion shaped the life of Angela Davis from southern Jim Crow segregation and Klan terror, to integrating white elite educational sites to leadership in the CPUSA's Che-Lumumba Club and alliances with the commanders of Oakland's Black Panther Party, and co-leadership in the Soledad Brothers Defense Committee. Davis's capacity to think and function under difficult or dangerous conditions, while demanding civil and human rights, was shaped by her early upbringing. Raised in an influential family with powerful networks, she still was vulnerable to anti-Black violence that radiated throughout the Jim Crow south and beyond. In public talks and interviews, Davis does not often speak about her father, Frank Davis. Mr. Davis was trained as a school teacher but became a businessman who operated the only Black gas station and downtown parking lot in a segregated city where Blacks were prohibited from buying gas from whites or parking their cars in "white" lots. Almost all of Black Birmingham that owned cars knew Frank Davis, according to Davis. Her father recommended that she go north to integrate white schools. Sallye Bell Davis raised and politicized Angela Davis. Her mother brought her four children to NYC each summer to stay with family friends as she completed her master's degree in education at New York University. Davis was a disciplined student; her mother, an educator and organizer trained by the CPUSA, became a role model for the youth, although Davis would say that it took decades before she realized her mother's impact on her life trajectory. Davis entered the world of Black militancy in her mid-twenties which was largely after southern Black children and teens had avidly protested and faced the terrors of police, dogs, and white nationalists amid government neglect or collusion. Her baptism as a "red-diaper" baby and the networks wielded by the CPUSA and CPSU would spare her from the (near) drownings plaguing Black radicals and revolutionaries who swam against a tsunami of repression. Mrs. Sallye Bell Davis was a lifesaver.

Mrs. Davis

Sallye Bell Davis began organizing with the CPUSA in the 1930s; the CPUSA had roughly 100,000 members.[1] During the Great Depression, poverty, labor exploitation, and hunger, and police (both state and private agencies hired by corporations or "robber barons") had constituted a matrix of oppression and depression. Workers were out of work and often on strike. Families became homeless. Farmers saw banks foreclose on their lands. Whatever white families and communities suffered from the stock market crash, Black families and communities suffered worse – denied aid and protections given to whites, they found scarcity compounded in their lives. Severely disenfranchised by capitalism, they were also devastated by white supremacy and Jim Crow laws and legislation.

Through their parents, Angela and her younger sister Fania recognized that their household experiences of anti-Black violence were shaped not only by victimization but also by agency. Black families were constantly grappling with white supremacist terror; many chose to have weapons for self-defense. Parents explicitly or implicitly by their actions "trained" their children for survival, and the ambitious and middle class, for "success." Mrs. Sallye Davis, mother of four, two daughters and two sons, was the primary tutor for politics, at least for her daughters. A "red-diaper" baby in postwar United States required at least one communist or communist-leaning parent. In the Davis family, the most radical parent was the mother, not the father. Mrs. Davis profoundly shaped the political worldview of her daughters—first-born Angela and third child Fania.

Although the mother favored the trappings of the Black bourgeoisie more than her daughters, *Angela Davis: An Autobiography* notes that Mrs. Davis did not force her daughters to become high school debutantes or participate in cotillions. Rather than cajole or coerce, she brushed off her disappointment when they declined the social rituals of elites. While the Davis sisters rejected elite social life, they seriously pursued their studies. Both of their parents had been trained as educators or school teachers. The Davises were not poor; they had means and time to invest in formal education that was unequally distributed based not just on race but also on class. A skillful political organizer, one of the many but rarely heard of Black women resisting anti-Black racism and labor exploitation, Mrs. Davis synthesized the contradictions of being a member of the Black (petite) bourgeoisie and communist organizations; she embraced civil rights agitation.

Sallye Davis's public presentation was shaped by education, employment, home ownership, and appearance—colorism was a component of anti-Blackness in the twentieth century (and remains so today). Mrs. Davis shared with her daughters the conventional personal beauty of light skin (or white adjacency), which society—before, during, and after the chant of "Black is beautiful!" and the heydays of that declaration—associated with greater intelligence and moral virtues.[2]

Sallye Bell Davis was a foster child, likely with a white father. Davis recalls that her mother, who had a passion for learning, was an agricultural laborer in a troubled home: "My mother ... had to run away from her foster parents to be able to get a high school education, because she grew up in the country, in the deep country in Alabama." After securing her education, befriended by Black teachers in Birmingham, Sallye Davis worked with the CPUSA in the 1930s and 1940s. She organized for workers and against repression. An officer of the Southern Negro Youth Congress, Sallye Davis also worked with both the CPUSA and the NAACP organizing defense for the Scottsboro Nine case. The Black teens, migrant laborers during the depression, were falsely accused of raping two white women (sex workers) and also hopping trains as hobos in the depression; the Black youths fought back after white male teens attempted to throw them off a moving train designating it as "whites only." The black youths were arrested, tortured and sentenced to execution. The CPUSA rallied (later followed by the NAACP) to mount a vigorous legal defense and international campaign to save their lives. The Scottsboro case, which became an international human rights case, expanded its influence beyond the Jim Crow south and drew the NAACP out of its timidity and into the legal battles to save the lives of the Black youths; it registered the CPUSA as an international actor against anti-Black violence and persecution.

Mrs. Davis combined Black maternal nurturer and Black communist activist. She became a force and a role model that shaped the ethical trajectory of her first-born, Angela, and the developing advocacy for social justice. The agentic, intellectualized pro-communist Black family in the Jim Crow south had strong female leadership, largely shaped by the mother's leftist politics and communal commitments. The sensibilities shaped by the Black petite bourgeoisie do not appear to have determined Mrs. Davis's approach to "care" and leadership; perhaps because of her links to sharecropping, foster care, familial fugitivity, and homelessness, Sallye Davis's relationship to class and classism was complicated. Sallye Davis constructed herself into an educator and teacher, passing on to her daughters independence, determination, and courage to follow political paths for Black liberation and equality. Although the Davis parents rooted their children in economic stability within the Black (petite) bourgeoisie, their analysis of structures of economic exploitation was known to their children, as shown in Angela Davis's reflection: "[I]t's taken me a long time to recognize the extent to which I walked down a path that was carved out for me by my mother, because I always saw myself resisting my parents, as children often do, but my mother was an activist."[3]

Born in Talladega County, raised as a rural laborer, a teen, she ran away to Alabama's growing city Birmingham in 1931 to escape her foster parents' demands that she quit school to work full time. Taking odd jobs, Sallye Bell lived in a segregated Young Women's Christian Association (YWCA) until a local school principal took her into their home. In 1935, she won a scholarship to, and later graduated from, Miles Memorial College.[4] During the 1930s, she was a dedicated activist. By the early 1940s, she was a central leader in the civil rights and economic rights movements—movements that Angela Davis would describe as "left causes." Fueled by battling anti-communism and racism in a formerly Confederate state, Sallye Bell Davis's legacies centered on education and human rights advocacy.

Sallye Bell met her future husband, Frank Davis, when both were "country people", though his family owned land, whereas hers worked it. Reinventing themselves through college and teaching careers, they moved from the rural areas to the growing city of Birmingham. Frank Davis was from Marengo County and attended Raleigh, North Carolina's Saint Augustine's University. After the teachers married and started a family, the father purchased a small business, a gas station, while Mrs. Davis taught first grade. Like all loving and gifted Black parents, they provided care for their children and community within a hate-filled society. Creating a nurturing home within a Jim Crow war zone was a daunting task. Nonetheless, the parents were determined that their children learn to navigate between and bridge the white and Negro worlds.

A rapidly industrialized city, Birmingham was disfigured by racist anti-Black violence. The majority of Blacks in Alabama, a quarter of the state's population, lived and labored in rural areas, where Blacks were exploited in agricultural labor. A few were property owners. In *An Autobiography*, Davis shares fond memories of childhood summer visits to her paternal grandmother's farmhouse sanctuary. Land ownership created havens for Black families and communities where siblings and cousins roamed with freedom, ate from gardens and orchards, and played beyond the sight of hostile whites. Black land, a buffer zone from Jim Crow, offered some respite in nature—gardening, fishing, or hunting as communities strove for self-sufficiency and prosperity. Country life had its hazards, but it appears to have offered more autonomy for Blacks than city life structured by Jim Crow.

From Birmingham, Sallye Davis built ties with other middle-class Negro families. She also forged political, educational, and financial bridges with affluent white families—some of whom were communists—that would prove highly beneficial to the family. As a young child, Angela Davis would socialize with Black and white communists who traveled to Birmingham to organize with the Southern Negro Youth Congress. However, as a teen and young woman, she would consider the CPUSA "conservative," as the party of her parents.

A reform-minded radical, an elementary teacher in segregated schools, constrained by practicalities and domestic responsibilities, Mrs. Davis in a number of ways sharply contrasted the California Black revolutionaries who would later inspire her daughters (although she was similar in ways to mentor Charlene Mitchell). *Angela Davis: An Autobiography* describes the mother's compassionate, familial commitments that resonated with the middle-class homemaker and educator. The kind, conscientious elementary school teacher distributed, discarded, and washed—and sometimes new—clothing of her children to the poor. As a maternal figure focused on education and social uplift, Mrs. Davis's deep commitment to social justice and Black equality would create networks that years later would prove indispensable in assisting her imperiled daughter after she became a political fugitive and political prisoner.[5] There must have been idyllic moments for the Davis family that climbed into the middle class. The first of four Davis siblings, Angela Yvonne, was born on January 26, 1944. Her younger siblings followed some two years apart: Benjamin (1945), Fania (1948), and Reginald (1950). Angela and Ben spent their first years in the mixed-income Black community of public housing. There her mother organized for tenants' rights and reliable delivery of heat and water. In 1948, the year Fania Davis was born, the family transitioned from the projects on Eighth Avenue to integrate a predominantly white middle-class neighborhood. They moved into a spacious Queen Anne home. Angela and her younger three siblings grew up and played among fruit trees planted in their large yard.

An Autobiography reveals that Davis's mother "had many friends who were members of the Communist Parties." That network of friends made the party seem a protective part of Angela's childhood and eventually influenced her decision to join the communist Che-Lumumba Club, as opposed to Black militant organizations in California that were rooted and based in working-class and impoverished Black communities. Sallye Davis's communist networks opened academic doors for her children and strengthened defense networks for Angela, the future fugitive, prisoner, and defendant. Friendships with Birmingham Black communist families, the Jacksons and Burnhams, existed in the 1940s and 1950s. The Jackson family was forced out of Birmingham as police sought to imprison the father for anti-racist activism; the family relocated to New York City. By the 1950s, the Burnhams as communists were also forced to relocate to New York City. Progressive New York grappled with the 1951 treason trial of Julius and Ethel Rosenberg for nuclear espionage; persecuted and prosecuted by New York attorney Roy Cohn, an associate of Senator Eugene McCarthy, the Rosenbergs were convicted. In 1953, Julius and Ethel Rosenberg were electrocuted at Sing-Sing Prison in Ossining, NY. The first peace-time execution for treason in the twentieth century had a chilling effect on activists aligned with the communist party, including Black families in Birmingham.[6] The 1950s McCarthy Senate Hearings's "witch hunts" lasted until 1954, when President Eisenhower requested an Army investigation and censorship of Senator Eugene McCarthy. US domestic anti-communism aligned with US-CIA destabilization of foreign socialist, communist, and labor union-led governments. That year, the young Angela turned ten, and the battles consuming her most were the ones in the segregated school yard of the local Negro school.

Underresourced Schools

In September 1948, precocious four-year-old Angela—whose mother had already taught her to read—enrolled in Carrie A. Tuggle Elementary School. The young Davis became more aware that they had acquired an elegant, hard-earned home by integrating into hostilities. All of the children experienced the trauma of a Jim Crow childhood marred by racism, policing, Klan terror, and substandard schools. Despite a Jim Crow childhood, or because of it, Davis's parents ensured that their children had resources, connections, and upward mobility tied to affluent white progressive networks. Davis might *not* have achieved the same educational outcomes and employment if her family had stayed in the projects or if she had graduated from the local underresourced Black high school (Davis had to repeat her sophomore year at her Manhattan private high school she integrated because of the vast difference in schooling and development). She could have attended Fisk and become a pediatrician which was the desire in her early teens. Impoverished Black children appear to have resented and targeted students with more resources. *An Autobiography* suggests she was mocked by darker Negro schoolchildren because of her light skin and "good hair" and their assumptions that she thought herself better than them;[7] targeting select students, painful taunts raged at a pecking order of color, caste, and classism rather than white supremacy and poverty in the 1950s. By the 1960s, older youths in the Black Panther Party would fight white nationalism, capitalism, and imperialism.

Having never experienced poverty and hunger, or lack of adequate resources, and, as a child, horrified at the existence of child poverty and hunger, she stole coins from her father's pockets—change to be used at his Birmingham gas station—hid the money, and carried it to school, to distribute among the poor children at Tuggle Elementary who were not properly fed before school and who could not afford the school lunch.

Tuggle Elementary all-Black staff were beholden to a white school board that divested from their education in order to promote Jim Crow segregation, racism, and inferiority complexes. Fights among segregated Black children in middle school escalated into high school homicides. For Davis, the violence from elementary school carried over into high school, and intensified so much at "Parker [High]… it verged on fratricide" with near daily fights, and tragically, a schoolmate knifing another student to death in the school yard. Davis reflects: "We seemed to be caught in a whirlpool of violence and blood from which none of us could swim away."[8] Davis's parents' decision to send all of their children to private schools in the north might have also been based on safety issues.

When Angela turned fifteen, family outmigration for the Davis children became the norm. Leaving Birmingham's all-Black segregated and underresourced schools was ironically triggered by the 1954 Supreme Court *Brown v. Board of Education* desegregation ruling against "separate but equal schooling." The schools were separate but never equally funded by taxpayers. (Alabaman schools were not desegregated until 1963 when Davis was a sophomore at Brandeis University.)

Tuggle Elementary School received limited financial resources from a white school board. Keeping good teachers who could survive Jim Crow contempt was not easy. Most deferred to racists, setting an example of submission for their Black pupils. Angela Davis recalls a verbal confrontation a Black teacher had with a white school board member: "Once a Black teacher did fight back. When the white men called him 'Jesse' in front of his class, he replied in a deep but cold voice, 'In case you have forgotten, my name is Mr. Champion.' He knew, as the words left his lips, that he had just given up his job."[9] As heroic as Mr. Champion's claim to respect was, the lack of public support among adults for him troubled Angela: "Jesse Champion was a personal friend of my parents, and I was appalled by the silence that reigned among the Black community following his act. It probably stemmed from a collective sense of guilt that his defiance was the exception and not the norm."[10] The humiliation led to violence within Birmingham's Black community. Witnessing the internalized hatred among her peers, Davis writes: "It hurt me." Her memoir records the assaults:

> The fight in which my girlfriend Olivia got stabbed with a knife. It hurt to see another friend, Chaney—furious when a teacher criticized her in front of the class—stand up, grab the nearest chair and fly into the teacher with it. The whole class turned into one great melee, some assisting Chaney, others trying to rescue the teacher, and the rest of us trying to break up the skirmish.[11]

The child who early in her youth envisioned herself as a pediatrician became a peacemaker in school. Reflecting upon the violence at the segregated school, she describes the rage of schoolmates as self-inflicted wounds in the absence of political critiques, redirecting them from the structural sources of their pain. The children were "folding in on ourselves, using ourselves as whipping posts because we did not yet know how to struggle against the real cause of our misery."[12] The lack of mobility, even for the middle class—trapped in segregated environments with the poor, struggling alongside them with substandard housing, public services, and public education—impressed upon them the need to break out of confinements.

Screenings of white troops and veterans during the US invasion of Vietnam would lead to the first documentation and studies of a "new" health disorder called "Post-Traumatic Stress Disorder" (PTSD).[13] White feminists would append the disorder to (white) rape survivors. Birmingham Black children struggling under Jim Crow law in under-resourced schools, constantly dishonored or threatened as Blacks, were confronted with PTSD but with few to no resources to cope with it. The Davis children, though, had a buffer: their well-connected parents and influential white allies facilitated the purchase of a spacious Queen Anne from which they could rent out rooms to supplement their income. Davis's parents – as formally trained teachers – could help with homework and structure informal study to stay abreast at school, if not at the head of the class.

White Supremacist Terrorism

White flight and terrorism followed the entry of the Black middle class into previously white neighborhoods. The Davises had been one of the first Black families to move into the "whites-only" zone. There was violence in the projects and violence in the suburbs. They were distinct and related. Those whites who could not or would not move from the city's suburbs in "white flight" represented an enemy formation for young Angela Davis, who, along with other neighborhood children, went on the offensive. The Black children would taunt the "old, racist couple"—the Montees—and "the people with the hateful eyes"—who refused Blacks/Negroes civility and refused to move out. When Pastor Deyaberts and his wife bought the house next door to the Montees, crossing the visibly invisible line of segregation, the Klan bombed their home in the spring of 1949. Angela was five years old, living with her toddler siblings in a war zone: "I was in the bathroom washing my white shoelaces for Sunday School the next morning when an explosion a hundred times louder than the loudest, most frightening thunderclap I had ever heard shook our house." Davis recalls medicine bottles falling from shelves and shattering on the floor, which "seemed to slip away from" below her as she "raced into the kitchen and [into] my frightened mother's arms."[14] *An Autobiography* describes the anguished and angry gathering of Blacks who "came up the hill and stood on 'our' side, to glare" at the bombed-out Deyaberts' home: "Far into the night they spoke of death, of white hatred, death, white people, and more death. But of their own fear they said nothing. Apparently, it did not exist, for Black families continued to move in."[15] Fear existed. So, too, did armed self-defense and Black rage against murderous racists.

Around age twelve, Angela Davis would learn of a boy, three years older than her, who was tortured and murdered in the adjacent state of Mississippi. The August 28, 1955 sexual violation, torture, and lynching of Emmett Till, in Money, Mississippi, created another Black mother militant—this one with a murdered child. Mamie Till Mobley retrieved his mutilated and bloated body (he had been thrown in a river weeks before he was retrieved) and held a funeral in Chicago. Ten thousand mourners attended the open-casket funeral. Some maintain that the Black fourteen-year-old murdered for the "crime" of whistling at a white woman, had a lisp; reportedly, his mother had taught him to conquer it by whistling his words. Tortured, murdered, and thrown into a river to decompose, the boy's mutilated body was captured and frozen in the photographs from the open casket funeral in Chicago.[16]

Negro/Black publications such as *JET*, as well as the international press, published the photo of the mutilated teen in his coffin on the covers of or inside their publications; magazines in brown paper wrapping were mailed to Black homes and businesses throughout the United States. Emmett's murder was the spark that led to Rosa Parks's refusal to relinquish her seat on a segregated Montgomery, Alabama, bus. On December 4, 1955, the Montgomery bus boycotts commenced, with Rosa Parks and Rev. King, Jr., the same year that the US military and CIA became involved in destabilizing Vietnam after the Vietnamese forced France in 1954 to relinquish its former colony.

An Autobiography rarely references these seismic events in civil rights and human rights. The memoir reflects a childhood shielded from political engagement but emotionally terrorized by bombings that personally threatened Davis's life and the lives of her family and community. The proactive engagement of her parents included working with an armed community of watch patrols largely comprised of fathers collectively protecting their homes. In Davis's family circles, it also included discouraging children from civil rights organizing, sending them out of the south to prep schools in the north—thus sparing their children from not only attacks but also confrontations with racist atrocities. Young liberation activists, as nonviolent "child soldiers" or "shock troops," did enlist in the campaign to break the back of Jim Crow. Yet those students tended to stay in the south as child soldiers for Black human rights (German Jewish philosopher Hannah Arendt, while living in New York City, chastised Black parents for "using" their children in the civil rights struggle; Ralph Ellison's cutting response became a mini-tutorial.[17])

Among the first Black families to own a grand home in a white neighborhood, the Davises took in boarders, as noted before, during their early years of home ownership. Family mobility into previously all-white communities manifested as an individualized desegregation movement. Their refusal to submit to Jim Crow norms met retaliation: vandalism and bombings by the Klan. Negroes renamed the city "Bombingham." As the bombings continued, they christened the neighborhood, where their house proudly stood as a prime target, as "Dynamite Hill." Angela, Ben, Fania, and Reginald, the Davis children, share vivid memories of the trauma. The church their family attended was destroyed by the Klan because it had integrated discussions about integration:

When I was 11 and Fania was 7, the church we attended, the First Congregational Church, was burned. I was a member of an interracial discussion group there, and the church was burned as a result of that group. We grew up in an atmosphere of terror ... it's important to recognize that there were reigns of terror throughout the 20th century.[18]

Attacks against Black churches or houses of worship where nonviolent activists met to organize were common during the southern movement. The violence often went unpunished and made armed self-defense a practical necessity and, in fact, a deterrent from violence, arson, and death. Despite the weapons that their families had for self-protection, churches that the Davis sisters visited or attended became piles of burnt timber and ash. Angela's church, a few blocks from her home, sat across from the home of a prominent Birmingham attorney: "Arthur D. Shores, an amazing civil rights lawyer, who worked with Thurgood Marshall to bring down the system of segregation through litigation … [survived but his] home was bombed twice." For Angela Davis, "litigation," following and practicing the law to obtain civil rights, could mean a death sentence for Blacks.[19]

Referencing the September 1963, 16th Street Birmingham bombing tragedy where Klansmen killed four young girls—Angela Davis was studying in France at the time as a Brandeis undergrad, and her younger sister was attending a private high school in New Jersey and preparing for Swarthmore—Fania Davis candidly speaks about Jim Crow terrorism scarring her childhood and growing up in Birmingham: "Some very, very good friends of mine were killed by bombs, bombs that were planted by racists. I remember from the time I was very small …. the sounds of bombs exploding across the street, our house shaking. I remember my father having to have guns at his disposal at all times … at any moment … we might expect to be attacked."[20]

Author of 2019 *The Little Book of Race and Restorative Justice: Black Lives, Healing, and US Social Transformation*, Fania Davis contributes her narratives that align with those of her older sister: "We were fortunate. Bombs never struck our home, but they struck the homes of families all around us. We often were wakened in the wee hours of the morning by the terrifying sounds of bombs exploding."[21] Noting how Bombingham fathers purchased and carried weapons to protect their families, four years Angela's junior, Fania defers to her sister's account of the violence: "My sister remembers, I was too young, but she remembers there were times when my father heard noises and grabbed his gun and went downstairs to make sure that there were no Klanners lurking in the bushes."[22] The siblings archive their accounts for the public, normalizing *personal* or *familial* armed self-defense as a rational response to lethal threats from violent racists: "My father participated in armed patrols because they had to protect the community. They'd get out every night, in shifts of course, with their weapons and they'd drive around the community to make sure that there weren't any strange racists there, because they bombed houses all over."[23] "They bombed houses all over" is not hyperbole. Between 1957 and 1962, "Bombingham" suffered fifty unsolved bombings. During that same five-year span, Vice President Nixon met with Rev. King, SCLC leader Ralph Abernathy, and NAACP leader Roy Wilkins to spearhead the Civil Rights Act of 1957, the first civil rights legislation since reconstruction.[24] It is possible that bombings accelerated as protests to civil rights legislation.

Police Violence

The heart of the anti-Black violence in Birmingham resided not with rogue KKK but with state employees. Police violence destabilized Black communities. Bombings were attributed to Police Commissioner Eugene "Bull" Connor, who headed the police forces and controlled Birmingham's city government. While serving as the Commissioner of Public Safety in Birmingham, Connor, a white nationalist, worked with the leadership of the Ku Klux Klan to terrorize Black citizens. Connor would, among other atrocities, advertise and promote bombings on the radio in order to deter civil rights activism and integration. *An Autobiography* details the ruthless violence of the police commissioner:

> Connor—would often get on the radio and make statements like, "Niggers have moved into a white neighborhood. We better expect some bloodshed tonight," and sure enough, there would be bloodshed … in my neighborhood, all of the men organized themselves into an armed patrol. They had to take their guns and patrol our community every night because they did not want that to happen again.[25]

Davis's outrage imprints civil and human rights violations on the pages as she puts Connor on trial and establishes guilt despite his immunity from prosecution. Years after his death, Davis, through her writings and speeches, defined Bull Connor, making infamy his legacy as a police commissioner who championed white rights like a fascist. The autobiography prints him on the page as a Jim Crow terrorist who destroyed the lives of Black children. The police turned Black self-protection into a Sisyphean task.

Years after Connor's reign of terror, the Birmingham Public Library used the Freedom of Information Act (FOIA) to post digital copies of FBI reports from the Alabama Special Agent in Charge (ASAC) and Klan informants. The people's archive, freely available to the public, reveals the May 12, 1961, report days before the Congress on Racial Equality (CORE) brought its civil rights crusade through Birmingham. The Alabama Knights, KKK, and Birmingham police all opposed the planned Freedom Rides for May 14, 1961. The ASAC dutifully informed superiors what FBI Klan informants knew about the police commissioner:

> Page said that Eugene "Bull" Connor, Police Commissioner, Birmingham, had stated, to whom not known, "By God, if you are going to do this thing, do it right." Referring to the Klan intervention with the CORE organization, Bull Connor further indicated when trouble broke out he would see that fifteen to twenty minutes would elapse before police officers would arrive at the scene. Bull Connor said if Negro members of CORE enter bus depot restaurant, Klansmen are to start an incident and blame the incident on the Negroes, thus allowing a fight to begin. Bull Connor said if they attempt to enter the rest rooms in the bus depot they are to beat them and "make them look like a bulldog got ahold of them." Then remove the clothes from the person and leave the individual nude in the rest room. If a nude person attempted to leave the rest room, he would be immediately arrested and it would be seen that this person went to the penitentiary. Bull Connor said

if any Klansman is arrested, he is to insist that the Negro was at fault but that if any sentences are given to Klansmen, he would insure that they would be light. Connor stated no member of the Klan is to carry his identification card and only persons who have pistol permits were to carry their pistols … Birmingham PD not being advised UACB in view of Cook's talk with Shelton and Connor's alleged statement to Klan Members. It is believed that if this information were furnished, it would be turned over to the Klan immediately and the informant would be immediately compromised. Local military agencies advised. All Birmingham informants alerted.[26]

The Davises' Black communities did not need a police report to alert them to organized terror campaigns waged by white state employees. The family mulled its options and decided to stay in Birmingham. They could have moved to New York City to join the Burnhams and Jacksons, close family friends whose parents were Black activists also aligned with the CPUSA. Frank Davis, though, was determined that racists would not push him off his property and out of the state that he and his family had lived in for generations. The Davis children would continue to be exposed to systemic violence from white Klansmen, police, and suburbanites, and social violence within the segregated and impoverished sectors of Black communities and schools.

Mama's Girls

An older Angela Davis would acknowledge how her strong-willed radical mother served as her most important role model in her youth.[27] Mother and daughters, the Davis women, were cut from the same fine cloth of Black bourgeois intellectuals—courageous advocacy for communism or socialism, and a passion for social justice. Their graduate degrees from elite universities, the phenotypical "bright" equated with links to white genealogy, the fashionably attractive, and strong will were embodied in the confident, if not proud or idealized, Negroes/Blacks assimilating into the "American dream" and the pecking order within Black communities and segregated sites. Their radical politics for structural change was the one disruptor in the narrative of assimilation.

Since their activist mother had built a protective framework from the ground up around her children, she created a scaffold of postwar leftist connections that would serve her daughters well. Progress through education remained her primary goal for her four children and her students. Mrs. Davis's three decades of civil rights activism, from 1937 to 1967, put her in touch with luminaries from the southern movement who organized in Alabama: Rosa Parks, Coretta Scott King, Ralph Abernathy, and Stokely Carmichael.[28] As a university student, Angela Davis expressed little interest in or desire for her mother's communist party or the Southern Civil Rights movement led by Southern preachers, attorneys, sharecroppers, and SCLC. However, during her fugitivity and trial, the young Angela Davis would become the beneficiary of networks and skills honed by an older generation that had learned from civil rights battles in the south and fought Jim Crow terrorism. A trained educator, their mother taught in the southern public schools while attaining a graduate degree at a northern elite university in Manhattan, New York University (NYU). Her connections and alliances predicted that the futures of her children would not be confined to Jim Crow Alabama. Angela would be the first to depart, being offered scholarships in 1958 at both the Historically Black College/University (HBCU) Fisk University in Nashville, TN (where her father enrolled in graduate courses) and a private Manhattan school with boarding in New York City. An American Friends Service Committee (AFSC) scholarship program for southern Black students was designed to integrate northern elite white private schools. Although there were multiple factors to consider, Angela Davis followed the path already set by her mother's NYU graduate degree studies and chose New York.

Education outside of the south would create a different trajectory. The affluent and well connected among Black families had the easiest access to funneling their children out of Jim Crow segregation and away from the Black poor into the north and toward integration into the middle class. The most dishonored, overly policed and impoverished were the Black poor and working classes, and radicals who rebelled against racism. Groomed to embody the managerial caste for the Black mass, Angela Davis leaned left while remaining in the talented tenth formation. Promoted by W. E. B. DuBois in his 1903 *Souls of Black Folk*—until he was betrayed by Black elites during the McCarthy era—the talented tenth encompassed Black elites with diverse political leanings. Angela Davis was, in fact, one of the talented tenth of formally educated Blacks who would integrate white elite schools and then provide leadership to the Black mass. The revolutionary Blacks, who largely did not have her background in formal education, were leading movements that the talented tenth could join and follow or attempt to steer and (re)direct.

Sallye Davis had fought Jim Crow, anti-communism, Dixiecrat lawmakers, and Klan terrorists as a seasoned activist who approached issues with an analytical perspective and steely resolve to resist the violence of the bellwether state. Angela Davis notes of her early upbringing: "It took me a long time to recognize that my mother was really the primary influence in my life during my years as a young activist. I saw myself as also rebelling against my parents. And later I recognize that she had carved out the path, in a sense, the whole trajectory that I have followed. She was an activist in the campaign to defend the Scottsboro Nine. She joined the Southern Negro Youth Congress that was a formation that was led by black communists. W. E. B. DuBois spoke at one of their most important gatherings."[29]

Davis, years later, would note the impact of Sallye Davis's politics:

I absorbed all of that by osmosis ... [without] realizing that it had come from my mother. But when I myself ended up on the FBI's most wanted list and in jail ... my mother and other members of my family were my most important advocates. My mother traveled all over the country speaking out on my behalf. As a matter of fact, there are photographs of her holding my sister's, one-year-old or nine-month-old, because my sister is in Europe traveling, urging people to join the campaign for my freedom and my mother's carrying the baby, and has her fist ... I said, "Yeah, yeah, yeah. I am walking in my mother's path."[30]

When her eldest child was incarcerated and preparing for trial, Mrs. Davis moved to California and began to raise funds and travel to speak and advocate for Angela; her younger daughter Fania also devoted herself full-time to the National United Committee to Free Angela Davis. Both Sallye and Fania Davis would embark on international speaking tours for the legal defense. Sallye Davis, as grandmother, also helped to raise Fania Davis's baby daughter while the child's mother traveled to speak for her sister's legal defense.

3

Student Assimilationists and Rebels

In 1954, the federal government determined through the US Supreme Court ruling in *Brown v. Board of Education* that segregated schools were unconstitutional. The court's May 17th unanimous opinion stated: "To separate them [children in elementary, junior and high schools] from others of similar age and qualifications solely because of their race generates a feeling of inferiority as to their status in the community that may affect their hearts and minds in a way unlikely to ever be undone."[1]

Brown v. Board of Education indicated to the Black middle class that "another world [was] opening up" to them.[2] Following the desires of their white constituents, Jim Crow lawmakers dismissed the ruling as an advisement from northern white liberals and communists. In 1957, Daisy Bates, president of the Arkansas state of the NAACP, recruited young Black activists, the Little Rock Nine, to challenge segregated schools in Arkansas; they set the precedent for the nation's enforcement of federal law.[3] The benefits of *Brown v. Board*, like most civil rights gains, were limited and skewed toward those best positioned to benefit: children of Black elites who had networks with influential white progressives. Black parents organized to integrate southern schools despite the opposition from state and local governments that sided with violent racists. President Eisenhower (re-)established law and order to quell white violence in 1957 by sending U.S. National Guard troops to Arkansas to enforce and protect the integration of Little Rock's Central High School; he thereby upheld the US Supreme Court's determination in the *Brown v. Board*[4] ruling that race-based "separate but equal" public school systems were unlawful.

Those battles were painfully fought in the south. Some Birmingham Black middle-class parents, though, decided to keep their children out of a desegregation war zone and thus sought schooling in the private sector, and in the north; sheltered from public schooling, white mobs and Klansmen, and lack of material resources, Angela Davis and her siblings would be educated in New York and New Jersey. Davis, as an adult, understood the Trojan Horse embedded within *Brown v. Board*—the quality and autonomy of students would be diminished, along with employment sectors for Black teachers and administrators:

[I]n the process of desegregating the schools in Birmingham, Alabama, great damage was done to the existing structures of education. … I know this from my mother who complained a great deal about the reconfiguration of the schools … [there was a pattern in which] the best Black teachers were sent to the white schools and the worst white teachers were sent to the Black schools … the predominantly Black schools … in the final analysis, it was very difficult to recoup in that respect. Now, as an individual, I think I benefited greatly from this decision [*Brown v. Board of Education*], although I'm not sure it was meant to benefit individuals per se—but rather to lift up communities.[5]

The first Alabama student to go north for schooling on an AFSC grant in the 1950s was a fourteen-year-old Black girl from Montgomery who had a recommendation letter from Rev. Martin Luther King. Over seven years, AFSC helped Black families from seven southern states send more than sixty-five students to be fostered by white northern families in New York, New Jersey, Connecticut, and Pennsylvania while they attended private schools whose tuition AFSC paid. Graduates of the program attended Harvard, Oberlin, Sarah Lawrence, and other private schools.[6]

By 1959, it was Angela Davis's turn to migrate out. Her father Frank Davis coached her into the transition to the north. Davis describes him as "a major influence" in her education: "He's actually responsible for my decision to finish high school in New York."[7] After being accepted in the Fisk University/Meharry Medical School early admission plan, Davis, at age fifteen, had decided to be a pediatrician; she would have graduated at nineteen and then would "go to Meharry across the street, and I would be a doctor by the time I was 23."[8] Frank Davis, who had taken courses at Fisk after graduating with a BA at the HBCU Saint Augustine's University in Raleigh, NC, thought his eldest child was too young for arduous practice as a physician at that age, as Davis recalls: "[H]e looked at me and he said, 'Fisk? I don't think so.' … then I got a list of all of the clothes that I would have to bring, including the long formals and the white short formals …. I said, 'Hmm, I think I'll go to New York.'"[9]

CIA Agents Schooling Students in 1959

The year 1959 was a pivotal year. The Cold War was hot, and given that, the First World was trying to control or expand its accumulations of racialized colonies, and the Second World of the Eastern bloc or Union of Soviet Socialist Republics (USSR) was attempting to modernize without being threatened with atomic bombs (the United States had dropped two in Japan in the closing weeks of the Second World War); the so-called Third World of Africa, Middle East, Asia, Latin America, and the Caribbean would be the sites of wars and assassinations to force former colonies to align with the interests of their former colonizers, the globe's only standing empire: the United States. In 1959, Cuban guerrillas led by Cuban attorney Fidel Castro and Argentinian physician Ernesto "Che" Guevara did the unthinkable in the minds of war hawks: they defeated the dictator Batista, who had controlled the island nation through brutality, torture, and organized crime syndicates backed by US mobsters. The guerrilla armies and intellectuals defeated the most powerful nation in the world—the United States, which was propping up dictatorships and apartheid regimes through CIA assassinations, covert funds, and mercenaries.

When Angela Davis left the Jim Crow south to enroll in a private NYC high school, her future ally was then her ideological foe as a daughter of a communist organizer. Gloria Steinem rose to prominence within the Central Intelligence Agency (CIA) shortly after graduating from Smith College. She had come from a home with parental instability and limited means but reinvented herself and shaped her own trajectory. Thus, the future iconic feminist was a global traveler (post-grad she traveled in India extensively) and returned to elite educational sectors in the United States in order to shepherd students into Cold War antagonisms largely directed or manipulated by the CIA. Steinem's official employer was the National Student Association (NSA). Postwar, the United States formed organizations as global projects to steer capitalism. In 1947 it formed the NSA and the CIA (which during the Second World War had been named the Office of Special Services). The NSA, as a front to steer students into anti-communist commitments, was managed by the Independent Research Service (IRS). IRS co-directors Leonard Bebchick and Gloria Steinem were well-educated intellectuals and skilled writers which was the norm for the CIA. They published a 1959 "educational" pamphlet, *A Review of Negro Segregation in the United States*, celebrating the successes of integration of white and Black students in US colleges and universities. The pamphlet argued that the atrocities that Angela Davis faced in the Jim Crow south were not that relevant because the US government was effective in moving past anti-Black racism. Rather than focus on income inequality, labor exploitation, and white nationalism, *A Review of Negro Segregation in the United States* celebrated an integrationist project—embodied in the high school and university educational trajectory of the Davis children—and depicted the United States as a progressive, pro-integration nation with pockets of white nationalists. *A Review* was developed to counter the appeal of socialist youths and Second and Third Worlds' countries which celebrated the victories and independence of the 1959 Cuban revolution. In 1960, a delegation from the Cuban revolution visited the United States for the first time; when their accommodations near the UN were withdrawn, at the invitation of Malcolm X, Fidel Castro and the Cuban delegation stayed at the Theresa Hotel in Harlem. The NSA publication with its glossy, cheerful images, black-and-white photos of well-groomed interracial youths studying together or posing as beauty pageant contestants, wanted students to believe that capitalism was the only option for the future and that racism was fading.

A Review of Negro Segregation was propaganda for international students, including those from Soviet satellites, who were gathering in Vienna at a Youth Festival. With a foreword by Senator Hubert Humphrey (D-Minnesota), future vice president in the Johnson Administration,[10] *A Review* described the IRS as "a non-profit, privately financed educational association of students and recent graduates, formed for the purpose of providing objective information to young Americans interested in the Vienna Youth Festival."[11] Difficult to locate today in public libraries, the sophisticated forty-nine-page pamphlet of CIA Cold War propaganda claimed that slave-holding presidents were noble and triumphantly heralded the United States as overcoming "negro segregation" without the need for civil rights protest movements or self-defense or anti-racist control over policing.[12] In fact there is no real mention of the movement in which activists and nonactivists—such as Emmett Till—were violated or murdered.

Deflecting attention from anti-Black, roiling racist atrocities soiling the international reputation of the United States required that educators and mentors reassure students that the system was improving, and that seductive socialist/communist propaganda that decried US racism was ill-informed. The NSA pamphlet minimized US racist violence by deflecting from the Montgomery Bus Boycott, Rev. King, segregated housing, schooling, employment sectors, police violence, and terrorism. The pamphlet projected a progressive north as a promised land, juxtaposing it against a backward south and reassuring that just as in the antebellum age, the north would win again. *A Review* does not mention objective history such as the 13th Amendment legalizing slavery for those duly convicted of crime, and that the rise of convict prison leasing after the war meant that Blacks died at faster rates than they had on plantations because they were worked to death as prison property of the state. *A Review* also failed to note the betrayals of Reconstruction in the 1877 "compromise" that withdrew federal troops from the south; those troops had been sent to protect emancipated Blacks from racial terrorists, confederates, who had lost the war but would engage in terrorist tactics to reassemble white nationalist power. Hence the Black codes became Jim Crow segregation.[13] The NSA's fervor for anti-communism wedded it to the white nationalism it supposedly repudiated. Ironically, Vladimir Lenin's 1913 description of US segregated schooling is reflected in the CIA's *A Review of Negro Segregation*:

> In the United States of America, the division of the States into the Northern and Southern holds to this day in all departments of life; the former possess the greatest traditions of freedom and of struggle against the slave-owners; the latter possess the greatest traditions of slave-ownership, survivals of persecution of the Negroes, who are economically oppressed and culturally backward (44 percent of Negroes are illiterate, and 6 percent of whites), and so forth. In the Northern States Negro children attend the same schools as white children do. In the South there are separate 'national,' or racial, whichever you please, schools for Negro children. I think this is the sole instance of actual 'nationalization' of schools.[14]

Steinem's writing shaped perceptions of racial integration as a seamless endeavor—rendering the civil rights *movement* unnecessary for human rights. She promoted international confidence in the US government and white civil society, portraying both as inherently *not* hostile to Black Americans. At the 1959 seventh World Youth Festival in Vienna, she studied and exploited the resentments Europeans had for their behemoth neighbor, the Soviet Union, that overshadowed and dominated the borders of Finland and Austria. (Austria signed a 1955 neutrality treaty as a détente maneuver to distance itself from both the United States and the USSR.)

Steinem was a gifted, attractive young anti-communist woman selected by the CIA to steer progressive students. Her 1959 IRS report celebrated the United States as a non-racist or anti-racist democracy. At the student festivals, Steinem would gather and analyze information on students attending communist-sponsored international events or forums; identify potential assets based on their willingness to promote US ideologies (pro-capitalism or anti-communism); offer monetary reimbursements; engineer extortion or "blackmail"; and cultivate ignorance among "useful idiots." Hundreds of international university students receiving IRS funding were unaware that the CIA paid for their flights and accommodations all the while surveilling them and shaping their political loyalties to defend Western capitalism and hegemony by deflecting critiques of US racism and poverty.[15]

The NSA (and the United States) was portrayed as encouraging not repressing civil rights. *A Review of Negro Segregation* is published eight years after the US government punished the signatories of the 1951 *We Charge Genocide* document, authored by the Civil Rights Congress, a Black cadre of the CPUSA. Delivered to the UN by Paul Robeson, the document depicted US crimes against the "Negro people." The text circulated throughout the globe. In 1964, Malcolm X, el Hajj Malik el-Shabazz willing to work with civil rights organizations supported delivering the document to the United Nations. *A Review of Negro Segregation* had hoped to bury, if not counter, *We Charge Genocide* and disappear it, as its pages veiled or ignored Emmett Till, Rev. King, Rosa Parks, the Montgomery Bus Boycott, civil rights demonstrations, and lynching. Steinem,[16] the lead author, marketed CIA Cold War propaganda for the United States. She turned historical objectivity into promissory memories in which the formerly enslaved—with family members working to death through postbellum convict prison leasing, or dishonored and disappearing through exploitation, poverty, incarceration, and police brutality—now had a promising future:

> Negro and white students study and socialize together at Lincoln University, Missouri. On many campuses, Negroes are gaining acceptance in social fraternities and sororities. They are especially active participants in local and national student organizations, particularly the National Students Association (NSA), which has had Negroes elected to its highest offices.[17]

Promoting the text at the 1959 Youth Festival, Bebchick and Steinem minimized negative perceptions of the United States and reassured that the trajectory of US democracy was following the path of human rights. The following year, the 1960 Freedom Riders launched their campaign for the states to follow federal law and end discrimination. The violence arrayed against the courageous civil rights activists—white supremacists and police attacked and firebombed buses and passengers to stop desegregation—dispelled *A Review*'s mythmaking.

The CIA's propaganda promoted the promise of Black assimilation absent beatings, lynching, rapes, fire hoses, police dogs, batons, and Klansmen (uniformed and plain clothed). State propaganda fought an ideological war against not just the Soviets but also the CPUSA, civil rights militants, and rebellious students. Multiracial progressivism and Black American leadership were materializing and it did not have to be radical, according to CIA propaganda, because the changes were coming from the federal government and northern liberal elites (who would have been recruiting grounds for the CIA). *A Review* targeted future leaders within their countries:

[W]ith every step forward the Negro takes, the whole nation moves ahead, for along with segregation many other, more subtle forms of discrimination are being cast out. Every law against segregation, every Supreme Court decision, every municipal ordinance and Interstate Commerce Commission ruling, speaks not only of outlawing prejudice against Negroes, but bans discrimination against any person on the ground of race, color, religion or ethnic origin.[18]

The CIA agents sought to destabilize Soviet credibility and alliances with Third World students engaged in anti-colonial struggles. US students who were members of the NSA did not know that the CIA was covertly funding and steering them. Both US and British "intelligence" targeted western European students to dismiss or diminish their critiques of racism, capitalism, and colonialism. Intelligence gathering sought to infiltrate or destabilize the student "left" in the Americas, Europe, and Third World. Steinem's work ethic and intellectual skills at gaslighting the left were impressive; although she was outed as a CIA operative in 1967, she would still be asked to head the CPUSA's fundraising campaign to free Angela Davis in 1971, when Davis was put on trial. Perhaps Steinem's adjacency to state power is what made her essential in the defense trial of Davis, a rising star in the CPUSA, during the Cold War era.

Progressive, Private Educational Railroads into the North

Under the heading "Pairing Southern Students with Northern Families Taught Everyone," the AFSC describes its endeavors from 1957 to 1965 as a "deep involvement with the civil rights movement" through a "unique program born in 1957, when a violent backlash began against the civil rights movement to desegregate the South." According to the organization, its staff and supporters confronted Jim Crow "resistance to integrated schools"; its belief that "'access to the best knowledge available' is a right for all people" led to the creation of the Southern Student Program,[19] an alleged oasis that coexisted with a Jim Crow war zone around southern school integration (although, in the 1970s, white Boston families violently and viciously opposed school integration and Black students still faced emotional and psychological alienation and aggression in liberal white schools).

On November 14, 1960, in New Orleans, armed US marshals protected four Black girls: Leona Tate, Tessie Prevost, and Gaile Etienne desegregating McDonough 19 School; and Ruby Bridges desegregating William Frantz School. After her six-year-old daughter passed an advanced placement test, Lucille Bridges, who had insisted that Ruby be tested, enrolled the child in a white elementary school five blocks from their home (as opposed to the Black elementary school that was several miles away). Ruby Bridges, at age six, became the first Black child to integrate a white elementary school in the United States. White mobs greeted the child daily to throw objects, curse her, and threaten to kill her: a white woman displayed a coffin with a Black doll inside; another white mother yelled she would poison the child. Born the year *Brown v. Board of Education* was declared law, Ruby was only permitted to eat food brought from home because the white male federal marshals guarding her thought she might be poisoned.

Marshals escorted her to the restroom. Ruby spent the year confined in a classroom, the only child with the one white teacher from Boston, Barbara Henry.

Civil rights battles were waged in different states on multiple fronts with diverse combatants and allies. White supremacist bombers, screaming mobs, and violent police enforcers waged war on southern Black children. In the north (with the exception of Boston in the 1970s) the violence and racist aggression were low key; battles continued, but more on an emotional landscape. Affluent white high schools such as Manhattan's Elizabeth Irwin High School, which Angela Davis attended, recruited a few Black students through the AFSC integration programs. Wealthy white students Davis met in high school invited her to their second homes in the Hamptons on weekends; at the dinner table they insisted that their Black maids leave the kitchen to greet her, presumably the first Black teen that wealthy white teens had ever brought home. Outside of the Jim Crow segregated south, Davis found herself as an anomaly—no longer targeted by physical anti-Black violence but now the signifier of the progressivism and anti-racism that *A Review* celebrated and the object of curiosity to the people who created privileged educational zones that she had entered and within which she would remain.[20]

As noted earlier, the "talented tenth" concept was popularized in DuBois's *The Souls of Black Folks*—and later repudiated when he was persecuted as a communist or radical—and had been engineered by white philanthropists seeking to create a managerial elite to quell Black rebellion and steer Black masses (elite HBCUs Morehouse and Spelman are named after white wealthy donors, respectively Henry Morehouse and Laura Rockefeller Spelman, of the Missionary Home Baptist Society.[21]) In the name of progress, white elites and their Black supporters depoliticized Black education after the Civil War, when everyone was radicalized, and during Reconstruction when the convict prison lease system emerged to work Blacks to death in northern industries' investments in mining, forestry, lumber, and industrialization of the south. Robber barons expanded their great wealth by exploiting Black labor: J. P. Morgan had been a war profiteer during the Civil War.[22] Corporate leaders as capitalists—Rockefeller, Carnegie, Cornell—funded colleges and universities that often bore their names.

Funded by corporate magnates, as noted earlier, the all-white American Baptist Home Mission Society (ABHMS) coined the term "talented tenth" in 1896.[23] King's alma mater Morehouse College is named after ABHMS secretary Henry Morehouse. Rockefeller Spelman was an abolitionist. In theory, philanthropic intervention or charitable gifts by capitalists can address racist oppression and poverty.

During Reconstruction, the Rutherford-Hayes compromise allowed the US government to pull out federal troops sent to quell white supremacist terrorists from killing emancipated Blacks and stealing their land; in exchange for withdrawal of troops, southern Congressional reps voted to make Rutherford president of the United States. W. E. B. DuBois's 1935 *Black Reconstruction* describes how federal interventions in the south favored capital – corporate wealth – not Black workers or laborers who would engage in a 'General Strike' during the civil war. Angela Davis would briefly meet DuBois at the home of Herbert Aptheker and his daughter Bettina Aptheker, lifelong friend of Davis; at the time late in his life, DuBois had joined the CPUSA.[24]

Angela Davis came of age during some of the most transformative movements in US contemporary history. Unlike King[25] and DuBois[26]—both with PhDs from prestigious institutions, respectively Boston University and Harvard—she encountered Marxism while studying in her leftist high school. As a CPUSA member, and a red-diaper baby, she was anti-imperialist and opposed the United States's unpopular war in Vietnam—a war that would lead to 58,000 US casualties and 2–3 million Vietnamese deaths.[27] As a teen in a "foreign land"she was part of the migration of Black elites not just in the United States but throughout the globe. The class similarities—despite the cultural differences between these elites representing oppressed nations and communities— suggest that the freedom movements had multiple layers of complexities and contradictions.

Cold War Educational Alliances with African Elites

In the late 1950s, when Davis was finishing high school and preparing for university, Tom Mboya, the co-founder of the Republic of Kenya, was introduced to Cora Weiss, a Jewish intellectual and activist who navigated multiple political alliances.[28] Mboya convinced Weiss to support African students enrolling in US colleges and universities. Together they secured funds for the first flight which brought eighty-one students (thirteen women) to southern segregated colleges. According to Weiss, "Establishment" organizations, such as the African American Institute and the Institute for International Education, "pilloried" the endeavor, accusing the Africa education fund of "lowering the standard of education" by bypassing African elites (who could study in Britain) in order to bring in "kids from the bush." Centrists and conservatives argued that the students would lack sufficient funds and refuse to return to their home countries where they could become the colonial managerial elite, an international version of the talented tenth. However, recruited students began studies in colleges in the Jim Crow south "at white Christian colleges that wouldn't take American Blacks"; however, in the white missionary tradition of "saving heathen souls," conservative and white nationalist Christian colleges enrolled "Africans because they were foreigners."[29]

Reportedly, 778 students came from Kenya and East Africa in the early years of international students traveling to the United States. Weiss asserts that "the African students were the wedge that opened the door to African Americans in southern white colleges."[30] A transverse migration emerged among global Black elite students. Southern US students were leaving the south for the north. International Black students were leaving Africa for the US south. Weiss makes no reference to the roles of southern civil rights educational activists such as James Meredith (the first African American student to integrate the University of Mississippi), Medgar Evers (applicant to University of Mississippi law school), and Martin Luther King, Jr. (doctorate in theology from Boston University). Apparently, Black students needed a "wedge," one constructed or directed by elite whites. A future supporter of Angela Davis and Gloria Steinem, Weiss would also raise funds to endow the Rutgers University Gloria Steinem Chair in media studies (the inaugural chair was Naomi Klein), after supporting African students to

gain entry into southern white colleges; essentially, they "worked their way north …
[and] graduated from northern schools."[31] Black prominent entertainers such as actors
Harry Belafonte and Sidney Poitier, sports star Jackie Robinson, and others supported
fundraisers to recruit African students to the United States. Still, it was a Massachusetts
white liberal senator who provided substantial funding through his family foundation
and, as a Cold War liberal, facilitated educational elites entering the United States. Tom
Mboya, through Cora Weiss's connections, met with Senator John F. Kennedy. Through
that meeting he was able to secure $100,000 (which would be approximately $1 million
today) from the Kennedy Foundation.[32] At some juncture, elite Black American and
African students would meet not only at HBCUs such as Howard University but also
at white liberal schools. Davis's ties to the CPUSA (through family, the Apthekers, and
Elizabeth Erwin) made her early education shaped more by communists with ties to
the USSR than to liberal intellectuals as staunch loyalists to the United States. However,
over time she would blend the two sectors.

The US American Administration, of course, was anti-communist and anti-
Soviet, and anti-Third World liberations. The United States's destabilization of
Brazil's democracy led to a military junta; its list of interventions included the Bay
of Pigs invasion of Cuba, the 1961 assassination of Patrice Lumumba, war atrocities
in Vietnam, attempts to kill Fidel Castro, assassinations of Che Guevara, and later
Amilcar Cabral. (In 2023, the daughters of Malcolm X, and civil rights attorney Ben
Crump announced that they would be filing a lawsuit against the NYPD, FBI, and CIA
for the 1965 assassination of Malcolm X el Hajj Malik el Shabazz.)

The Black elites had some privileges with which they could negotiate schooling
and alienation at relatively privileged settings. The Davis sisters, to whatever degree
they understood the international flow of Black elite students from abroad, were aware
that they could weaponize a hierarchy of blackness established by whites and turn that
global reality into a performance play to mock white nationalists at home.

Student Tools for Mocking Jim Crow: Become a Faux International Elite

As a student, Angela Davis's internationalism and interests focused on Europe not
Africa. She was not a Pan-Africanist. She first studied French and later German
philosophers. Davis grew up in two starkly different cities: "Bombingham" with its
primitive racism and New York City with sophisticated racism. She and her siblings
traveled as children from Jim Crow to Gotham each summer with their mother as
she completed her graduate degree at NYU. *An Autobiography* details no bombings or
police violence in NYC directed at the Davises. Each time Angela Davis returned to
the south from the north, she became "more keenly sensitive to the segregation" of a
Jim Crow childhood in Birmingham. *An Autobiography* recounts her first Birmingham
bus ride with her teenage cousin "Snookie." One day, as a child, Angela Davis raced
for her "favorite place, directly behind the driver" with her older cousin "cheerfully
urging" her to accompany the teen to the back of the bus, but the child had made up
her mind; only when the teen said that she would have an accident if she did not reach

the (fictitious) restroom in the back of the bus did the child relent and accompany her. Davis, years later, reflected:

> I imagine the whites were amused at her dilemma, and the Black people were perhaps just a little embarrassed about their own acquiescence. My cousin was distraught; she was the center of attention and had no notion of what to do .... When we reached the back and I saw there was no toilet, I was angry not only because I had been tricked and lost my seat, but because I didn't know who or what to blame.[33]

Daily insults were constant. As a child, Davis fought to preserve her dignity. Although other middle-class Black children lived in cocoons of Black enclaves where whites rarely ventured, Jim Crow childhoods remained scarred by white militias, police, and Klansmen who terrorized Black families with beatings, rapes, murders, and bombings. Most (middle-class) Black parents shielded their children by discouraging them from activism. None of the Davis children participated in civil rights protests. Still, violence invaded schools and churches.

Fania Davis, Angela's younger sister, was a pugilist who constantly battled Jim Crow:

> I found myself—even as a 10-year-old—just going into the white bathrooms and drinking out of the white-water fountains, because from a very early age I had a fierce sense of right and wrong. My mother would be shopping somewhere else in the store, and before she knew it, the police were called.

An Autobiography describes the sisters' protests against racism in their personal lives. The older sister proposed a plan to mock a Birmingham segregated shoe store by pretending they were "foreigners"—speaking French, or imitating a French accent, they would ask to see shoes: "At the sight of two young Black women speaking a foreign language, the clerks in the store raced to help us. Their delight with the exotic was enough to completely, if temporarily, dispel their normal disdain for Black people." As the sisters began to laugh, the clerk serving them responded nervously, whispering, "Is something funny?" at which point Angela Davis spoke to him in English and explained the "joke." *An Autobiography* notes, "All Black people have to do is pretend they come from another country, and you treat us like dignitaries." Without purchases, the sisters left the store laughing. The teens were able to pull off the stunt against Jim Crow without being physically accosted by white workers or police. Class privilege was mobilized along with white American fantasies about or preferences for "exotic" Africans. Having the wealth to shop in middle-class stores, performing as international Black/African elites was a form of confrontation that vastly differed from classes encouraged by Malcolm X, SNCC, and King to further civil and human rights. Two young Black women took pleasure in sweet revenge against racist whites—their class, coloring, and foreign language skills provided the props for a theatrical victory (whether or not the Davis sisters informed their mother at the time of their performance is unclear).

During the Jim Crow era, segregationists understood the "nonthreatening" African "guest" students to be visitors—not "competitors" for jobs, land, mates, or education.

They also considered them to be different from Negroes or Black Americans. Africans or Blacks from the continent, Latin America, and the Caribbean represented international trade and commerce to white American businesses. Despite "Whites Only" signs and protocol, the store wanted to sell to the Africans belonging to white southern colleges. The Davis sisters must have known that the store was not strictly "Whites Only"; if so, no salesperson would have served them; the police would have been called if Angela and Fania Davis did not immediately leave when told to do so. (Under Jim Crow, whites did not have a stable metric for labeling Mexicans, Asians, Native American in the "whites" and "coloreds" dichotomy, hence a light-skinned Black could have been seen with some ambiguity.) The "color line" was not consistent or uniformly enforced. The sisters explored and tried on merchandise while secretly mocking white shopkeepers who violated or bent white supremacy strictures because they craved currency. The teens triumphed by posing as affluent (they likely had shopped in similar or better stores in the north). Their stylish clothes, self-confidence, coloring, French (not African) language marked them as attractive and white-adjacent; speaking a European language, a colonial language that was not English, they posed as exotic hybrids. Poor, darker-skinned Blacks coming from laboring in the fields would not have been able to cross the threshold into the store to pull such a stunt. If they had entered the store, their outcomes would likely be police brutality, arrest, jail, and further beatings. Davis's story resonates with middle-class Black readers who have been racially profiled or rudely ignored in white-run stores and businesses.

Yet the victory could be pyrrhic if it comes at the cost of class solidarity. Poor Blacks lack the financial means to enter into stores to make such purchases, fake or real. Archie Mafeje notes in his 1993 *Africa Review* article, "Black Nationalists and White Liberals: Strange Bedfellows,"[34] and civil rights activist and SNCC mentor Ella Baker notes in her June 1960 article, "Bigger than a Hamburger" that the civil rights movement needed to be about more than consumerism or the "right" to buy goods, homes, and automobiles that affluent whites possessed.[35] Baker had suggested to SNCC activists not to become a youth wing of the Southern Christian Leadership Conference, headed by a then more moderate King, but to keep autonomy in order to reject capitalism and imperialism while remembering that impoverished Black laborers and workers could not afford to buy a restaurant hamburger.

Student Mobility and Vulnerability

The Davis daughters went back north to their respective schools. As the south roiled with racist threats and violence against Black school children, national and international newspapers and television footage disseminated the spectacle of white American families rioting to keep Black youths from learning. In the southern battles to desegregate Jim Crow public schools, Black children were spat upon, and Black teen girls, with their starched skirts and pristine blouses, were tripped to fall into broken Coke bottles smashed in hallways and school sidewalks. Parents in the middle-class Black community knew the networks to avoid underresourced Black schools and resourced violent white schools. *An Autobiography* offers no accounts of Birmingham

Black school children battling racist white children, or the Davis children actively involved in civil rights protests. Hence, the perspectives of Freeman Hrabowski provide context for the childhood narratives of *An Autobiography*. Both Davis and Hrabowski, whose parents were friends and lived in middle-class integrating neighborhoods, excelled past the norms of their peers (Black and white). Freeman Hrabowski would serve as president of the University of Maryland, Baltimore County, and Davis would be honored as the presidential professor at UC Santa Cruz. Such students integrated US society as "shock troops" for the north, leaving Jim Crow behind. Their battles were significantly different from the Black students in the south who risked their health and/or their lives to integrate southern schools; students dropped out of school or were expelled for participating in Freedom Rides, or voter registration drives to battle Jim Crow and white nationalist terror.

Precocious learners, six years apart in age, Angela Davis and Freeman Hrabowski started school at age four. Mrs. Hrabowski, Freeman's mother, was Angela's favorite teacher in Birmingham and knew that her parents had enrolled Angela in the AFSC program to integrate Black southern children in northern schools. AFSC adapted the template of the postbellum nineteenth-century white philanthropists in the American Baptist Home Missionary Society as white progressive elites created a conduit for their Black counterparts in the south to enroll their children in northern prep schools. Colleges or universities in the AFSC system included those that had enrolled Black elites in the previous century: DuBois went to Harvard; Mary Church Terrill and Anna Julia Cooper to Oberlin. Freeman Hrabowski asserts that both Angela Davis and he had mothers who were teachers, and the middle class provided invaluable assets for advancing in education (and up the economic/cultural ladder). For Davis, Hrabowski, and others in their social circle, "the idea was education was critical, was absolutely critical."[36] They also understood that in that era and today, parental education was central for surviving and thriving; Freeman Hrabowski observes: "Angela and I were both fortunate to be children of middle-class parents ... your mother's a teacher ... we're all affected, influenced by our experiences ...."

Hrabowksi describes the 1963 integration of Birmingham schools – which took place four years after Angela Davis had left Birmingham for New York City – as "a traumatic experience." He recalls how "white families came out when the Black children were to go into the high school ... and threw rocks." The Hrabowski parents were close to Davis's parents. Both Mrs. Davis and Mrs. Hrabowski were militant activists, but Mrs. Hrabowski appears to be the only mother that permitted her child to engage in direct action protest and to have had open confrontations with governmental bodies. In 1948, she was fired from teaching for leading a protest for pay equity for Black teachers in Jefferson County, Alabama; Mrs. Maggie G. Hrabowski had formed a Black group demanding to be paid the same wages as white teachers. As the spokesperson for the organization, she met with the board of education to discuss pay equity demands. She was fired not for organizing a strike but for attempting a Black–white dialogue with the all-white school board members. The offense was treating whites as peers, not as superiors. Later, Ben Hayes, the Black superintendent of Black schools, would hire her to teach in the Birmingham school system.

Just as Angela Davis's parents had considered the HBCU Fisk for her, the Hrabowskis considered Morehouse for their son, but he chose to attend the HBCU Hampton University.[37] Using the same AFSC program, both families enabled their children to escape substandard southern Jim Crow schools, violent white families and teachers, and anti-Black terrorism. While Angela Davis and her siblings integrated elite liberal New York and New Jersey high schools when they turned fourteen, Freeman integrated a school in Springfield, Massachusetts (where he was thoroughly miserable).[38]

Although Freeman Hrabowski remembers that Black families "didn't think that at that time we'd ever see schools changing or integrated in our city" because Birmingham was a "stronghold of segregation," he recalled the Davis family as optimistic and celebratory about *Brown v. Board of Education*: "the *Brown v. Board of Education* victory was one of the most important legal victories in our recent history."[39] Maintaining that economics, politics, and social standing were as important as quality of school education, and that civil rights or legal rights could not "accomplish all that needs to be accomplished in the quest for freedom," Davis still understood legal rulings and electoral victories as forming "a new terrain for us to rethink the possibilities of the future." Angela Davis remained adamant about the centrality of education: "I see the *Brown v. Board of Education* victory as reconfiguring the terrain of our quest for freedom."

The Davis and Hrabowski parents were all trained educators. Both fathers, though, were unable, as Black men, to earn decent wages as teachers. Mr. Davis opened his own business. Mr. Hrabowski worked at a steel mill, earning additional money by reading and writing office invoices and reports for his illiterate white supervisors. The Hrabowski parents also tutored Blacks working at the steel mill, helping them to obtain their GEDs.[40]

Birmingham's Black bourgeoisie settled in two communities: Tannersville and Smithville. The Davises lived in Smithville, the Hrabowskis in Tannersville. Those "two worlds" forged reserves; isolated from white conservative racists, they created "another universe" in which Black propertied families would "see things downtown ... [and not] think that they were connected in any way" with their lives in the isolated Black middle-class worlds. And the Hrabowski family fantasized about better schools, new textbooks, well-paid teachers, and the absence of racist whites attempting to control their worlds.[41] In their interviews with Julian Bond, neither Freeman Hrabowski nor Angela Davis discusses how the Black middle-class enclaves remained connected to underresourced, impoverished Black communities, in the city projects and countryside, beyond charitable giving and educational endeavors.

Freeman Hrabowski and Angela Davis were likely in Massachusetts at the same time while he was at boarding school and she attended Brandeis University. For Hrabowski, boarding and attending a white Massachusetts school proved stressful. He describes school in Massachusetts as "intellectually, academically rich and socially devastating because [whites] would never speak to me, not even the teachers .... It is an awful feeling for a child to feel ignored completely, invisible. It was worse than being hated. I didn't exist."[42] Whereas Hrabowski was alienated from affluent white students and their families, Davis describes boarding as an expansive experience marred by patronizing whites who nonetheless wanted proximity to the racially-fashioned debutante.

As noted earlier, she was familiar with the liberal racism of the north because she had accompanied her mother and siblings to New York City when Sallye Davis attended summer graduate classes at NYU. Davis's Black and white childhood friends (several Black families had relocated from Birmingham or the south) and the metropolitanism of New York City cushioned her against isolation. Her high school, though, did not include her Black friends tied to a familial network. During the school year, without family and childhood friends, isolation was a norm: "once I arrived at Elizabeth Irwin High School, I was the Black girl, the Negro girl from the South."

Acclimated to New York City from childhood, familiar with CPUSA and progressive youth networks, Angela always had friends and attracted people who desired to assist her. Lonely, she was never left as an isolate. Most of Angela's time was spent studying; she and Freeman Hrabowski left underresourced Black Birmingham schools and were academically behind their white affluent classmates. Disciplined and hardworking, they soon began to excel. Both shared an affinity to European bourgeois culture, which they inherited from their educator mothers, who seemed to be enamored with European cultures. Affinities for European classics—perhaps as a respite, substitute, or improvement upon white US Americana culture—led prominent Black Birmingham families—such as those of Angela Davis, Hrabowski Freeman, and Condoleezza Rice—to introduce their children to European literature, language, and culture. Mrs. Sallye Davis focused on French culture for her eldest daughter. Mrs. Rice favored Italian culture, naming her daughter—who would become Secretary of State and an architect of the invasion of Iraq under false pretenses of weapons of mass destruction—after the Italian opera phrase "*condolcezza*." Mrs. Hrabowski chose Russian culture and would punish her son with reading assignments in Russian literature, introducing the middle-schooler to Dostoevsky—as well as Ralph Ellison's *The Invisible Man*.[43] French, Italian, and Russian were the gateways to escaping intellectual Jim Crowism for the precocious students. These young students would emerge as intellectuals across an ideological spectrum of politics spanning Marxism, rightist conservatism, and liberalism. Childhood friends, Rice and Freeman remain close, according to Freeman. The political spectrum covered by the three—from reactionary military hawk through liberal university administrator to abolitionist feminist and communist—reveals the political diversity within the Black middle classes and how internal opposition to Black revolutionary struggle could be a stable norm within Black communities.

Despite the impressive resources available in some white schools, Angela Davis noted the value of Black schools: "I can remember from the time I was very young, first grade, celebrating Black history, Negro History Week. Every time we sang the American National Anthem, right, we also sang the Negro National Anthem." For Davis, Black schools were unique because teachers encouraged students to study how "Black people had made major contributions … [and] gave us all a sense of pride and … tools with which to resist the imposition of racial inferiority."[44] For Hrabowski, Black teachers and mentors instilled in their students self-respect and an awareness that, although they lacked resources in their schools, and white elite schools would be more academically challenging, they could meet higher standards as long as they could work "as hard as necessary" with the attitude that "I'll kill myself to get there."[45]

Davis, Rice, and Hrabowski all received doctorates (Hrabowski at age twenty-four) and became notable professors (Hrabowski at the University of Maryland, Davis at UC Santa Cruz, Rice at Stanford University). Both Davis and Rice had influential internationalist mentors, European Jewish academics who had fled Europe to escape the Nazis. Davis's mentor was Herbert Marcuse, a German Marxist who had worked for the Office of Strategic Services (OSS) during the war against the Nazis and Third Reich. Condoleezza Rice's mentor was Josef Korbel, a Czech anti-communist who fled Prague after the 1938 Munich Agreement and German invasion (the father of Clinton Secretary of State Madelene Albright, Korbel secretly converted his family to Catholicism in 1941). Rice met Korbel at the University of Denver, Colorado (the Rice family had left Birmingham for Colorado); her father had vilified Martin Luther King, Jr., as an "outside instigator" because of his civil rights organizing. Rev. Rice blamed Rev. King for the murders of the four girls—Addie Mae Collins, Denise McNair, Carole Robertson, Cynthia Wesley—who died in the bombing of the 16th Street Baptist Church. Mr. Rice also worked in education while his daughter attended a private Catholic girl's school.[46]

Despite ideological differences—radical, liberal, conservative—no significant public political discord appears to exist among Birmingham's former children who were scarred and survived Jim Crow. Ideology was subordinate to belonging: the scholars were socialized among the Black middle class and were trained in white high schools and universities open to certain forms of integration. All embraced and mentored their students in politics—"radical," "liberal," or "conservative"—that aligned with political norms. Condoleezza Rice and Angela Davis would defend their respective US Presidents, Bush and Obama, when they were condemned or criticized for treating Black and poor people as disposable.[47] For Hrabowski, ideological differences were insignificant before the unifying drive for educational success: "growing up in Birmingham … we can be very close, supportive and yet have different points of view on different things. What we had in common in all those situations [was] the power of education to transform lives … that's a theme you're going to find in any of those families."[48] The transformation of Angela Davis's life would begin in 1959, in Manhattan, at an experimental progressive private school, where affluent white parents and communities persecuted or offended by McCarthyism wanted to raise their leftist children in peace. But there would be links to her past in Birmingham. The eldest child of the Davis family was close to the eldest child of the Burnham family, Margaret Burnham. These gifted and strong-willed daughters raised by Black communist mothers—Sallye Davis and Dorothy Burnham—would reunite when Davis was arrested in Manhattan in October 1970. Having just earned her JD, Margaret Burnham rushed to the Women's House of Detention and presented herself as Davis's attorney. From there, Burnham would move to California to serve as one of Davis's six defense attorneys. Exceptional allies were available to Angela Davis. Still, aspects of negotiating her reality and identity as a Black boarder in a white home, and one of the few, if not only Black students in a private school, were a burden to shoulder often alone.

4

From "Bombingham" to the Big Apple

Angela Davis joined a high school communist youth organization in Manhattan in 1959 with her schoolmate Bettina Aptheker, the daughter of famous communist historian and CPUSA central committee leader Herbert Aptheker, dubbed a "father" of Black studies and friend of W.E.B. DuBois. Davis was an excellent candidate for the American Friends Service Committee scholarship. One of three Black students among the over thirty students awarded grants to private schools in the north, Davis would become deeply acclimatized to the international city that she had only visited with her mother and siblings during summers. Her dashed hopes for middle school and high school in Birmingham had left Davis feeling hemmed in: "At fourteen, in my junior year, I felt restless and exceedingly limited. The provincialism of Birmingham bothered me, and I had not yet been swept up into the Civil Rights Movement to the extent that it could forge for me a solid raison d'être."[1] According to Davis, she had neither the vocabulary nor analytical tools to understand her feelings: "I simply had the sensation of things closing in on me—and I wanted to get out." What worried her, to some extent, was that the grace time of childhood was ending and the rite of passage into becoming an acceptable "young lady" was upon her:

> The time was fast approaching when, in order not to be outcasts, girls my age in middle-class circles had to play an active role in the established social life of the Black community. I hated the big formal dances and felt very awkward and out of place at the one or two such events I attended. I had to get away. One way or another, I was going to leave Birmingham.[2]

Deciding between the early entry program at Nashville, Tennessee's Fisk University, an HBCU, and the AFSC northern high schools, Davis chose the latter. As noted earlier, she had wanted to be a pediatrician and planned to pursue that goal by studying at Fisk, ranked among "the most academically prestigious Black universities in the country."[3] But her father advised her that she was too young to plan a future as a pediatrician at Fisk's Meharry Medical School.[4] DuBois had attended Fisk, before enrolling at Harvard. Angela Davis described the school as "the University of the Black Bourgeoisie par excellence." (E. Franklin Frazier's *Black Bourgeoisie*[5] had been published in English translation in 1955; it is unclear if Davis had heard of or read the book before choosing schools and weighing the contradictions of Blacks consumption and wealth under racial capitalism.) She was clear about impending difficulties if she remained in the south: "I could predict that my disinclination to become involved in purely social affairs would create enormous personal problems. Probably if I did not pledge a sorority, I would remain an outsider."[6] The social demands of an HBCU would not provide Davis the space she needed. New York City offered a massive container within which she could rest, nest, and roam; there would be social demands, but only those made by white liberals and progressives, which, in theory, would be less demanding; and the political demands made by teen leftists and schoolmates such as Bettina Aptheker, would give material relevance to the teen's political perspectives.

The fifteen-year-old embraced the contributions and contradictions of the Black bourgeois culture she rejected. Yet what Davis did not seek in northern white schools or in Europe were young, seasoned Black activists. Black militants were emerging from HBCUs and some predominantly white institutions. Often, they were trained in multiracial formations such as CORE, SNCC, SCLC, and SNCC. Focused on the youth wing of the CPUSA, in the absence of any notable links to or interests in the Black church, mosque, fraternity, sorority, secret societies—that is, without Black culture—Angela Davis's template for organizing was determined by the youth wing of the CPUSA. New York City white activists as intellectuals would care for and tutor her, introducing her to the world of Marxism as seen by the CPUSA and the CPSU. Her home life with anti-war theologians, working to deter armed conflicts during the Cold War, introduced her to international politics.

Boarding with the Melish Family

A Harvard- and Cambridge-trained Episcopal priest, Rev. William Howard Melish, was ousted from his downtown Brooklyn parish in 1957 at about the same time that Angela was being recruited to New York City with an AFSC scholarship. Rev. Melish lived in Boerum Hill with his wife and three sons. His father, Dr. John Howard Melish—a controversial leader in the Episcopal church during the 1940s–1950s—was removed from his parish in 1949 by Bishop James P. DeWolfe of the Diocese of Long Island. DeWolfe would close Holy Trinity Church in 1957, relieving Howard Melish of his duties as rector. Wisconsin Senator Joseph McCarthy had denounced Rev. Melish, who would sponsor Angela Davis during high school, for chairing the National Council of American-Soviet Friendship. Rev. Melish enthusiastically supported US peace with the USSR and civil rights. His AFSC was among the organizations that worked in tandem with the CPUSA. Melish had told Angela's mother about the Quaker scholarship program for southern Black students to come north. The AFSC ticket out of Bombingham had been stamped with Sallye Davis's networks and working friendship with the radical Episcopal priest. Despite losing his parish, and being called before the House Un-American Committee, Melish offered to host Angela Davis in his family home in Brooklyn Heights during her high school years in Manhattan. The stability and care of the Quaker family that embraced Davis furthered the Black teenage girl's journey of self-recognition and self-possession and mitigated her childhood rage at and fear of whites that she had grown up with under Jim Crow.

Beyond the reach of HBCU social demands, Black parental, protective measures, and Black petit bourgeois conventions, Angela Davis had more autonomy than she had ever experienced before. According to Rev. Melish, his family directly introduced the fifteen-year-old to radical anti-racist politics through political forums and salons regularly held at the Melish home.[7] The adults consistently invited the teen to join them in discussions. Melish found the teen to be apolitical when she arrived in New York; she appeared to be disinterested in organizing or political events and struggles. Herbert Marcuse would make the same assessment when he met her as an undergraduate at Brandeis. Yet the constant flow of foreign and US visitors in and out of the Melish home created a salon for international politics and peace activism, and dynamic conversations among communist, religious, and civil rights leaders. The Melish home became the fifteen-year-old Davis's second home and source of schooling. At the Melish home, Davis was exposed to political ideas, debates, and philosophies. In Birmingham, her mother's friends and visitors offered a younger Davis an opportunity to listen and learn, but it's likely that Davis rarely participated. Her surrogate Brooklyn home determined that she was old enough to join in the dialogue and debates with adult visitors who spoke about world affairs and US domestic and foreign policy; they encouraged her to do so as a peer.

Their anti-racism and the refusal to be intimidated by anti-communism cost the Melish family dearly. Still, the family generously welcomed the Alabaman teen into their fold and became surrogate caretakers. The parents and their three sons—John, William, and Jefferson—offered a highly educated, affluent white surrogate family. The eldest sons chaperoned Angela to and from school in Manhattan.[8] After she graduated from high school, the parents, Howard and Mary Jane Melish, would continue to be members of the Davis family's political networks. The Melishes visited the Soviet Union multiple times. Years later, Howard Melish, with Angela Davis and Sallye Davis, raised funds for Anne Braden's Southern Conference Education Fund (SCEF).

Student Activism

As a teenager, Angela Davis remained ambivalent about formally joining the CPUSA for several years. Decades later, she spoke about her hesitancy: "I ... did not initially join the Communist Party when I first became a political person because I had a tendency to see communists as being my parent's age ... I didn't see it as an option for myself as a young person." Davis adds: "[I] changed my mind." Her activist mother taught her daughters to "dare to be different" by being principled; for Davis, "she reminded me of that ... over and over again, that I should not be afraid to stand up for what I believed. So that, even though there were difficulties, ah, my mother immediately supported me."[9]

First in New York, and later California, the Melish, Aptheker, Mitchell-Alexander, and Marcuse families, among others, actively supported Angela Davis. Integrating white families, social networks, and a virtually all-white high school meant entering a portal into another world. This was a marginalized or demonized "leftist" world, but it was also a world of power shaped by the hegemony of white progressives who were eager to be helpful to the young recruit from Birmingham who showed so much promise. Downtown Brooklyn and Manhattan became "home" for several years. White, Jewish, and Black leftists, urbane intellectuals, international and multiracial cultures eclipsed Jim Crow. The affluent sectors of Manhattan and Brooklyn Heights, not the New York City ghettoes, became Davis's chrysalis. *An Autobiography* makes little mention of Harlem, the Bronx, or Bedford-Stuyvesant, which were overwhelmingly Black and Puerto Rican—mostly impoverished but with enclaves of wealthy Blacks.

Davis writes of encounters with few Black political radicals and theorists before 1967. She describes meeting DuBois in Manhattan through the Apthekers when in high school. At Brandeis, she recounts Malcolm X speaking on campus; but after the first thrill of hearing whites castigated by the eloquent speaker, she found his lecture disappointing and Malcolm X lacking pragmatic policies to move the races toward reconciliation. (Malcolm X would become one of the key inspirations for the Black Panther Party.) While living in New York City during high school, Davis could have visited the Audubon Ballroom in Harlem/Washington Heights or heard Malcolm speak at Temple No. 7, the Harlem Mosque where he presided, from 1952 to 1963. (Davis's future colleague poet June Jordan, born in 1936, met with Malcolm X when she was in NYC.) Both sites were a subway ride away from Elizabeth Irwin High School, taking the A train or #1, 2, or 3 trains. Martin Luther King, Jr., also frequently visited and spoke in New York City, where there was strong support for the southern movement, particularly among unions with Black members.[10] *An Autobiography* says little about King, who frequently visited NYC and met with New Yorkers In Friendship allies Bayard Rustin, Ella Baker, and Stanley Levison, during Davis's formative years in New York. Malcolm X's Mosque and the Organization of Afro-American Unity (formed after he was pushed out of the Nation of Islam) were located in Harlem. Davis engaged student activism with her school peers in local protests at segregated stores such as Woolworth; these protests were met with civility, not fire hoses, dogs, Klansmen, or police violence. Literature and philosophy moved the young Davis more than civil rights agitation. *The Communist Manifesto*—which focuses on labor exploitation, not racial integration—inspired Davis.

Elizabeth Irwin High School was heavily influenced by activist parents, mostly "leftist," affluent Jewish parents who had survived McCarthyism. The high school students were encouraged to engage in civil rights advocacy. They picketed and engaged in sit-ins at segregated businesses like Woolworth's with the Advance Club, a youth organization linked to the CPUSA. Angela Davis and Bettina Aptheker joined Advance and participated in protests on a regular basis. It was likely there that they first met Mike Zagarelle, who had begun organizing with Advance at the age of fourteen. By age eighteen, Zagarelle was the president of the club and a CPUSA member. Born the same year as Davis, he lived in the Bronx with his Jewish parents and on modest means. On scholarship, Davis attended Elizabeth Irwin. Zagarelle attended the public High School of the Arts in Manhattan (and later Hunter College for several years). Picketing Woolworth's Manhattan segregated lunch counters created bonds across class, gender, and race.

Davis socialized with other teens in Manhattan; her childhood friends tended to be other red-diaper babies, e.g., the Burnhams and Bettina Aptheker. Her social activism and political engagements focused around the CPUSA, which consistently worked to attract teens or young activists. The Progressive Youth Organizing Committee (PYOC) was established in April 1959. In 1961, the PYOC formed the W. E. B. DuBois Club in San Francisco. Herbert Aptheker and his daughter Bettina were powerful organizers among California students and the DuBois Clubs. In other states such as Illinois, white students dominating the DuBois Club appeared reluctant to have meetings on the south side of Chicago, the predominantly Black or brown communities in the Windy City.

An Autobiography makes little to no references to New York City's public housing, poverty, and inferior schools for Black and brown communities; or Black activists and the agency of Black churches or mosques. Apparently, the young Angela Davis, as had been the pattern in Birmingham once she moved to a middle-class enclave, was sheltered and isolated from the conditions that impoverished and working-class Black youths experienced in New York. Police violence and gangs (theatricalized in the 1961 *West Side Story*) are also absent. The Black violence and poverty of the Jim Crow south of her childhood are vanquished by the memoir as readers focus on Davis's social environment. The Black violence and poverty in the north go unmentioned. Black leftists integrated middle-class communities with concerned, if not always politically conscious, whites. Davis gradually realized that her educational trajectory indicated that she might never call Birmingham "home" again, and the youthful desire to be a Black doctor or pediatrician to care for the Black community receded.

Despite the progressive politics and constant educational tutelage, in her first year of high school in the north, Davis was struggling. The teachers and head of school decided that she needed to repeat her sophomore year and receive a private tutor in French in order to reach competency. Angela Davis had begun to teach herself the language before she moved to Manhattan. Incredibly disciplined and focused, Davis labored until she excelled. Failing in French, she decided to concentrate in that major. With the assistance of a native French-speaking tutor, Davis, demonstrating her discipline and grit working on an uneven field, eventually took high honors.

Leaving Birmingham for Manhattan's West Village and Brooklyn Heights was still stressful. Her white schoolmates called her "Angie" (Davis was either the only, or one of two Black students in Elizabeth Irwin; *An Autobiography* mentions little about Black students at the school). Books were close friends. Literature spoke to her. Interested in activism, but not intensely involved, Davis understood that she had more license and safety to protest in the north and with fewer (lethal) penalties. For the young bibliophile, text proved more impactful than picketing on the street. *An Autobiography* reverberates with the eagerness of a young convert awakened through Marxist literature:

The *Communist Manifesto* hit me like a bolt of lightning. I read it avidly, finding in it answers to many of the seemingly unanswerable dilemmas which had plagued me. I read it over and over again, not completely understanding every passage or every idea, but enthralled nevertheless by the possibility of a communist revolution here. I began to see the problems of Black people within the context of a large working-class movement. My ideas about Black liberation were imprecise, and I could not find the right concepts to articulate them; still, I was acquiring some understanding about how capitalism could be abolished.[11]

For the teenager, the final words of the *Manifesto* created "an overwhelming desire to throw" herself into the communist movement. Courage would be required in any challenge to capitalism, Davis writes in her memoir: "communists disdain to conceal their views and aims."[12] The CPUSA followed the CPSU foreign policy line of peaceful coexistence. The more excitable teen, though, recited Marx and Engel's battle creed: "They [communists] openly declare that their ends can be attained only by the forcible overthrow of all existing social conditions. Let the ruling classes tremble at a Communist revolution." Davis concludes the revelation with the adage repeated by millions for over a century by the time she stumbled upon it: "The proletarians have nothing to lose but their chains. They have a world to win."[13] That she herself was petite bourgeois seems irrelevant to her. Her conviction gave her (self-)confidence in the future and her own place within it: Victory would be inevitable.

By graduation, Angela Davis had mastered French and planned to major in French at Brandeis. Poised and polished in ways that would have eluded her in the Jim Crow south, she decided to follow the pattern of Elizabeth Irwin graduates and applied to Brandeis University, the new elite Jewish university in Massachusetts. Davis received a full scholarship. Davis was also admitted to Mount Holyoke College (with less funding). Despite her mother's preference for the older, prestigious "WASP" Seven Sisters college, Davis chose the innovative, mixed-gender university with graduate programs, educational diversity, and international students. In spite of the appearance of ease and comfort, and her poise in following the trajectory of white leftist elites, her vulnerabilities still materialized. The terrorism of the Jim Crow south could reach into the consciousness. Although "sheltered" in elite schools, the violence against Black and liberation movements had no boundaries. Refusing the vibrancy of Black urban culture that resisted white nationalism, Davis never sought out Black militants in NYC while a high school student.

In 1960, when Davis was a senior in high school in Manhattan, Fidel Castro was received by Malcolm X in Harlem. *An Autobiography* makes no mention of this historic event. Some 2,000 Harlemites celebrated in the streets outside the Hotel Theresa. The ten-person delegation – denied their mid-town Manhattan hotel accommodations when Castro was to speak at the UN after the triumph of the Cuban revolution against the "Yankees" – was nevertheless elevated by Malcolm and Harlem, thwarting US attempts to embarrass the Cubans. Fidel Castro made his address to the UN. Philadelphia Panther veteran Rosemari Mealy's *Fidel and Malcolm X: Memories of a Meeting* is a seminal text of the 1960 meeting between Malcolm X and Fidel Castro at the Hotel Theresa.[14,15,16] The book, reprinted in 2014 by Black Classic Press, was published in 2019 by *Letras Cubanos* for the Havana Book Fair and 62nd commemoration of the

Malcolm/Fidel meeting at the University of Havana. Unlike the Cuban government and people, Davis and the CPUSA considered Malcolm a "narrow nationalist," although the 1965 posthumous *Malcolm X Speaks* was edited by George Breitman, a communist and founder of the US Socialist Workers Party. Davis failed to see Malcolm X as an internationalist and a revolutionary in her youth and for years while teaching as an academic. El Hajj Malik el Shabazz was assassinated several months before Davis graduated from Brandeis.

5

Traumatic Awakenings in Devastated Children

Birmingham Children's Crusade

When Birmingham, Alabama, moved to the forefront of the civil rights movement, Angela Davis was in France. Her mother was teaching and tutoring Freeman Hrabrowski, whose mother, also a school teacher, was a friend of Sallye Davis. Freeman, while still a youth in Birmingham, decided to become a civil rights activist. His narrative, offers a glimpse into the choices that Davis did not take while a youth in Birmingham elementary, middle and high schools. Her absence then in political struggle might have become an impetus that would later propel her into risk-taking alliances with Black militants, once she became a University of California doctoral student.

As a child, Freeman Hrabrowski was able to do what Angela Davis was discouraged from doing, and/or avoided: direct confrontational action to further civil rights resistance. He did this in part by challenging his parents and accepting the risks of being vulnerable to white nationalist violence and police violence in order to further the goals of the movement. In his 2014 oral history interview with Julian Bond, Hrabrowski candidly shares his experiences of trauma while organizing in Bombingham. His PTSD and recollections reveal and trace the Jim Crow indignities and assaults from which the Davis parents shielded their children. Angela Davis suffered family or collective trauma from living in Bombingham, but she never joined mobilizations to confront white supremacists; hence she never suffered combat trauma. Once she moved to New York, her distance from the physical war zones allowed her to retain physical safety even if psychological fragility remained. Children who functioned as foot soldiers, strategists, and survivalists in what SNCC called the "second civil war" lacked physical distance as a buffer zone from material and emotional terrorism. (The older and less confrontational Southern Christian Leadership Council [SCLC], formed in 1957—three years before SNCC emerged in 1960—referred to the civil rights struggle as the "second Reconstruction.")

Birmingham's Black middle class was nervous about the upcoming 1963 Birmingham Children's Crusade. Some members, such as Condoleezza Rice's father, objected to Rev. Martin Luther King, Jr., and "outsiders" leading demonstrations in Birmingham. Jim Crow was devastating and lethal. Yet the Black middle class, in more privileged enclaves, could shelter in their homes and communities—protect themselves and their private property with guns. (Today, the police murders disproportionately target Black people who lack wealth—George Floyd, Michael Brown, Eric Garner, Breonna Taylor, Ayana Stanley Jones.) Sending children away from war zones is a global phenomenon. Recognizing the United States as a war zone of anti-Blackness is seen as a controversial statement. What Davis did or did not, does or does not, recognize as a war zone appears to have shifted over the decades. Housed and schooled with highly educated white elites, escorted to and from high school by one of the Melish sons daily, she lived in a protective zone and is protected by influential whites. In *Faces at the Bottom of the Well*, Critical Race theorist Derrick Bell reflects that when he was stopped by a white patrolman late at night in the deep south, the Harvard law professor understood that by dropping the name of a powerful white judge, the white officer would know that he, as a Black man, "belonged to" a more powerful white man, and so any anti-Black violence would have to be explained to the white supporter understood as "owner."

As was Bell, Hrabrowski was in the deep south, but he was not traveling through, and he did not have a white protector. Nonetheless, the teen was swayed by SNCC organizers that civil rights protests in Birmingham had to be accelerated, and that with most of the adults willing to risk their lives as activists imprisoned, the children would have to take their place. The Black middle classes had been "impressed" and also "very frightened" by the influx of college-educated Black youths from Atlanta, Washington, DC, and elsewhere descending on the city. Birmingham's Black elite were torn; they were "proud of all these young smart people of color from other places" but also worried about police and Klan reprisals after the organizers left the city to organize in other towns.[1] That is, the residents had no plans to replace the "outside agitators" who risked their lives and freedoms to challenge Jim Crow segregationist violence in a state where they did not reside. Hrabowski notes how contemporary memory defiles historical objectivity: "[E]verybody today can act as if, oh, Dr. King was wonderful and all that, but there were a lot of people who were saying this man is getting above himself."[2]

Local police had locked up most of the adult nonviolent activists struggling to end segregation in Birmingham. Rev. King's Southern Christian Leadership Conference (SCLC) direct action coordinator James Bevel pondered how the movement could continue without adult engagement and leadership. Bevel decided to petition Birmingham's Black activist leaders to see if they would permit elementary, high school, and college students to become leaders in the Birmingham movement. Some wondered if this was an appropriate option and if the students were ready to take on such a grave and dangerous responsibility. *An Autobiography* describes schoolmates in Tuggle Elementary School and Parker High School—trapped in segregated, underfunded schools—inflicting trauma and fratricidal violence on each other, as discussed in Chapter 3. Nonetheless, the students who stayed in the segregated and impoverished zones likely formed the ranks of Black child activists who emerged as foot soldiers and fought against segregation and police/Klan terror. Davis's 1974 *An Autobiography* offers a more guarded and disciplined narrative than Hrabrowski's candid interview some forty years after repression. Hrabrowski's autobiographical reflections need not reflect poorly on any party, such as the CPUSA; he was not a member of or beholden to any organization. He has no need to shape a narrative to conform with the tenets of a party. His insights into how young students became political activists, not just victims of state violence and social dysfunction, differentiate the (petite) bourgeois youths who were politically absent or passive from lumpenproletariat youths who police incited to harass and attack the protesters. (Similar "black-on-black" violence was inflicted on civil rights leader Fannie Lou Hamer, as discussed in Chapter 1, when white prison guards instructed Black prisoners to beat her with a black jack—refusal meant that they would be beaten—for Hamer registering Blacks to vote.)

From May 2 to May 5, 1963, the Birmingham Children's Crusade against segregation and racism fought Jim Crow. National and international news captured Police Commissioner Bull Connor turning fire hoses, attack dogs, and clubs on the children. With cameras flashing and film footage mounting, 1,000 Birmingham children, some as young as eight, marched to the mayor's office to call for the integration of schools, buildings, and businesses. Negro school administrators and teachers tried to stop the children from protesting. When they locked the school gates and blocked students with high chain-link fences, students scaled over or tunneled under fences. Older children helped younger ones out of confinement. Six hundred students, mostly younger children, were arrested on May 2. By May 8, SCLC and the Black community had reached an agreement with Birmingham businesses to integrate public facilities and schools by September.

For Hrabowski, the height of the civil rights movement was when Dr. King and the SCLC came to Birmingham to ask children to go to jail in order to desegregate southern schools. Freeman Hrabowski describes the traumatic campaign for children and their families. The Davis family had close friends whose children were jailed as activists. The Davis children were studying in the northern high schools or in Europe at the time of the Children's Brigade. Hrabowski chronicles not only the brutality of jailing nonviolent child protestors in Birmingham, but how he became one of those children. Every night, Freeman's parents had brought him to the Alabama Christian Movement meetings at a local Black church. Disinterested in the planning for civil disobedience, the high school sophomore did his math homework to the sounds of freedom songs. According to Hrabowski, the music was like "rap" and filtered into his head: "all of that was a part of me."[3]

When time came for the children to engage in mass protests, Freeman sought to participate. His parents demurred, but he thought that if he and other children had been daily listening to, and internalizing, the civil rights protest plans, they should be able to participate. Middle-class Black parents often said "No" to their children participating in civil rights marches. Hrabowski stated that this was out of concern for their children's safety but he does not imply that working-class or impoverished families lacked concern for their children. Angela Davis says that her parents gave her female gender as an excuse for keeping her home.[4] Yet her brothers also appeared not to participate in on-the-ground activism. Parents also had fears about employment. The board of education had threatened to fire employees whose children joined civil rights marches or who were arrested while protesting. Freeman Hrabowski, although forbidden, continued to argue for his right to march.[5] When his parents told him that he could not join the Children's Brigade, Freeman called them "hypocrites."[6]

An Autobiography offers no such form of rebellion against parental authority—other than Davis dating and contemplating marrying a white German man who was also studying at Brandeis and would accompany Davis to Europe to enroll in the Frankfurt School. As for Freeman, his parents sent him early to bed so that he could reconsider his tone. Children and youth influenced their elders to accept the militancy of the young. They debated with their parents or snuck out of the house to protest. They were devoted even when frightened and determined to continue to transformative movements. Young Freeman Hrabrowski understood that he must negotiate with his parents for his right to "strike" against Jim Crow:

> You do not disrespect your mama, especially your daddy. ... Mama could be a little more lenient when Daddy in the wrong, but you don't do your daddy. And they were not pleased ... it was early the next morning that they came in after spending a sleepless night and told me I could go ... that experience taught me that you really don't have to be traditionally courageous to do something that has some meaning, because I was not courageous. I wanted to be helpful because I wanted better schools. And I wanted to be able to drink out of the water fountain and go to the bathroom and all the basic stuff and go to Kiddyland, you know—and not be seen as second class. I knew that.[7]

Attending planning meetings at his Black church helped the tenth-grader cope with stress and violence; confronting injustice, within community, can be cathartic or healing. Singing or humming freedom songs—"'Let nobody turn me around, turn me around' ... was amazing and that gave you courage to keep going."

Being in high school, Hrabowski led the younger children and ended up speaking to Bull Connor.[8] Hrabowski notes his fear as he narrates the encounter with one of the most dangerous men in the state, describing Connor as "this guy with this red face" snarling "What do you want, little nigra?" Shaking, the youth addressed Connor as "suh," and replied: "We want to kneel and pray for our freedom." Connor then spat on Hrabowski and pushed him toward the paddy wagon. Connor's rage and that of white police attacking children created international publicity as international media captured the horrific violence waged against Black children. As noted in Chapter 4, *An Autobiography* writes into history the white supremacist police chief's atrocities. This form of "literary activism", recalls material struggle; it cannot replace, but it can complement Freeman's activism in educational endeavors for objective history to shape collective memory. Enraged by defiant Black children seeking citizenship rights, Connor created a bloody media spectacle for photographers. The press released photos and pictures that embarrassed "his city," the southern states, and the United States throughout the globe.[9] It was a media coup against Alabama's White Citizens' Council formed in Selma in 1954.

For Hrabowksi, Connor " hadn't thought about being mean to those children" but allowed his rage to create a public embarrassment for Birmingham and demonstrate that Connor "was out of control." Hrabowksi saw Connor "as a terrible man": "I hated him."[10] It was the violence in the jail against the school children who protested—the caging of them, after their arrest, with young predators—that shaped the unforgivable. The children that Hrabowski led were confronted "with the bad boys ... the ones that have the knives. We don't have any knives. We don't cut people and things like that." Hrabowski doesn't query what white guards would allow youths to have knives in jail if they thought the youths would use them against the guards. The white police encouraged the jailed youth who were violent to attack the youth protestors.[11] Children in Hrabowski's care "were crying for their mama." They had brought their Bibles to jail, so Hrabowski read to them frequently, using Christianity as a shield and sword to stop verbal or physical assaults against the children by guards and prisoners. Hrabowski became the Captive Maternal[12] who, as caretaker, functioned to stabilize and protect the children: "Any time ... somebody would say they were going to—or begin to do something to my children, I'd start reading aloud—'The Lord is my Shepherd, I shall not want.' Everybody respects the Bible. ... I would have my kids singing songs. They'd leave them alone doing that." Hrabowski was constantly vigilant, "especially with those who were really scared, and trying to keep one or two who were ready to fight from getting into that."[13]

When Julian Bond asks Hrabowski in his interview if the "other inmates [were] clearly rough, rough guys," Hrabowski merely states that "it was not good" and acknowledges that he had "blocked" memories of those youths. His lessons from the protest and arrests were about the agency of the youth and their need for training: "a twelve-year-old, an eight-year-old, can think much more clearly than we think. They need teaching and training, but ... they can really appreciate the difference between right and wrong and can make decisions...."[14]

The March on Washington and Birmingham's Tragedy

The August 28, 1963, rally for jobs and freedom in Washington, DC, became *the* civil rights event of the century. It was largely performative and controlled by the Kennedy Administration. It was brilliantly planned by radical and socialist Black leaders to coincide with the anniversary of the murder of Emmett Till.[15] The war resistance was embedded in the narrative: awareness of the March on Washington has its origins in the brutal slaying of a Black child. (The anniversary of Barack Obama's acceptance of the DNC nomination in 2008 was scheduled for the anniversary of the March on Washington, and thus is also tied to Till's murder by white nationalists and their exoneration for that murder.) A. Philip Randolph inspired this historic March on Washington, which provided a platform for Rev. Martin Luther King's memorable "I Have a Dream" oration. King's dream for a nonracial democracy was transcendent and transformational, a call for whites and Blacks to live together in harmony or détente. SNCC's John Lewis also stood on stage; the Kennedy Administration threatened to pull the microphone plug if he spoke about white terrorism against nonviolent protesters. James Baldwin was there but was banned from speaking, as the Kennedy Administration feared an inflammatory speech.[16]

Some 250,000 people attended the 1963, March on Washington for Jobs and Freedom, several months after the Birmingham Children's Crusade.[17] It was an international event. But despite the intense effort the Kennedy administration invested in choreographing an international spectacle of optimism and civility, there were other interpretations of US political struggles. Third World communists challenged the optics projected by the First World.

Exiled from the United States, pursued by the FBI for offering protections to civil rights activists after leaving Cuba, former NAACP North Carolina leader, Robert Williams—who authored *Negroes with Guns* with his wife Mabel Williams—left Cuba for China. Once befriended by the Communist Party he encouraged Mao Tse-tung to issue an August 28, 1963, statement of support for Black US freedom struggles: "The fascist atrocities of the US imperialists against the Negro people have exposed the true nature of so-called American democracy and freedom and revealed the inner link between the reactionary policies pursued by the U.S. Government at home and its policies of aggression abroad."[18] Williams had convinced Mao to publish the statement at the time of the historic March on Washington where Rev. Martin Luther King, Jr., delivered his "I Have a Dream" speech. Mao bluntly stated the colonized oppressed right to rebellion:

On behalf of the Chinese people, I wish to take this opportunity to express our resolute support for the American Negroes in their struggle against racial discrimination and for freedom and equal rights.

There are more than 19 million Negroes in the United States, or about 11 per cent of the total population. They are enslaved, oppressed and discriminated against—such is their position in society ...

I call on the workers, peasants, revolutionary intellectuals, enlightened elements of the bourgeoisie and other enlightened persons of all colours in the world, whether white, black, yellow or brown, to unite to oppose the racial discrimination practised by U.S. imperialism and support the American Negroes in their struggle against racial discrimination. We are in the majority and they [imperialists] are in the minority. At most, they make up less than 10 per cent of the 3,000 million population of the world. I am firmly convinced that, with the support of more than 90 per cent of the people of the world, the American Negroes will be victorious in their just struggle. The evil system of colonialism and imperialism arose and throve with the enslavement of Negroes and the trade in Negroes, and it will surely come to its end with the complete emancipation of the black people.[19]

There appears to be no similar Soviet statement condemning US racism that asserts the right to Black self-defense and to have international allies in order to overthrow their racist oppressors. The Soviets' "peaceful coexistence" policy doctrine could not embrace the advocacy that the Chinese Communist Party asserted for oppressed Blacks, even though that Communist Party had expelled external aggressors and colonizers.

Black Girl Soldiers Are Assassinated

Less than three weeks after the historic March on Washington, white power militias, which had detonated several explosive devices since the march, bombed Birmingham's 16th Street Baptist Church. Between Sunday School and church services on Sunday, September 15, 1963, the bomb exploded. Of all of the historic atrocities that occurred that year, this one had the greatest impact on Angela Davis. The 16th Street Baptist Church was an organizational base for CORE, SCLC, and Rev. King. King's aides and associates, Rev. Ralph Abernathy and Rev. Shuttlesworth, were central to the SCLC and civil rights movement campaigns. (Rev. Abernathy, who would head SCLC after King's assassination, visited Davis when she was in jail; he and Rev. Fred Shuttlesworth, whose daughter had attended Birmingham schools with Davis, supported her during her incarceration and trial.)

The political assassinations of Cynthia, Denise, Carole, and Addie Mae were often discussed by Angela Davis and Fania Davis. The murdered girls were organizers. They were changing clothes in the women's/girl's bathroom before giving their presentation on youth organizing for the Children Crusades' civil rights campaign when the bomb blew up the 16th Street Baptist Church.

All four child activists had closed-casket funerals. No one was to repeat the galvanizing horror of Mamie Till Mobley's 1955 funeral for Emmett Till. Davis pointed out that people remembered Emmett Till's name but would not remember that of the Birmingham girls. Yet one should note the full context. People best remember Emmett Till's name, not just because of his gender but because of the frightening disfigured image of him in his coffin. None of the Birmingham parents would agree to do what his *mother* Mamie Till Mobley did: exhibit a mutilated child (or in this case their body parts) as a declaration of war against a society or state that permits white nationalist terrorism. (Emmett's father, Louis Till, had been hung in Europe during the Second World War, convicted of raping and murdering an Italian woman. John Edgar Wideman researched the case and in his fiction *Writing to Save a Life—The Louis Till File* raises queries about the rape and murder charges.) Mrs. Till Mobley demanded and organized an open-casket funeral for her sexually abused and murdered child. Her political protest to God and/or humanity was not so much about gender but a function to resist war. The parents of the slain Birmingham girls, Birmingham clergy, and Rev. King did not want to incite a response. They wanted decorum for the funerals. Grief without rage was to be the norm. So they instructed no "politicization" of the burials. However, clergy and families could control the services, but they could not control the streets. Grief, expressed by all genders, in varied ways, would clash with National Guard and state police who used military tactics to put down an insurrection. As noted above, some Black Birmingham residents sought to burn the city. Perhaps a few were related to the youths in jail who threatened Black child civil rights activists?

Robertson's private family funeral took place on September 17. The other funerals soon followed. Rev. Martin Luther King, Jr.'s eulogy at the church funerals for three of the girls (the fourth family wanted complete privacy) spoke to the memory, promise, and sacrifices of Addie Mae Collins, Carol Denise McNair, and Cynthia Diane Wesley. King was mournful and castigating: "These children—unoffending, innocent, and beautiful—were the victims of one of the most vicious and tragic crimes ever perpetrated against humanity. … And yet they died nobly. They are the martyred heroines of a holy crusade for freedom and human dignity." For Rev. King, in death

> [the children] have something to say to every minister of the gospel who has remained silent behind the safe security of stained-glass windows. They have something to say to every politician who has fed his constituents with the stale bread of hatred and the spoiled meat of racism … to a federal government that has compromised with the undemocratic practices of southern Dixiecrats (Yeah) and the blatant hypocrisy of right-wing northern Republicans.

Noting Blacks' acquiescence to oppression, and lack of activism, King asserted that the girl martyrs "have something to say to every Negro (Yeah) who has passively accepted the evil system of segregation and who has stood on the sidelines in a mighty struggle for justice. They say to each of us, Black and white alike, that we must substitute courage for caution." For King, it was not the specific murders that the nation needed to focus on but "the system, the way of life, the philosophy which produced the murderers."[20] Three thousand multiracial mourners came to pay their respects. Reverend King's eulogy forbade singing, shouting, and demonstrations.

After the bombings, Governor Wallace ordered 300 state police to assist local police in controlling the city. While Black youths threw bricks at cars with white drivers and passengers, white police shot at Black protesters, including sixteen-year-old Johnny Robinson, whom they shot in the back and killed as he fled from police through an alley. White teens shot at and killed Blacks as well. Fifteen miles from Birmingham, they shot Virgil Ware, age thirteen, who died on the handlebars of his older brother's bike as his brother peddled down a street. The white teens, Larry Sims and Michael Farley, who shot Ware in the cheek and chest, were convicted of second-degree manslaughter and were sentenced to two years of probation. The Alabama governor also called in the National Guard to stave off insurrections as Black residents began to burn Birmingham. According to K. Kim Holder, distinct differences exist between a *riot*—the dismissive label used by police and state against dissidents; a *rebellion*—a spontaneous eruption or confrontation against daily indignities and scarcities; and an *insurrection* sparked by the murder of kin or community folk. Whichever descriptor is applied, the bereaved extended beyond the personal family and expressed more than mourning and prayers for the mass murder of Black children in a church during Sunday sermons.

This was not exceptional, although horrific. Angela Davis maintained: "Many people assume that the bombing of the 16th Street Baptist Church was a singular event, but actually there were bombings and burnings all the time."[21] Rage at the mass child murders simmered for years. The FBI derailed investigations of the September 15, 1963, 16th Street Baptist Church bombing. On May 13, 1965, the agency identified four Klansmen, from a rogue Cahaba faction that considered the conventional Klan too mild in repression. The four alleged culprits were Thomas Blanton, Herman Cash, Robert Chambliss, and Bobby Frank Cherry. FBI Director Hoover obstructed justice by burying the investigative files and closed the case in 1968 without pursuing prosecutions. Hoover then sealed the files. Alabama Attorney General William Baxley reopened the case in January 1971 (while Davis awaited trial in the Marin County Jail). Threatening to expose the Department of Justice for protecting terrorists, Baxley obtained original FBI files withheld from the 1960s Birmingham prosecutors. J. Edgar Hoover's failing health likely facilitated Baxley's legal prosecutions. Those prosecutions, years after the murders, signaled progress to some. Chambliss received a life sentence for Carole's murder; Blanton and Cherry were convicted of murder in 2002.[22]

Davis Women Reflect on Death

Angela Davis enrolled in a Brandeis study abroad through the Hamilton College language program. As a French literature major, she was off to France for a brief prep before her final destination, Paris. Her undergraduate year in France would shape her international vision and cosmopolitan perspectives. But her study abroad would also be devastated by the bombs that exploded in Birmingham. The trauma would impact her perceptions of racist and political repression and self-defense. Sallye Davis told her eldest child not to come home to Birmingham after Angela told her she desperately wanted to leave France that September day, after reading the American newspapers that sold out in Biarritz and covered the carnage of the bombing of the 16th Street Birmingham Baptist Church. Divided by an ocean, devastated and alone, the nineteen-year-old was one of countless Black youths seen as prey. Her mother gave her the words to process the trauma: "Bloody Sunday."[23] That trauma would create a reservoir of rage and resolve for a future fight when she returned to the United States.

Since the bombing took place when Davis was in a foreign country, she was stranded in her grief in a western European country. Paris prided itself as the center of Western civilized culture, yet its citizens could not seem to grasp the gravity of the bombing deaths. Mourning and organizing around the 1963 Bloody Sunday, Angela insisted that the public recognize the four young girls murdered as activists and remember their names: Cynthia Wesley, Carole Robertson, Denise McNair, and Addie Mae Collins—whose sister, Sarah Collins, survived but lost her right eye. Hundreds searched through debris for survivors. Finding the decapitated or dismembered bodies of Addie Mae, Denise, Carole, and Cynthia, survivors and community responders also located twenty injured people, including Sarah, who was blinded with twenty glass shards embedded in her face and one eye. Condoleezza Rice was in church a few blocks away from 16th Street Baptist.[24] Rice's biography states that she, as an eight-year-old, heard and felt the shock of the bomb that killed her playmate Carol Denise McNair.

Angela Davis's recollections of Black grief, frustration, and rage in the aftermath of the bombing often center on memories of girlhood friendships, female activism, and maternal grief; little to no mention is made of the Black rebellion. Victimization centers the tragedies and makes it memorable. The Birmingham bombing would prove an unforgettable, haunting event for all of the Davis women. Their memories confirm, overlap, and contradict each other as the mother and her two daughters have recounted the trauma over the years. In one memory, Sallye Davis, upon hearing the explosion from her home, contacts Alpha Bliss Robertson and drives her to the Sunday School class to find Carole. Instead, the women find debris and parts of the children's bodies. In another memory, Carole Robertson's mother asks Sallye Davis for a ride to a "Friendship and Action" meeting, a new organization formed by Black and white parents and teachers to develop grassroots anti-racist activism amid school desegregation, and to allow Birmingham School children to meet each other. In all memories, all four girls are activists who had helped to plan or participated in the successful May student uprising that defeated Bull Connor, a fierce adversary of Reverend King's. Each girl had survived the crush of high-powered fire hoses and dogs. In the iconic photos of a war zone, one sees boys and girls defying the beatings and water pressure that could knock you to the ground or rip off a layer of skin. Connor had thought that police violence would quell the nonviolent dissent against Jim Crow; instead, that violence had "filled the jails in Birmingham in a way that reenergized the Civil Rights Movement like nothing since the Montgomery Boycott."[25]

In her collective remembrance of this tragedy, Angela Davis notes erasure:

> The time in the country my mother and I spent remembering that terrible day three decades ago—"Bloody Sunday", she calls it—was both healing and frustrating. As we spoke about the girls as we had known them, it occurred to me that the way the memory of that episode persists in popular imagination is deeply problematic. What bothers me most is that their names have been virtually erased: They are inevitably referred to as "the four Black girls killed in the Birmingham church bombing".

For Angela Davis, the theorist, the fact that the deceased were girls made it difficult for the public to remember and state their names. She cites the 1964 tragedy in Neshoba County Klan murders: "when James Chaney, Michael Schwerner and Andrew Goodman were killed in Mississippi … [then over a] decade earlier, Emmett Till was found at the bottom of the Tallahatchie River. These boys, whose lives were also consumed by racist fury, still have names in our historical memory. Carole, Denise, Addie Mae and Cynthia do not."[26]

Over decades, Davis repeatedly returned to the Birmingham tragedy in her narratives. The carnage waged in the civil rights movement in the Jim Crow south dominated her stories of violence more so than her stories about state violence against the Black Panthers. Panthers responded with armed self-defense against white nationalists and police forces. The Birmingham murderers were not official police sent to "neutralize" their opposition. The murdered victims were girls who were not politicized against capitalism and imperialism and so understood to only want integration, and "first class citizenship," not revolution and decolonization across the globe. For most, as Davis notes, the four "function abstractly in popular memory as innocent, nameless Black girls' bodies destroyed by racist hate"; however, for Davis, they function as civil rights activists who should not be forgotten as such through memories shaped by a patriarchal lens.

The personal and familial grief and rage of Sallye, Fania, and Angela Davis intertwine. Yet only Mrs. Davis was physically in the war zone of Birmingham. Only she felt the physical reverberations of the bombs. Her daughters were shaken by the emotional and psychological aftershocks that radiated beyond the state and the country. Sallye Davis saw the carnage; she did not have to imagine it. Mrs. Davis comforted other mothers and children wailing, and the stoic or sobbing Black men staring at the wreckage. Those who witnessed or survived the bombing and the aftermath had a different PTSD than those not present at the crime scene. Her daughters' memories, from the Northeast or in Europe, rely upon the press and the memories of their mother. The parents physically fought against the Klan and police terror. Their daughters would do so once they became politicized by Panthers in California. Still, those experiences would be woven into the past even if they were absent for the atrocity.

Angela Davis uses the term "war" to describe the bombings. The siege on Black Birmingham residents reflected characteristics of "low-intensity warfare" or counterrevolutionary paramilitary training that the CIA and US military provided for repressive regimes; one of the bombers in the 16th Street Baptist Church was, unsurprisingly, a Marine veteran.[27]

Thinking about the bombed 16th Street Baptist Church while in Biarritz, France, Angela Davis felt at a loss while visiting a resort past its prime, but populated by affluent white American students and white Europeans. Without family and a society to share her devastation, her need for consolation turned into regret over her choice to travel to Paris: "If I had not been in France, news would not have been broken to me about the deaths ... in the 'objective journalism' of the *International Herald Tribune.*"[28] If she had not been in France, she would have been in Massachusetts—distant but still close enough to a Black American community in New York or Boston, which could recognize and absorb her grief. In Biarritz, Davis could not communicate with those around her; she was "living among people so far removed from the civil-rights war unfolding in the South that it made little sense to try to express to them how devastated I felt. I wrestled in solitude with my grief, my fear and my rage."[29] That grief and rage would erupt later in the war she wanted to fight and win; that war would not be in the deep south of her origins. Several months later, when Davis witnessed French nationals weep inconsolably at the assassination of President John F. Kennedy, she offered no condolences and showed no remorse for her indifference. Parisians mourned Kennedy in November 1963 but had failed to recognize the terror of four political assassinations that September. Angela Davis remained haunted: "I carried around in my head for many years an imagined representation of the bombing's aftermath that was far more terrifying than any cinematic image of violence I have ever encountered." Imagining the girls as fallen comrades, Davis saw, in her mind's eye,

[the] fixed eyes of Carole's and Cynthia's bloody decapitated heads and their dismembered limbs strewn haphazardly among the dynamited bricks and beams in the front yard of the stately church. ... My own private imagination of what happened that day was so powerful that years would pass before I felt able to listen to the details of my mother's story.[30]

In Paris, Davis was free to participate in anti-racist demonstrations against police violence. She read Sartre's and Fanon's writings on torture and colonial terror against Algeria. She built theoretical and political bridges between the anti-colonial struggles in Algeria and the anti-racist civil rights battles in the United States. By the time she herself went to trial in 1970, Jean Paul Sartre's apartment would be bombed by the paramilitary OAS.[31] In Paris, Algerian students were beaten and thrown into the Seine to drown.

Davis's memoir focuses on the girl casualties, emphasizing their civil rights activism: at the time of their deaths the girls were preparing to speak about civil rights at the church's annual Youth Day program. She writes that she learned from the newspapers and news from home about the Black rebellions, uprisings, and riots in northern, mid-western, and western cities: Detroit, Michigan; LA and Watts, California. *An Autobiography* says little about that violence in her hometown, Birmingham. The conventional Black bourgeoisie—restrained as well as isolated in middle class enclaves—did not drive downtown towards danger in order to offer risk-taking solidarity through rebellion; they would be neither witnesses to nor collaborators with outraged Blacks as "lumpenproletariat" attempting to burn sectors of Birmingham to the ground.

Through a historical and feminist lens, Davis chastises the public for gendered amnesia concerning the names of the slain girls: Addie Mae Collins, Cynthia Wesley, Carole Robertson, and Denise McNair. Emphasizing gender in Black political history, Davis helped to pave the path for the "Say Her Name" movement twenty years before it was formed after Sandra Bland's death in police custody in Texas. Trying to fathom a mass murder that scarred her life, Davis grappled with September 15, 1963. Over the years, her focus shifted: from attempts to personally grapple with the agency of white supremacist terrorists who traumatized, and so transformed her, from her distant safety in France into becoming a stoic militant who wanted revolutionary comrades and later distance from the bloody battles for justice. Davis functioned to preserve history, but objective history was not always aligned with her public memories. It became imperative to remember the names *Carole, Cynthia, Addie Mae, Denise*. But there is no recollection of the children who fought with them and little to no mention of the riot or rebellion that followed their murders. Her narratives—part memory prompts, part feminist critiques—focus on girlhood friendships and grieving mothers and serve to input the agency of female actors and their grief into history. In dialectical struggle with King's sermon, seeking and offering comfort Davis asserts that the girls "did not die in vain … history has proven over and over again that unmerited suffering is redemptive." King asserts this within the template of Christianity. Davis is not a Christian. One might argue that she is a communist, hence the assertion. But there is no definition of "redemption" and the girls were not Marxists engaged in class struggle. King offers a balance: he chastises those who refused to fight and to share the suffering and sacrifice.

Decades after the 1963 mass murder in the church, Birmingham Black girls who survived the Klan and bombing became recognizable political figures. Despite their shared origin story in Bombingham, their politics were diverse and spanned from radical to reactionary. All had been traumatized in childhood by white supremacists. Two were raised by a communist mother; one by a conservative father who, as a Black paster, blamed Rev. King for the deaths of the four girls, denouncing King as an "outside agitator" responsible for the murders and church bombing. While Angela and Fania Davis organized for Black equality and human rights, and the freedom of political prisoners (from Davis to Nelson Mandela), Condoleezza Rice worked in the republican administrations of arch-conservatives; from her offices in the federal government, she spread false information about weapons of mass destruction in order to garner public support for the United States to invade Iraq and destabilize the Middle East after "9/11." (Years later, Rice would campaign for the confirmation of arch-conservative Supreme Court Justice Brett Kavanaugh for the Trump Administration.) Birmingham girls who could play with each other grew to become Black women with antithetical politics, ranging from visionary through pragmatic to predatory. Not participants, all—like so many others—were beneficiaries of soldiers (Christian or not) in the second civil war; the southern civil rights movement had forced the United States to open its doors to Blacks, women, people of color, LGBTQ communities, and many others. Noncombatants who were beneficiaries of the sacrifices of frontline southern activists could also become casualties of war.

Tracking the Rise of Resistance

Angela Davis was a high school senior when SNCC was founded in 1960, inspired by the sit-ins in Jim Crow college towns, such as the HBCU Shaw College, the alma mater of Ella Baker. SNCC aligned with community-based organizations the 1962 Freedom Rides and the 1963 March on Washington. They fought for voting rights and the 1964 Civil Rights Act and the 1965 Voting Rights Act. Early key SNCC leaders and mentors include John Lewis, Bernice Johnson Reagon, Stokely Carmichael, Julian Bond, Ella Baker, Rubye Robinson, and Fannie Lou Hamer. Carmichael was also an aide to Rev. King. SNCC and SCLC worked together on a consistent basis. In 1966, students increasingly protested against the Vietnam War and the draft.[32] Video footage captures Carmichael chanting "Black Power!" after his twenty-seventh jailing (and beating) for nonviolent protest for civil rights. His cries for "Black Power!" at a June 1966 Greenwood, Mississippi, rally were caught on camera as footage that show Carmichael and Rev. King standing together, with the latter expressing visual discomfort as he realizes that the nonviolent movement of interracial activists was fading under violent repression.

Replacing integrationist John Lewis (who would later become a prominent liberal-centrist US congressman), Carmichael became SNCC chairman in 1967. The original SNCC had recruited multiracial "shock troops" against a white supremacist south. Now whites were asked to organize their own communities and lead them beyond white supremacist violence and discrimination and anti-Black exploitation. As Black identity and militancy grew in the face of anti-Black violence and terror, largely ignored by the federal government, H. Rap Brown quipped that "[v]iolence is as American as cherry pie."[33] His inflammatory speeches flowed with Carmichael's exhortations. SNCC would dissolve by the early 1970s. Its leadership had gone "Panther";[34] the disintegration of the integrated liberal nonviolent cadres was a response to the brutality of being beaten, jailed, sexually assaulted, attending funerals of the murdered.

Urban uprisings overtook US cities as a response to segregation, poverty, and police murdering Blacks. In 1965, Harlem, NYC, and Philadelphia, were burned following white police officers brutalizing and killing Black people. Watts, CA, was also torched in 1965. In 1966, in North Omaha, Nebraska, the National Guard needed three days to quell the rebellions against racism. In 1967, after the police and the Michigan National Guard failed to quell a rebellion in Detroit, the US 82nd and 101st airborne were deployed.

In varied sites, groups referred to themselves as "Black Panthers" after learning about rural Alabama militants and self-defenders in the south. Inspired by the Lowndes County, Alabama Black communities, Black rural communities trained or protected the students coming from out-of-state colleges to organize voter registration drives. Several nonviolent/unarmed activists had been murdered, including white and Black organizers such as Goodman, Swerner and Cheney, and Viola Liuzzo. Carmichael was routinely beaten and imprisoned by white racist police due to his work in the southern civil rights movement with SNCC and with Martin Luther King, Jr. in SCLC. Black communities were attempting to vote and Black citizens were being murdered for doing so. It was only rational that they made preparations for their security and safety and to protect their civil rights. The southern-based Deacons for Defense and Justice in Louisiana and North Carolina NAACP chapter leader Robert Williams started a gun club to protect nonviolent civil rights activists.[35] Malcolm X represented in the north, with his adage "By any means necessary," the right to self-defense. Southern, midwestern, northeastern Black intellectuals and radicals influenced the rise of the California Black Panther Party for Self-Defense, and various other nonactivist and activist formations thousands of miles away from activist working-class students from Merritt College. The posthumously published memoir *The Autobiography of Malcolm X*—Malcolm (el Hajj Malik el Shabazz) was assassinated in 1965[36]—was edited by Alex Haley, reportedly a paid FBI informer on Malcolm X. The California Panthers would differ from the Alabama Panthers. The way in which self-defense—intellectual, emotional, spiritual, material—was practiced would begin to shift as well. Fania Davis, years after becoming a Black Panther who physically fought to save the life of her husband and herself and child while pregnant, would find an equivalency in diverse forms of aggression. Fania Davis's memories of the church bombing are as pained as her older sister's. Boarding in New Jersey, Fania Davis describes the bombings as her "origin story." Domestic terrorism in effect gave birth to the radical who would unambiguously join the Black Panther Party in San Diego, where she and her older sister were enrolled in a doctoral program in philosophy in order to work with the Marxist theorist Herbert Marcuse. Fania Davis recalls that she was fifteen when Cynthia Wesley and Carole Robertson were murdered in Birmingham: "two close friends were killed in the Birmingham Sunday School bombing carried out by white supremacists trying to terrorize the rising civil rights movement." Her recollections are more personal and less guarded than those of her sister, who later bore the weight of public discourse symbolizing political dissent and memory of girl-child martyrs who registered sympathetically to the larger public. Fania Davis recounts how she blocked the front door to the family home in Birmingham to bar her brother's white college classmate from entering, when she was on break from college. She defines her action as a form of "racist bias" as opposed to a reflex action to trauma. Expressing remorse for "racist bias," Fania Davis states that her actions reminded her of segregationist

Alabama Governor George Wallace, who blocked the Courthouse door against Black peaceful protestors. She conflates her "power" as a Black female student who belongs to no powerful political entity to that of a white nationalist who encouraged his supporters to rule as pure whites or devastate through anti-Black violence. A young Black female student and an old white supremacist governor can act out of emotions or enact performative politics; there is no material basis for finding an equivalency between the two. Days before the 16th St. Baptist Church bombing, Governor Wallace, in a *NYT* interview, had stated that "fancy funerals" would stop (Black) integrationists. In Fania Davis's memories, the Dixiecrat governor's inciting whites to murder civil rights activists would become the equivalent of a Black student's emotional desire to repel whiteness and create sanctuary within her family home.

Part II

University

Undergrad

Brandeis Undergraduate in a Changing World Order

On January 17, 1961, President Eisenhower bid farewell to the nation while Angela Davis was preparing for university. Eisenhower warned the public that democracy against "the military–industrial complex," expanding with the combined interests and machinations of the military establishment and the arms industry, would seek to dominate the US political economy, ideology, and democracy itself. (Mike Davis's 1990 *City of Quartz* coined the phrase "prison industrial complex; with the end of the Cold War and Soviet Union, Angela Davis moved away from CPUSA leadership and turned to abolition, co-founding Critical Resistance in 1998.[1])

That fall, Angela Davis enrolled in Brandeis University. Founded in the postwar 1940s, the institution offered a progressive mission for educating Jewish students following the German Holocaust. Its Waltham campus was situated several miles outside of urbane Boston in a state that prided itself as being home to some of the best universities and colleges in the nation. Formed in 1948, as a bold innovation in higher education, Brandeis University boasted an early board that included Albert Einstein and later First Lady Eleanor Roosevelt. The board sought to create a Jewish-sponsored nonsectarian university open to all ethnic and racial backgrounds, an intellectual repudiation of Nazism. Einstein was the board's first choice as university namesake, but he was unsettled by marketing and the founding board's rejection of radical thinkers to lead the school. The board settled on the first Jewish Supreme Court Justice, Louis D. Brandeis. A sitting justice at the time, Brandeis was seen as a brilliant progressive and human rights advocate. When Angela arrived as a first-year undergraduate, she was older than the school, which was continuously undergoing construction.

Angela Davis's experiences in a private university formed by Jewish families and communities in 1948 with memories of the German Holocaust mirrored her experiences in the private high school formed by progressive Jewish families persecuted or threatened by McCarthyism and anti-communism. Davis's experiences, from fifteen on, were based in socialization in environments where there would be few Black students and few working class and poor students. She became the "exceptional Black" in all formal education once she left Birmingham—high school, university, graduate school (Frankfurt) and doctoral studies (UC San Diego). She still felt racial discrimination. Her 2014 interview with Julian Bond notes that her analysis of white liberal racism was underdeveloped during her early student years. Her parents had schooled her in southern Jim Crow culture, but she lacked instruction in liberal racism and there was a void in her seeking Black culture and intellectualism in nearby Black communities, e.g., Harlem. Some Black students integrating privileged white zones addressed their isolation by organizing with under-resourced Black communities or moving into those communities and commuting to campus. Angela Davis was not one of those students. She took refuge in books.

The first year at Brandeis was filled with classes, studies, and work study: refiling books in the university library and working at the campus coffee shop Chomondeleys. For spending money, Davis also worked at a "two-bit soda parlor in Waltham." *An Autobiography* notes that that year, she settled in as a first-year student with international students; she shared collective fears of a mounting Cold War conflict. Rebuffing the Cubans' attempts to remain nonaligned, in 1961, the United States/CIA coordinated the assassination of Congolese leader Patrice Lumumba, Prime Minister of the Democratic Republic of the Congo, yet failed in the Bay of Pigs invasion into Cuba to destroy that liberation movement. In October 1962, unable to reverse the Cuban revolution and Cuba's growing ties with the USSR given the United States' violent responses to socialist states in the Americas, President Kennedy was drawn into the October 1962 missile crisis with Soviet Premier Nikita Khrushchev. Fearing a nuclear holocaust, Brandeis and other students fled the campus for their parents' second homes far from cities.

From its founding following the Second World War, and the German Holocaust, Brandeis offered to Jewish students what it refused to offer to Black students: an educational grounding in their historical culture and struggles, and a route to accumulate power for self-protection and advancement. Brandeis boasted its proximity to cities that were home to the largest Jewish communities in the United States. Yet that was also true for Black Americans in an era when Harlem remained a Black cultural capitol and Boston a site for Black radical intellectuals. Brandeis did not emphasize its links to Black communities within NYC and Boston. But the campus undergrads were organizing for change.

During her sophomore year, in 1962, Davis traveled to the international youth festival in Helsinki, Finland, to witness and participate in the international student progressivism. As noted in an earlier section on the CIA's NSA, international festivals were cultural battlegrounds during the Cold War with competitive conflicts between the Western or European First and Second Worlds. Third World was where the bloody battles were fought as liberation movements defended themselves against colonialism and genocide. Finland had conflicted relations with its eastern Soviet neighbor. Its government was agitated by the Soviet presence as was the United States and the CIA. Undergrads Angela Davis and Alice Walker attending the festival might not have noticed Gloria Steinem. It is very likely that the observant Steinem would have noticed the two attractive young Black women students in the nearly all-white US contingent, shaped by scores of students recruited through the National Student Association. Davis's international trip was likely funded by Brandeis or donors with ties to the

CPUSA. Walker likely received a scholarship through her school, Smith College, Steinem's alma mater. The CIA funded Steinem's recommended recipients. The Brandeis scholarship student with side jobs was now an international jetsetter. Davis's parents were middle class and provided her with the basics; they had three younger children to put through college (all apparently received academic or athletics scholarships). Students not sponsored by CPUSA/CPSU or affluent families could seek funding from the NSA/IRS for their European trips. There is no indication, though, that Davis's travel was sponsored by the CIA organization.

Traveling to the Youth Festival in Helsinki via a Brandeis charter plane to London, Davis took advantage of a stopover in Paris to explore the city. Algerians in France were demonstrating for independence during the height of the Algerian Revolution. Davis continued to Finland to join the 8th International Youth Festival. The festival was supposed to be an international gathering to promote communism and socialism; it was sponsored by the Soviet Union. Communist China and North Korea participated in the planning committee dominated by the USSR, yet later retreated from the USSR in part over its "peaceful coexistence" policy with the West during a time at which NATO and the United States were sending militaries or mercenaries to kill freedom fighters resisting colonial domination. *An Autobiography* largely focuses on Europe and the United States; not much is known about Davis's positions on the Sino-Soviet bloc or African liberation movements, i.e., "colored nations" in antagonism with Western imperialism and Soviet conflicts with the United States.[2]

At Helsinki, where the two Black women sophomores stood out, Steinem was in the process of disrupting the festival that she had recruited students to attend. Discrediting the Soviets and their support for anti-capitalist, anti-colonial formations that challenged United States and NATO hegemony was key. From 1958 to 1962, Independent Review Service (IRS) leveraged CIA interests through the National Student Association (NSA). Students, without their knowledge, were the intellectual foot soldiers in the Cold War. Steinem embraced being a covert operative, describing to the press in 1967—when she was exposed as an agent—that she only worked with liberal and "forward thinking" CIA agents.[3] Despite several decades of CIA-sponsored assassinations, coups, and genocides, Steinem's loyalty never wavered; she was a loyalist: "I never felt I was being dictated to. … The CIA was the only one with enough guts and foresight to see that youth and student affairs were important."[4] Liberals, (neo)radicals, feminists, and the CPUSA would protect Steinem after her association with the Agency was exposed to the public. Those beholden to her for encouraging white liberals to support Angela Davis (afterward Steinem published Davis's writings in *Ms. Magazine*—the publication's original funding is tied to CIA assets), including academics and feminists, dismissed the objective history as largely irrelevant to the present moment.

The coastal city Helsinki, Finland's capital, was forced to concede annexed territory to the USSR, creating Helsinki's tense relationship with the Soviets. Known as the beautiful "white city" due to the color of its massive stone buildings, Helsinki sought a nonaligned coexistence between the East and the West. The Youth Festivals were viewed by the nation as public relations and propaganda parties, as well as economic revenue. The first six international Youth Festivals were held in the Soviet Union. Seeking a broader tent, Soviets posited neutrality and tried to appeal to Western and Third

World students with international youth festivals in noncommunist territories. The CIA, however, wanted to damage the USSR's appeal to international youth. Following the template set by CIA propaganda, the British government issued a statement for its students to avoid the World Federation of Democratic Youth and the International Union of Students due to the USSR's attempt to use the festivals to "exploit young people" through communist propaganda. Angela Davis was one of some 14,000 youths representing 137 countries/nationalities at the 1962 Helsinki World Festival of Youth and Students for Peace and Friendship. Pro-communist, her interests aligned with the Soviet bloc and Cuba. *An Autobiography* mocks the CIA disruption and surveillance in Helsinki.

The Finnish mainstream media and political parties boycotted the festival. The "anti-festival" was marked by "racist youth disturbances, which the police quelled with horses, batons and tear gas"; white supremacist disruptions reportedly coincided with "anti-communist counter-festival … culture, art and music as weapons of political combat." The CIA funded a counter-festival to promote capitalism or free enterprise; jazz musicians Archie Shepp and Bill Dixon performed and NYC Museum of Modern Art flew in abstract paintings for the exhibit. Finnish racial animus against Third World youth led to street confrontations; white Finnish citizens engaged in silent boycotts, heckling, and fights fueled by anti-communism and by racism against "non-Nordic" visitors.[5] Although the CIA released reports of its role in cultural disruptions, it claimed no credit for the violence. *An Autobiography* mentions frequent violent disruptions at the youth festival: "In keeping with the dictates of the Cold War, the CIA had planted its agents and informers in all the strategic areas of the festival, including the delegation from the United States (a fact later admitted by the Agency)." According to *An Autobiography*, disruptions ranged from the kidnappings of the East German delegates to tear-gas bombs exploding "on crowds during mass events" as "Hell's Angels types picked fistfights with delegates in the streets of downtown Helsinki."[6]

The festival lasted two weeks. The Helsinki festival had an immense impact on Angela Davis. The cultural programs reflecting liberation struggles in Africa, Latin America, Asia, and the Middle East were the most moving events for the Brandeis student. It was in Helsinki where she was smitten by the beauty and militancy of brown and Black Cuban women. Of all of the cultural programs, the Cubans stole the show and her heart. They displayed an African-centered Caribbean culture bold and strong enough to wage a 1959 successful revolution against the Batista dictatorship backed by the US empire and the Mafia. Angela Davis—along with communist, liberal, and conservative students—watched, as did secret police from the United States and USSR, young Cubans satirize the invasion of their nation by foreign capitalists, organized crime figures from the United States, and wealthy Cubans that turned an island home into a playground for whites to indulge in, and profit from, gambling, drugs, and prostitution. In plays, songs, and dances, Cubans narrated their oppression, rebellion, and victory through liberation. The leadership roles of women and girls deeply appealed to the eighteen-year-old Davis: "long before women's liberation had been placed on the agenda, we watched the Cuban militia women zealously defending their people's victory."

An Autobiography describes how one performance epitomized Cuba's "infectious dynamism" as "the Cubans did not simply let the curtain fall" but, reflecting "life and reality", they "continued their dancing, doing a spirited conga right off the stage and into the audience." One of many youths "openly enthralled by the Cubans, their revolution and the triumphant beat of the drums," Davis joined the conga line, recalling that the Cuban performers and revolutionaries pulled "the timid ones, perhaps even the agents" into movement "brought into Cuban culture by slaves dancing in a line of chains."[7] Delighted, Davis danced as Finns watched "in disbelief at hundreds of young people of all colors, oblivious to traffic, flowing down the streets of Helsinki." Such spontaneity of the student cultural exchange, especially with the Cubans, inspired the US students organizing for solidarity with Cuba and socialist states, to the consternation of the CIA, and likely Gloria Steinem. Davis had her first taste of global culture; it would not be her last.

An American (Black Woman) in Paris

After studying French literature at Elizabeth Irwin High School and Brandeis University, Davis became a student of "one of the greatest French poets, Yves Bonnefoy"[8] when she studied abroad during her sophomore year in France. Alabama's segregated Black schools did not provide or mandate foreign language studies in high schools. To a 2019 Brandeis audience Davis confided that she "had to learn three years of French and one year in order to catch up" with her classmates in Elizabeth Irwin. *An Autobiography* states that she repeated her sophomore year because she was so behind but became excellent, taking highest honors, in French by the time she graduated from high school. Since French was a prerequisite for graduating from Elizabeth Irwin High School, Davis devoted herself to study: "I became so immersed in the language and culture that I decided that I didn't want to become a doctor after all. … I liked the humanities." At Brandeis University, Davis had excellent French teachers and, after her first year, would travel to study in France for the summer.[9] The immersion in European American and European culture became the "life of the mind," which was transformative for Angela Davis. She left the south for the north in order to escape virulent racism and then left the north for Europe on the same mission:

> The way I think about it now, I made this journey from the south to the north in search of some kind of freedom. And what I thought I would find in the north wasn't fair. I discovered new forms of racism that I could not at the time articulate as racism. But I can remember in high school, I would always get invited to people's houses into their summer houses because many of the people were pretty wealthy … [often] they would ask the [black] servant to come and join them … there were these really awkward moments that I didn't know how to explain … before we had developed a vocabulary to talk about the influence of racism. I think I began to imagine France as that place [of respite from racism].[10]

The teenager avidly studied French literature, culture, and language as an escape from white supremacy. Europe was racist; France violently so, particularly against the nations and peoples it had racialized and colonized. Yet US Black Americans had sought racial refuge in France for decades. Notable celebrities and entertainers sought refuge there: Josephine Baker, Richard Wright, James Baldwin, Nina Simone. Carrying the ID of an "American," Davis could wave the US passport, imprinted by an alpha American Eagle, and receive a "pass" of sorts, as a citizen of the most powerful or imperial nation in the world. That was not true for other Blacks or racially denigrated people:

> I have this in my mind that if I could only make it to France, I would find freedom. And my first trip to France was at the height of the Algerian Revolution … women from Martinique who told me that I had to be really careful because the police might think that I was Algerian. And there were police attacks, there were rallies.

She went to France seeking sanctuary and found solidarity.[11]

Davis could read French authors in original French texts while monolingual American students would wait months or years to read the same books in English translations. French writers in the 1960s were globally read. Jean Genet,[12] Frantz Fanon, and Jean Paul Sartre shaped the cutting edge of global left intellectualism. After her French language studies in France during the summer of 1962, Davis prepared for the Sorbonne. A few exceptional Black scholars had made the journey into European studies decades before Davis: DuBois studied at Friedrich Wilhelms-Universität zu Berlin, 1892–4; Anna Julia Cooper received her PhD from the Sorbonne in 1924. Privileged US students studying in Europe increased in popularity after the Second World War. Students stayed in French homes while attending university. Most students were white and bourgeois and could more easily find housing and accommodations.

The Nazi occupation of Paris and the French Resistance shaped Parisian culture and anti-communism. Parisian women fighting in the French underground were captured, tortured, and sent to Nazi camps. There, militant communist women expressed contempt for Jewish women, whom they viewed as noncombatants—as passive, apolitical victims.[13] High school sophomore Davis read *The Communist Manifesto* and her life and consciousness altered; yet *An Autobiography* does not mention Davis seeking out women or students in the French Communist Party or socialist parties. The French Communist Party was formed in 1920 out of the socialist worker's party; it was opposed to colonialism. (Vietnam liberator prime minister/president of Vietnam, Ho Chi Minh, had been educated in France and would later engage in a liberation war to oust French colonizers; the 1954 Geneva Accord was implemented; Vietnam was to be a free nation; then the United States waged war against Vietnam until 1976.) Davis did encounter international university students from Algeria and Martinique—nations that shaped the theories and texts of Frantz Fanon's *Black Skin, White Masks*, and *The Wretched of the Earth*.[14]

"High Culture"

During the 1950s and 1960s of Black protests and anti-colonial uprisings, Angela and Fania Davis used their French skills to pose as non-US Blacks in order to challenge white segregationist storekeepers in the Jim Crow south. Their posture as the affluent children of diplomats from Martinique or North Africa was a ruse against Jim Crow. Ironically, the ruse would not have worked in France because the people they were imitating—although a step up in the US anti-Black pecking order—were colonized by France; hence, in France they would be a step down and not "exotic." However, in France, US Blacks were exotic. Davis would find that she could benefit from exoticism and degrees of acceptance based on colorism, racial identity streams, and multilingualism in European languages. Her fluency in French impressed more than shopkeepers in the United States, whereas her fluency in the language of "Black militancy" and Black suffering enlightened or captivated Europeans. Davis aligned with militant networks fighting colonialism and imperialism. During the liberation wars against French colonialism, Algerian students, workers, and women were violently attacked in France. Angela Davis faced racist discrimination and problems with stable housing in France as well, but she was neither a laborer nor a "colored" colonized by France and, when necessary, could speak in US English to signify that she was a citizen of *the* imperial state. "Colored" laborers and workers needed to send wages back home to feed, clothe, and educate their families. American students were not in France for that purpose. The Black elites followed in the footsteps of the more privileged and monied white elites: take a year abroad, refine European language skills, become socialized into European bourgeois culture. Davis's desire for French culture flattered the French, who looked down on colonized Blacks in Haiti, Senegal, and Martinique but found Black Americans "refreshing" and "fascinating." The allure was partly based on entertainment and empire—Louis Armstrong and Miles Davis, and Black jazz players in general had impressed the French for decades. Blacks as US cultural ambassadors were used during the Cold War; Steinem had deployed them— Louis Armstrong, Marian Anderson—at the international youth festivals. Born and raised in Martinique, Frantz Fanon attended medical school for psychiatry in France. He was treated generally with contempt; hence Black skins wear white masks. Angela Davis's personal strengths became social power through academic training and employment.[15] Creativity endeared Black artists to the French. Black rebels would demand international solidarity, which was not always forthcoming.[16] Decades after philanthropist Josephine Baker's risqué performances, during the rising appreciation of Nina Simone and James Baldwin (both would support Davis after her arrest), Davis, having fled US racism to seek freedoms in France, would personally find a welcome that nonetheless also made demands.[17]

According to Alice Kaplan, while in Paris the young Angela Davis shared the self-conscious beauty of Jewish or Christian white women, Susan Sontag and Jacqueline Bouvier, respectively.[18] The linkage of the three women reflects gradations of a western European femme phenotype lauded in American culture as personal beauty: the Catholic Bouvier; the Ashkenazi Jew Sontag, the light-skinned Black/Colored Davis. A ranking order (pre)exists in Kaplan's narrative but is not articulated: all physical traits are on a continuum of "white beauty" and all ranks are not equal. Davis's personal beauty diverged from hegemonic norms, the Afro being the most striking departure. Sontag's and Bouvier's standardized personal beauty was along the continuum of European culture. Davis's beauty was adjacent. (A complete departure would feature Nina Simone as the representative that strays beyond the norms of European idealized and racialized beauty.) This narrative of course is about students, so Simone would be exempt, but some African and US students who favor Simone.) For Kaplan, all three women shared intellect, and acculturation aligned to western European norms. However, their politics, material realities in struggle, had different registers under hierarchy shaped by Eurocentrism and imperialism. Admiration for female appearance and education could eclipse attention to diverse political functions. Bouvier, the future wife of President John F. Kennedy, set the gold standard of European cultured beauty in the United States and abroad. The multilingual student who would become First Lady following the 1960 US presidential election would help to promote the American Alliance for Progress and tour Puerto Rico, Mexico, Venezuela, and Colombia with the president, a campaign that took place at the same time that the US State Department and CIA (which reports directly to the president) were orchestrating invasions, coups, and assassinations to create pro-US corporate-military friendly governments. Anti-Semitism filtered Sontag's beauty; her consciousness led her to openly oppose the US war in Vietnam and to remark at a 1965 *Partisan Review* symposium that "the white race is the cancer of human history."[19] Angela Davis's light brown skin and reddish hair granted a hyper-visibility marked by the illicit and the desirable, differentiated by contrast to the "common" dark-skinned Black or African. Such unwanted accolades proved to be an effective shield for Davis when her racially ambiguous markers would be emphasized (by Cuban elites and others) to differentiate Davis from other Blacks and militants.[20]

Some scholars attribute Angela Davis's "fearlessness and sense of justice" to her studies in France, where she allegedly developed "her analytic tools, her understanding of politics and language."[21] That attribution erases the context and history of Black anti-racist agency which are not an extension of European theory. Davis's 2019 Brandeis interview seems to express that perspective that elevates observation and textual study—rather than shared material struggles—as the main drivers of radicalism. Despite the shared struggles against fascism in which Davis's parents' generation would have fought in Europe, Davis appears to have not located a strain of Black-American militancy while abroad.[22]

French Terrorism against Anti-colonialists in France

In Paris, Angela Davis's community of young women students and friends included former schoolmates from Elizabeth Irwin and Black girlfriends who had lived in Birmingham before moving to New York City. Harriet Jackson, whose communist father was driven underground, joined Davis in France, as did her white schoolmate Florence Mason, who had been a CPUSA Advance Club member with Angela Davis in high school. Studying at the Sorbonne when the defeated French army and paramilitaries returned from Algeria, Davis witnessed firsthand the dispossessed, bitter colonial elites who repatriated without their lifestyles of Arab servants and resources, defeated by a people's insurrection that pushed them off colonized land. Davis would read Fanon's account of the physical, military, and psychological effects of torture and of the counterrevolutionary war in Algeria.

Protected by her bald eagle-passport, Angela Davis scrutinized political violence spilling from the colonies into France. On July 5, 1962, Algeria's Independence Day, Algerian cafes flew the nation's new flag and passed out gratis couscous. The French *Organisation de l'armée secrete* (OAS)—using tactics of domestic terrorism deployed by US Vietnam vets who formed underground white nationalist terrorist cells in the States[23]—shot up Muslim Parisian cafes. *An Autobiography* describes a young paratrooper, near Davis's apartment, standing at his window "spraying the street with bullets" from a military assault weapon.[24] Watching domestic terrorism abetted by police was a flashback to Birmingham. However, in Paris, foreign students and workers seemed to lack what protected Davis as a child: family elders in organized and armed community patrols.[25] Parisian street wars of repression witnessed by Angela Davis were a precursor to the urban cities she longed for when she later studied at the Frankfurt School in Germany. In France, her consciousness sought intertwined international freedom struggles:

> To be an Algerian living in Paris in 1962 was to be a hunted human being. While the Algerians were fighting the French army in their mountains and in the Europeanized cities of Algiers and Oran, paramilitary terrorist groups were falling indiscriminately upon men and women in the colonialist capital because they were, or looked like, Algerians.[26]

Most of the victims might have been African and Arab males, but that is not clear given that war crimes against women and children – which would include torture and rape (men and boys were raped as well) – were underreported and largely undocumented by those victimized.[27] Mostly targeted were Arab neighborhoods or university protestors:

> In Paris, bombs were exploding in cafés frequented by North Africans, bloody bodies were discovered in dark side streets and anti-Algerian graffiti marred the sides of buildings and the walls of métro stations. One afternoon I attended a demonstration for the Algerian people in the square in front of the Sorbonne. When the *flics* broke it up with their high-power water hoses, they were as vicious as the redneck cops in Birmingham who met the Freedom Riders with their dogs and hoses.[28]

Davis's provincial, southern industrial city, Bombingham, had prepared her for the European metropolis's rabidly racist colonialism. Her mind had imprinted Addie Mae, Cynthia, Carole, and Denise; their spirits accompanied her walks to witness Parisian carnage.

Returning to the States: Another Bloody Sunday and Immersion in Brandeis

After Angela Davis returned from France to Brandeis, she threw herself deeper into her studies. Finishing papers and plans for postgraduation on the East Coast, she read newspaper reports of campus protests on the West Coast. During her last semester at

Brandeis, the second "Bloody Sunday" occurred. In 1965, in Selma, Alabama, SNCC's voting drive was attacked by white police and Trooper James Fowler shot and killed SCLC Jimmie Lee Johnson at a peaceful protest.[29] SNCC then asked Reverend King to co-lead peaceful demonstrations with John Lewis on March 7. State troopers and police rioted when the marchers would not turn back at the Edmund Pettus Bridge; they beat scores and hospitalized fifty peaceful civil rights advocates that day as camera crews filmed the melee. The world witnessed the second US "Bloody Sunday" as another national disgrace. With federal protection, marchers finally crossed the bridge on March 21, 1965.

While an undergraduate at Brandeis University, Davis had met the Berlin-born philosopher, Herbert Marcuse, in 1962. Davis was majoring in French studies and focused on contemporary French literature and philosophy. Marcuse's personal biography of ethnic (Jewish) and political repression in some ways parallels Davis's biographical narrative and likely informed his personal commitment to her. Davis formally met Professor Marcuse on the Brandeis campus, fresh from her travels to European countries adjacent to the Soviet bloc. She knew who he was and she was intrigued by his work; that he held status as a "rock star" of the student left didn't hurt. As a sophomore, she discovered Marcuse's *Eros and Civilization*—a theoretical text that synthesizes Karl Marx and Sigmund Freud. First published in 1955 (reprinted in 1966), *Eros and Civilization* argues for a non-repressive and non-materialistic society.

Marcuse taught in Brandeis's Department of History of Ideas (the title mirrors the "History of Consciousness" at UC Santa Cruz where Davis would complete her illustrious academic career in the first decade of the twenty-first century). During her sophomore year Marcuse was teaching in Europe. During her junior year, she was studying in France. The first semester of her senior year, he recommended an independent study with her on the pre-Socratics, studying the genealogy of European philosophy to David Hume and the Enlightenment. Stating "We hadn't yet reached Kant," Davis recalls the semester as "one of the most exciting intellectual experiences of my life." Marcuse advised Davis to enroll in his graduate seminar on Kant's *Critique of Pure Reason*. She hesitated, protesting that she only had one semester studying philosophy. He insisted. She enrolled and then he asked her to present the first paper of the graduate seminar. The paper, according to Davis, "was on Hume as the predecessor to the development of Kant's critical theory." After that experience, Davis says that she "was totally hooked."[30] She was elated to find a brilliant fount for theory. In the 2019 discussion at Brandeis, Davis described what she had received as a student: "I'm so happy I came to Brandeis because … I discovered Herbert Marcuse, I discovered what I really wanted to do." Her detailed notes on Marcuse's lectures are in the Harvard papers. They are so exact that Davis reflects: "I could probably rewrite the lectures from my notes." Davis confides that she "fell in love with not philosophy per se, but philosophy is [*sic*] critical theory as a way to think about the world, not in terms of what exists, but what can possibly be."[31]

Before she became his mentee, Davis had attended his lectures, when she approached him in her senior year, she said, "Professor Marcuse, I think I'm really interested in philosophy, but the problem is I haven't taken any courses in philosophy."[32]

When asked about their mentor-to-mentee relationship, and what Marcuse saw in Davis, she replies in 2019 at a talk at her alma mater:

> I think he just saw curiosity. I was really deeply interested ... I came to Brandeis ... because [of] the intellectual atmosphere. ... I don't think I had ever experienced anything like that before and it has remained with me ... you had to spend hours and hours reading, and thinking, and discussing ... that's a great thing. I tell my students now "You won't realize until much later that this is the only time when you can devote all of your life to reflection and reading, and thinking."[33]

The stellar student sought out the Marxist theorist and began to study the pre-Socratics, Plato and Aristotle. After independent study with Professor Marcuse, young Angela turned toward political theory, auditing his undergraduate course on European political thought in addition to his graduate seminar on Kant's first *Critique*. Their meeting and tutorial were pivotal for Angela Davis's development as a theorist. Her first travels to Europe led to observations of Cold War clashes between capitalists and communists. If the honors student had not taken tutorials and seminars with Marcuse as an undergraduate, she might not have spent two years of graduate study at the Frankfurt School in Germany. Davis had mastered French literature, not the German language and political theory, while at Brandeis. Marcuse provided her with a letter of introduction to philosopher Theodor Adorno and facilitated Davis's entry into the Institute for Social Research, likely as the first Black US female student.

In 1965, Angela Davis graduated from Brandeis University. That year, Marcuse retired from the university and was planning his move to California to teach at UC San Diego. The most influential academic in Davis's intellectual formation, and for her generation, Marcuse's gravitational pull for young students opened doors into political theory and liberation struggles. Famous among leftist theorists and student radicals, vilified by conservatives and the CPSU, and later largely forgotten, the radical theorist used his prestige and connections to assist students.[34] A beneficiary of Marcuse's largesse, Davis's life reflected his radical rock-star trajectory. His star faded because radicalism, following repression and cooptation, went into decline. Her star continued to rise.

Marcuse's "Most Famous Student"

Angela Davis's interactions with the famous philosopher in critical theory, Herbert Marcuse (1898–1979), shaped not only her university studies but stages within her intellectual and political life. In the first stage, she began as his undergraduate student at Brandeis University in her senior year. She graduated, in the second stage, to attend the Frankfurt School—to which he directed her for advanced study, and vouched for her enrollment. In the third stage, Davis left Germany to enroll in the doctoral philosophy program at UC San Diego with Marcuse as her advisor. Undergrad, MA graduate, doctoral studies: this standard academic trajectory within the professional professoriate was shaped by a (in)famous radical Jewish leftist theorist. Philosophy, critical theory, radical thinking, and praxis with the leftist or post-Marxist theorist revealed transformational stages for Davis: caterpillar, cocoon, chrysalis. Davis was indebted to Herbert Marcuse. Marcuse was indebted to Davis. Their intellectual and political studies would prove beneficial to both.

An Autobiography says little about Marcuse; this is odd because he is likely one of the greatest influences on her intellectual and philosophical development. Marcuse died in 1979 in Germany; his ashes were interned in a cemetery in the United States for decades (only when a graduate student doing research on Marcuse noted that there was no grave for the Marxist theorist and professor was a ceremony and internment held in Germany—which Marcuse might have protested). Marcuse had a significant impact on Davis's intellectual formation and an incredible impact on the American and European left. Davis's association brought her notoriety as a student, but there was also the aura of celebrity and authentic commitment to radical thinking and transformations. Marcuse had many students, including prominent scholars such as Bettina Aptheker, who would become Davis's colleague at UC Santa Cruz for decades, and notorious radicals and martyrs such as Sam Melville, who was killed at Attica. However, his "most famous student" was a young Black woman who was raised in the segregated south.

"The Man"

Herbert Marcuse[1] grew up in a comfortable family in Berlin as a privileged, gifted youth who belonged to a stigmatized ethnic and religious minority. There may have been empathic recognition between the Jewish professor and his Black student.

Both came from persecuted ethnic and racial groups whose families still managed to accumulate and maintain status despite devastating race wars. Marcuse was confronted with pogroms and the Nazi Holocaust, Davis with Jim Crow and Klan terrorism. After fighting in the First World War, Marcuse joined the German Social Democratic Party and later completed his doctorate at the University of Freiburg in 1922. He worked alongside Jean Paul Sartre as the research assistant of Martin Heidegger, who became a Nazi.[2]

Nazism forced Marcuse from Germany in 1933 to Geneva where, at the invitation of Adorno and Max Horkheimer, he joined the Institute for Social Research (Frankfurt School).[3] He immigrated to the United States, obtaining citizenship in 1940.[4] In New York City, he taught at Columbia University; his research focused on anti-Semitism, racism, fascism, totalitarianism, dissent, persecution, and war—the travail devastating Germany and Europe. After the December 1941 attack on Pearl Harbor, Marcuse joined the Office of Strategic Services (OSS) in Washington, DC. When the US entered the Second World War in December 1942, President Roosevelt's Coordinator of Information, William Donovan, formed the Research and Analysis Branch (R&A) with 900 scholars (which grew to 1,200), which was described as "first-class minds" without "political commitments" eager to serve the war effort. R&A members included Marcuse, Arthur Schlesinger, Jr., Ralph Bunche, seven future presidents of the American Historical Association and five of the American Economic Association, and two Nobel Laureates.[5] As would be the case for his "most famous student"—Angela Davis—Marcuse's radicalism did not preclude him from aligning or working with non-radicals based in academia.

OSS men analyzed Nazi Germany with "scientific objectivity"; their research contributed to the Nuremburg trials.[6] (Marcuse, Franz Neumann, and Otto Kirchheimer's intelligence reports would later be compiled and published, in 2013, as *Secret Reports on Nazi Germany: The Frankfurt School Contributions to the War Effort.*) In 1945, the OSS dissolved; it was reconstituted in 1947 as the Central Intelligence Agency (CIA), which, during the Cold War, would persecute Marcuse, the Black Panthers, and US radicals. There is no indication that the CIA persecuted Davis. Working at the US State Department, Marcuse was pushed out by 1951. After teaching at Columbia and Harvard, in 1954, he settled at Brandeis. There he met and taught Angela Davis and her former Elizabeth Irwin high school classmates. Professor Marcuse candidly observed that his excellent student at Brandeis was gifted but seemed apolitical and disinterested in activism. As an undergrad, Angela Davis presented as the opposite of Marcuse's more militant white students (who also enrolled in the UC system); these activists were engaged in insurrectionist speech and acts to advance liberation struggles in the 1960s and beyond.[7] Some of the white students, such as Bettina Aptheker, participated in the southern civil rights movement, which Davis had avoided. Radicalized by the repressive violence and murders against US activists or Third World liberation movements, some formed underground cells.[8] Their names—and deeds— would be eclipsed by "Angela," who, unlike the Weather Underground and Panthers, engaged in no illegal protests or acts against the state and its police and military forces.

When Marcuse was teaching full-time at Brandeis, he publicly condemned the US imperial wars in Southeast Asia and US racism, two years before Martin Luther King,

Jr., delivered his sermon, "Beyond Vietnam: A Time to Break Silence," at Riverside Church in Manhattan, on April 4, 1967 (King's assassination occurred on the anniversary of that sermon the following year). Dissatisfied with the professor's public stances for justice and human rights and his opposition to capitalism and imperialism, Brandeis offered him a yearly renewable contract as he reached the retirement age of sixty-five. He rejected it for UC San Diego. Originally, UCSD had a small liberal arts college; its liberal arts departments had three faculty in philosophy and four in literature in 1963. The philosophy department invited Herbert Marcuse to attend its 1964 symposium "Marxism Today." The Brandeis professor "was well known in academic circles as a social and political theorist, a critic of postindustrial society, and a committed but non-dogmatic Marxist." Out of the symposium event, Marcuse was invited to teach in the UCSD philosophy department. UCSD offered him a (potentially renewable) three-year "postretirement appointment"[9] while Brandeis pushed him toward retirement.

Although Marcuse had warned in his text *Soviet Marxism*, written for the OSS, that the Soviet state had turned "Marxism" into "state Marxism," or "Soviet Marxism," that did not deter his doctoral student Angela Davis from joining the CPUSA in 1968. In Marcuse's analysis, the CPSU presented itself as the stand-in for the proletariat, or for workers and laborers. Hence, in theory, it could speak for the proletariat. If this were true in the USSR, then, logically, it would be true in the United States; i.e., the CPUSA in the states could speak not only for the proletariat but also for the Black masses, because the party knew their interests better than the workers and/or the Blacks—understood as racially oppressed workers—did themselves. The vanguard as party elites would steer the masses and attempt to absorb them within or adjacent to more established organizations. The party under Gus Hall, the same leader that would lock out Davis's cadre in 1991 when they sought to liberalize the CPUSA and address LGBTQ and feminist rights, saw other leftist organizations as potential competitors. The derisive use of the term "the central committee" came to represent concentrated control over decision-making and anti-democratic leanings within the CPUSA and CPSU. In both formations, party leaders consolidated power into an official "voice" to represent the proletariat. The working class would "rule" via the will of the governing elites. The CPSU, under siege by the West, sought control of its satellite countries; the "Stalinist" CPUSA defended the USSR and its 1955 Warsaw Pact (a response to the formation of NATO); and Davis, after her 1972 acquittal, would serve on the CPUSA central committee for nearly twenty years as that organization expressed the "will" of the people.[10]

The Frankfurt Institute

Three years after participating in the 1962 Soviet-sponsored International Youth and Student Festival in Helsinki, Davis moved to Germany. She had Marcuse's support. An earlier biographer, Marc Olden, suggests that Davis's decision to study in Germany was (partially) influenced by her desire to continue—despite parental objections—her romance and relationship with a graduate student from Germany studying American cultural studies, Manfred Clemenz.[11] Angela Davis had met her first partner at Brandeis.

Manfred returned to Germany with Angela Davis after they both graduated from Brandeis. The couple enrolled in the Frankfurt School to study with Theodor Adorno. They considered marriage, to the consternation of their parents. Black and white parents were apprehensive or hostile to interracial and intercontinental marriage between their gifted children. Biographer Regina Nadelson speculates that while studying abroad at that time, the young Davis also suffered from depression and anxiety and began to see a clinician, the father of her European boyfriend.[12] Davis's and Clemenz's names appear on graduate student projects and publications, which indicates that they were both enrolled at the Frankfurt Institute at the same time and worked together on class assignments. Both studied with Adorno and Oskar Negt.[13]

The Institute for Social Research had relocated to Geneva from Frankfurt, Germany, when Adolf Hitler consolidated power in 1933. Two years later, moving to New York City, it merged with Columbia University. No longer working for the OSS, Herbert Marcuse joined the Institute, beginning his US teaching career in 1952 at Columbia. By the 1950s, Horkheimer, Adorno, and Pollock had returned to West Germany, while Marcuse stayed in the United States and eventually secured a position at Brandeis University. In 1953 – around the time Marcuse was pushed out of Columbia, largely due to anti-communism – the Institute for Social Research permanently returned to Frankfurt, West Germany. Recommending that Davis study with Theodor Adorno (1903–69) at the Frankfurt School in Germany, Marcuse wrote a letter of introduction to Adorno. She applied and was accepted. Adorno's "resignation" as to the possibilities of political struggles and liberation movements led to disagreements between him and Marcuse. Adorno would argue that leftist members of the 1960s student movement were reverting to fascism in their increasingly confrontational protests in Germany. In response, from 1965 to 1967, while Davis was enrolled in her graduate degree program, Marcuse argued that Adorno and other Frankfurt School faculty theorists had

> given up on the proletariat revolution that Marx had predicted. Not only had the European working class failed to execute their "historic task" of ushering in socialism, many were rapidly becoming fascists. Much of the Frankfurt School's initial efforts, then, were spent deriving the position from which a critical theory of society was at all possible.[14]

Failing to sufficiently factor into his analysis the forces of racism/anti-Blackness and patriarchy, Marx incorrectly believed that "the standpoint of the proletariat" would allow one "to decipher the future of capitalism and predict its demise."[15] Adorno—who did a series of public radio addresses in 1960s Germany—developed the "critique of capitalism into a critique of Western 'instrumentalist' reason in general, thereby making it unclear not only from what standpoint they were speaking, but also to whom they were speaking."[16] Philosopher Nicole Yokum reflects:

> Adorno and Horkheimer's *Dialectic of Enlightenment* famously claims that the form of reason dominant in modernity, instrumental rationality (means-end

reasoning), helps to explain how the Enlightenment ended up reverting into fascism. According to them, "enlightened" thought contains the seeds of its own demise, insofar as it's all about subsuming particulars under categories (ignoring and doing violence to what makes them unique), so that things all become replaceable, like laborers in the capitalist economy. They link this to trends in Western philosophy, too. But they take the Holocaust as the emblem of the "regression into barbarism" and they are really not thinking about colonialism and imperialism. Marcuse … was the only one at the time who was taking colonialism into account, at least a little bit.

(December 6, 2022 notes to author)

In Frankfurt, Davis established her credentials as a stellar student. Negt described her as the most outstanding among the 120–150 students attending his seminar. While in Germany, Davis also began organizing with an activist socialist student group.[17] (That group, co-led by Manfred Clemenz, would organize from 1970 to 1972 for Davis's acquittal and decry that she was a "militant" who would have knowingly participated in an effort to clandestinely free Black political prisoners.)

After two years of study in Frankfurt, Angela Davis was preparing for final exams. Observing US rebellions from a great distance, pondering her contributions to a Black freedom movement that she had yet refused to join, her tutelage on violence was shaped by the perspectives of a spectator and a scholar in Europe. The Frankfurt School theorists had experienced and survived Nazi Germany by fleeing to the United States and working for the US Department of State during the Second World War. The US they fled to for safety and democracy was the same nation and imperial project that systemically stole and degraded Black lives. It is likely that the Frankfurt School was not teaching Fanon or Mao, texts the Panthers and militants were studying in their own "schools"; genocide, anti-Black violence and Jim Crow terrorism could be seen as analogs but likely not templates for theory. Davis studied in Europe with German Jewish men grappling with the horrors of Nazism and fascism, but she likely did not fully comprehend those experiences; and, she lacked experiential knowledge in radical organizing and poverty—the experiences of Black laborers, workers, rebels whose insights into US repression expanded but did not fully restructure dominant narratives taught by European scholars.

Defending Marcuse in California

The *San Diego Union*'s June 11, 1968, editorial "This Is an Order!" demanded that the University of California investigate Angela Davis's Marxist mentor and advisor, Herbert Marcuse. Marcuse, unlike Davis, was not aligned with the CPSU. Unlike his most famous student, he was not a communist; he was a critical theorist who studied Marx. His critiques and opposition to capitalism and Stalinism rendered him an "enemy of the state"—actually two states: the United States and the USSR.

Supporting civil rights and leftist student movements, Marcuse also opposed the US war in Vietnam, CIA and military recruitment on campuses, and university grants funded by the Defense Department. Incensed at his presence on campus, reactionary US veterans escalated their warfare against anti-war and anti-racist activists. They became so reactionary that, though they had fought the fascists and Nazis during the Second World War,[18] they were now promoting Nazi ideas and violence during the Cold War against the civil rights movement and the anti-imperialist war movement. Balanced journalism found Marcuse to be "far less active in civil rights and antiwar movements than ... Benjamin Spock and two-time Nobel Prize-winner Linus Pauling, who were highly visible in newspapers and on television news."[19] Yet he became a primary target, likely because he was a Marxist. Marcuse had introduced her—after she read *The Communist Manifesto* in high school—to Marxist philosophy. Mentored for CPUSA leadership, Davis chose orthodoxy and was not deterred by the rigid structure and managerial ethos described in *Soviet Ethics*, if she even read it. That CPUSA General Secretary Gus Hall was a Stalinist did not negatively impact Davis until the Soviet Union collapsed and Hall sought control by locking out reformers, including Davis and Charlene Mitchell (several hundred members, including many academics, left the party that day).

Angela Davis and the CPUSA were clear; they spoke to the factory working class and the laboring class (Chicano/Latinx farm workers) as well as disaffected middle-class student militants (such as Davis) of all racial backgrounds.[20] For Davis's advisor also had an analysis of culture. For Marcuse, contemporary society was "unfree and by its very nature repressive," and Marx's worker as revolutionary agent had been seduced by consumerism and marketing, accumulating stuff, distracted by consumption and materialism; its vanguard role was not predictable. Yokum notes that the Frankfurt School and Marcuse studied cultural products, e.g., radio, magazines, movies, etc., and how consumption of capitalist goods and cultural commodities fed into the working class's identification with capitalist ideology that masked domination.[21] Marcuse discussed how people enamored with apparently elegant or sexy split-level homes rendered their working-class lives *just* comfortable and luxurious enough to bind them to capitalism.[22] Marcuse did not fully note, and likely the CPUSA underplayed, the entrenched white supremacy and anti-Blackness in the United States and global working classes. (Anti-racists overlooked how liberation movements could also become commodities, as images of sleek, attractive, articulate, and affluent Black radicalism became sold as simulacra, e.g., in the Blaxploitation film industry and other sectors.) Contrary to the CPUSA, the white male worker did not constitute the progressive vanguard, as Marcuse's 1964 *One-Dimensional Man* warned:

> [L]iberty can be made into a powerful instrument of domination. The range of choice open to the individual is not the decisive factor in determining the degree of human freedom, but *what* can be chosen and what *is* chosen by the individual. Free election of the masters does not abolish the masters of the slaves.[23]

Disenfranchised "students, artists, Third World peoples, and U.S. racial minorities" embodied Marcuse's concept of "revolutionary potential."[24]

Soviet Marxism condemned Stalinist Marxism (as noted, the CIA supported the text). The CPUSA likely considered Marcuse a pariah but left the verbal bashing to the Soviets or CPSU. The CPUSA was attempting to recruit Marcuse's student into the CPUSA.

Marcuse's undergraduate courses, such as "The Present Age," focused on contemporary thinkers. Under student pressure, he offered a course on Karl Marx but discouraged graduate students from writing on Marx given the conservative job market. A year after Angela Davis arrived on campus, in 1968, San Diego County citizens began to protest Marcuse and his anti-war students. Marcuse had visited Socialist German Student Organization Rudi ("Red Rudi") Dutschke, who was shot in the head by a reactionary during a student demonstration. Following that gesture of compassion and solidarity, on May Day, leftist students of the University of Paris carried banners reading "Mao, Marx, et Marcuse!" and occupied a lecture hall. International media began to refer to Marcuse as the "Father of the New Left" and "Angel of the Apocalypse."

That year Governor Ronald Reagan referred to student protestors as fomenting a "climate of violence" on and off campus. In mid-May, Marcuse and his wife Inge Neumann (Franz Neumann's widow) traveled to Germany and France, where he had been invited to speak at an academic conference. It was while in Berlin that the Marcuses visited the gravely wounded Rudi Dutschke in his hospital room. Soon after their visit, the *Bonn Advertiser* quoted a "well-informed" unnamed source who claimed that Marcuse had invited the West German student radical to bring his wife and son to San Diego. Furthermore, according to the *Advertiser*, Marcuse had offered Dutschke a teaching assistantship at UCSD. The story was picked up by *Newsweek*, the *New York Times*, and the *San Diego Union*, which was sufficiently provoked to write its "This Is an Order!" editorial calling for an "investigation." Even before the Marcuses returned to La Jolla, threatening letters were mailed en mass to the professor, UCSD administrators, and Chancellor William McGill. Marcuse informed *New York Times* reporters that he and his wife, upon visiting with Rudi Dutschke in the hospital, had recommended to the student leader that he recuperate in the United States with his wife and young son but not enroll in a US university for formal study given the political hostility. (Dutschke did not survive the attack by his right-wing assailant and died soon after the visit.)

While in France in 1968, during student and worker protests, Marcuse attended a UN Educational, Scientific and Cultural Organization (UNESCO) conference on Karl Marx in Paris. When student activists occupying the École des Beaux Arts asked him to speak to their gathering, he assented and brought "greetings from the developing movement in the United States"; Marcuse "praised the students for their critiques of capitalist consumerism."[25] Constant negative news about Marcuse drove headlines. The UC administration was being pressured to act. William McGill had been named to the UCSD chancellorship on June 21, 1968. The American Legion lobbied McGill to fire Marcuse and offered to buy out the professor's contract. The Regents' agenda for its September UCLA meeting included Marcuse's reappointment and the "Dehumanization and Regeneration in the American Social Order" course that UC Berkeley's Free Speech Movement wanted for Panther Eldridge Cleaver, author of *Soul on Ice* (Cleaver was hired to give ten lectures in a thirteen-week course).[26] The day before the Regents' September 19 meeting at UCLA, the *Union* editorial linked Marcuse to Cleaver, reprimanding the Regents if they permitted

[the] world-infamous Marxist [Marcuse to use] the facilities and prestige of the University of California to preach everything contrary to the American tradition, heritage, and Constitution ... [and] Eldridge Cleaver, rapist, revolutionist, and advocate of militant violence, to lecture at Berkeley and Irvine campuses.[27]

Highlighting ideologically driven attacks from conservative news outlets, *The Nation* championed Marcuse and critiqued the propaganda that the professor was "fomenting dissent." It noted that San Diego County had "twenty-one military bases and retired military personnel." Marcuse had supporters within the academy that resisted a "purge" and the return of McCarthyism. The Pacific Division of the American Philosophical Association elected him its president. UCSD faculty negotiated with the administration for contract renewal while the majority of faculty supported his reappointment. His students began target-practicing to offer him armed protection.[28] In 1968, Marcuse's most promising student began purchasing guns.

According to John Burke, the *Union* slandered Marcuse for "inciting students," although Marcuse never sought to influence student opinions. He did not know until later, after they had created defense units and strategies, that his students were taking up arms to counter death threats against him. He spoke with students who sought him out, yet he did not proselytize. Burke recalls Marcuse saying, "if my words are enough to disrupt society, then society is in bad shape."[29] A faculty committee began investigating Marcuse in October, the month UCSD students had invited Eldridge Cleaver to speak to a mass of 4,000 on campus. Cleaver led students in chanting "Fuck Ronald Reagan!"[30] Provocative and performative—decades before he (d)evolved into an arch-conservative Christian republican—Cleaver taunted Governor Reagan through the press: *"I challenged Ronald Reagan to a duel and I reiterate that challenge tonight, ... And, I give him his choice of weapons. He can use a gun, a knife, a baseball bat or a marshmallow. And I'll beat him to death with a marshmallow."*[31]

In 1969, Reagan would continue to pressure for Marcuse's removal. He would turn his ire on the professor's stellar doctoral student. The Regents were formed in 1868 and for over a century were plagued by corruption, insider dealing on contracts, and considerable unethical and anti-intellectual conduct. After appointing William French Smith as UC Regent in 1968, Governor Reagan demanded that UC Regents fire Davis as a UCLA instructor-professor in the philosophy department. Marcuse was still teaching at UCSD in spite of Governor Reagan and the Regents' attempts to fire him. Some speculated that Davis was targeted by the Regents because it was easier to destroy her budding academic career, as an avowed member of the CPUSA, than that of an august European left thinker who was not a party member; perhaps attacking Davis was one form of retaliation against her mentor.

Threats against Marcuse increased. That fall, students guarded the entry to his lectures. Students searched unregistered persons who wanted to enter his large survey courses and recruited a friend not enrolled at USCD to sit with his weapon and monitor Marcuse's large class. The widower Marcuse's future third wife—after Inge Marcuse's death—graduate student Ricky Sherover attended Saturday target practice with students who defended Marcuse.[32] Whereas Adorno's students in the Frankfurt

School allegedly protested his lack of support for the student movement, Marcuse's students constituted a vanguard to protect their radical professor.

Rather than denounce conservatives' attempts to remove him from his teaching post, Marcuse apologized to UCSD Chancellor McGill for the "trouble" he was "causing." Witnessing what happened to her mentor, Angela Davis would take the opposite strategy the following year when conservatives tried to oust her from UCLA. As reactionaries threatened to kill Davis, she would vigorously challenge the Regents, the governor, rightist ideologies, racism, and sexism.

On November 22, the Regents and Governor Reagan met in the same gymnasium where Cleaver had spoken a month before. Several hundred students and faculty, including Marcuse, waited quietly outside. One hundred students watched from the balcony while a vote was taken to determine the status of Marcuse's course "Social Analysis 139X." The Regents voted to limit guest lecturers to one lecture in credit courses and struck Marcuse's course from the list of courses taken for credit. Students walked out and rallied. Marcuse protested the Regents' action, stating he would no longer serve on administrative committees. On February 3, 1969, the faculty committee investigating Marcuse reported that he ranked highly among sociologists and political theorists, but not philosophers, and was considered a highly gifted teacher; the committee recommended that UCSD renew Marcuse's contract.[33] McGill's "policy on post-retirement appointments" limited Marcuse's continuance as faculty; the policy went into effect in June 1970. The February 17 *Union* ran headlines of McGill's announcement and the second bombing of San Francisco State College's administration buildings. The next day it reported protestors firing tear gas and cherry bombs and shattering windows at UC Berkeley. Republican Assemblyman John Stull petitioned for Chancellor McGill's dismissal. The San Francisco Police Department guarded the regental executive session on McGill's decision to rehire Marcuse. Reagan advocated that Regents take control over postretirement appointments. Jonas Salk and prominent academics sent a telegram in support of McGill. McGill notified Marcuse of his 1969–70 contract. Marcuse was seventy-two when the contract expired in June; seventy was mandatory retirement age. UCSD, however, allowed him to retain his office on campus and teach informally.

Thousands of students were inspired by Herbert Marcuse, the courageous academic intellectual with the mass appeal of a "rock star" for the New Left. Davis modeled Marcuse. Yet her adjacency to the armed rebellions of Black militants – not her philosophy – allowed her stature to surpass, among the global left, both those faithful to the CPUSA and those derisive of it. She rejected Marcuse's critiques of the hypocrisies and spiritual emptiness of capitalist consumerism *and* communist conformity. During the Cold War, Davis was in "good standing" with the Soviets whom the vilified Marcuse criticized. The Soviet's official paper *Pravda* castigated Marcuse. Its 11 million readers read descriptions of Herbert Marcuse as a "werewolf," and denunciations of his criticisms of Soviet rigidity and repression. The Pope hated Marcuse's call for a revolution based in "erotic liberation":

In 1969, Pope Paul VI condemned him by name, blaming Marcuse—along with Sigmund Freud—for promoting the "disgusting and unbridled" manifestations of eroticism and the "animal, barbarous and subhuman degradations" commonly known as the sexual revolution. The hostility that Marcuse aroused was ideologically ecumenical.[34]

Marcuse urged students to think critically about the world and to reject unhealthy social and political orders driven by alienation, technology, and ideology. This did not win him academic friends in the White House or the Kremlin. Rejecting the title "Father of the New Left" and the celebrity status that comes with such appointments, the professor remained a protective and political mentor for Angela Davis, Fania Davis, Bettina Aptheker, Mario Savio, and scores of other students who chose to align with and learn from him.

Marcuse would support Davis throughout her incarceration and trial with a defense mounted by the CPUSA. Angela Davis makes little reference to Marcuse until after her departure from the CPUSA and his commemorations in 2003, when his remains were finally located by a diligent grad student writing about the critical theorist. As noted earlier, the German graduate student realized, through his research, that there was no grave for Marcuse in Germany or in the United States. The industrious student tracked down the philosopher's ashes to a New England moratorium where they had sat for nearly a quarter of a century. Marcuse had been forgotten. Herbert Marcuse had died in Germany in July 1979 after suffering a stroke; his death had garnered little public notice. With news accounts of a graduate student "finding Marcuse," interest in him was renewed. Angela Davis was sought to speak about his life and attend his "repatriation" for burial in Germany. (It is likely that Marcuse, who had survived the German Holocaust, might have preferred being buried in England, to the right of Karl Marx rather than on German soil.) Although the CPSU had attacked Marcuse years earlier, Davis appears to have offered no public critique. After her acquittal, and leadership in the NAARPR/CPUSA, she had lost touch with the autonomous thinker. Only decades later would she offer commentary, noting that he "engage[d] directly with ideas associated with movements of that period" and that his "reference to 'feminist socialism' in the latter essay ["Marxism and Feminism"] predicted the important influence of anti-capitalist and anti-racist feminism on many contemporary movements, including prison abolition, campaigns against police violence, and justice for people with disabilities."[35]

Dissertation Prospectus: Immanuel Kant

Despite turmoil, Angela Davis immersed herself in academic studies. In the 1967 to 1968 academic school year, she completed her doctoral course work with excellent grades.[36] She found that she had clearly "benefited both from [Marcuse's] deep knowledge of European philosophical traditions" and insistence that students stay involved with the world. After course work was completed, Davis began to work on the dissertation. (Davis's 1974 dissertation on Immanuel Kant from Humboldt University in East Germany is not available in digital format, nor was it made available to researchers who approached Humboldt University; the university cited Davis's privacy rights.) The dissertation prospectus was titled "Toward a Kantian Theory of Force."

The dissertation is organized into four parts: I. The Principle of Morality versus the Principle of Legality; II. The State as the Custodian of Coercions; III. The Role of Force in History; IV. A Kantian Theory of Force. Davis writes that in the concluding section, she seeks "to delineate a more far-reaching notion of the importance of force for Kant" by exploring the theories of force in the writings of Fichte, Hegel, and Marx.

Marrying scholarship with activism might or might not be possible in a dissertation theorizing context and addressing contemporary political struggles. Davis's "Toward a Kantian Theory of Force" focuses on the development of morality through the state or against state repression. She writes: "The importance of the category of force in Kant's political and moral philosophy has been virtually ignored. Indeed, scant attention has been directed to his *Metaphysical Elements of Justice*." Davis notes that she would "remedy this deficiency by shedding some light on these works via the concept of force." She proceeds to identify the "various functions of force" as "legal coercion, illegitimate violence (crème and revolution) and war as an action prohibited by reason yet necessitated by historical progress." Her stated problem for interrogation is the "conflict between historically necessary force and its historically desirable abolition." Davis wants to explore if Kantian political theory and philosophy of history contain or recognize forms of violence that stabilize or reproduce, to undermine his "rationally organized society based on freedom." The paradox, as she notes, appears to be that "certain forms of violence must prevail" if Kant's goal of justice is to be achieved.

Angela Davis posits two choices for Kant's theory, queries which her dissertation would explore and attempt to answer: was Kant's concept of force homogeneous enough to encompass diversity and antithetical functions, due to the theoretical paradigm of material conditions, *or* was "a rupture and contradiction within the very concept of force itself" the issue? Kant posits a dualism between morality and legality, theory and history. Discussing self-coercion, coercion, and force, Davis argues that "force is an essential element of freedom. It is the link between the theory and practice of freedom." Davis writes that Rousseau asserted people "must be 'forced to be free'." In a Kantian sense, "the threat of force can bring about external freedom only, i.e., the freedom to act without fear of arbitrary intervention by another." Only the external conditions exist, so this is not a moral freedom. Moral freedom "is the internal conformity with the moral law" which is not affected by external coercion.[37]

If Kant argues "that only a legal order can lay the empirical base for the unfolding of morality in the empirical individual," then, Angela Davis asks, what is his "view of the relationship between morality and legality?" She asserts that legality "can never enter the realm of freedom." But humans need law in order for their societies to evolve, so Kant's concept of justice comes from the template of moral law: a belief that "the state should ... be a collective moral being."[38] Grappling with a dilemma that she states most philosophers have shirked, Angela Davis tackles "the analysis of the morality-legality dualism" as "the problem of justified coercion by the state." So the question is: what is the state? As an aggregate of external legal relations based on a social contract, the state is about coercion primarily, and only secondarily concerned with "the moral maturation of its members." If, however, the state is "a collective moral being"—an idea or ideal—then "its task of protecting the external freedom of its members as a precondition of their moral development is the primary concern."

The coercive means are secondary to the goal which is moral development; per this thesis, coercion on an evolutionary trek would fade away as humans became more moral, hence Kant's idealism. Davis writes that her thesis seeks "to determine whether the relationship exists" between the "Idea" or theory of the state and the material state in the twentieth century.

The "objective necessity of history forces men, through war, to make his entrance into … society."[39] In sum, Davis argues that "Kant's view of history as force" mandates a rejection of his theory of morality as outside of the boundaries of time. If war becomes a precondition for history, then "history and morality are directly opposed to one another"—a fact Angela Davis notes is "untenable." She asserts that "morality has a historical dimension" unexplored by Kant.[40]

The dissertation prospectus was submitted to the UCSD philosophy department at a time when Davis observed that Marcuse's grasp of theory and "the fearless way he manifested his solidarity with movements challenging military aggression, academic repression, and pervasive racism" were unparalleled. That hold on theory helped Davis to hone her theoretical skills to bridge the world of conceptual thought with the world of political activism, specifically politically dissent. Her professor identified academia/theory and activism as distinct partners in a dialectical dance: "Marcuse counseled us always to acknowledge the important differences between the realms of philosophy and political activism, as well as the complex relation between theory and radical social transformation."[41] One can assume that Davis is arguing that the state, in theory, has the right to legal enforcement of its law; and evolving morality, in theory, can emerge in opposition to repressive law; hence both the state and the citizenry that opposes its repression would, in theory, have the "right" to use force. In the state's case it would be legal; in the militants' case it would be illegal. Which party, though, possesses the moral high ground? What is the argument for state laws, i.e., legal codes that exist to cultivate morality and ethical behavior in society?

For Davis, Marcuse was a reminder "that the most meaningful dimension of philosophy was its utopian element. 'When truth cannot be realized within the established social order, it always appears to the latter as mere utopia.'"[42] He taught his students to reject the "unmediated translation[s] of theory into praxis." Marcuse believed that the student rebellions were neither "revolutionary" nor "pre-revolutionary"; rather, he argued, they formed an era in which student militancy "demanded recognition of new possibilities of emancipation" that brought in the immediate moment or the future "fresh air that would certainly not [be] the air of the establishment."[43] It is not clear how Marcuse approached *student* rebellions as being a catalyst (or utopian element).

Just as Kant's notion of "man" had gender, racial, and class connotations, Marcuse's notion of the "student" was shaped by the elite white male students at the Frankfurt School, Columbia, Harvard, Brandeis, and UC San Diego. There is data showing Marcuse being criticized by feminist students for his lack of an analysis of gender. Fania Davis Jordan and Angela Davis were likely his only Black students, or, at least, were the only ones mentioned in Marcuse's legacy of teaching. The sisters are also Black *women*, which is a phenomenon under-analyzed in *An Autobiography*. Yet, their experiences as Black graduate students, of course, did not typify the *Black experience* in an era in which less than 5 percent of Black Americans had a college or university degree.

Herbert Marcuse, Angela Davis, Fania Davis, and many others in academia faced death threats from racist and anti-Semitic vigilantes and police departments. However, there was always resistance. Demonstrations led by feminist, gay, Black, Chicano, Asian, American Indian, and white anti-war protesters rattled the social order.[44] Police forces and vigilantes worked violently to quell unrest. The concept of a Third World campus at UCSD seemed sensible, but the organizing was not sustainable. It had no adequate self-defense component. As anti-war protests on the campus became more heated and violent, repression became more intense.

As the doctoral student worked on her thesis, she found that German (Jewish) philosophy provided a paradigm to analyze moral freedom in the contemporary struggle amidst state and police repression of Black liberation and worker movements. For Davis, radical struggles would deliver progress but not denouement: "Marcuse did not always agree with particular tactics of radical movements of that era, he was very clear about the extent to which calls for Black liberation, peace, gender justice, and for the restructuring of education represented important emancipatory tendencies [that] helped to push theory in progressive directions."[45] One wonders if the ultimate goal is to help theory become more "progressive."

As Davis studied Marcuse's *An Essay on Liberation* (1969) *and Counterrevolution and Revolt* (1972),[46] other women students working with Marcuse began to critique his lack of gender analysis (and edited his 1974 "Marxism and Feminism" paper presented at Stanford University).[47] Marcuse's "*An Essay on Liberation*" references militant Third World organizations, *not* the USSR or CPUSA, as the potential future of "revolution":

> In Vietnam, in Cuba, in China, a revolution is being defended and driven forward which struggles to eschew the bureaucratic administration of socialism. The guerrilla forces in Latin America seem to be animated by that same subversive impulse: liberation. At the same time, the apparently impregnable economic fortress of corporate capitalism shows signs of mounting strain: it seems that even the United States cannot indefinitely deliver its goods—guns and butter, napalm and color TV. The ghetto populations may well become the first mass basis of revolt (though not of revolution). The student opposition is spreading in the old socialist as well as capitalist countries. In France, it has for the first time challenged the full force of the regime and recaptured, for a short moment, the libertarian power of the red and the Black flags; moreover, it has demonstrated the prospects for an enlarged basis. The temporary suppression of the rebellion will not reverse the trend.[48]

Impressed by Marcuse's optimism, Davis would assert that a key part of his legacy for people was an increased capacity to imagine a holistic and shared future. Marcuse and Davis likely underestimated the rise of reactionary or protofascist forces stemming from the Vietnam War. As students demonstrated against the Vietnam War, veterans—who felt betrayed by a Republican administration that "caved" in to anti-war protesters, and "inferior races"—waged domestic warfare, reconciling with the Nazis against whom they had fought in the Second World War.[49] According to Davis, "political imagination reflects the possibilities" for future productive struggles.[50] Her professor who had introduced her to philosophy provided relevant lessons: "The insistence on imagining emancipatory futures, even under the most desperate of circumstances, remains—Marcuse teaches us—a decisive element of both theory and practice."[51]

Marcuse's esteem for his most (in)famous student would lead him to give unwavering support when Davis was arrested in 1970 and incarcerated in a small, cramped cell in the Marin County Jail. The professor's draft notes for the January 31, 1971, *NBC* interview about Angela Davis evinced a steadfast belief in her innocence and exceptionalism.[52] For Marcuse, his undergraduate and graduate student philosopher was assuredly *nonviolent*. Marcuse noted the complexity and rigor of her educational background, one shared by white European/American elites: "She was my student in philosophy and political theory. In lectures and seminars, we discussed the great texts which have shaped the history of Western civilization: from the Greek philosophers to Hegel and Nietzsche; from the political theorists of ancient Greece to Marx."[53] Marcuse restated previous assertions about her exemplary scholastic achievements—"because it may help to explain her development, her life" and described her as "the best or one of the very best students I had in more than 30 years of teaching."[54]

Marcuse humanized Davis to a media and white society that hounded her. To Herbert Marcuse, the young Angela Davis was "an extraordinary student not only because of her intelligence and her eagerness to learn … but also because she had that sensitivity, that human warmth without which all learning and all knowledge remain 'abstract,' merely 'professional,' and eventually irrelevant."[55] His loyalty to "the left" was unwavering but unconventional. For some, the German-Jewish philosopher was a thorn in the sides of the "establishment." For others, he rejected orthodoxy in Marxism and critical theory. His philosophical reflections could be considered "abstract scholarship." Yet his militant students took theory to heart and engaged in political dissent and organizing in order to change the material struggles of liberation. Marcuse was attacked because he "championed student militants against the Establishment … decried 'increasing repression' under the Nixon Administration … [and] refused to turn his back on his former pupil Angela Davis."[56] He confides to Davis her impact on his critical thinking:

> Frederick Douglass one day hits back, he fights the slave-breaker with all his force, and the slave-breaker does not hit back; he stands trembling [and] calls other slaves to help, and they refuse. The abstract philosophical concept of a freedom which can never be taken away suddenly comes to life and reveals its very concrete truth: freedom is not only the goal of liberation, it begins with liberation; it is there to be "practiced." This, I confess, I learned from you.[57]

Some observers felt that Herbert Marcuse's "consistent espousal of radical action [was] an offense to liberals who have opted for sensible gradualism and modification rather than eradication of the political culture."[58]

For fifteen years, Marcuse supported Angela Davis as she evolved from an undergraduate into a graduate student and critical theorist. He and his wife Inge Marcuse visited her in jail and offered support throughout her trial; the couple celebrated her acquittal. Angela Davis did not finish her dissertation on Kant with Marcuse, who was pushed out of UCSD by June 1970. After her acquittal, Davis traveled to East Germany and obtained her doctorate from Humboldt University. Humboldt University's illustrious alumni include Karl Marx, Friedrich Engels and G.W.F. Hegel, W. E. B. DuBois, Albert Einstein, and Walter Benjamin. The dissertation (as of the last inquiry in 2019 made by a German graduate student returning from studies in Massachusetts) remains sealed and unavailable to the public.

8

1967 Entry Points

Welcome to the Hostile California

California was not the Deep South. Still, it expressed the same stale violent hatred for Blacks. It particularly resented the migrations of southern Blacks newly entering into the state. California police departments recruited their white employees from the Jim Crow south, asserting that the new recruits knew how to "handle negroes." In addition to its racism, the state prided itself on the greatest collection of Research I universities. Gradually its high schools, colleges, and universities became sites of student-led rebellions that followed the Black-led southern civil rights movements. But the postwar boomers—now young adult students—had grown up, from 1955 to 1969, watching, on television, protesters against Klan and police brutality being beaten bloody, having their clothes and skin torn off by high pressure water hoses or police canines, or murdered by joint forces of Klan and white supremacist police. In the mid- to late 1960s, television was filming a stream of flag-draped coffins coming home from Vietnam.[1] On television sets and in newspapers, the southern civil rights movement dominated headlines.

White UC Berkeley students Mario Savio and Bettina Aptheker[2] led the Free Speech movement so that civil rights organizers returning from the south could display pamphlets on campus alerting students to human rights violations. Aptheker had befriended Davis in high school in NYC. Along with Savio, Aptheker had volunteered for the 1964 Freedom Summer, alongside students from HBCUs such as Howard University, to join the shock troops desegregating the south. Other students were radicalized in peace movements where police, National Guard, and civilians (such as construction workers) beat them mercilessly for being white traitors, class traitors and traitors to America. The Vietnam war draft, ostensibly for all fit males who had turned eighteen, kept schools, campuses, and students uneasy and on edge.

On January 2, 1967, Republican Ronald Reagan was sworn into office as Governor of California. Until Governor Reagan began cutting funding to public universities to subdue student rebels, California boasted some of the best schools in the nation. UC students were considered to be some of the brightest university students in the nation. They were also becoming some of the most militant. Their radicalism stemmed from varied sources, some of it from critical thinking, countercultural desires or outrage against injustice. Leisured students grappled with their privileges and moral mandates that they engage with a world where inequality, imperial wars, and threats of nuclear war created resources they took for granted while impoverished families suffered. The civil rights movement was also migrating onto their campuses. Civil rights, workers' rights, and environmental rights movements were emerging. Over three hours north of San Diego, Santa Barbara had suffered a massive oil spill in late January that year. Some 80 to 100,000 barrels of crude oil wrecked Southern California beaches; the next month, another spill closed the harbor.[3] The nascent environmental movement began to emerge alongside the increasingly militant civil rights and anti-war mobilizations. San Diego was anchored in a zone of military bases and minutemen strongholds, bordered by Pacific waters and Nevadan deserts, with Oregon to the north and Mexico to the south. California's environmental beauty was the backdrop to battles royal. Unrest and polarized politics in California, the bellwether state for the nation, was the norm.

Named the "Golden State" in 1968—for 1840s gold mines, yellow poppies, and optimism—California displayed dark hostilities towards its small oppressed Black population. Besides replicating the deep south's anti-Black policing, San Diego was also home to several marine and navy bases whose occupants were predominantly white, militarized and hostile to Blacks—particularly militant Blacks. In July, Angela Davis would fly to California to begin her doctoral studies at UC San Diego and reunite with her younger sister Fania Davis Jordan, a graduate of Swarthmore College. The sisters were enrolled in the same graduate program to study philosophy with the German leftist theorist Herbert Marcuse.[4]

Reactionary Governor Represses Radicals

Ronald Reagan began his political trajectory in reactionary politics as an arch anti-communist in the 1940s, when he headed the Screen Actors Guild (1947 to 1952 and 1959 to 1960). Reagan transformed himself from a B-grade actor into a wealthy and well-connected anti-communist demagogue in order to become electable as governor of California from 1967 to 1975 (later, he would be elected president of the United States in 1980). In his leadership role, he undermined actors' abilities to bargain as a union against movie companies. Reagan successfully purged progressive and pro-union workers by arguing that communists were infiltrating Hollywood. The same argument would be used twenty years later against the University of California. Reagan so regularly provided names of suspected communists to the FBI that he earned an "informer's code number, T-10."[5] Since the 1950s, Reagan had been the key spokesperson for propaganda for the CIA-front Crusade for Freedom. The Crusade functioned as the domestic counterpart of Radio Free Europe. Crusade propaganda was endorsed by the publishers of the *Washington Post, New York Times*, and Hearst Corporation who also worked with the CIA.[6] When it came time to fire or retire Herbert Marcuse from teaching at UC San Diego and Angela Davis from teaching at UCLA, Reagan used political connections and funds to "buy" loyalty to sway members of the Regents not sufficiently enthusiastic about imposing reactionary mandates onto higher education.[7] Before he would eliminate Marxist or communist professors, in *his* universities, Reagan would neutralize student rebels and Black Panthers.

On February 21, 1967, several Black Panthers, wearing Black berets and carrying shotguns, rifles, and pistols, appeared at the San Francisco International Airport as bodyguards and escort for Betty Shabazz, the widow of Malcolm X, who had been invited to speak to Bay Area communities. Police took notice but did not intervene. There was an oversight. The conservative governor, Ronald Regan—who displayed considerable animus toward Blacks and communists—was on the grounds holding a press conference and tour. The greatest weapons the Panthers wielded was not their guns; it was their bold intellectualism. Their most effective pedagogical tool was not political education committees. Their greatest asset was the creative, striking, highly influential *Black Panther Party* newspaper, which promoted Panther analyses and causes. The most pressing cause would be to get Huey P. Newton out of jail. The newspaper disseminated information about Panther political platforms and recruited Panthers and allies; the Panther paper had striking art by Douglass Emory and brought positive and negative (from police and conservatives) attention to the BPP.

In April 1967, Martin Luther King, Jr., denounced the war in Vietnam at New York City's Riverside Church, citing US imperialism and condemning capitalism (the following April, he would be assassinated). In 1967, Newark, NJ, and Detroit, MI, went up in flames. When the local police failed to contain Detroit, they called out the National Guard. When the National Guard failed to suppress the Detroit rebellion, orders were given to the 82nd and 101st Airborne, which was used overseas to destroy guerrilla liberation movements in the Third World. The US military was also deployed to inflict successful occupations of US cities.

On May 2, 1967, the Black Panther Party had paraded with guns at the Sacramento Capitol to display their right to not be terrorized or deterred from offering protections by predatory police. Panthers with loaded pistols, shotguns, and rifles entered the State Capitol, in Sacramento, while Governor Ronald Reagan was giving a tour and press conference. The white school children on the grounds mistook the Panthers for a rifle club and gleefully greeted them. Misunderstanding the layout of offices, Panthers mistakenly entered the chamber with the assembly in session (which was illegal). Black Panther Party's co-founder Bobby Seale read a statement protesting an assembly bill to ban the carrying of loaded weapons within city limits. State police escorted the Panthers out and arrested them. Newspapers and media widely reported on their bold confrontations with police and government. The FBI and the Central Intelligence Agency (CIA) became increasingly focused on the Black Panther Party, after the Sacramento incident in close proximity to a reactionary, anti-communist governor. Several months later, that summer, from Europe, Angela Davis decided to come home into the fray.

Newton's June 20, 1967, pamphlet, *In Defense of Self-Defense*, would have alienated the CPUSA (which Davis would join in 1968):

The power Structure inflicts pain and brutality upon the peoples and then provides controlled outlets for the pain in ways least likely to upset them or interfere with the process of exploitation. The people must repudiate the channels established as tricks and deceitful snares by the exploiting oppressors. The people must oppose everything the Oppressor supports and support everything that he opposes. ... If Black people go about their struggle for liberation in the way that the oppressor dictates and sponsors, then we will have degenerated to the level of groveling flunkies for the oppressor himself. When the oppressor makes a vicious attack against freedom fighters because of the way that such freedom fighters choose to go about their liberation, then we know we are moving in the direction of our liberation. The racist dog oppressors have no rights which oppressed Black people are bound to respect. As long as the racist dogs pollute the earth with the evil of their actions, they do not deserve any respect at all, and the rules of their game, written in the people's blood, are beneath contempt.[8]

Davis wanted to meet Huey Newton. Eventually they would meet when she moved to California. He would obtain his PhD at the same university, UC Santa Cruz, and in the same program, the History of Consciousness, that would hire her as a full professor once she returned formally to the academy. Newton's striking violence against members of the Panther Party and in Oakland communities, and against women, did not deter their mutual alliance that lasted until his death in 1989.

London Stopover—the "Dialectics of Liberation" Conference

When Angela Davis chose, after graduating from Brandeis, to study critical theory in Germany, she continued her pattern of isolation from Black communities and militant liberation movements. Her frustrations were mounting as she finished her studies at the Frankfurt School:

> While I was hidden away in West Germany the Black Liberation Movement was undergoing decisive metamorphoses. The slogan "Black Power" sprang out of a march in Mississippi. Organizations were being transfigured—the Student Non-Violent Coordinating Committee, a leading civil rights organization, was becoming the foremost advocate of "Black Power." The Congress on Racial Equality was undergoing similar transformations. In Newark, a national Black Power Conference had been organized. In political groups, labor unions, churches and other organizations, Black caucuses were being formed to defend the special interests of Black people. Everywhere there were upheavals.[9]

In her sightline were multiple Black Power organizations; rather than the agency and needs of the rank-and-file, she focused on the leadership. In London, before departing from Europe, she would meet her first Black internationally known US militant.

From Frankfurt, Davis traveled to London in July 1967, to meet with intellectuals and activists at a conference for leftist thinkers, her last stop before flying directly to the United States. She was frustrated with Frankfurt and her life. The rebellions and organizing against racism, exploitation, and war were mounting in the United States, often under the leadership of young Black militants. In Germany, she could read about the rise of the BPP and organize at the university and with local groups, but it was not the same. The epicenter for struggle was Third World liberation, internal and formal colonies. The premier empire to be challenged was the United States. Her birthplace. She could not fully comprehend movements from across the Atlantic Ocean, movements within which she had never participated. Having completed her graduate degree, stopping in London allowed her to see her professor Herbert Marcuse and to meet civil rights icon Stokely Carmichael (Kwame Ture). Both would be speaking at the "Dialectics of Liberation" conference in London, a conference on theory dominated by white intellectuals. In London, Davis would ask Carmichael/Ture for connections to US "movement" leaders or Black militants. Arriving in California, she phoned the list of Black leaders given to her by Carmichael/Ture only to encounter disconnected phone numbers or people who immediately hung up the phone, considering her call a prank or police ensnarement.

When Angela Davis met Carmichael/Ture in London, he embodied the southern civil rights movement and was one of the most prominent leaders in SNCC, where he would be an active member and leader from 1960 to 1970. By the time he met Davis at the "Dialectics of Liberation" conference, the Student Nonviolent Coordinating Committee (SNCC) was transitioning into an all-Black Student militant *National Coordinating Committee* (SNCC). The acronyms remained the same and confusion followed. Carmichael came to London as a proponent of "Black Power." His co-authored book with Charles Hamilton, *Black Power: The Politics of Liberation in America*, was published in January 1967 by the powerful corporate press, Random House.[10] Carmichael/Ture had spent seven years of organizing in the bloody south, without the protection of the federal government to quell racist violence against and murders of civil rights activists.[11] Born in Trinidad (birthplace of Black Marxists/communists Claudia Jones and C.L.R. James), Carmichael was enrolled in Howard University in Washington, DC, before he left school in 1960 to fight the southern civil rights movement. He had risked his life for Black liberation for years. As Kwame Ture, he would co-lead the Black Panther Political Party and briefly align with the Black Panther Party (for Self-Defense) or BPP. Under the leadership of Oakland/Newton, Ture was antagonized or intimidated; he left California and turned towards organizing in anti-colonial movements in African nations.

Weeks leading up to the London conference had been dominated by news coverage of US urban uprisings and rebellions around the globe. Students were protesting for rights; workers engaged in massive strikes. The stated objective for the 1967 conference was to "create a genuine revolutionary consciousness by fusing ideology and action on the levels of the individual and of mass society."[12] "Dialectics of Liberation" was described as a "unique expression of the politics of modern dissent, in which existential psychiatrists, Marxist intellectuals, anarchists and political leaders met to discuss … the key social issues of the next decade."[13] Although the definition of the gathering seemed more geared toward college or university students—children of the (white) bourgeoisie that the CIA's NSA sought to harness to an imperial project—Davis welcomed its emphasis on analysis and organizing. Meeting and interacting with activists and intellectuals proved more fruitful for her than being cloistered in the library, reading texts for class or discussions with other students: "I learned more about the new movement there in

London than from all the reading I had done." Black radical activists who attended the conference, such as Carmichael (Ture), had organized for years with impoverished Black communities terrorized by the Klan, but they might not have easily seen themselves reflected in the description of the conference. Excited to get closer to US activism beyond her studies, Davis might not have recognized that the activists whose participation meant so much to her would likely not see their peoples' struggles in the conference papers. Speakers analyzed violence tied to "personal alienation, repression and student revolution" and "guerrilla warfare" that sought to "free man from mystification, from the blind destruction of his environment, and from the inhumanity which he projects onto his opponents in family situations, in wars and in racial conflict."[14] The specificity of anti-Black violence proved elusive to some but not to all.

From the conference hall, Angela Davis listened to Marcuse's keynote on the "primary aggressiveness" between the haves and have-nots. Carmichael raised the roof with a fiery call for Black Power and new ways of fighting individual and institutional racism. Networking with the "Dialectics of Liberation" presenters and academics, Angela Davis pushed past the conference setting to accompany speakers on their visits with militant leaders in London's Black communities. Although not a pan-Africanist, she observed the similarities and mutual needs between impoverished and oppressed communities on both sides of the Atlantic: "Between conference sessions I spent my time with Stokely and Michael X's group, accompanied them to meetings in London ghettoes, helping on occasion to pull the gatherings together. I was struck by the degree to which West Indian communities in London were mirror images of Black communities at home."[15]

Although impressed by some Black activists that she met in London, particularly Carmichael/Ture[16] and Michael X, Davis nonetheless departed from the "Dialectics of Liberation" conference with the view that Black liberation movements needed more developed analyses. Her years of analytical training in white universities in the Northeast or Europe, in the absence of Black communities or engaged struggles, could present blind spots, but, in her mind, the Black liberation movement needed more Marxist theory, and her white university peers and faculty more experiential knowledge of Jim Crow segregation, racist economic exploitation, and Klan terrorism. She thus became the nexus between the two, but that bridge did not inherently have the multidimensional scaffolding to clearly view Black revolutionary struggles in the crosshairs of counterrevolutionary police forces within an empire.

Angela Davis viewed racist conflict and colonialism through a mirror of politics that seemed to have overemphasized the emotions and underemphasized the intellectualism of Third World antagonists to empire: "These warm, receptive, fiery, enthusiastic people were also searching for some way to avenge themselves."[17] It is not clear if *An Autobiography* is referencing Carmichael/Ture at the London Conference. Davis could not have been infantilizing Marcuse's keynote; the German Marxist had leveraged her academic career as a philosopher, getting her into the Frankfurt School. Carmichael/Ture as a prominent SNCC leader was radicalized by white supremacist murders, beatings, and imprisonment of civil rights activists, largely undeterred by the government. He had organized intensely with the Lowndes County Alabama Panthers; they had trained him along with SNCC civil rights leaders such as Ella Baker and SCLC leaders such as Martin Luther King Jr. Carmichael/Ture had served several tours of duty on the frontlines of what SNCC called the "second civil war." Davis had been vulnerable to bombings of her Black middle-class neighborhood Birmingham but not exposed to the battlefields. Domestic property protection is not the equivalent of a revolutionary struggle in someone else's state or town that you have never visited before, but for which you are willing to risk your life so that the community obtains some fragment of freedom.

SNCC and the Southern Christian Leadership Council (SCLC) factions separated in the southern movement due to the rising call for "Black Power!" As the multiracial turn-the-other-cheek Student *Nonviolent* Coordinating Committee dissolved into the Black Power Student *National* Coordinating Committee (as noted above the acronym "SNCC" became confusing), the new SNCC would become more interesting to California Black Panthers.

Sitting through days of the conference and meeting Black activists in the city of London, Davis formulated structural analyses; describing US Black communities and leaders, she asserts: "As in the United States, there was a natural inclination to identify the enemy as the white man. Natural because the great majority of white people, both in the United States and England, have been carriers of the racism which, in reality, benefits only a small number of them—the capitalists."[18] That assertion is debatable. The Frankfurt School, where she studied for two years, attempted to analyze why German workers embraced the Third Reich and its racist wars. Non-capitalist "Aryans" and the working class and laborers joined their *Führer* in genocidal wars for racial purity. The psychological impulse seems understudied here; Fanon's *Black Skin, White Masks* and Sander Gilman's *Difference and Pathology: Stereotypes of Sexuality, Race, and Madness* could offer additional insights beyond class analyses (the influential *The Authoritarian Personality* by Adorno, et al. was published in 1950).

Davis's analysis offers a unifocal explanation for exploitation and misery: capitalism. Hence, she regarded analyses that centered on anti-Blackness as limited. "The man" was the capitalist state, and the true enemy of the people and of "our" (i.e., Black) people: "Because the masses of white people harbor racist attitudes, our people tended to see *them* as the villains and not the institutionalized forms of racism, which, though definitely reinforced by prejudiced attitudes, serve, fundamentally, only the interests of the rulers."[19] Racist attitudes also produce existential wealth that becomes linked to material wealth and police violence—e.g., see Cheryl Harris's 1993 "Whiteness as Property," *Harvard Law Review*. The "rulers" are capitalists, not all whites. Adhering to CPUSA critiques, economic oppression steered Davis's theory. Over decades, feminism and gender critiques would be added to Davis's analyses, but anti-Blackness and Afropessimism were banned as analytical tools, as descriptors reduced to Black victimization by white supremacy but not by whites. The narratives centered lynching and white supremacist murders which included children—Emmett in 1955, Addie Mae, Carole, Cynthia, Denise in 1963—and adults such as Medgar Evers who was assassinated on June 12, 1963, in Jackson, Mississippi. (George Floyd protesters in 2020 could more easily describe the impact of capitalism and racism, but not always the specificity of anti-Black terror—an analytic often dissipated in the language of "people of color" and general "racism.") As a graduate student in Europe, Davis was eager to return to the United States in order to both experience and help lead Black rebellion. Hence, she joined the CPUSA. She worked with the Panthers formally as a member in an education committee for several weeks but became the international icon for "the Panther."[20]

A decent living wage benefits all if all are equally employed. Economic exploitation is impacted by anti-Black aggressions shaped by the social order and personal and psychological disorders—if one can refer to white nationalism as a disorder. Anti-Blackness drives redlining, substandard medical care, mass incarceration, police violence, and mortality rates of Black mothers and infants during childbirth. The "white man" became "the man" in the political lingo of the era as a signifier for white supremacy and patriarchy. Critical thinking about racism has evolved since Davis was a graduate student. She had heard Malcolm X speak at Brandeis University as an undergrad. At first thrilled and amused at his quips against whites/white supremacy, she became dismissive as noted in *An Autobiography* published in 1974. (Davis was invited by Malcolm's daughters to give the 2023 keynote on the anniversary of Malcolm X's February 21, 1965, assassination in the Audubon Ballroom in Washington Heights.) She notes in a 2019 conversation at Brandeis University that as a student, her era did not have the language for critiquing more subtle and pervasive forms of racism. Malcolm X, though, had that language; it was incisive, disruptive, and assertive: house slave vs. field slave, "ballot or the bullet," "by any means necessary"; "fox in the hen house"; "there is no such thing as a 'second class citizen.'" It was language that Davis refused; and so *An Autobiography* largely dismisses Malcolm as a performer and refuses to recognize him as a critical theorist. (Contributions from academics that deepen the discussion include legal theorists Harris's "Whiteness as Property";[21] and white supremacy as "existential wealth"; Derrick Bell's critical race theory on the permanence of racism and "interest convergence"; as well as Frank Wilderson and Jared Sexton's critical theories in Afropessimism, and other analyses of anti-Blackness.)[22]

At the time of the 1967 conference, led by leftist bourgeois white males, Davis mused about Black (out)rage: "When white people are indiscriminately viewed as the enemy, it is virtually impossible to develop a political solution."[23] *An Autobiography* recalls her schoolyard observations of Birmingham's Black working class and poor students' violence against each other: "I was learning that as long as the Black response to racism remained purely emotional, we would go nowhere. Like the playground fights at Parker High, like the sporadic heedless anger of those who fell under police clubs in Alabama—it would solve nothing in the long run."[24]

Settling In: UCSD Campus Organizing

Entering San Diego in 1967, within miles of the Mexico border and Tijuana, Angela Davis, with books and luggage in tow, settled into the sprawling system of the University of California. Multilingual, she read news and literature, in English and French, focusing on radical philosophers Jean Paul Sartre, Frantz Fanon, and Albert Memmi. Renting rooms in the home of a young white couple—fellow graduate students—she shared their San Diego beachside home and played with their toddler.

That pristine sanctuary provided space and quiet to study, think, and write while engaged in play witnessing a secure childhood that had never been offered to Black children under siege and segregation. The quiet was a stark contrast to the explosions on "Dynamite Hill." At a distance were the Black communities in economic and political struggle and corralled by the police. Davis's initial organizing in San Diego centered on campus politics. With Black UCSD students, "Liz" and "Ed," she helped to form a Black Student Union. While trying to bail out radical student protestors opposing the war in Vietnam, she was arrested. Kept for hours at the station, she and another white student vocally asserted their rights until they were released. Then campus organizing and reforms gradually faded away and Davis became more interested in Black communities.

An Autobiography notes Davis's strategy to go forward beyond the campus by meeting Black community-based activists, learn from them, and engage every Black militant organization. Hence, she needed the list from Carmichael/Ture, but it was not useful. Black Power formations were competitive and in conflict (the FBI and local police would stoke conflict into deadly antagonisms). Davis was a useful ally; she brought the sensibilities of higher education and European culture—a great representation of the "good Negro" and the Black (petite) bourgeoisie, which was her lifestyle even though her commitment was to communism. However, her ideas were not picked up much outside the academy. The "grounded" community that lived among impoverished and working-class Blacks, if they were militants, was not reading Kant. They were reading Marx, Malcolm, Mao, Stokely, and Fanon. Davis's perspective that focusing critique on white racism was a misstep would not resonate with those harassed or beaten by (white) cops and prison guards, aka, "the man." Angela Davis—as an excellent young student—came home to seek out Black Power, yet there were varied forms. Within decades through networks shaped by CPUSA, liberals, powerhouse publishers, academia, pop culture, and liberal funders and celebrity platforms, Davis would be able to not just *define* Black Power. From her student years, and decades with the CPUSA/CPSU and academia and publishing sectors, Angela Davis—in relation to Black struggles and Black power—would, for the conventional public, be able to enact Huey P. Newton's definition of power: "power is, first of all, the ability to define phenomena, and secondly the ability to make these phenomena act in a desired manner."

The focal point in California would be the well-being of the cofounder of the Black Panther Party for Self-Defense, formed in 1966 in Oakland, California, by Huey P. Newton and Bobby Seale. On October 28, 1967, Huey P. Newton was shot, seriously injured and incarcerated after a shooting incident with two white police officers; one died. Officer John Frey would die from his injuries and Newton would be jailed and charged with the murder of a white police officer; charges would be dropped to involuntary manslaughter and, later, Newton's attorneys Charles Garry and Fay Stender would get him off on a technicality when the presiding judge failed to recognize Newton's statement that he had passed out from being shot in the stomach and did not see who shot the arresting officers. Davis describes this period as a transformative one, during which she transitioned from seeking experiences and knowledge in Europe and being "sporadic and disconnected" to becoming focused and disciplined. Those efforts entailed not just academic study but also engagement with and *advocacy for* young Black militants seeking transformative politics.

The next month, Davis attended a November Black Youth Conference held at the Second Baptist Church in Watts. Keynote speakers included SNCC (transitioning into the Student *National* Coordinating Committee) leader James Forman and CPUSA leader Franklin Alexander, brother of Charlene Mitchell. Davis was later invited to a small house meeting where Alexander and Ralph Featherstone discussed their recent trip to Africa. There Davis met representatives of the Black Panther Political Party (BPPP), a study group linked to SNCC. The BPPP was her first association with "Panthers" as she joined the study group for a brief period.

In a flurry of months, Davis met with SNCC. She also became familiar with the Afro-American Association group, a study group at UC Berkeley, and the Black Panther Political Party. Davis worked with the Los Angeles branch of the Black Panther Party. She met and split from the cultural nationalism of Maulana Karenga, a founder of US and Black cultural studies who created the holiday Kwanzaa. (Allegedly, Karenga demanded that Black females walk behind him in order to honor "African" traditions; more tragically the US was accused of killing Panthers John Huggins and Alprentice "Bunchy" Carter at a Black student UCLA campus event.)

As activist support groups moved at increasingly accelerated rates, responding to violence from white supremacists and US police forces, Davis provided support where she could while she worked on her dissertation: as discussed in the previous chapter, the study of Kant's theory of force or violence and morality. Davis was analyzing the dialectic between the demands for freedom, which would employ force to enable moral development, and the demands of state legal codes that would use coercion or violence to structure their vision of a moral society. Police violence against political dissent was a fact, not merely a theory. Davis's daily university life of the mind was woven into research on an eighteenth-century Enlightenment philosopher. Instead of a rational order, the US state was creating chaos and violence.[25] Davis continuously confronted the disorder and violence by informing the public, through the media and protest marches, of police killings of political leaders resisting government agencies working to destabilize liberation movements:

> There was terrible repression during that period. I had never experienced anything like that in my life. And I realize, looking back, that we lived in a war zone. I could receive a telephone call from someone with whom I was active in SNCC for example and she or he might say, "My house is surrounded by the police. Call as many people as possible because we need support." That was quite usual. So that we expected, ah, every moment that we might be confronted with … armed attack. I don't know if I can get that across, that feeling today, except by saying that it was as if we were involved in battle. … We know that J. Edgar Hoover orchestrated a national assault on the Black Panther Party in particular and other organizations that were militant representatives of the Black community at that time. There were many people who, as a result of that repression, call the period fascist. I was one of those who was opposed to arguing that we lived in an era of full-blown fascism.[26]

Davis's definition of "fascism" would have been influenced by the Frankfurt School faculty and Marcuse, as Jewish theorists studying and debating how the Nazi regime could have emerged in "civilized" Europe. What some might see as an "existential battle" is a central theme here. During early childhood, Davis's family home was rocked by the aftershock of Klan bombings of Black homes, and parents (fathers) needing to create armed patrols at night to seek and deter arsonists and bombers. There is the "lull" in Europe where alienation becomes so entrenched for Davis in France, and somewhat in Germany, that distancing from the civil rights movement becomes a form of disassociation and an identity crisis. The death threats track Davis, while police follow and harass her, once she publicly announces herself as both a communist and an ally to Black militants. San Diego police attempt to kill her sister Fania Davis Jordan and brother-in-law Samuel Jordan because they are BPP members. Her fugitivity, bounty, capture, imprisonment, and trial—all are zones of hyper-vulnerability to extreme mental and physical violence. The distance between the Panthers and Davis would grow after August 1970 when Davis separated from Black militants, during her underground and trial (severing with co-defendant Ruchell Magee) in order to save her life first from the death penalty and later from decades or life in prison.

There was growing support among the public for radicals and Panthers as news leaks informed that US tax dollars were funding lethal state warfare against dissidents; yet no matter how many congressional hearings, stolen and leaked government files, and later Freedom of Information Act (FOIA) documents verified that Black militants were being illegally hunted by police forces—FBI, CIA, Drug Enforcement Agency (DEA)—it was insufficient to stop the violence.

Newton and Seales's Black Panther Party participated in study groups that integrated study, activism, and direct delivery of care to impoverished communities. The Afro-American Association included UC Berkeley doctoral students Cedric Robinson (author of *Black Marxism*), and Vice President Kamala Harris's parents, affluent or scholarship students from India and Jamaica earning their doctorates at Berkeley or Stanford. Newton and Seale briefly joined, but, finding little connections to the needs of Black working class and impoverished communities, left the group.

The Free Huey! Campaign heralded Newton as a leader, brilliant theorist, warrior, and potential martyr ("Set our warrior free!" was one of the Panther chants concerning Newton). Huey Newton's writings were published in pamphlets and in the *Black Panther Party Newspaper*. His iconic stature was intentionally cultivated and promoted by Kathleen and Eldridge Cleaver in an attempt to save his life. They were successful. What Newton became later, in his violent attacks against "East Coast" Panthers and crime-boss predation against Black communities, was another story.

FBI Counter-revolutionaries

COINTELPRO, the FBI lethal counterintelligence program, took the lives of Fred Hampton and Mark Clark in a December 4, 1969, assassination raid in Chicago, IL. While Davis was in jail in Marin County, California, the FBI and LAPD framed and falsely accused the leader of the Southern California Panther Party, Elmer

"Geronimo" Pratt, of a murder he did not commit, using a Black police informant as a "witness." Pratt was convicted in a Los Angeles trial and endured twenty-seven years in prison (upon his release due to attorneys Johnnie Cochran, Panther leader Kathleen Cleaver, and Stuart Hanlon, the US government issued a financial settlement to Pratt but did not acknowledge any wrong-doing). The FBI and the NYPD also framed Dhoruba bin Wahad, making a financial settlement after nineteen years of imprisonment—again, with no acknowledgment of state illegalities or admission of police/FBI criminality.

While the CIA was covert in destabilizing and neutralizing opponents, the FBI was overt. Headed by J. Edgar Hoover, the FBI orchestrated direct attacks on Black radical activists. Hoover's infamous memorandum designated the Black Panther Party as the number one threat to the internal security of the United States. In 1967, the FBI put out a lethal directive against Black dissidents.[27] FBI Director J. Edgar Hoover planned to "expose, disrupt, and otherwise neutralize" Black organizations that were seeking radical political-economic reforms. His primary target would be the most militant and inspirational of the groups, the Black Panther Party. COINTELPRO originated under Hoover to cripple and dismantle the CPUSA. Re-envisioned by federal and local police forces, it unleashed a racial animus that the white-led CPUSA had never faced. The 1967 directives had five objectives as the FBI functioned to neutralize progressive opposition to state and police:

1. Prevent the coalition of militant Black nationalist groups ... the first step toward a real "Mau Mau" in America, the beginning of a true Black revolution.
2. Prevent the rise of a "messiah" who could unify, and electrify, the militant Black nationalist movement.
3. Prevent violence on the part of Black nationalist groups ...
4. Prevent militant Black nationalist groups and leaders from gaining respectability, by discrediting them to ... the responsible Negro community ... the white community, both the responsible community and to "liberals" who have vestiges of sympathy for militant Black nationalist ... Negro radicals. ...
5. [P]revent the long-range growth of militant Black nationalist organizations, especially among youth.[28]

Panther Identity

Conventional scholarship and east coast Panthers—such as academic K. Kim Holder and Black Liberation Army (BLA) vet and author Dhoruba bin Wahad—recognize Angela Davis as a close ally to the BPP Oakland leadership before and after the party was split into factions in which sectors of the "West Coast" California members of the Black Panther Party became antagonists of the "East Coast" or New York panthers. Eventually, Oakland Panthers led by Huey Newton would be associated with organized crime and death squads targeting Panthers who maintained the practices of "self-defense" and "revolutionary struggle." During and after 1970, Oakland leadership, despite its apolitical criminal behavior, appeared to have more immunity from police raids and arrests than Panthers aligned with the underground. Having rejected revolutionary struggle, Oakland Panthers also seemed to have avoided FBI COINTELPRO violence, wiretaps, and police criminality routinely practiced by the LAPD in southern California and the NYPD in New York City.[29] Over decades, the BPP became one of the most powerful emotional, political, and visual signifiers of Davis as Panther or Panther adjacent. However, it is difficult to find sources from that era that identified her as a member of the Black Panther Party before, during, or immediately after her incarceration and trial. It is much easier to trace the membership/leadership of other Black women associated with the BPP; consider for example, Kathleen Cleaver, who left Barnard College in NYC to organize with SNCC in Atlanta, GA, and met Eldridge Cleaver at an organizing event. She returned with him to Oakland, CA, and joined the Central Committee of the BPP. Davis writes in the foreword to *Comrade Sisters* that she was a rank-and-file member of the California-based BPP; in her 2021 and 1988 editions of *Angela Davis: An Autobiography*, Davis writes that she was asked to work on the political education committee but soon left. The narratives around the BPP are vague. Davis did work with the BPP for several days or weeks. Specifics are not given. "Rank-and-file" refers to the mostly anonymous community-based activists who rise early to cook and serve breakfast to impoverished children and families and later wash dishes and mop floors. Rank-and-file stood on street corners for hours to sell the influential and financially stable *Black Panther Party Newspaper*, hawking to students and community members to hand over 25 cents for a paper.[30] From 1968 to 1971, *The Black Panther Party Newspaper* was the most widely read US Black newspaper; its weekly circulation was 100,000–300,000. A major educational tool for party members as students of revolutionary struggle, the party mandated that each member study the newspaper before they could sell it.[31]

Scandal! NSA Is CIA

Whether or not Angela Davis remembered Gloria Steinem from Helsinki, Davis learned upon her 1967 return to the United States that the leftist *Ramparts Magazine*—read on UC campuses—had an investigative scoop on CIA infiltration of student movements. The exposé by Sol Stern turned a small leftist magazine into a buzzword for revelations about the CIA's use of students as Cold War pawns through the National Student Association (NSA). The scrappy start-up *Ramparts* delivered its journalistic bombshell in February 1967 before Davis's summer return.[32] Its exposé on the NSA and Independent Research Service (IRS) stemmed from leaked documents provided by former NSA director-turned-whistleblower, Michael Wood.[33] *Ramparts* rattled the progressive and mainstream press. When the *New York Times* and the *Washington Post* picked up the story then it became "real" news. The mainstream press described Wood as an idealist unknowingly recruited by the NSA/CIA, after his impressive work for a Watts anti-poverty youth program following the 1965 riots. Wood's civil rights work as a white middle-class student with considerable skills drew the attention of CIA handlers. Once hired, he began to note irregularities in mission and funding. After asking questions that remained unanswered, he was informed by a senior administrator that the organization was a front for the CIA. Months before his termination, Wood began collecting NSA documents and then turned them over to *Ramparts*. When the major press released the story, the State Department acknowledged that the CIA had subsidized NSA international activities to undermine communist students and, for years, used the NSA as a Cold War "front." The *Washington Post* and *New York Times* then ran follow-up stories, with sympathetic interviews with an unapologetic Gloria Steinem who had worked for the CIA since the 1950s, as a key handler for student trips to international youth festivals.[34] In the furor that followed these revelations, liberal and conservative students debated the implications of CIA officials illegally purchasing student leadership in a contest against the Soviets.[35]

Acknowledging that since the 1950s, the CIA had funded NSA students and administrators,[36] NSA President Eugene Grove argued that US students were treated as (potential) assets but *not agents*. The *Times* offered a blunt interpretation: "[T]he CIA has infiltrated and subverted the world of American student leaders over the past fifteen years. It has used students to spy ... to pressure international student organizations into taking Cold War positions, and has interfered in the internal workings of the NSA."[37] These funds helped to attack Black radicals and communists such as Paul Robeson.[38] Despite global evidence of US-sponsored Cold War coups, human rights abuses, and assassinations to stop anti-colonial liberation movements (which the major press downplayed), Steinem steadfastly and stoically maintained that the CIA "was completely different from its image; it was liberal, nonviolent, and honorable."[39] She expressed no regrets for associating with an agency known for international war crimes. Instructing the agency to stop secretly funding private student groups, President Johnson closed the NSA. Several years later, Gloria Steinem became the leading public face of the feminist movement, securing sufficient corporate capital to launch *Ms. Magazine* and the Ms. Foundation.

Ramparts published its investigative report in the same year that the CIA assisted in the capture and murder of Ernesto "Che" Guevara in Bolivia. The Argentinian's nickname comprises the title of the "Che-Lumumba Club" that Davis joined in 1968 when she became a member of the CPUSA. The second half of the Club name comes from the CIA-assisted assassination of Patrice Lumumba, who led and won a freedom movement in the Congo.

Police intelligence created the NSA in order to woo "the best and brightest" undergrad and grad students into becoming future anti-communist leaders who thought of themselves as not racist but fair and open-minded.[40] Despite the embarrassing 1967 NSA closure, the International Commission Jurists, Radio Free Europe, United Auto Workers, and National Education Association were also funded by the CIA; the agency's reach into civil society was impressive.[41] It was also lethal. Karen M. Paget's 2015 *Patriotic Betrayal* suggests that information that the CIA gathered about student political opponents to repressive regimes may have been delivered to state officials leading to the subsequent arrests, imprisonment, and executions of student rebels and opponents. Paget cites nations where governments eliminated students: Iraq,[42] Iran,[43] South Africa. (US democratic and republican administrations supported the apartheid regime by funding white mercenaries to kill African liberation forces.)

As future president, and Davis nemesis, Ronald Reagan noted students were most likely to protest for civil and human rights; thus they became one of the most problematic sectors for state control. Within the sphere of US influence and foreign policy, the government of Mexico used snipers to kill students in 1968 when university and prep school students took over a plaza chanting that they wanted a freedom revolution not the Olympics.[44] The National Student Association appeared designed to render young radicals and progressive students to vulnerable authoritarian and militarized regimes. White middle-class students and activist leaders were massacred in the United States at Kent State University and Jackson State University in 1970. Those listening to Crosby, Stills, and Nash's *Four Dead in Ohio*, or later to the Isley Brothers' rendition of *Ohio*[45] linked to the artistry of Jimmie Hendrix's *Machine Gun*, were surviving or losing friends to the US war in Vietnam and the domestic warfare in the United States against anti-war and anti-racist protestors. Black Panthers were targeted for torture, imprisonment, and assassination in a variety of zones. Panther recruits and Black radical organizers included males evading the draft or returnees from US warfare into Vietnam. While some Panthers engaged in breakfast, literacy and medical programs (also attacked by the FBI and police), others sought university deferments or, after their tours of duty, used their GI Bills to enroll in college and university. Others sparked rebellions as diverse soldiers, including Black radicals, engaged in pacifist mutiny, or alternatively rebellion in the ranks through "fragging."[46] The "Third World" students in the "Global South" mirrored, in some ways, the vulnerability of the "colored" students of the internal colonies of Western nations; the norm was that nonconformist radical youths were expendable.

As did other Black elites who could be distinguished from revolutionary rabble, Angela Davis had value and a specific appeal to white liberals aligned with the state's counterrevolutionary cadres. (There appears to be no record of Gloria Steinem raising hundreds of thousands of dollars for defense funds in the 1970s for any other Black political prisoner.) At the time of the exposé, the *New Yorker* asserted that the NSA supported civil rights because the second NSA president was a Black Catholic, James (Ted) Harris (1948–9); its fourth president was the Jewish civil rights and anti-war activist, Allard Lowenstein (1950–1). NSA supported SNCC, the Selma, Alabama march, and the 1965 Voting Rights Act. Within and beyond the CIA, the NSA was seen as "socially progressive, anti-colonialist, and sometimes even socialist."[47]

Philosophy Professor and Communist Target

California, like Alabama, was not safe for Black people, particularly those outspoken about their legal rights. The Davis sisters had integrated a white zone of formal education. They were not domestic laborers or factory workers; they were leisured intellectuals in white, affluent enclaves. That class distinction was not sufficient to spare them from harassment and violence. San Diego was more violently hostile than New York City, Waltham, MA, France, or Frankfurt—Davis's homes since she turned fifteen. (Given NYPD brutality against the Panther party, and its alleged collusion with the assassination of Malcolm X in Harlem, NYC is the exception.) California was the headquarters of the revolutionary Black Panther Party for Self-Defense (BPPSD), founded one year after Watts, CA, burned in a 1965 Black rebellion.

Graduate students with stipends and financial support from parents prioritized their academic studies. An untested political novice, Angela Davis sought to enter a fray between political radicals on one side and paramilitary police forces and white supremacists on the other side. She could have taken the "fifth" when the chancellor asked if she were a member of the CPUSA. She could have worked with the NAACP, not the BPP. But California was where people went to reinvent themselves. The impetus now for Black struggle was revolution, not integration. Within two years, the name "Angela Davis" would appear in newspaper headlines declaring and denouncing the arrival of a sophisticated intellectual, yet novice activist, who publicly identified as a communist and maintained alliances with Black militants. Although Davis did not live in underresourced Black neighborhoods, occupied by police as "ghettoes," she was still vulnerable to the violence and dishonor arrayed against Black Panthers and Blacks in general.

UCLA's Diversity Hire

At the University of California Los Angeles (UCLA), Leon Letwin was chair of the Equal Opportunity Commission. Professor Letwin was an integrationist who worked to bring African Americans and other minorities into UCLA School of Law. In the fall of 1969, UCLA enrolled forty-seven special admissions students, three times the number recruited in 1967. Letwin and the Equal Opportunity Commission committee members sent a memo to the vice chancellor, indicating that they were seeking critical thinkers who would be attractive to minority students. Hence, recruitment of faculty was tied to diversifying and retaining underrepresented students. Between 1968 and 1969, UCLA hired sixteen Black, three Chicano, and thirty-eight Asian professors. Despite "growing Jewish resistance" to affirmative action, Letwin continued to push for change.[1] One of his star future hires would be Angela Davis. For some Black or Latinx students, the immense pressure of outperforming white peers as the "model minority" was compounded by student militancy or class status. Angela Davis, her siblings, and cohorts from Birmingham had college-educated parents, so they were not "first-generation" students. They were members of the Black elite; that their parents leaned toward social reforms and the CPUSA made them even more intriguing than apolitical or nonpolitical Black students. Still, their conduct on campus, just like their appearance, would have to be near flawless, particularly given their commitments to social justice.

In March 1969, Angela Davis had received offers from Yale and Swarthmore. The smaller and more elitist university and college in the northeast were not as compelling as the University of California. The state and the university were at the epicenter of activism for political change. Davis chose to stay in California in order to remain connected to political struggles. When Princeton University forwarded her application on to the UCLA philosophy department, UCLA offered Angela Davis a lectureship to teach in its philosophy department the same month. When she accepted, Angela Davis became the first Black woman to teach in the philosophy department at the University of California. Davis was accustomed to stress and performing under a spotlight or microscope. She had faced immense pressures to prove herself and her intellectual worth in her elite white high school, at Brandeis University, the Sorbonne, the Frankfurt Institute, and UCSD. UCLA would be added to the growing list of trials and triumphs. By the time she stepped on campus to teach in the philosophy department as a young Black female professor integrating UCLA, Professor Davis had already mastered the skills of academic excellence.

Returning to the UCLA campus from her summer 1969 trip to Cuba, the new professor diligently prepared for her philosophy classes only to find herself outed as a communist by an FBI undergraduate informant. Although not targeted for elimination or neutralization as were the Black Panthers and communist labor militants, the FBI took note of Davis's hire and worked to undermine her. UCLA student William Divale had been recently outed as a paid FBI informant who conducted surveillance on his professors and fellow students, some of them serious activists against the war in Vietnam and racist repression. Divale wrote an opinion editorial in the student paper *The Daily Bruin*. Possibly to deflect negative attention from himself, he alerted UC that a communist professor had been hired. Rather than deny her CPUSA membership, Angela Davis decided to go public to test the legality of McCarthyism (seasoned CPUSA advisors such as Dorothy Healey recommended that she take the fifth and refuse to answer any queries about her political party affiliations). The response was virulent and violent. Davis recalled that "racists and anti-Communists throughout the state responded with furor. Threatening calls and letters poured into the Philosophy Department and into the offices of the Communist Party." That opposition went beyond verbal harassment: a "man broke into the Philosophy Department offices and physically attacked [Department Chair] Don

Kalish." The university had to install a "special telephone" to screen calls before they were forwarded to Davis. With her life in danger, campus police were on constant alert. Professor Davis recalled: "Several times they had to check out my car because of bomb threats I had received."[2]

After the FBI's campus informant Divale wrote the July 1969 *Bruin* op ed. on the "mystery communist," the FBI began targeting Davis, Letwin, and other UCLA professors. Letwin was a former CPUSA member who had resigned from the party before joining the UCLA faculty. Harold Horowitz, Ken Karst, Leon Letwin, Henry McGee, and Arthur Rosett drafted academic resolutions to support Angela Davis. Letwin was likely instrumental in hiring Henry McGee, whose father had been president of the Chicago chapter of the NAACP; McGee became the first Black UCLA law professor.[3] Several weeks later, the *Daily Bruin* published an exposé about a recent UCLA graduate, William Divale, a paid FBI informant, who had testified before the government's Subversive Activities Control Board (SACB). Divale had spent his four years at UCLA writing extensive surveillance reports against alleged campus communists. Shunned by students, in his letter of defense he stated that he was not anti-communism per se; rather, he opposed CPUSA manipulations and intrigues. Seizing an opportunity to deflect attention from himself, Divale offered an example: the UCLA Philosophy Department had hired an unnamed communist as faculty.

When asked by the UC Board of Regents if her party affiliation was communist, Davis readily replied: "Yes, I am a Communist. And I will not take the Fifth Amendment against self-incrimination because my political beliefs do not incriminate me; they incriminate the Nixons, Agnews and Reagans."[4] Angela Davis's eloquent and courageous response—vetted by CPUSA attorneys—to the Regents' McCarthy-like letter was a salvo against an academic inquisition:

> [My] answer is that I am now a member of the Communist Party. While I think this membership requires no justification here, I want you to know that as a Black woman I feel an urgent need to find radical solutions to the problems of racial and national minorities in white capitalist United States. ... It goes without saying, of course, that the advocacy of the Communist Party during my period of membership in it has, to my knowledge, fallen well within the guarantees of the First Amendment. Nor does my membership in the Communist Party involve me in any commitment to principle or position governing either my scholarship or my responsibilities as a teacher.[5]

By October 6, 200 students had enrolled in her philosophy course. After the Regents' attack on Professor Davis, 2,000 showed up for her class in solidarity. The lecture audience was ten times the enrollment. The university relocated "Recurring Philosophical Themes in Black Literature" to Royce Hall auditorium. Later, a student referendum showed that 81 percent of the students voted for Professor Davis to keep her position (more positive votes than in the earlier referendum, which reported that 67 percent of the students supported the withdrawal of US troops from Vietnam). "Recurring Philosophical Themes in Black Literature" was a unique UC class offering in 1969. Professor Davis's lectures centered political philosophy and Black existence:

Are human beings free or are they not? Ought they be free or ought they not be free? The history of Afro-American literature furnishes an illuminating account of the nature of freedom, its extent and limits. Moreover, we should discover in Black literature an important perspective that is missing in so many of the discourses on the theme of freedom in the history of bourgeois philosophy. Afro-American literature incorporates the consciousness of a people who have been continually denied entrance into the real world of freedom, a people whose struggles and aspirations have exposed the inadequacies not only of the practice of freedom, but also its very theoretical formulation.[6]

Despite the distractions of job discrimination, Professor Davis gave impeccable and brilliant lectures for hundreds of students that grew into several thousand as supporters sought her out in their opposition to Regental authoritarianism. Her lecture, later published as "Unfinished Lecture on Liberation—II," was pathbreaking:

One of the striking paradoxes of the bourgeois ideological tradition resides in an enduring philosophical emphasis on the idea of freedom alongside an equally pervasive failure to acknowledge the denial of freedom to entire categories of real, social human beings. In ancient Greece, whose legacy of democracy inspired some of the great bourgeois thinkers, citizenship in the *polis*, the real exercise of freedom, was not accessible to the majority of people. Women were not allowed to be citizens and slavery was an uncontested institution. While the lofty notions affirming human liberty were being formulated by those who penned the United States Constitution, Afro-Americans lived and labored in chains. Not even the term "slavery" was allowed to mar the sublime concepts articulated in the Constitution, which euphemistically refers to "persons held to service or labor" as those exceptional human beings who did not merit the right and guarantees otherwise extended to all.[7]

Angela Davis's philosophical analyses aligned with her employment predicament: without naming race or Blackness, the three-fifths clause of the US Constitution chained "other people" to abuse, violence, and exploitation to expand its national project; without naming Davis's race or gender, Reagan's Regents were at war not only with her communist ideology but also with her Blackness and female gender. Confident that she had grounds for a successful lawsuit based on employment law and First Amendment and civil rights, Davis continued to teach her classes. However, Governor Ronald Reagan—anti-communist, white conservative/reactionary—by waging war against a young, Black female communist academic, helped to create and cement her iconic imagery and legacy of a radical for justice.

CPUSA California leader Dorothy Ray Healey had advised Davis to take the Fifth Amendment, as Healey had in the past at her job sites to avoid being fired and impoverished. A white radical feminist, Healey grew up in poverty. Her working-class militancy focused on union strikes for Black and brown laborers in factories and fields. Healey likely thought an employment battle against the governor on behalf of the professoriate was not critical at the time. Still, Angela Davis wanted to be the test case. Healy brought her to a meeting with CPUSA attorneys to craft a legal strategy. Using Davis as a test case elevated the profile and the relevance of the CPUSA, but that garnered attention would be a fraction of the international spotlight that would be focused on Davis after the Marin County raid. (Healey had attempted to reform the CPUSA in 1968 following Nikita Khrushchev's denunciation of Stalin and the Soviet invasion of the Czech Republic; she left the CPUSA after Davis was acquitted in 1972 and, with Michael Harrington, cofounded the Democratic Socialists of America [DSA]).

The primary task of Davis as doctoral student was to complete her studies, write and defend her dissertation, and prepare for a career as a university professor. Although she labored at those tasks, and defended herself from conservatives and reactionaries, including then California Governor (and future US president) Ronald Reagan, Davis was constantly pulled toward political engagement. In addition, Davis had not completed her dissertation and was serving in the capacity of what today would be "predoc" or visiting instructor. (She would complete her dissertation at the Humboldt University; based on researchers who visited the university, as noted earlier, the dissertation is not available for the public.)

UC Regents clamored for Davis's intellectual head on a platter as Regan promised a purge of UC dissidents and communists. When the chancellor eventually supported her right to teach, Mrs. Millicent Veronica Hearst, the grandmother of SLA captive and guerrilla Patty Hearst, and the mother of media tycoon William Randolph Hearst,[8] worked with Governor Reagan to have the chancellor removed. Angela and her legal team still assumed that she would teach that fall in philosophy at UCLA. She believed that she would prevail on the merits of an employment discrimination case charging the Regents with discrimination based on race, gender, and ideology. An alliance for Davis had grown among faculty hostile to the evisceration of their First Amendment rights and autonomous governance to hire and tenure their colleagues. They began to develop strategies to defeat Regental autocracy.

In *post45*, Casey Shoop provides an in-depth analysis of Professor Davis's firing by the UC Regents and the UCLA faculty's strategic war plan to battle the Regents' usurpation of faculty powers and violation of First Amendment rights. On October 3, 1969, Los Angeles County Superior Court ruled that the Regents violated Angela's First and Fourteenth Amendment rights. Regents bypassed faculty and administrative governance to fire her by executive decision. UCLA Chancellor Young formed a "secret" Ad Hoc Committee on February 17, in which seven faculty were tasked to investigate allegations against her. Chancellor Young's letter to the committee focused on three allegations: Angela Davis indoctrinated students in the classroom, engaged in political activism off-campus that impeded her obligations as faculty, and made public statements that demonstrated opposition to academic freedom. The Ad Hoc Committee vindicated Angela on the first two charges. The third "highly subjective charge" was used to terminate her employment. The Ad Hoc Committee determined that on occasion her public speeches "offended 'good taste'"; it also stated that

a concept of academic freedom that rejects traditional academic values presents no threat unless it becomes prevailing doctrine; and it is our unanimous conviction that the best way to prevent it from becoming prevailing doctrine is to allow its free and lawful expression in competition with the philosophy embodied in the principles and resolutions adopted by the AAUP and the Academic Senate.[9]

Davis's October 24, 1969, Berkeley speech argued that academic freedom is "kind of an empty concept"; the context of her remarks demonstrated the rightist push by the majority of the Regents to quell speech. The speech addresses academic freedom and educators fired for their radical ideas. Davis asserts that the freedom to teach and learn "is totally impotent if it is not accompanied by the freedom to act in a way that is consonant with the principle." She notes the irony that recent violations of academic freedom "are the result of and are reinforced by the continued violation of real, concrete freedoms in the society." Davis then lists these aggressions against professors:

> There's Marvin X at Fresno State, who is being denied the right to teach because he sees the path of Black liberation as being the construction of a Black nation. There's Dangerfield in Los Angeles, who is being denied the right to teach in a Black high school, Manual Arts, because he sympathized with the demands of the students and of the community to make that education relevant to the community, relevant to the Black liberation struggle. There's Saul Castro, who has attempted to do the same thing for the Chicano community. He is being denied the right to teach.[10]

Denouncing the Regents as "unscrupulous demagogues" who hoarded university knowledge to deploy "in the service of the prevailing oppression," she castigates the Regents as "committed to the immoral usurpation of power which rightly belongs to those who have the knowledge and the experience to pass rational ... judgments about the way in which education ought to be carried out."[11] Essentially, Davis battled the Regents for unilaterally seizing the powers and authority of current and former faculty and university administrators. A professoriate army agreed with her. On February 5, 1970, she spoke in Santa Barbara, pivoting to attack white nationalist professors in the university, singling out UC Berkeley psychologist Arthur Jensen, who posited that Blacks held inferior IQs. Davis noted the differential enforcement of academic freedom, defining it as a hypocritical political weapon that "while stripping political dissidents of their right to free speech, simultaneously protect[s] the research into the 'genetic inferiority of Black men.'"[12] The Regents rejected the Ad Hoc Committee's findings that Davis in fact was correct: if Jensen's racist hierarchies were protected speech, her anti-racist and anti-state violence analyses should be protected as well. They issued their statement:

> The Regents hereby relieve the President of the University, the Chancellor of the Los Angeles campus and all other administrative officers of any further *authority* or responsibility in connection with the reappointment or non-re-appointment of Acting Assistant Professor Angela Davis, and direct that the Board of Regents, acting as a Committee of the Whole, review the record relating to this matter and recommend appropriate action to the Board at its next regular meeting.[13]

All parties involved might not have realized the powers of the Regents. Interviewing UCLA historian Gary Nash, Casey Shoop analyzes Angela Davis's case and how faculty at UCLA supported her. The UCLA Academic Senate issued a resolution to condemn the Regents and its 1950 anti-communist policies. Adamant that Davis's original two-year teaching contract be retained, the UCLA Senate began a strategic chess game:

> 1,673 faculty members had already petitioned the Regents, remonstrating against "that revolution, the unprecedented action of the board of Regents in summarily suspending the power of administration offices and intruding upon the process of evaluation of academic qualifications by peers, which is essential to a great university," and then had called upon the regents "to withdraw from a course fraught with peril for the future of the university."[14]

Shoop observes that the most striking feature of the academic battle was "the large-scale mobilization by student protestors" and the Academic Senate creating the Angela Y. Davis. Fund Committee to solicit funds from faculty and staff for her teaching salary. Wages the Regents denied for fall 1970 could be privately raised. UCLA Professor Nash led the committee: "We asked for three quarterly installments at the following rates: assistant professors ten dollars, associate professors twelve, and full professors fifteen [...] Between July 6 and July 30, when I made out the first check, which was for support of her July salary, 287 contributors had sent checks for a total of $4,505." Angela Davis received one check before the August 7, 1970, Marin County Courthouse tragedies. For Shoop, those tragedies do not "eclipse this heroic act of faculty collectivization in support of their most precarious member." The Faculty Senate defied the Regents. The Senate sought a confrontation that they were confident they could win. With their own resources, the faculty censored the Regents and the rightist governor who intruded into their academic terrain. Faculty anticipated the Regent's future moves. Professor Davis "would have shown up on campus. Her preferred course, supported by the philosophy department, would have been open to students ... students would have swarmed the course." If the registrar followed the dictates of the Regents and refused to assign a classroom, progressive faculty planned for the course to be taught in the quadrangle bordered by the philosophy department building and the architecture school. According to Nash, funding and outdoor accommodations "would in effect have thrown the ball back into the Regents' court. What would they do to silence her? What would they do to punish students who took the course? What would they do to hundreds and hundreds of faculty members who were supporting her salary while she taught?"[15] Two thousand students showed up for her lecture on Black freedom. Some might have been merely curious about this novel Black woman philosopher, but others, many others, likely appeared in solidarity. The students are the consumers and the products of the university. Their middle-class or affluent parents were taxpayers. Whatever their political affiliations, as important as those might be, their right as elite whites is that they had the freedom of choice to be taught by diverse instructors and professors. That was the education that was being purchased: contemporary, culturally cosmopolitan, informed.

Materialist Philosopher: Freedom for the Soledad Brothers

Angela Davis had spoken at public rallies, denouncing police and National Guard violence against protesters. Davis consistently and vigorously denounced the imprisonment and persecution of the Soledad Brothers; she did so at times using Panther vernacular. The iconic photo of Davis carrying a placard to "Free the Soledad Brothers" while marching with Jonathan Jackson is striking. The Soledad Brothers Defense Committee (SBDC) was initiated by George Jackson and his attorney Fay Stender (who had also represented Huey Newton, as well as other incarcerated Blacks) to defend San Quentin prisoners George Jackson, Fleeta Drumgo, and John Clutchette. All three Black men were charged with killing a prison guard in retaliation for white guards murdering Black prisoners (all defendants were exonerated, Jackson posthumously). For philosopher and educator Davis, the writings of Frederick Douglass about freedom (in or out of captivity) materialized in the theoretical writings of George Jackson, who had politicized Davis into abolitionism. Her solidarity activism to free and save the lives of the Soledad Brothers became a materialist response to academic theories on freedom and enslavement and the agency of Black rebel captives.

The day the UC Regents announced its decision on Davis's UCLA renewable teaching contract, Angela Davis was at an SBDC rally. According to Davis, not "long after the demonstration had come alive," reporters informed her that the Regents would not renew her contract.[16] Her attorneys had expected that verdict and planned to counter it. Angela Davis, though, used her own personal employment case to draw attention to life-threatening repression of incarcerated Black men. She deployed a political strategy of skillfully weaving into news coverage the First Amendment violations at an elite white university and the racist repression of poor and working-class Black prisoners. Activists and protesters held "a press conference on the sidewalk outside the State Building" to counter the apparent media "policy of minimal or no coverage of the Soledad Brothers movement." When the press posed questions, Davis "made a point of phrasing" her responses with each sentence referencing her UC firing *and* "the repression of the Soledad Brothers and other political prisoners."[17]

Davis had grounds for a successful lawsuit based on employment law and First Amendment rights.[18] The Supreme Court had ruled in the 1967 *United States v. Robel* that the anti-communist McCarran Internal Security Act violated the right to free association or First Amendment rights. Davis fulfilled her original contract, teaching her classes for the academic year. Her contract was not renewed because of her alliance with militant activists, specifically the imprisoned Soledad Brothers and Black Panthers. Davis's alliance with Black liberation organizations such as the Panthers became more noteworthy than her membership in the CPUSA. Numerous white academics and intellectuals had joined the CPUSA as students or faculty, and faced discrimination and employment insecurity due to McCarthyism and anti-communism. However, they did not have to contend with the violence that was arrayed against the Black Panthers, outside and inside prisons. The coordination of that violence, and impunity and immunity with which police forces deployed it, increasingly appeared as a war orchestrated by the US government. The FBI was implicated in the murders of two

Panthers on the UCLA campus, and the deaths and incarceration, through frame-ups, of dozens more. Because Davis was an advocate for, but not a member of, the Black Panther Party, there was distance between her human rights advocacy and their political identity. Angela Davis's victimization through employment harassment and freedom of speech rights was relatable to the general public. Allegiance to revolutionary struggle was not palatable to liberals or most progressives. Davis, through her CPUSA membership, was not aligned with revolutionary movements given the CPUSA/CPSU "peaceful coexistence" mandate. The definition of "revolutionary" in an era of mass resistance—material resistance—against racism, capitalism and imperialism was more abstract for academics, but less abstract and more concretized for those who participated in daily chores of serving and protecting the people.

Still, Angela Davis's popularity among progressives and radicals grew because she courageously refused to lie or hide her Communist affiliations, or turn her back on the Panthers. While the academic employment trial was litigated and fought in the press, Americans were consuming it as pretty tame fare compared with the other headlines in the news that made mainstream America clamor for "law and order." In August 1969, the Manson family's gruesome murders—conducted as they were attempting to start an anti-Black race war—included targeted Hollywood actress Sharon Tate (the eight-month pregnant wife of filmmaker Roman Polanski) and her friend, coffee heiress Abigail Folger. (In 1971, Saundra Pratt, the eight-month pregnant wife of Panther Elmer "Geronimo" Pratt—who was framed by the LAPD and FBI and on trial for the murder of Carol Olsen—was also murdered, but garnered less attention.) In October, National Guardsmen clashed in Chicago with anti-war protestors in the Weathermen's "Days of Rage" as hundreds of thousands took part in anti-war demonstrations across the United States.[19] On November 3, President Nixon's request that the "silent majority" support the war in Vietnam was diminished by Seymour Hersh's November 1969 exposé on the March 1968 My Lai massacre.

Protest movements continued to grow throughout 1969. Warren Burger was sworn in as Chief Justice of the Supreme Court to mark a liberal era; yet, repressed populations continued to seek militant expressions of opposition to police forces and poverty. Radicals began to gain more visibility. The Weather Underground took over the Students for a Democratic Society (SDS) national meeting in Chicago. One of the more fascinating moments, and movements, was the emergence of the radical LGBTQ formations seeking queer liberation. Protesting students raged against the Vietnam War and, from their trainings in elementary school, worried about a nuclear holocaust in a war with the Soviet Union. Free speech and anti-war movements raged on throughout 1969. UC Berkeley became a battle ground—not just around free speech and the war in Vietnam, but also around the use of land and environmental protections and students' rights.

The UC Regents had developed the 1956 Berkeley Long Range Development Plan, which authorized the purchase of land for dormitories and parking spaces. The land was acquired in 1968, but UC lacked sufficient funding for development until the following year. In spring 1969, the alternative weekly *Berkeley Barb* publicized a collective park planting and creation over the upcoming weekend. Scores of students and community members came to the site to clean it of debris and plant flowers and gardens. When told to vacate, most left. In defiance, some stayed, creating a tent city (politicized in ways that the Occupy Movement would emulate forty years later). The university demanded they leave. The occupiers resisted. On May 15, 1969, at four-thirty in the morning, Governor Regan sent three hundred California Highway Patrol and police to evict everyone from the two-plus acres and to enclose it with a cyclone fence.

From UC Berkeley, thousands had gathered—first, for speeches—at Sproul on the UC Campus, and then marched to the park where they fought the police. They rioted; the smartest and best of the UC students were among those who overturned cars, set fires, and threw bottles, rocks, and bricks. Deputies from the Alameda County Sheriff's office were called in. Some 128 people were hospitalized, and one student, James Rector, was killed by buckshot. In the police version, UC student James Rector was an assailant, throwing rebar off a rooftop at police when he was shot through the heart. In the activist version, Rector was standing on the roof watching the melee trampling the gardens he had helped to plant. He became a martyr of a people's movement. If, in fact, he had made speeches about the police as unlawful killers and referred to law enforcement as "pigs," then he was on Reagan's radar; the communist affiliation might have been the lesser of the offenses Reagan wanted to prosecute.

Reagan's National Guard remained in Berkeley for seventeen days, camping in People's Park. Reagan had publicly denounced the Berkeley administration and faculty as "weak" for permitting student demonstrations. The university's Vice Chancellor offered to reserve one-fourth of the lot for the People's Park, and agreed to inform People's Park creators prior to construction of the parking lot. Reagan considered that a capitulation. Reagan described UC campuses as "a haven for communist sympathizers, protesters and sex deviants." At a press conference, an animated faculty member confronted the governor about his use of violence: "You can't run a university by bayonet." Reagan disagreed, admonishing faculty and administrators: "All of it [violence] began when some of you who know better, and should have known better, let young people decide what laws they were going to obey." The following year, in an April 7, 1970, interview, the governor reportedly stated of UC student protesters: "If it takes a bloodbath, let's get it over with. No more appeasement." The governor's public exhortation for a "bloodbath" was reminiscent of Birmingham police commissioner Bull Connor's calls for bombings. California police and guard understood the message. With little fear of reprimands from the state or federal government, militarized, the guard increasingly conducted violent crackdowns.

The violent battle over the People's Park and the killing of an unarmed student by the state led Davis to publicly proclaim that she would rather be a "Sister" than a "Professor." She chose the mass in protest over the academy's authoritarianism, a 180-degree departure from what Marcuse characterized as an apolitical bookish student at Brandeis. Reagan and the Regents seemed determined to make sure that she lived up to her word. The People's Park confrontation and tragedy would embroil Davis in a free speech struggle in which her off-campus free speech condemning police violence would be used by UC Regents to justify nonrenewal of her teaching contract.

Presidents Nixon and Nguyen Van Thieu met for peace talks concerning Vietnam; negotiations were led by Secretary of State Henry Kissinger. Repression was ripe on campuses poised on the "cutting edge of change." In Los Angeles, Angela Davis's life was also in the crosshairs. White police officers and Black Panthers carried weapons and monitored her classes and walked her to her car. The police worked during her normal campus teaching and office hours and then left. Black militants stayed and saw her safely home, just as white male students brought guns on campus to protect Marcuse against right-wing organizations like the San Diego Minute Men.

By March 1970, California National Guard was spraying burning chemical powder on students protesting the Vietnam War. That spring term, political protests and chaos ensued and shaped the discussions of militant students and activists. On March 6, 1970, the Weather Underground blew up three of its members (two escaped) in one of their parents' West Village Manhattan brownstone. The bomb was meant for a Ft. Dix military dance in New Jersey as a protest against the Vietnam War. On March 17, newspapers covered the charges against fourteen officers for suppressing information to the public and their commanders about the My Lai Massacre. On April 29, the United States invaded Cambodia; anti-war protests increased. Several days later, 12,000 demonstrated in New Haven, CT, to free Black Panthers Bobby Seale and Ericka Huggins and seven of their compatriots—on trial for the torture and murder of a young Black drifter who had joined the Panthers and was mistaken for a police agent. The wars at home and the wars abroad were intermingled, and violence was escalating. It was a circular firing range: the more Vietnamese and Cambodians were massacred, the more students rebelled; and the more students rebelled, the more National Guardsmen were bringing the militarist war to campus.

Killing the Revolution

Herbert Marcuse asserted that the revolution died on May 4, 1970, when the National Guard shot and killed four white, middle-class students at Kent State during student protests against the war in Vietnam.[20] Weeks later, Black students at Jackson State University in Jackson, Mississippi, died when white police shot up the women's dormitories and campus because the Black students protested the National Guard having murdered white youth at Kent State. In Jackson, a high school student and Jackson State sophomore were killed by "stray" bullets. Months later, the FBI and Jackson Police Department, with a Thompson tank, stormed the Republic of New Afrika house. Located down the street from the university, RNA members – including followers of Malcolm X and some former Black Panthers – had publicly declared their second amendment rights and warned the white police force to stop violating and killing Black civilians. In the pre-dawn raid, the police shot tear gas into the house and gunfire was exchanged, with wounds inflicted on both sides; one police officer died of his wounds. Nine RNA members were convicted of murder and imprisoned.

It is not certain that Marcuse's pronouncement was verifiable. The "revolution" could have died on April 4, 1968, with the assassination of Martin Luther King, Jr., or

April 6, 1968, when the Oakland police killed seventeen-year-old Bobby Hutton. Then there was December 4, 1969, when the Chicago Police Department and FBI executed the assassinations of Fred Hampton and Mark Clark. The National Guard killings occurred on May 4, 1970, at Kent State. On August 7, 1970, Jonathan Jackson executed the risky raid at the Marin County Courthouse where guards killed that seventeen-year-old rebel, two Black incarcerated men, and one white judge, while injuring others. On August 21, 1971, prison guards shot and killed George Jackson. On September 13, 1971, the National Guard killed thirty-nine people to quell the imprisoned seeking human rights in the quashing of the Attica prison rebellion.

Marcuse likely called the end of the proto-revolutionary era when he saw the National Guard indiscriminately shoot *white* students who rebelled against their class, making the phrase "class suicide" less theoretical and more material. Yet the national shock waves reverberating across the nation mourned the loss of white children, both the activists and non-activists who were "collateral damage" in the civil rights and human rights struggles.

At Kent State in Ohio, the shooting of thirteen students led to four fatalities, nine wounded; students were demonstrating against the Nixon administration's incursion into Cambodia during the US war against Vietnam. Popular music memorialized the killing sprees, which some defined as "fascism."[21] Some of the shot and wounded or killed were not protesting, but walking across campus, as was the case in Jackson State. Activists who survived the bullets were charged with murders committed by the guard and commanded by the governor. Four days after Kent State, 1,000 mostly white students marching in lower Manhattan to protest the killings of students were beaten by white construction workers on Wall Street. Class war and proto-fascism met student rebellions against imperial wars, poverty, and racism. On May 9, 100,000 students marched on Washington to end the Vietnam War. On May 15, white police shot Black student protesters who had retreated into a women's dorm at Mississippi's Jackson State University. Claiming that they saw a sniper (later investigations provided no evidence of one present), forty officers shot out the windows of the building, killing two Black students and injuring twelve to twenty others.[22]

National Guard violence on white campuses—mandating that students retreat from their alliances with Third World peoples—unfolded parallel to police violence against historically besieged Black communities. The violence was accelerated for Panthers. Carl Hampton could join the National Committee to Combat Fascism but not the BPP because of the moratorium on membership. Recognized by the party and authorized to sell the party paper, he returned to Houston, TX, to create an adjacent party until formal membership was open. On July 27, 1970, in Houston, Texas, Houston Police Department snipers shot and killed Carl Hampton, who was organizing "People's Party II," an unauthorized branch of the Black Panther Party awaiting formal authorization from Oakland headquarters. After Chicago Panther leader Fred Hampton's 1969 police-FBI assassination, Oakland headquarters had suspended the opening of new Panther branches and member recruitment. A Houston Grand Jury exonerated the police, saying that Hampton and People's Party II members fired first. Community members testified that upon hearing that armed men were on the roof of a nearby church, the Black men walked outside the party office with weapons; rooftop police snipers fired upon them as soon as they entered the street to search for a threat. Marcuse had offered prescient theory with an imperfect timeline. Keenly affected by the deaths—state-inflicted murders—Angela Davis's rhetoric about police violence increasingly used the vernacular of the Panthers until she was fired for "unbecoming speech." After her arrest, she would continue the defiant language until, in preparation for her trial, she returned to the language of the CPUSA's peaceful coexistence and the language of Oakland Panthers—who, at the 1969 Conference to Combat Fascism, mandated (in order to not alienate liberals or government) that the words "cops" and "police officers" replace "pigs" and that cadres refer to themselves as "progressives," not "socialists" or "revolutionaries."

Part III

Political Activism

10

Not Your Mother's CPUSA:
The Che-Lumumba Club

1968 Conflicts and Antagonisms

In January 1968, celebrity Eartha Kitt denounced the Vietnam War to FLOTUS Lady Bird Johnson at a White House "ladies' luncheon"; the First Lady cried and President Johnson used his administration's policing apparatus to blacklist Eartha Kitt (who played the role of the first Black Cat Woman on the TV series *Batman*). In January 1968, the Viet Cong began the Tet Offensive against South Vietnam and the United States. On February 8 of that year, white police killed three Black students at Orangeburg, SC protests for civil rights. Four days later, Black Memphis, TN sanitation workers went on strike after two of their workers were crushed to death in the back of a garbage truck, seeking shelter from a storm after being denied access to the "Whites Only" workers' center. At least one thousand workers participated in the strike as garbage collected on the streets. On March 16, the My Lai Massacre occurred in Vietnam (the war crime would be hidden from the public until 1969).

On April 4, Martin Luther King, Jr., was assassinated in Memphis, Tennessee, while supporting the Black sanitation workers on strike. Cities burned in the wake of his murder. James Earl Ray confessed to the murder but quickly recanted. Coretta Scott King refused to accept official accounts of her husband's assassination. Davis's activist family was spared the roiling tragedies that stalked the King family.[1] Two days later, police shot and killed seventeen-year-old BPP member Bobby Hutton; unarmed and shirtless—but not stripped of his pants as Eldridge Cleaver had suggested—Lil' Bobby was surrendering after an ill-conceived shootout with Oakland police, initiated by Cleaver.

On April 4, 1968, while mimeographing leaflets in the SNCC office, Angela Davis heard of Rev. Martin Luther King, Jr.'s assassination. She immediately joined activists to mobilize against police violence against Black communities:

> [W]e realized, being in L.A., that if we did not move quickly, that the Los Angeles Police Department would use [King's murder] as an occasion for a massacre … immediately after the assassination, [police] set up machine guns on top of the roof of the downtown police station, the Parker Center.[2] The young activists decided that a "shelter inside" strategy to get people off the streets would be the

best plan to increase survival rates. [W]e decided [to] … organize a campaign to ask all of the merchants in South Central to close in deference to the memory of Dr. King and then we put up picket lines at all of the stores that didn't, including some of the large stores at the malls.[3]

On April 11, President Johnson signed the 1968 Civil Rights Act to expand upon the provisions of the June 2, 1964, Civil Rights Act. On May 17, the Catonsville Nine—which included Catholic priests, brothers Daniel and Phil Berrigan—burned draft records with napalm to protest the Vietnam War in Catonsville, Maryland, inspiring other acts of civil disobedience against the war.

Political crises and tragedies continued. On June 5, New York Senator Robert Kennedy was assassinated in Los Angeles during a speaking event for his presidential campaign. Sirhan Sirhan, the Palestinian gunman, confessed to the murder, stating that he opposed Kennedy's plans to extend the occupation of Palestine. Living in Los Angeles at the time, Davis observed of CPUSA members: "[S]ome of my comrades were directly investigated because Sirhan Sirhan's car was once outside of a meeting that was called by communists … it was a very strange connection."[4]

Despite facing death threats from white nationalists and supremacists, Davis earned her MA degree at UCSD with honors in July. In August, she was helping the BPP to organize protests to "Free Huey!"—an endeavor led by Kathleen and Eldridge Cleaver—as Huey Newton was facing a death sentence after being charged with the shooting death of police officer John Frey.

In August 1968, Chicago police rioted outside the Democratic National Convention (DNC) in response to protests against the U.S. war in Vietnam and police aggression. Esquire magazine had hired French author Jean Genet, and US authors William S. Burroughs and Allen Ginsberg, to cover the DNC. Genet would later create a fundraising tour on university and college campuses to raise defense funds for the Black Panthers (Angela Davis would serve as his interpreter). In opposition to the ticket of Richard Nixon and Spiro Agnew, Senators Hubert Humphrey and Edmund Muskie were nominated for the President/Vice President Democratic Party ticket. On August 20, 1968, the Soviet Union invaded Czechoslovakia. Following the CPUSA Stalinist line, Davis supported the invasion, going along with the CPUSA/CPSU narrative: the tanks and warfare were a just use of force and the dissidents were reactionaries not worthy of defense. Davis joined the CPUSA in 1968, the year the Soviets invaded Czechoslovakia, stabilizing their "satellite" countries to limit US influence and infiltration. Hundreds of thousands of socialists and progressives—not just capitalists and conservatives—viewed the invasion as a militarist incursion that threatened the Czech Republic and "people's movements" throughout Eastern Europe. While outraged CPUSA members left the party, Davis joined. Some argue that a sizable percentage of those members who quit were actually infiltrators—FBI agents or informants.[5] However, the oppressive nature of the occupation disillusioned many leftists who had supported the CPSU.

In September, Huey P. Newton was sentenced to prison for killing Oakland police officer John Frey. His attorney, Fay Stender, filed an appeal to reverse the conviction. That month, J. Edgar Hoover declared war on the BPP, naming it the "greatest threat to the internal security of the country."

Working with the CPUSA

In 1968, a dynamic Black family recruited Angela Davis to the CPUSA. Charlene Mitchell, who had joined the party as a teenager soon after the end of the Second World War, was a dynamic leader and strategist. Davis found that Charlene Mitchell, and her younger brothers Franklin and Deacon Alexander, wielded a practical synthesis of race and class based on their early childhood poverty and labor in racist Chicago "ghettoes." Davis also appeared to develop a strong friendship with Kendra Alexander.[6] Kendra Alexander's life was more privileged given her white Canadian mother, a nurse who divorced Kendra's Black father but maintained a middle-class lifestyle that enabled her daughter, as a college student, to maintain some class connection with Angela Davis. Kendra Alexander would also be the other Black woman who joined Angela Davis in weapons training. Dorothy Ray Healey knew what the young people in Che-Lumumba were doing, but never informed the New York-based central committee because she feared that they would expel all of the young militants and decimate the numbers of the Southern California party.[7] Outwardly projecting an adherence to the CPUSA central committee dictates emanating from the East Coast, Angela Davis, Franklin, and Kendra Alexander were developing a small arsenal and training in the California hills for self-defense. Davis began buying guns around 1968 and contributed her weapons to the general collection stored often in a house where she did not live. Che-Lumumba Club leaders likely strayed from CPUSA protocols and ideology ("peaceful coexistence" doctrine) when Davis was purchasing and storing weapons unlocked in a communal house where she did not reside.

By the 1960s, the CPUSA had been overshadowed by New Left parties and civil rights organizations. Angela Davis joined the Che-Lumumba Club when there were less than 3,000 CPUSA members nationwide. The most prominent organizations were SNCC, Students for a Democratic Society (SDS), and the BPP; later, militant organizations inspired by the Panthers would form, including I Wor Kuen, La Raza, Young Lords, White Patriots, and the American Indian Movement (AIM). Young communists and/or socialists distrusted, and so did not join, the Soviet-aligned CPUSA; SNCC and the BPP were considered to be more relevant in meeting the needs of oppressed peoples in the United States and colonized Third World countries, and Black communists or Marxists in the Panthers or prisons – not CPUSA members – were seen as the vanguard for defeating the imperial United States. In Davis, the CPUSA found a perfect opportunity to display and showcase youthful Black leadership within its half-century-old organization.

Through meetings and study groups, Davis gradually came to know the multiracial women's leadership of California's CPUSA headed by Healey and Mitchell. When Angela Davis rejected the BPP to become a member of the all-Black Che-Lumumba Club, her rising trajectory toward the upper echelons of the party did not appear to be shaped by the Women's International Democratic Federation (WIDF) based in the Soviet bloc.

Davis chose a form of Black radicalism structured and administered by an older white-dominated but multiracial leadership. The CPUSA had access to an Eastern European USSR think tank, organization and haven with funding to foster international solidarity. The more revolutionary and incendiary Panther party and its offshoots, Black Liberation Army and Republic of New Afrika, were not serious competitors. For Davis, in that era, only one party offers a "true path of liberation for Black people" and "leads toward a complete overthrow of the capitalist class in this country." She was convinced that the CPUSA deployed "Marxist-Leninist principles in the struggle for liberation." The BPP and other youth-led formations embraced Marxist-Leninist principles, yet were more focused on racially driven violence and anti-colonialism. Davis's descriptions of the Che-Lumumba Club in her autobiography reflect CPUSA strategic organizing: the club was Panther-adjacent without the liabilities to police and vigilante violence that the actual Panthers endured (or, they quit the party, or perished as party members). Black youths echoed the claims made by Fred Hampton and others devoted to the BPP—they would "die for the people." The CPUSA had no such public declarations; police were not killing them with impunity. A party that originally formed with the phrase "Self-Defense" in its title had to drop the phrase in order to increase its capacity to withstand or dodge police forces' terrors.

Angela Davis joined the Che-Lumumba Club in 1968 after weeks of meetings and after working with the Panthers on their political education committee, likely for several weeks (the three editions of *An Autobiography* do not offer detailed narratives or time/date stamps); her then friend and partner Deacon Alexander was challenged by Panthers who found his membership in the Che-Lumumba Club to be incompatible with his membership in the BPP. Creating the Che-Lumumba Club within the CPUSA to recruit Black militants likely originated with Charlene Mitchell,[8] who ran for president on the 1968 CPUSA ticket, with Mike Zagarell as vice president. CPUSA leadership gave permission for Mitchell to form a Black-brown club named after revolutionary leaders assassinated by the Joining the Che-Lumumba Club in 1968, Angela Davis entered two political families: the party family, CPUSA, and the personal family, Mitchell-Alexanders. The primary founders and members of the club were Charlene Mitchell, Franklin Alexander, Kendra Alexander, and Deacon Alexander. They were, largely, a family.

Charlene Mitchell and her younger brothers, Franklin and Deacon, as well as her sister-in-law, Kendra Alexander (who was married to Franklin), were the backbone of the club. Kendra became one of Davis's closest women friends. Mitchell sat on the central committee of the CPUSA and had joined the CPUSA at the age of sixteen. She and her siblings grew up with limited resources in a Chicago "ghetto." As teenagers, they followed their trade unionist father's militancy and joined the CPUSA. Recruiting young Black members into Che-Lumumba, as an offshoot of a largely white CPUSA headed by Gus Hall, at the height of Black Power! Black activists seeking sovereign political movements were not trying to integrate white-dominated formations.[9]

The Che-Lumumba Club was one of several formations used by the CPUSA to recruit youths into the party. In the 1960s, Gus Hall[10] had announced that the party would create "a Marxist-oriented youth organization to attract non-Communists as the first step toward their eventual recruitment into the party."[11] Bettina Aptheker helped to lead the formation of DuBois Clubs in California, one formed on the UCLA campus in 1962. Due to failing membership and government harassment, the DuBois Clubs disbanded in February 1970. (Che-Lumumba Club would exist until Angela's

Davis's acquittal.) Having worked with the Advance Club in high school, Angela Davis was familiar with the Black-led Che-Lumumba Club's structure and strategies.

During the administrations of Dwight D. Eisenhower and John F. Kennedy, the CIA was directed to plan or assist in the destabilization or assassinations of Third World socialist-communist leaders to further US corporate and military interests. In 1961, the US CIA-led invasion of the Bay of Pigs failed to depose Cuban President Fidel Castro. That year, Congolese President Patrice Lumumba was killed by a firing squad in the Congo. Lumumba, the political prisoner elected as Congolese president at age thirty-four, fought for his people controlling their resources, labor, and culture. After he was killed, the United States and Belgium (members of NATO) protected the despotic thirty-year reign of Joseph Mobutu, installed by the United States and Belgium after Mobutu had Lumumba executed. This allowed Belgium and the United States to expropriate the Congo's vast mineral wealth (particularly its uranium)[12] as Mobutu became a billionaire, looting his nation's reserves, and the people became impoverished. The leading figure in pan-African liberation movements, Lumumba had been supported by Cuba, which provided training and troops to African liberation movements, and the USSR. Six years later, in Bolivia, the CIA helped to locate the Argentinian physician who became a guerrilla liberator in Cuba and helped to depose the dictator Batista in 1959; in 1967, Ernesto "Che" Guevara was tortured and executed and his body disappeared in Bolivia. The National Security Archive[13] reports his murder and the absence of a trial:

> On October 9th, 1967, Ernesto "Che" Guevara was put to death by Bolivian soldiers, trained, equipped and guided by U.S. Green Beret and CIA operatives. His execution remains a historic and controversial event; and thirty years later, the circumstances of his guerrilla foray into Bolivia, his capture, killing, and burial are still the subject of intense public interest and discussion around the world.[14]

CIA declassified documents assert that with "Guevara no longer in Cuba … there is no doubt that Castro's more cautious position on exporting revolution, as well as his different economic approach, led to Che's downfall."[15] This self-serving deflection by the Agency cannot mask that Castro did not murder Che; the CIA did.

Davis recalls that in that era, she understood that Lumumba's and Guevara's sacrifices, as international leaders, represented the convergence of struggles against racism and capitalism:

> Having especially followed the theories and practices of Black communists and anti-imperialists in the United States, Africa, the Caribbean, and other parts of the world, and having worked inside the Communist Party for a number of years with a Black formation that took the names of Che Guevara and Patrice Lumumba, Marxism, from my perspective, has always been both a method and an object of criticism … the terms "Marxism" and "Black Marxism" [are not] oppositional.[16]

The revolutionary heroes held nuanced critiques of the Soviets' "peaceful coexistence" with the West and the United States, a policy put into place in 1959, several years after Nikita Khrushchev publicized Stalin's crimes. CPUSA ideologies were aligned with the CPSU's "peaceful coexistence" policy; that policy was at odds with Third World revolutionaries' desperate freedom struggles; or, as Guevara stated to the UN after the assassination of Lumumba, liberators would be happy to comply with "peaceful coexistence" if the United States and counterrevolutionaries would stop killing freedom fighters and their allies. Dorothy Healey had described Gus Hall as a "Stalinist"[17] because he demanded strict adherence to the party line. Mitchell used the names of slain revolutionary leaders who were known for spontaneity and creative militancy; their names would attract Black and brown young radicals to the newly formed "Che-Lumumba Club." According to Mitchell, she learned from the CPUSA the capacity to form movements: "the ability to link struggles and the ability to understand time, place and circumstance ... understand the interrelationships of what is going on with those things, then we will be able to move."[18]

By 1968, Davis the graduate student considered herself to be "almost a full-time activist."[19] Living in Los Angeles, she worked with Los Angeles SNCC, which formed the political study group the Black Panther Political Party (BPPP). Some readers erroneously conflated the BPPP with the Black Panther Party (BPP). The third edition of *Angela Davis: An Autobiography* dispels some of the confusion. Whether Davis was a member of the *activist* BPP that promoted self-defense from police violence and created breakfast programs[20] for impoverished urban families is addressed in the 2021 edition, which states that Davis was asked to work with the BPP political education committee. In addition, the BPPP held study groups; its roots were tied to Stokely Carmichael (Kwame Ture) and the Alabama Lowndes County Black Panthers.

While Davis and activists were trying to minimize violence, the LAPD was attempting to incite it. Outrage on the streets would "justify" police infliction of mass injuries, arrests, and deaths. Davis recounts how radicals sought peace as law-and-order forces fomented antagonisms:

> [W]e were actually trying to prevent a riot, prevent the outbreak of violence, but the Los Angeles Police Department obviously wanted violence. We ... learned later that they had developed new technologies and they had new weapons and they wanted probably to try them out and so they actually dropped off a young black man whom they had severely beaten, in front of our offices ... we had to get him to the hospital and so forth, but we realized that it was provocative. They wanted us to riot and we were doing everything we could to involve people in an organized, non-violent protest.[21]

According to Davis's California communist mentor, Dorothy Healey, Davis received special permission from the CPUSA to join the "Black Panther Party." Healey likely meant the Black Panther *Political* Party (author's emphasis), which, as stated earlier, was a study group and part of SNCC. *An Autobiography* recalls the chauvinism and ideological divisiveness that Davis experienced in the SNCC-led Panther party on the West Coast.[22] SNCC's BPPP was so riddled with internal conflict under the leadership of James Forman that it expelled Franklin Alexander. Angela Davis left weeks later, disaffected by the expulsion of her close friend and mentor. A similar departure occurred when the BPP expelled Franklin's younger brother, Deacon Alexander; then too Davis left. Some might think that the brothers were "infiltrating" the parties in order to steer them toward the CPUSA analytical framework and that Davis, without them, did not feel comfortable with the alliances she had formed with the BPPP and the BPP.

The Panthers faced the most lethal violence from the state, based on its revolutionary potential and anti-Black animus. However, other student activists, including white students aligned with the CPUSA, were also surveilled, harassed, and threatened. These students recognized shared precarity. News coverage also began to note state repression against students. The Left followed press coverage of the August 6–7, 1969, congressional hearings on the CPUSA infiltrating the SDS. University of Chicago student Gerald Wayne Kirk testified that Youth Communist League (YCL) leader Mike Zagarell recruited him to infiltrate the SDS. Zagarell, in an earlier interview with the *Harvard Crimson*, emphatically denied that the CPUSA infiltrated other organizations.[23] Kirk, who was Black, volunteered in 1965 to collect intelligence for the FBI on SDS, the DuBois Clubs, and the CPUSA after watching a protest on campus devolve into chaos. He testified that the CPUSA encouraged students or youths to participate in demonstrations against the war and for civil rights. According to Kirk, youth leadership of the CPUSA departed from the ideology and party line of their elders:

> [V]iolence was not at all looked down upon as a method of promoting this confrontation … we were told several times, for instance, by Franklin Alexander and Kendra Alexander of the DuBois Clubs that violence was an integral part of the revolution and we should not be afraid of it and, if we had to fight someone, do something that would be a violent confrontation, we should not at all shirk that responsibility.[24]

Kirk testified that the FBI never asked him to infiltrate the Panthers. He did not mention Davis's name but asserted that her mentors and close friends, Franklin and Kendra Alexander, legitimized and encouraged students' willingness to engage in armed struggle. It is not clear how much credence can be given to FBI informants whose interactions with activists depend on deception. Yet, in her memoir, *California Red*, Dorothy Ray Healey notes that California communist youths were purchasing and practicing with weapons, going into firing ranges in the hills for target practice. They saw themselves as providing a logical strategy for self-protection and group and individual survival. It is not clear how much influence the Alexanders had on Angela Davis concerning the necessity of weapons. She briefly dated Deacon Alexander, considered Kendra Alexander one of her closest friends, and saw the older Franklin Alexander as a guiding mentor. When his sister Charlene relocated to NYC, Franklin Alexander became the key leader in Che-Lumumba and an advisor to Angela Davis. Alexander was likely more receptive to armed self-defense than Mitchell, who focused on labor organizing. Pre-politicized to armed self-defense as a child growing up in "Bombingham," Davis accepted, in that context, the need to protect private property, family, and personal safety – rights that were legally sanctioned (structurally for whites) by the Second Amendment. Pragmatic Black politics under Jim Crow required self-defense and guns in the home. Davis's guns, or some of them, would be located in a communal house for Black radicals. Davis likely had heard of, or read, Robert and Mable Williams's 1962 *Negroes with Gun*.[25] The speeches and texts by Malcolm X and Fanon advocated and/or analyzed armed self-defense, but Davis was unimpressed by Malcolm; reading Fanon's 1952 *Black Skins, White Masks* and his 1961 *The Wretched of the Earth* provided psychoanalysis on anti-Blackness, critical analysis of colonialism, and details on the Algerian war of independence against colonial France.

Panther deaths were overshadowed by the mass killings of Vietnamese in the Southeast Asian war. The atrocity of US troops' mass murders of elderly, female, and child villagers—with the Orwellian logic that "in order to save the village [from communism], one must destroy it"—fueled a growing rage within the anti-war movement and against the establishment and governing authority in all of its guises. Also, in April 1969, twenty-one New York City Panthers, the entire New York Panther leadership, were indicted, with thirteen arrested in New York County on charges of conspiracy. *People v. Lumumba Shakur* became the legal title for the "Panther 21" case. An NYPD memorandum announced the Panther 21 arrests as closure or a "summation" of coordinated police and FBI attacks dating back to the organization's founding in 1966.[26]

CPUSA Ambassador to Cuba

When Angela Davis visited Cuba as a graduate student the summer before she began teaching philosophy at UCLA, she served as a goodwill ambassador for the CPUSA in international alliances with communist parties and nations embraced by the Soviet Union and destabilized by the United States. Davis's travels no longer focused on Europe but Cuba. The previous summer, her sister Fania had visited the island nation, part of the Soviet satellites, and a target of the CIA's Bay of Pigs fiasco of an attempted coup in 1963. The United States' refusal to allow Cuba to remain nonaligned during the Cold War drove the independent nation into an alliance with the Soviet Union. Both Angela Davis and her comrade and close friend, Kendra Alexander, from the small collective of the Che-Lumumba Club, visited Cuba on a CPUSA delegation. Angela Davis became interested in Cuba after her sister Fania Davis and their friend Victoria Mercado participated in the summer of 1968 orange harvest to support the Cuban economy and engage in people's diplomacy to deter or minimize CIA assassinations and a crippling embargo. After the sustained aggressions from the United States, Cuba had become a Soviet satellite, a small island to the south of the behemoth United States.[27] Angela Davis and Kendra Alexander were eager to volunteer their work in the coffee and sugarcane fields to help harvest 10 million tons of sugarcane. In 1969, SDS and the Cuban government had formed the Venceremos Brigades to foster relations between US progressives and Cuba under the strain of the US embargo. Angela Davis and Kendra Alexander were two of the only three people of color in that Brigade.[28] As Fania Davis had the year before, Davis did agricultural labor. As a member of the CPUSA—backed by the CPSU, which heavily financed and militarily supported Cuba—unlike Fania, Angela was privy to political meetings and discussions that went beyond the standard educational sessions for US Americans and solidarity tourists. Few graduate students had her clearance to meet with heads of state. Cuban officials were not welcoming to all Black radical activists; minimizing Black liberation in their ideology and practice, they found Davis to be more suitable as a guest than they found Black revolutionary nationalists such as Stokely Carmichael (Kwame Ture) to be. Unlike Ture's pan-Africanist revolutionary positions, Davis's Che-Lumumba remained aligned with the CPSU.

In 1969, Angela Davis visited Cuba and was greeted warmly. The same government that arranged for Black Panther leader Eldridge Cleaver—who had fled the United States after a parole violation and a shootout with police following Martin Luther King, Jr's assassination—to be sent to Algeria welcomed Davis with enthusiasm. Komboa Ervin and Carmichael/Ture also voiced critiques of racism in Cuba. A Panther vet who hijacked a plane to Cuba was sent to Czechoslovakia, where he was arrested by the CIA in Eastern Europe; Ervin was extradited to the United States and imprisoned for a life sentence. Eventually paroled, the author of *Anarchism and the Black Revolution* became a critic of authoritarian states. Enamored with Cuba, Angela Davis praised the newly formed socialist-communist nation for its advances in "the destruction of the material base of racism."[29] Davis optimistically asserted that "only under socialism could this fight against racism have been so successfully executed."[30] Upon returning to the United States, she noted in her report to the CPUSA that Castro had personally informed her that the Cuban state was moving away from "emphasizing armed struggle to mobilizing mass movements."[31] Thus the Soviet "peaceful coexistence" mandate of the 1950s along with the 1930s "popular front" mandate was de-emphasizing liberation struggles in the colonial south, while seeking rapprochement with the Western capitalist states and—the most powerful and lethal of them all—the American empire. "Peaceful coexistence" was embraced by the CPUSA, the *Partido Comunista de Cuba* (PCC), and promoted by the CPSU. Che Guevara had addressed the UN following the 1961 CIA-assisted assassination of Patrice Lumumba, anti-colonial liberator and president of the Congo, stating that international anti-colonialists were happy to abide by "peaceful coexistence" if the Western forces and CIA stopped killing them. Two years later, Malcolm X outraged the white public and Elijah Muhammad of the Nation of Islam when he referred to President John F. Kennedy's assassination as "chickens coming home to roost" given the US involvement in Lumumba's assassination.

For Davis, having observed and mourned – while a student – the assassinations of Patrice Lumumba (1961) and Che Guevara (1967), joining an international communist party that prohibited direct confrontation with the state authorizing these assassinations would be more pragmatic than following a BPP/BLA code for armed self-defense. Davis tacitly accepted the Soviet policy of peaceful coexistence just as she uncritically defended Cuba without noting contradictions or context. Davis became a champion of Cuba, describing her journey there as "a great climax" that brought meaning and purpose to her life: "the Cubans' limitless revolutionary enthusiasm had left a permanent mark on my existence."[32] Her memories of that fervor, and the alternate worldview embraced by revolutionary Cubans, would sustain Davis during first battles with the UC Regents and Governor Reagan over her being fired as a communist philosopher, and, later, the much greater battle for her life and freedom from incarceration.

CPUSA Assistance

At the January 1970 CPUSA National Committee, Charlene Mitchell and Louis Weinstock, in two separate reports, gave updates on the "problem of reacting to the growing repression against the mass movement, especially the Black Panther Party, and the perspective of a national center to coordinate the many defense activities." Mitchell provided an update on preparations for a national emergency conference in defense of the BPP "under sponsorship of a group of noted citizens." Weinstock listed defense activities of national organizations and of ad hoc committees, focusing on New York, which included the "National Lawyers Guild and other attorneys, 200 in all, ... defending some thousand persons, including selective service and military cases." Weinstock also raised a "major question": whether a central defense structure is possible, despite the ideological differences existing on that front.[33] The answer would unfortunately prove to be "No."[34]

The CPUSA, through support and advocacy, sought to be the vanguard unifier of different left factions; it was the oldest radical formation and had the most resources and developed international networks. But its attempts to *steer* the BPP, and mitigate its outspoken and confrontational tactics, were largely unsuccessful. The CPUSA also lacked charismatic leadership that appealed to radical youths. It did not daily address the material and physical needs of impoverished Black communities as the BPP did when they delivered clothing, education, and food through breakfast programs, as well as security against racist police forces. The BPP, not the CPUSA, fired the imaginations of Blacks, and others, who desired a restructuring of the political-economic and social order. The Panthers *inspired* people to mobilize and resist. The CPUSA, through its Black formations such as the Che-Lumumba Club, set a primary mission based in solidarity, persuasion, and tactical assistance through the organizing.

There were intergenerational overlaps between the CPUSA and the BPP. The father of Black Panther Roberta Alexander (she is discussed in the chapter on Black Panther doppelganger women) knew Jessica Mitford and the CPUSA DuBois Clubs. Through those connections, Alexander was introduced to Bettina Aptheker. Alexander had enrolled in UC Berkeley late in 1964, and Aptheker helped her to navigate the large institution and find spots with the most supportive teaching assistants (TAs). The 1964 Free Speech movement led by Bettina Aptheker and Mario Savio politicized Alexander.

Since the Panthers rejected CPUSA "parental" authority, so the CPUSA offered assistance in fundraising, legal aid, and influential protective networks for mobilization, conferences, and protests. The CPUSA's political committee issued an OPEN LETTER TO THE MEMBERSHIP from the National Committee on January 18, 1970:

Dear Comrades: The tempo of mass struggle in our country sharply accelerated in the 1960s. There is no doubt that the 1970s will witness even more intense and widespread struggles. New sections of the people are continually drawn into the fight against the war. The Black Liberation Movement constantly seeks new avenues to challenge the system of racist oppression. Mass movements among Chicanos, Puerto Ricans, Indians, are steadily growing. With the hard-fought GE strike, the most massive confrontation in decades between labor and capital at the point of production has begun. Women's struggles against their oppression are rapidly increasing. Among youth, opposition to ruling-class policies continues to spread in many fields. Movements for defense of the democratic rights of the Black Panthers and of other victims of racism and repression are mounting. The Nixon Administration, in the face of this tidal wave of opposition, is resorting to ever-greater demagogy, while taking a new turn to the Right. It organizes extreme Rightist forces to attack the peace movement. It coordinates the efforts to exterminate the Panthers. It seeks to shackle the mass media. It prepares major anti-labor legislation and promotes unemployment as its answer to inflation. It is moving toward political and economic polarization all down the line. The perspective is for much sharpened struggle. What is required to halt the reactionary thrust that leads in the direction of fascism?[35]

The CPUSA's query on how to halt the national turn toward "fascism" suggests calls for "a new, more realistic direction"—a contrast to the BPP. How best to achieve this political realism: through, according to the CPUSA, the "widest unity of struggle, increasingly led by the workers." Yet the workers were divided by racism; white supremacy prevented white workers from aligning with Black and Chicano/Latinx workers and laborers. Glossing over the contradictions and racist realism, the party called for "unity ... based on the closest ties of labor and the freedom movement"; this could only be achieved if "the rapidly-growing Left [became]... a united force, understanding its mass responsibilities correctly." The call does not directly confront COINTELPRO and anti-Black/Brown/Red violence. The call advocates worker or class unity rooted in expanding the readership of the CPUSA newspaper:

> It is in this crucial situation for our country that the National Committee calls on every member to make a maximum effort, individually and collectively, to make a breakthrough in the circulation of the Marxist press—*The Daily World* and *The People's World*. We must secure 6,500 new readers of *The Daily World* and added numbers to *The People's World* among workers, Black, Brown and white, in the basic industries, in the Black community, among the activists in the mass movements. Achievement of this objective will make a tremendous contribution to our mass objectives. By reading the Marxist-Leninist press, these new readers will become consistent fighters for the mass line necessary to defeat reaction and move forward.[36]

Of course, this is not the sum total of the CPUSA response, but it is what dominated the speech of Gus Hall and Henry Winston as reported by the CPUSA *Public Affairs*.

Its faith in its literary publications and political analyses is assumed to be a match for a murderous COINTELPRO and the rise of political imprisonment based on political dissent, not on the condition of the worker or the subjugation of the Black. Although both workers and Red, Black, and Brown people were being incarcerated during this period, they were not targeted by COINTELPRO as a mass; only their radical leaders were targeted. Using Winston's language, the party elevates the role of print and eliminates the reality of risk:

> These "collective propagandists, agitators and organizers"—*The Daily World* and *The People's World* reach every day into areas we often cannot reach by any other means. With effort, thousands of these readers will become new members of our Party. And the Party must be built if the mass perspectives are to be achieved. The National Committee has singled out this press building campaign as key in the total work of the Party at this time. It is key to building a united Left and to building the Party. And these, in turn, are decisive for uniting the people, defeating reaction and opening a new path. Press building is not an "inner" task. It is the heart of the struggle to end the war, against racism and reaction.[37]

Cuban's Contradictory Allies

African Americans have been interested in Cuba and have supported Cuban independence movements from colonial rule in the nineteenth century. According to Lisa Brock, who traces Black American and Cuba relations back to Frederick Douglass,[38] after the Cubans' successful struggle to oust colonial Spain, the United States' invasion and occupation propelled the country into an island playground for the American Mafia and a dictatorship under Fulgencio Batista from 1952 to 1959.[39] The 1912 *Partido Independiente de Color* (Independent Party of Color) "inspired masses of peasants to rise against poverty and economic marginalization." Black Cubans who had fought against Spain's colonialism resisted the US and Cuban elites and were massacred by the thousands in "the 1912 Race War," which the Cuban government never fully recognized, mourned, or analyzed.[40] During the time of Angela's defense and acquittal, the nation exhibited an unwillingness to publicly address sexism, anti-Black racism, and discrimination against LGBTQ citizens.

Unlike other Black radicals and militants, such as Robert Williams, Stokely Carmichael (Ture), Eldridge Cleaver, and Huey Newton, who all spent time on the island, Angela Davis never publicly criticized the Cuban government or openly spoke about its limitations in terms of Black equality. First admiring Cuban culture and cultural resistance at the Helsinki youth festival in 1962, then hearing about her sister's visit on an early form of Venceremos Brigade, then in the company of Kendra Alexander visiting Cuba and representing the CPUSA through the Che-Lumumba Club, Davis remained an enthusiastic supporter of the nation led by Fidel Castro—the only, some said, truly victorious people's revolution in the hemisphere. The month after LA Panthers John Huggins and Bunchy Carter were murdered on the UCLA campus; in February 1969, Lorenzo Komboa Ervin hijacked a plane to Cuba, reportedly, to avoid being prosecuted for trying to kill a KKK leader. In Cuba, the Black radical was disillusioned. The Cuban government sent Ervin to Czechoslovakia (likely with Soviet permission). The Czech government turned Ervin over to US officials. In September 1969, he was charged with two counts of airline hijacking in the US District Court for the State of Georgia. Ervin became the first American to receive a life sentence for hijacking an airplane; after fifteen years, he was released through litigation and an international campaign.

International Solidarity with Cuba

On Angela Davis's 1969 delegation to Cuba, she and Kendra Alexander were two of the three people of color. Her reports following her trip were enthusiastically supportive of the Cuban nation and government. She offered gentle critiques of Cuba to the CPUSA based on gender discrimination or male chauvinism.[41] The CPUSA supported peaceful coexistence and opposed US foreign and domestic policies as pragmatic combatants in the Cold War. Unlike the Black revolutionary militants, the CPUSA, Cuba, and Angela Davis did not want revolutionary struggle.

Focusing on gender (not race), Angela Davis congratulated the Cubans on their improvements in race relations. After returning with Kendra Alexander to the states, Davis presented her report; no critique of Cuban anti-Black racism appeared in the 1969 report to the California CPUSA. Unlike the Black male militants who preceded her, Davis did not strongly question Cuba's position on discrimination against Black Cubans. She believed that a multiracial communist state was the only vehicle for the advancement of humanity. As a high-profile foreign dignitary, Davis would not have been available for an uncensored conversation with the "regular" Black Cuban who could critique Cuban government and society without consequences. As a multiracial state, which existed in the shadow of an empire known for toppling governments in favor of white corporations and white nationalist sentiments, Cuba was loath to open an official discussion on its national history of repression of Black Cubans.[42] The Cubans also saw in Davis the "mixed race" imago that aligned with their narratives of being African, Indio, and European, yet anti-Black practices and policies continued on the island.

Davis's communist affiliation, education, and personal comportment, rather than Black militancy, endeared her to Castro and the Cuban government. Davis had dismissed Black formations and leaders—such as Malcolm X—as "narrow nationalism."[43] The CPUSA cautioned against ethnic chauvinism and sexism, and straying from CPUSA analyses. It is not clear, in print, how Davis grappled with hegemonic white progressives who leveraged her as their exceptional Black person.[44] On some levels, Davis never questioned or challenged left authority figures that embraced her. Carmichael/Ture had confrontational debates with Fidel Castro in Cuba, as he rode for hours in the president's limousine arguing about the depressed status of Blacks in the communist nation.[45] The Cuban government never publicly castigated Black militant leaders from the United States; at times they forced the most incendiary and risky ones out of the country. Cuba "facilitated" the departures of

Williams, Newton, and Cleaver from the island. Williams would end up working with Chairman Mao in China. Newton, who would return to California, and Cleaver, who went to Algiers, were seeking asylum to escape the consequences of their violent choices unrelated to community protections. The Cuban Communist Party remained wary of "Black Power" movements, especially those headed by questionable leaders. Newton's and Cleaver's provocative rhetoric and erratic behavior made them unlikely ambassadors of Black liberation. They never met President Castro during their stays in Cuba.[46] Williams and Carmichael, though, carried a gravitas lacking in the Panther leaders. They met Castro and Cuban government officials but consistently argued that the needs of Black communities were insufficiently addressed, not only in the United States and throughout the globe but also in Cuba. Davis's reticence in publicly critiquing Communist Party officials or governments endeared her to governments worldwide, although it also made her vulnerable to critiques that she ignored the repression of groups and dissidents in Communist bloc nations.

11

Doppelganger Panther Women

Roberta Alexander, Fania Davis Jordan, Angela Davis

Pre-Panther Roberta Alexander, 1967

While Angela Davis was studying at UC San Diego, she and Fania Davis met a Black radical UC student, Roberta Alexander, who was also a "red-diaper" baby. However, Alexander is from a "mixed-race" household—Black father and white mother—and joined and remained with the Black Panther Party as a rank-and-file member for about a year, leaving in late 1969. She lived in a "Panther pad," engaged in delivery of care to impoverished communities, and used her academic skills to develop educational texts. Fluent in Spanish, Alexander could also converse and advocate with working-class Chicano/as in California who were monolingual. Enrolled as an undergrad at the prestigious UC Berkeley, she was mentored by graduate student Bettina Aptheker, Davis's childhood friend from Elizabeth Irwin. Alexander's high-risk activism explored the parameters for anti-fascist and anti-racist politics. She would join the BPP for one year and leave due to contradictions and harassment within the party and external violence from police forces. Alexander would be closer to Fania Davis Jordan's age and both women knew each other as students in the UC system. They shared similar narratives of precarity and political determination.

Roberta Alexander's narrative as a UC Berkeley student is unique. As had Angela Davis, Roberta Alexander enrolled in elite white institutions and did her year abroad in Europe. Unlike Davis, her family had meager financial means and her Black father was raised in part on a reservation and later became a manual laborer at age twelve. Roberta Alexander was the first in her family to go to university.[1]

In 1964, Roberta Alexander's father drove her to Berkeley and introduced her to older people on the left that he knew. Davis's friend and former schoolmate in Manhattan, Bettina Aptheker, befriended Alexander. Alexander recounted that Bettina Aptheker "had me over for dinner and helped me plan my classes, and [told me] who the TA's were, and who/what I should do."[2] Alexander's father was connected to the influential left, including British aristocrat-turned-British author and civil rights activist Jessica Mitford and National Welfare Rights Organization cofounder Roscoe Proctor, as well as other Bay Area activists.[3] CPUSA parents' connections to left and international elites—Aptheker, W. E. B. DuBois, Mitford, Proctor—created a network and a web that protected their children. These socialists and communists were well educated and influential among left liberals; they were also connected to Western European and Soviet elites. Alexander's parents were connected to the CPUSA DuBois Club at UC Berkeley.

During the fall 1964 semester, at the height of the Free Speech Movement co-led by Mario Savio and Bettina Aptheker, Berkeley students mobilized to support the southern civil rights movement. Alexander recalls how the protests for student free speech were tied to the southern civil rights movement. Freedom Riders[4] were returning to campus. They tabled on campus areas and nearby streets to inform other students about Jim Crow segregationist violence and resistance by students. Students who went south included Savio, the most prominent leader of the Free Speech movement. Alexander met Freedom Riders[5] returning from the south that summer she enrolled. The university and police mandated that students take down their educational tables. Students saw that as a violation of their right to free speech. A massive protest became a movement. Police arrested students occupying Berkeley's Sproul Hall. Seventeen-year-old Alexander informed the precinct that she was eighteen; she states that in order not to be separated from her friends and comrades who were eighteen or older—she would have gone to juvenile hall—she figured out a solution upon arrest: "I just gave them a different year."[6]

A member of the CPUSA DuBois Club, Alexander became politicized in her first year as an undergrad:

> I was very excited about the demonstrations passing out leaflets as a member of the W.E.B. DuBois Club early in the semester that the Free Speech Movement started … All it took was them to try to stop us setting up the tables, Mario Savio was one of the key figures, and we had rallies just about every day.
>
> Bettina Aptheker also spoke. I spoke once, as well, [I] started to get my feet wet a little bit.

Because Alexander wanted to study abroad in Spain in 1966 and 1967, and demonstrate against the war in Vietnam and for civil rights, she decided to major in Spanish. Progressive students feared the Franco regime, yet for Alexander, the Latin American regimes installed by the United States were much more brutal (e.g., the Kennedy Administration funded a coup that led to a military dictatorship in Brazil—CIA directors report directly to the US president).[7] Alexander notes how the university attempted to use her civil rights advocacy against her: "when I interviewed to go to Spain, they said, 'Well, you got arrested in the Free Speech Movement and you're going to a country that is a dictatorship.' And I said my purpose is to go study." Alexander received the fellowship and when she traveled to Madrid she found that Spain "truly was a repressive regime." She encountered multiple types of police forces; some were "called the *grises* because they wore grey, and they would be standing on corners with sub-machine guns." The students did not mingle easily with "other political people… we studied in… the *Facultad de Letras y Filosofia*… [Filosofía y Letras in the

Universidad Autónoma de Madrid]." To protect themselves during protests, Spanish students threw out leaflets from windows or balconies. If you did not see the leaflets, you would miss the demonstrations. They could not hand out leaflets or flyers on campus because demonstrating against the Franco regime and dictatorship could lead to arrest, torture, and disappearance.[8]

Alexander met progressive students in Spain and asked them how she could contribute as an activist. She was told to work with the American students. Three female US students set up a table in the *Facultad de Letras y Filosofia* to collect signatures in opposition to the US war in Vietnam. It would have been too dangerous to denounce Franco's Spain. They planned to carry the signatures to the (US) embassy. Alexander later realized the plan was naive. After a few days, the press came, asking the US students to contact them if they planned an action.

As was Angela Davis as a Black undergrad in France, Alexander was often depressed while in Spain: "I didn't find a boyfriend, and I unfortunately didn't study flamenco guitar ... whatever!" Organizing gave her purpose and a community of like-minded, ethical and daring students: "eventually, by the spring, I had quite a few progressive friends ... [who were] considered revolutionary at that time, and that was getting to be more and more fun." Her cadre planned large anti-war demonstrations on April 28, 1967. Roberta Alexander was asked to give a speech. She recalls hesitancy in her immediate response: "I don't know, maybe I'll write a letter and you can read the letter."[9]

The director of her program, Carlos Blanco Aguinaga, was the director of the exchange program. After fleeing Franco's fascist Spain in the 1930s, he grew up in the United States; studious and productive, he became a UC prestigious professor. When he learned that Alexander was a US activist, in October, he asked to meet with her in his office. Alexander recalls the conversation:

"Roberta, Ronald Reagan is coming to town and you could go over to the airport." And he starts drawing me a diagram of the airport [laughter], and he says, "And you can put a sign up under your coat, and then when he gets there, you can open up your sign against the war in Vietnam and against Ronald Reagan!" I know: "Man, this guy's crazy!" Fortunately, Ronald Reagan didn't come because I think I might have gotten home sooner [laughter] if he had actually come.[10]

Later, in a private meeting, the American Embassy told Blanco Aguinaga: "We can't protect your kids if they get involved in these demonstrations. So, you need to tell them to stay out of the demonstrations." Blanco Aguinaga then met with the student activists and informed them of the warning. Alexander recalls that after the meeting, she reminded him that students asked her to speak at the demonstration, to which he replied: "Roberta, I know you'll do the right thing."[11]

Alexander notes that the director did not tell her not to give the speech. On the day of the event, students had taken over a building; a sign hung from the fifth floor to the second floor, the banner blaring: "*Yanquis fuera del Vietnam!*" (Yankees out of Vietnam!). In 1967, she found that Europeans were "burning little American flags." Alexander enters the wall where she is to make her speech; it is at full capacity but the sound system is broken. Her collective reassures her that people will be quiet and able to hear the speech. The person who spoke before her was drowned out by loud conversations; according to Alexander, "it was just chaos." American reporters were asking her to translate Spanish. As soon as she walks on platform, the Black American receives a standing ovation. Everyone is quiet as she outlines her major points. When she finishes there is just applause. As she viewed it in her teenage mind: "I'm so popular because I'm just like [the] revolutionary student from the United States." Then five students told her that they all needed to make an emergency exit: "we have to run out the back way through this little forest where we have a taxi waiting for you … go to the train station, go straight to Andalusia … stay away for a couple of weeks, so this whole thing will cool down, and then they'll forget about you." Roberta Alexander described herself as "5 feet 10 inches… this color," and "so depressed" that she had been "just eating at all hours." Alexander took a taxi but to her apartment (officially she was allowed to live in a pension); a friend alerted her that police were looking for the student activists at their homes. The students then contacted Carlos Blanco Aguinaga and were invited to his home.[12] There, they planned their escape.

They collected their suitcases and found a special taxi to collect their luggage. The three women students were blond Caucasian (Roberta Alexander's friend), Japanese-Hawaiian (Carol Watanabe), and Black (Roberta Alexander) The cabby driving them to the director's office hears the radio announcement: *"El gobierno de España esta buscando estas mujeres—una chica de color, una Japonesa, y una rubia."* "The Spanish government is looking for a girl of color, a Japanese girl, and a blond girl." The driver looks in his rearview mirror, does not speak, but drops off the passengers. The students stayed at their director's house for several days. The women could not be easily and quickly arrested; according to Alexander, because of surveillance—what Alexander describes as "different levels of spies at the university"—it was difficult at first to arrest the American students. Also, the American Embassy continuously made inquiries about them to officials in Spain. Roberta Alexander decided that they should return to their apartments. The students were placed under house arrest in Spain; while imprisoned in her apartment, Alexander was able to give an interview to a Los Angeles, CA radio station. Although unable to contact her parents, they were able to hear her interview.

Answering a knock on her apartment door, she found plainclothes men asking if she were Roberta Alexander; she responded "Yes." They identified themselves as police and politely informed her that it was their duty to arrest her. Her arrest was based on speech violations undermining a fascist nation supported by the United States. Alexander walks with the police from her apartment toward the central jail, the *Puerta del Sol*. On their way, they stop for coffee. As was Davis's October 1970 arrest, Alexander does not attempt to flee and is met with a polite, nonviolent arrest. Because she is not a citizen of Spain but a citizen of the United States—the most powerful nation in the world— even though she is Black, Alexander has privileges as a university-educated American. In fact, all three students belong to US empire and elite educational institutions. The walk to the *Puerta del Sol* is mostly downhill and police and prisoners have to walk downstairs. Alexander describes the jail as "like a dungeon" and is the first among the American trio to arrive. Many students were preemptively arrested prior to May Day—in the medieval times it was the day to celebrate the arrival of spring; in 1899 it became known for international workers solidarity and the rise of socialism and marked vigorous demonstrations against labor exploitation and police violence. In the jail, Spanish students began singing "We shall overcome!" Alexander could join and support them, but because of her international standing based on citizenship, she was soon released and deported. Spain was not a US "colony" but it followed the dictates and desires of the US government. Roberta Alexander recalls: "it was more like I was kidnapped by the Spanish state under the orders of the American State Department. Because everybody we asked said [in response to:] 'Why are you arresting me?' 'We don't know. The American Embassy wants us to do it.'"[13]

The twenty-year-old students were placed on a train with a "row of police with … machine guns." At every stop, there would be *Guardia Civil*. They crossed the border to Hendaye, and found Carlos Blanco Aguinaga waiting for them – he had driven to their stop to provide money and to make sure they were taken care of. From there the three women students took the train to Paris. On board were immigrant workers, likely from Morocco; the women tried to tell them that they were being deported or abducted as they shared food with them. Their stories and absence from the university were appearing in newspapers. When they arrived in Paris with limited funds, they were figuring out how to secure assistance. That was when Alexander noted a crowd gathering. A man walked up to ask, "Are you Roberta Alexander, Carol Watanabe and Karen Winn?" The activists replied, "Yes." He then identified himself as a *CBS* correspondent and offered them a limousine ride to the Hotel George Cinq—what Alexander describes as "the fanciest hotel in Paris." There is one condition: that they give an exclusive interview to CBS at 5:30 am so that it would make the evening news in the United States. The activists agreed and were transported to the luxury hotel.[14]

In Paris, Alexander phoned her parents from the hotel. During the call she learned that her parents "had seen the CBS interview and were proud but nervous." According to Alexander, "there was reason to be afraid. Had it been Latin America it may not have turned out the same way." *CBS* shaped the interview as a "human-interest story," downplaying student militancy and US students, in study abroad programs, publicly proclaiming their denunciations of the Johnson administration's war in Vietnam. Whether it was to protect the students or to not rile the democratic administration, it worked. No police were deployed to harass or stalk the women. Returning to the states, the students went straight back to Berkeley. There would have been consequences if UC Berkeley students had been imprisoned, tortured, or disappeared. That fate had been inflicted upon many radical youths around the globe who challenged war and authoritarianism. Roberta Alexander and her collective belonged to UC Berkeley just as Angela Davis belonged to UC San Diego and UCLA.

Panther Fania Davis Jordan

A year after Angela Davis joined the CPUSA Che-Lumumba Club, her closest family member, Fania Davis, and her husband, Samuel Jordan, were threatened by the San Diego PD. Fania Davis did not join the Che-Lumumba Club (she would join the CPUSA when Angela Davis was arrested in order to work on the defense committee).

In 1969, Fania Davis Jordan with her husband Samuel Jordan became members of the San Diego chapter of the Black Panther Party. Married to an HBCU militant, Fania Davis Jordan, who followed her older sister to study for a doctorate in philosophy with Herbert Marcuse, chose a revolutionary organization. The political violence against the Davis sisters likely led Fania Davis to drop out of grad school (she would later become an attorney after working on her sister's defense trial). Both Davises would have their doctoral studies at UC San Diego with Marcuse derailed.

Arrest, court, media, and police records indicate that Fania Davis Jordan was a member of the San Diego Black Panther Party (for Self-Defense). The public and media at times conflated the sisters into one persona, identifying Fania as a CPUSA member when she was a Panther (later, Davis would identify as a Panther, after she left the CPUSA). San Diego police appeared to have attempted to kill Fania Davis, her husband, and their unborn child (Fania Davis Jordan was pregnant). Following an illegal mandate, San Diego officials and police decided that there would be no Black Panther Party in "their" city. The military town banned an organization that the federal government had not legally criminalized. Brutal repression was also used against student protesters. California fit the description that Malcolm had levied at the north; it was another version of Jim Crow and lynching. As the Klan had used lynching in the deep south, US police forces and prison guards used extrajudicial executions to neutralize Black militants. Samuel Jordan, a Black radical student at Lincoln University, along with his wife (who graduated from Swarthmore), and his sister-in-law Angela Davis, trained with weapons. The Davis-Jordans, though, would have regularly trained with Panthers. (In this way the Davis sisters diversified the security apparatus that in their childhood was largely led by Black men, such as their father.)

An Autobiography describes death threats against Angela Davis stemming mostly from white vigilantes and the mentally ill. Her name and image were publicized throughout the press, which largely denounced the communist, anti-war activist advocating Black liberation and the rights of the incarcerated. In 1969, police and detectives routinely surveilled Davis and made harassing traffic stops. Angela Davis's rising fear of the police led to stress. She increased her arms purchases with legally registered guns.

Court records for Fania Davis and Samuel Jordan offer a glimpse into the type of police terror inflicted upon members of the Black Panther Party in San Diego and in other US cities. During a November 17, 1969, domestic spat which police used as a pretense for interrogation or arrest, Davis's family members were vulnerable to becoming police homicides. While battling to keep her UCLA teaching position, organizing on behalf of the Panthers, Davis turned her attention what appeared to be the attempted murder of her sister and her brother-in-law, whom the police had charged with attempted murder of officers. The below condensed police report offers findings of fact that were not disputed by the defendants; the report reveals the level of police violence and threat that Panthers faced.

On November 17, 1969, 11–11:30 pm, Fania Davis Jordan was hitchhiking on Highway 101 in Del Mar. She was "nicely dressed" but without purse or shoes, "although she wore nylon stockings," according to San Diego Deputy Sheriffs Moorhead and Palmer. Palmer questioned Fania Davis, who said she was hitchhiking to go to a friend's house. Moorhead asked her if her car had broken down. She refused to speak with the deputies. They asked her for ID. She initially refused, but when they gave their police ID, she identified herself as Fania Davis, a UCSD graduate student who lived in Del Mar. Next, according to the report, "Samuel Jordan walked up between the deputies, grabbed Fania by the arm, jerked her toward him, and said 'Don't you ever do that again.'" He began to walk back on Highway 101 with Fania Davis toward their home. After Samuel Jordan ignored Moorhead's command that he stop: "The deputies caught up with Samuel and Fania and Moorhead asked Samuel for identification and an explanation. Samuel refused, commenting if he and Fania were white, the deputies would not be doing this." Rather than let the couple go, Moorhead stated that he feared Jordan might have a weapon beneath his loose knit sweater, reached down attempting to feel his waistband and asked if he had any weapons. Samuel jerked away and Fania hollered 'What's the matter with you guys, are you crazy?' Samuel said "These are fuckin' pig cops." When Moorhead and Palmer told Jordan he "was under arrest for delaying and obstructing [the] interview with Fania and for refusing to identify himself," and held Samuel Jordan by the arms for Moorhead to cuff him, Fania shoved Moorhead from behind and Jordan twisted free:

> Samuel backpedaled away yelling, "My name is Samuel Jordan. This is my wife. This is a family problem. Leave us alone." Moorhead did not believe this because Fania had said her name was Davis. (It apparently did not occur to the deputies to inquire of Fania whether she was married to Samuel or whether she needed help.)
>
> Moorhead again tried to arrest Samuel but he turned and ran toward and into the rear portion of a duplex on 26th Street. Moorhead chased him through the open door. Samuel grabbed a cancelled check from a coffee table and said, "This is my name, and you now know who I am. You know where I live. Get out of my house. You don't have a search warrant." Moorhead said it was too late for that, he was already under arrest. Moorhead and Samuel engaged in a struggle.
>
> During the struggle, Moorhead saw a shotgun in a bedroom and scissors on the coffee table. Samuel tried to work his way toward the bedroom. Moorhead feared Fania might use the scissors as a weapon, looked back and saw her jerk her hand from his gun. Samuel hollered for Fania to go get help. She ran out the door, returning in 15 to 20 seconds with a young white male, who left upon Palmer's orders.
>
> The deputies had dragged Samuel back into the living room and had him on the couch. Samuel was on Moorhead and Palmer was on Samuel.... Fania jumped on the pile, hitting Moorhead on the face with her hand causing a scratch. Samuel broke free and ran into the bedroom.
>
> Moorhead ran after Samuel drawing his revolver as he thought Samuel would get the shotgun. Samuel came through the door with the shotgun pointed at Moorhead. Moorhead fired 5 shots at Samuel, 4 of which were deflected when Fania hit his hand. One shot wounded Samuel in the shoulder.
>
> Samuel retreated into the bedroom. Moorhead heard what sounded like a round being jacked into the firing chamber of the shotgun.... He warned Palmer to take cover. Both deputies ran outside and took cover behind a large van. Palmer saw

a slender, tall person with an Afro style natural hairdo appear at the brim of the roadway in front of the driveway. Two shots were fired. Debris stung Palmer's face at the time of the second shot.[15]

Bearing a striking resemblance to her older sister, Fania Davis Jordan was under constant police surveillance by fall 1969. Angela Davis's media celebrity and police scrutiny—based on her assertion to her right to teach as a member of the communist party—had spilled over onto Fania Davis. On November 19, 1969, newspaper headlines proclaimed: "Red's Sister Jailed for Shooting."[16] The twenty-two- and twenty-three-year-old couple were traumatized at the hands of the San Diego police. Their previous experiences as organizers at Swarthmore for Fania Davis and Lincoln University for Samuel Jordan had not sufficiently prepared them for lethal police violence. Through the lens scrutinizing Angela Davis, newspapers routinely referred to Fania as the "sister of avowed Communist Angela Davis of UCLA." The Davis-Jordans were charged with "assault with intent to commit murder and assault on a police officer with a deadly weapon." The press used the graduate fellow to cast aspersions on the Marxist professor: "Mrs. Jordan, described by deputies as a student of controversial professor Herbert Marcuse of the University of California at San Diego, was an employee of the UCSD philosophy department." Filled with inaccuracies that criminalized the Davis-Jordans and, by association, Angela Davis, newspapers worked as public relations for the police department: "Both Jordans were accused of firing a shotgun at sheriff's deputies Burl Moorhead and James Palmer after the deputies went to the Jordan house in Del Mar because of a family fight."

Following the police-written script, the press depicted the Davis-Jordans as violent criminals, making little to no mention that Fania Davis Jordan and her husband had been fighting for their lives and family in their own home, which police entered without a warrant. The Black Panther Party in San Diego gathered members not from UC San Diego, where Fania Davis Jordan and Angela Davis were among a small number of Black students, but San Diego State, which had more working class and Black students. Yet, in the protection of the Davis-Jordans, young white and Black radicals were called upon to repel the police who did not have a search warrant and also did not have probable cause because a couple argued and did not want to speak with them. Activists knew their rights. Black Panthers studied their legal rights (including Second Amendment) although they were not well respected or enforced in anti-Black institutions such as policing and courts. The Davis-Jordans' defense attorneys understood the legal aspects of the fact-based narrative and pursued their defense in court and public: police had illegally trespassed into the Jordan apartment without a search warrant and tried to kill Samuel, placing a pregnant woman and their baby in danger. The legal entry notes that Fania Davis-Jordan fought the police and knocked the gun away as they shot at her husband at least five times, hitting him once. The struggle moved toward the courtyard. When Fania Davis yelled for a white neighbor to get help, he disappeared. Within minutes, an unidentified Black man with an Afro and a rifle shot at gravel near police, without hitting police. The police retreated while apartment neighbors watched. The anonymous Black Panther saved lives. Watching neighbors could be court witnesses if police brutality or executions took place. The unidentified man disappeared, never to be found. Police made arrests of the couple, charging them with attempted murder of police. With her sister jailed, and her brother-in-law shot and hospitalized before jail, Davis would have offered guidance and contacted CPUSA attorneys (the party had accomplished legal networks). Sallye Davis was also connected to the CPUSA (she would be mobilized again in August 1970 for her eldest daughter). Attorneys and family or party covered bail (the CPUSA had a cadre of skilled criminal defense and labor attorneys for half a century).[17] The Jordans were bailed out and would travel to Cuba, seen as a sanctuary, that summer.

In 1969, the SDPD tried to arrest if not kill the Davis-Jordans because they were Black Panthers. Soon after their arrests, without firing more shots, the SDPD effectively killed the San Diego branch of the Black Panther Party. Police forces used violence to terminate radical organizations. In 1970, the Desire Housing Projects in New Orleans' Ninth Ward were heavily impacted by police brutality and imprisonment of Black activists. Black Panthers worked to organize the community and provide services. However, white Louisiana governor John J. McKeithen banned Black Panther Party chapters in "his state." On September 15, 1970, one hundred New Orleans police, sheriff deputies and state troopers with assault weapons surrounded the Black Panther headquarters and shot 30,000 rounds into a building with twelve men, women and children, who miraculously were not injured or killed.[18] San Diego Police Historical Association footage from its police museum's 1970s archives[19] describes its YouTube video transcripts: "This video contains footage shot around San Diego during the July 13, 1969, Black Panther riots and other anti-war civil unrest that was common in the US in the late 1960's and early 1970's." The site also offers comments from police officers deployed against rebellions. SDPD Richard Bennett, an officer from 1961 to 2002, writes:

When riot formations were to be used, the face shields were brought to the scene from downtown. ... The race riots were a carry-over from the 1965 Watts riots, and every summer there was racial tension and clashes with the police. ... In the summer of 1969, we worked 12-hour shifts, with no days off for (I think) ten days. The Black Panther HQ was on Imperial Avenue. ... There was a lot of open hostility against the police in the late 60's. The riots quieted significantly when the first moon landing was televised. It was the first night of peace, and welcomed by us all.

Local, state, federal, and international police forces threatened the lives of Black Panthers and imprisoned activists.[20] The footage shows police with tear gas masks and canisters, as well as shot guns and boxes of cartridges, firing at Black civilians in the streets throwing bottles and bricks, and raiding homes and cars to make arrests. Footage shows the appearance of a Black intifada against white militarized police with full immunity to protect their violence.

The government protested on June 22, 1970, when the court dismissed the eighteen-count indictment against the Davis-Jordans; it was upheld by a Grand Jury on November 10, 1970, a year after the traumatic clash with the police. There was no time to celebrate. The previous month, Angela Davis had been arrested and incarcerated on conspiracy charges of kidnapping and murder following the Marin County Courthouse tragedies. Charged with attempted murder of two San Diego police officers, Fania and Samuel Jordan had traveled to the island sanctuary while Davis was a fugitive. Fania Davis had visited Cuba in 1968 for the summer orange harvest. Her older sister had met President Fidel Castro when she visited the following summer. The Davis-Jordans would have had the protection of the Cuban government. Angela Davis was a fugitive for ten weeks. The international news of Angela Davis's arrest in October 1970 reached Cuba. Fania Davis Jordan immediately left Cuba for New York City. She visited her sister in the Manhattan Women's House of Detention, the jail in the West Village situated blocks from the Elizabeth Irwin High School.[21]

Post-Panther Angela Davis

A month before the Marin County Courthouse tragedies, on July 7, 1970, BPP women leaders and political prisoners on the east coast, Joan Bird and Afeni Shakur—the mother of artist Tupac Shakur—were released on bail. During the Panther 21 trials, they would be incarcerated and later acquitted. In January 1969, Joan Bird had been tortured by the NYPD,[22] during interrogation in a Washington Heights precinct. She was charged and arrested for driving a car with Black Panthers who allegedly were seeking an armed confrontation with police.[23] The Panther 21 would be exonerated, acquitted by a jury that quickly recognized they were being railroaded by the state and that no evidence of illegal activity had been submitted by the prosecutor. The public would eventually learn that NYC Panthers, who included Dhoruba bin Wahad, had been framed by the FBI and local police, yet that knowledge would be mutedly discussed in the public after Panthers spent months or years in prison.

In the 2021 third edition of *Angela Davis: An Autobiography*, Davis's Preface addresses some confusion concerning the Black Panther *Political* Party (BPPP). Some readers (including my students) were confused by text that suggested that the third "P" had been dropped and the BPPP was conflated with the BPP, the Black Panther Party (for Self-Defense). Panthers have different recollections of Davis as a Panther (West Coast says Yes, or with Elaine Brown, Yes and No; East Coast states No). This raises the question which cannot be answered here: "What does it mean to be a 'Panther'?" In her preface to the 2021 edition of *An Autobiography*, Davis writes: "we need to engage in our relentless critique of centering the individual."

The cover of *Comrade Sisters: Women of the Black Panther Party* crops out the original photo in which Kathleen Cleaver, the first woman to sit on the Central Committee of the Black Panther Party, is one step down on a house porch upon which other Panther women are standing. Kathleen Cleaver (who received a JD from Yale after the party's demise) worked with attorneys Stuart Hanlon and Johnnie Cochran to secure Pratt's release from prison. Framed by the FBI/LAPD, as mentioned earlier, Pratt endured twenty-seven years of incarceration; the United States would issue a multimillion financial settlement for wrongful imprisonment but not acknowledge any wrongdoing. The photographic images were taken over fifty years ago by then twenty-year-old white photographer Stephane Shames. Shames and Black Panther vet Ericka Huggins are the editors. Ericka Huggins, the widow of John Huggins-slain by the United States on the UCLA campus in January 1970—stayed with the Oakland Panthers and developed its freedom school.

Davis became the symbol of the Black Panther woman decades later. In the twenty-first century, she began to pen forewords to the memoirs of Black women who were Panthers and organized and fought in the underground as revolutionaries in the Black Liberation Army (BLA) and the Republic of New Afrika (RNA): Assata Shakur's *Assata: An Autobiography* and Safiya Bukhari's *The War Before: The True Life Story of Becoming Black Panther, Keeping the Faith in Prison, and Fighting for Those Left Behind.* Shakur and Bukhari engaged in armed self-defense, revolutionary struggle, and war resistance. Davis was never targeted in the ways that Black Panther leaders and rank-and-file were. Police forces hunted, imprisoned, and/or killed Panthers. Davis's police files and the files for Governor Reagans's press conferences focus on the CPUSA. Geronimo Pratt's trial and Davis's trial occurred at the same time in California. Davis's trial dominated the media. Pratt bore the imago of the violent, militant "Panther." Davis was his opposite. Pratt was actually framed by the police/FBI because he was a revolutionary Panther. (Pratt was at a meeting in northern California—the FBI had taped the meeting and knew of Pratt's location—when a Black man shot a white couple on a tennis court in Southern California, killing the wife. A paid informant testified that Pratt was the shooter). FBI Director J. Edgar Hoover's hyperbolic and lethal designation of the Black Panther Party as the "greatest domestic threat" to US internal security was never directed at Davis.

Franklin Alexander was with Davis when she learned that her weapons stored in a separate house had been used by Jon Jackson in the August 7, 1970, Marin County Courthouse raid. Davis was impressed with the Panther breakfast program and other direct services to impoverished communities, *An Autobiography* does not describe her doing the work of the rank-and-file tasks stipulated or implied in the BPP 10-Point program.[24] Panther chapters were hierarchical and often patriarchal. (Kathleen Cleaver was the first and only woman on the central committee until she left the US with Eldridge Cleaver, in opposition to Newton, who installed Elaine Brown to head the BPP from 1974 to 1977 after he fled the United States to avoid criminal charges.) Rank-and-file members had to follow orders and complete assigned tasks. Those who failed to do so could be punished—compelled to do jumping jacks, push-ups, run around the block—or expelled. Davis functioned as an asset; with public and media visibility, UC doctoral and professorial status, she did not work or live as a "rank-and-file" activist. Even while demonized as a "Communist" by conservatives and reactionaries, she had prestige. Lacking political training from leaders such as James Forman, Bob Moses, Ella Baker—Davis would eventually find structured leadership that suited her when she joined the CPUSA in 1968. Black women had different responses to the movement: Assata Shakur rejected the civil rights mandate that the students could not defend themselves from physical violence from white supremacists and police; Kathleen Cleaver dropped out of Barnard to work at the SNCC headquarters in Atlanta, GA. Shortly after the BPP expelled Deacon, Davis left the BPP. *An Autobiography* does not share details about the educational committee, reading lists, syllabi or study groups.

Davis briefly worked with the BPP but was devoted to the CPUSA: the public tends to identify her with the Panthers although she had no BPP leadership role; whereas with the US communist party, she served as a leader for some twenty years.

However, Panthers were also communists. Black prisoners and revolutionaries would create a ragtag freedom army and seek Davis out as a public ally who was also relatable to the Black middle classes and white liberals based on her academic achievements and ethics. The rebel stars would fade in public memory as Angela Davis's rose, despite or because of her increasing distance from rebellion after August 7, 1970. Davis herself notes the contradictions: "I was a creation of the movement in many respects... both in terms of who I am and my own passion for justice but also a creation of the movement that developed around the demand to free me in terms of the iconography that that movement created and that doesn't have very much to do with me."[25]

Queering Radicalism: On Tour with Oakland Panthers and Jean Genet

Although no longer teaching and working on her dissertation, activism still remained important to Angela Davis. Her solidarity with LGBTQ communities broadened her human rights commitments. The June Stonewall riots against police in the West Village saw white, Black, and Latinx LGBTQ people fight police harassment and violence. Davis attributed Newton's statement in support of and alliance with gays and lesbians as the result of her tour with Genet. However, historians center Newton's transformation as stemming from NYC Panther Afeni Shakur (mother of artist and rapper Tupac Shakur, from the Shakur political family). New York City's June 28, 1969, Stonewall riot had no formal leaders as LGBTQ patrons and supporters prevented a police raid, arrests, and beatings of drag queens. On June 28, 1970, only the state of Illinois legalized same-sex acts. According to the marchers for the June Gay Pride, the '69 rebellion and '70 march "made them public, made them a people."

As the interpreter for French playwright and author Jean Genet's fundraising tour for the Black Panthers, Angela Davis witnessed Genet—dressed in a negligee and smoking a cigar—engage the homophobia of the all-Black male contingent led by David Hilliard. Following the report back to the imprisoned Panther cofounder, from prison, Huey Newton had penned and published "A Letter from Huey to the Revolutionary Brothers and Sisters About the Women's Liberation and Gay Liberation Movements" in the August 1970, *The Black Panther Paper*. Again, historians such as Hugh Ryan have noted the role of Panther Afeni Shakur in promoting alliances with the LGBTQ liberation movement. Targeted by COINTELPRO, Afeni Shakur, imprisoned at the Women's House of Detention, worked in solidarity with the Stonewall uprising leadership of Black transwomen/drag queens waging an uprising against police repression.

Jean Genet had first visited the United States in 1968, working as an *Esquire* "journalist." Along with Allen Ginsberg and William S. Burroughs, he covered the August 1968 Democratic National Convention. Machine boss Mayor Richard Daley instructed the Chicago Police Department to riot, with the backup of the US military, against anti-war protesters. Genet famously wrote of the experiences for *Esquire Magazine*: "The Democratic convention is being held right next to the stockyards, and I keep asking myself whether the air is being befouled by the decomposition of Eisenhower or by the decomposition of all America." In case some thought the French leftist intellectual was speaking in hyperbole, America's trustworthy news anchorman Walter Cronkite stated on air: "The Democratic Convention is about to begin in a police state, there doesn't appear to be any other way to describe it." The convention center was surrounded by barbed wire and guarded by military wearing tear gas masks and carrying bayonets and assault rifles.[1]

Jean Genet's reputation preceded his US arrival. According to Angela Davis, "many of us Black Americans" considered Genet an ally because of his anti-racist play, *The Blacks,* which had record-breaking performances in New York's Off-Broadway theaters.[2] Davis met Jean Genet in spring 1970 through the efforts of Black Panther Party leader Connie Matthews. While working for UNESCO in Copenhagen, Matthews had begun to support the Black Panther Party and Black power organizations in Europe. She then worked with the Oakland office, from 1968 to 1971,[3] as Huey P. Newton's personal secretary. Jamaican, schooled in London and Vienna, with a graduate degree in psychology, Matthews knew British and European culture well and was connected to both radical and elite networks. She coordinated international fundraising and speaking tours for the BPP, organizing a European tour for Bobby Seale in 1969. When Matthews asked Genet in 1970 to organize support for the Panthers in Paris, he replied that he preferred to do a US tour with the Panthers. Refused a US visa—likely because of his presence at the 1968 DNC Chicago police riot—Genet entered the United States illegally through Canada. He was never arrested or deported during his tour.

For several months, Genet and Davis met with David Hilliard and a contingent of Panthers. Collectively, they gave speeches and raised funds, attracting the "white intellectual Left over to the Panthers' side by speaking on coastal college campuses."[4] The Panthers needed to raise bail funds for Huey P. Newton, Bobby Seale, and other Panthers tied to the New Haven murder trial.

While Huey P. Newton and Bobby Seale were on trial, David Hilliard was in charge of the Black Panther Party.[5] Hilliard had invited Genet to the United States, hoping that the author could help popularize the cause and defense of the Panthers. During the tour, they held lectures at universities throughout the United States, targeting those which were largely white and elite.[6] Angela Davis was responsible for translating Genet's speeches, while still employed as a UCLA instructor in philosophy. Davis likely also helped to organize a party for Genet at the home of House Unamerican Activities Committee (HUAC) victim Dalton Trumbo, one of the Hollywood Ten; these blacklisted filmmakers had refused to testify before HUAC in Congress and had their film careers destroyed in the process. Despite being censored, Trumbo remained famous; while his uncredited work, screenplays, and two Academy awards were known within the industry to be authorized by him, he could not officially be recognized due to HUAC persecution and being blacklisted. Trumbo's opus included *Exodus, Roman Holiday, Spartacus,* and *Thirty Seconds over Tokyo,* although he was paid less for his work given the forced anonymity. Hollywood stars came to Trumbo's home in order to celebrate Genet and contribute to the fundraiser to pay for the legal defense of imprisoned Black Panthers. Davis would have one of her first exposures—one of many—with cultural or Hollywood celebrities. She recalled of her meeting Genet: "I remember [being] so excited to meet him. I knew his writings, he was a mythical character to me but, face to face with him, I had an almost motherly feeling. He was like a little boy, very kind and laughing a lot."[7]

Genet was a literary attraction in Europe and the United States. Whites flocked to hear him lecture about his plays, creative writing, and personal biography as a gay intellectual—orphaned as a youth, and then raised by French peasants, he became a military defector, petty thief, and prisoner until finding his path as a literary star championed by Sartre. The academic-inclined audiences did not want to hear about anti-racist white solidarity with the Black Panthers. Angela Davis understood that few whites were willing to support an organization that police and government had labeled "terrorist"; most defended white cops when Blacks were accused of killing policemen.

The inability to broaden and diversify the movement—to create a "great multiracial movement"—was frustrating. Although some student activists were interested to learn about the Panthers and the famous Jean Genet's support for them, most progressive whites who attended wanted only to hear from the French writer and to learn more about literature and his musings. Davis noted that they intentionally publicized Genet's lectures without mentioning the Panthers. Large crowds gathered for the famous playwright and author. Davis and the Panthers had a strategy for popularizing the anti-racist freedom struggle, though, with Genet as a willing participant in attracting audiences to be politicized into allies. For Angela Davis, the activists merely had to announce the author's appearance, and audiences would materialize: "We just said he would speak and a huge crowd came to hear him because he was Jean Genet, the great writer. He started saying he would talk about the Black Panthers and made a very moving appeal—a very theoretically advanced one, 'I'd say—about how to fight racism."[8]

Angela Davis recalls the campaign to tour with Genet at white universities to popularize support for Panther political prisoners as a Sisyphean task in cross-class and multiracial solidarity:

> On the campus, teachers and students alike would often demonstrate against the war in Vietnam … there had been a demonstration against Nixon's policy in Vietnam with ten to fifteen thousand persons; nevertheless, two weeks later, when we tried to arrange another demonstration to obtain the release of Bobby Seale, Erika [sic] Huggins and the "Soledad Brothers" (George Jackson, John Clutchette, Fleeta Drumgo) who were in jail, we only managed to gather two hundred persons, most of them Blacks.[9]

According to Davis, Genet had analyzed the role of white allies for decades prior to his invitation to come to the United States to support the BPP: "[He] made some proposals twenty years before that we just started to develop; for instance, the White participation in the struggle against racism." The audience, though, was restless when Panthers spoke. They did not want a session in solidarity strategies; they wanted a lecture on literature. "After a quarter of an hour, many members of the audience started to get upset and to whisper and, suddenly, someone even interrupted Genet asking him to speak, at last, of himself and his work! Genet answered: 'No, I'm not here to talk about literature or my books. I came to defend the Black Panther Party." Davis remembers that the white audience's response to Genet's tutelage for them to learn from the Panthers was "deeply shocking", for "half of the audience progressively left the place." That they refused to learn about the party proved to be "a real lesson" for the activists. Finding the tour educational yet noting "how much work had to be done to generate a real movement against racism," Davis gained insights into academia's aversion to radical politics:

> Many teachers I was familiar with were unable to attend such debates because, in a way, they felt Genet was accusing them of collusion. However, those who did stay were giving us something invaluable. Genet knew how to speak his heart without pity or condescension.[10]

Davis would assert that activists "learned how not to mistake solidarity feelings for feelings of pity among the representatives of the ruling culture." She observed that Genet—the orphan, thief, former prisoner—"already knew how to distinguish" solidarity from pity. Genet had many companions in this regard. White Yale students and community people were engaged in mass protests and clashes over the murder trial of Bobby Seale and Ericka Huggins. The Panthers had to ask white students and communities to stand down so that the National Guard would not come in and enact a massacre that would disproportionately affect Black individuals and communities.[11] For Davis, Genet's May Day Speech at Yale exhibited emotional intelligence that encouraged activism: "[the speech] even goes so far as to advocate the development of a 'tactfulness of the heart' when dealing with Black folks. … [For Genet] Blacks had silently been observing Whites for centuries … [while] Whites did not even realize they were being observed." An older Angela would advocate that "[w]hite folks have got to … [learn from] Black folks … Indians, Chicanos and the whole multicultural U.S. population."[12]

New York Times coverage of the May Day speech and rally included a quote from Charles R. Garry, Newton's attorney and Panther general counsel, in which Garry "described the relationship between Mr. Genet and the Panthers this way: 'He idolizes them. And they think he's outa' sight.'"[13] The Panthers produced the brochure *Here and Now For Bobby Seale: Essays by Jean Genet*. Genet's May Day speech was published later that summer. In a way, the Panthers promoted Genet as much as he promoted them. They formed an alliance—which Angela joined—that impressed and helped to mobilize campuses on the East Coast and prod and push them toward anti-racist consciousness, if not radicalism. Whatever the disappointments might have been, Angela had a front row seat to the mobilizations of thousands who, before, had only gathered in such large numbers for anti-Vietnam War protests and the funerals of beloved Panthers. Scholar Jacqueline Frost notes the magnitude of the final leg of the tour, which took place in a city and at an Ivy League university that was enveloped in rebellions and a Panther murder trial:

> Genet's May Day speech, the most famous of his public events in the States, was pronounced at around 4 p.m. before a crowd of twenty-five thousand who assembled themselves on the grasses of the New Haven Green opposite Yale's Old Campus. It was the first day of demonstrations for the release of the Panthers'

National Chairman, Bobby Seale, jailed in New Haven for his alleged involvement in the murder of Alex Rackley. After reading several lines of his text in French, Genet gave the floor to the Panther's Minister of Information, Elbert Howard, who read the entirety of the speech in English. An improbable duo, Genet must have appeared especially small next to "Big Man" Howard.[14]

Genet described how, on tour, white police ignored him—although he was illegally in the United States—but harassed his Black comrades. His May Day speech discusses the "the difficulties involved in convincing white people of their necessity" to join the anti-racist struggles. According to Genet, "[u]p till now, the Blacks found among white men only two means of expression: brutal domination, or a distant rather contemptuous paternalism. Another way must but found."[15]

The tour in which Davis was instrumental as a translator, interlocutor, and strategist influenced Black Panther co-founder Huey Newton to issue a statement on women's and gay liberation. Scholar Hugh Ryan notes the role of NYC panther Afeni Shakur, who wrote to Newton and organized a strike and rebellion in the Women's House of Detention (where Davis was detained in October 1970) in solidarity with the June 28, 1969, Stonewall rebellion in the West Village. At Stonewall, drag queens such as the transvestite (now, transgender) African American Marsha P. Johnson, fought against police repression and arrests of gay people.[16] Afeni Shakur wrote Newton about imprisoned women's alliances with queer rebels, and how jailed women burned their mattresses, lit cotton balls, and dropped the burning embers out of windows so that those fighting police harassment and arrest in the gay bar could see their solidarity. Newton's August 15, 1970, speech on gay and women's rights as an open statement for solidarity was unprecedented. He noted the rising "strong movements" surrounding women's rights and gay/lesbian movements and the "uncertainty about how to relate to these movements": "Whatever your personal opinions and your insecurities about homosexuality and the various liberation movements among homosexuals and women (and I speak of the homosexuals and women as oppressed groups), we should try to unite with them in a revolutionary fashion." Newton writes that he emphasizes "your insecurities" because he considers the confusion based on psychological and emotional defenses that lead to violence and alienation within revolutionary formations:

> [W]e very well know [that] sometimes our first instinct is to want to hit a homosexual in the mouth, and want a woman to be quiet. We want to hit a homosexual in the mouth because we are afraid that we might be homosexual; and we want to hit the woman or shut her up because we are afraid that she might castrate us, or take the nuts that we might not have to start with.

He speaks from his own vantage point as a Black cisgender male who routinely used violence to settle conflicts. Although Newton was unable to handle his aggressions and addictions, he counsels others to be self-reflective and to constrain their worst impulses that derail or destroy communities and movements:

We must gain security in ourselves and therefore have respect and feelings for all oppressed people. We must not use the racist attitude that the white racists use against our people because they are Black and poor. Many times, the poorest white person is the most racist because he is afraid that he might lose something, or discover something that he does not have. So, you're some kind of a threat to him. This kind of psychology is in operation when we view oppressed people and we are angry with them because of their particular kind of behavior, or their particular kind of deviation from the established norm.

Newton reminds that revolutionary struggle is a process that is always evolving (he does not note that it can regress or devolve) and that Panther text, including the 10-Point program, does not explicitly express homophobia or misogynoir or anti-Black misogyny:

As a matter of fact ... we say that we recognize the women's right to be free. We have not said much about the homosexual at all, but we must relate to the homosexual movement. ... I know through reading, and through my life experience and observations that homosexuals are not given freedom and liberty by anyone in the society. They might be the most oppressed people in the society.[17]

In a 1998 *Out Magazine* interview, Angela Davis would publicly acknowledge that she was a lesbian.

Crucibles

The concept of the "Black Panthers" as a community-based formation evolved out of poor Black sharecroppers in Alabama saving the lives of civil rights activists who were killed by white nationalists and Klansmen for their resistance to Jim Crow. Viola Liuzzo's murder in Alabama included an FBI informant being in the car with the Klansmen who shot up her car. Before her murder, white nationalists beat a white minister, James Reeb, to death in Selma, Alabama for organizing to end segregation. Liuzzo was part of the Selma to Montgomery march. The FBI slandered her as having been promiscuous with the Black teen civil rights organizer, Leroy Moton, that she was driving to the airport; he was injured but survived the shooting. King spoke at the funeral of the mother of five in Detroit. In February, he had spoken at the funeral of Jimmie Lee Jackson in Selma, after an Alabama state trooper shot Jackson in his stomach as he defended his mother from being beaten in a cafe during a civil rights protest.

Particularly after the assassination of King, the Black Panther Party as a concept and possibility in the minds of Black and nonblack youths was perceived and depicted by police as a threat to capitalism and imperialism. It was illegal for the CIA to spy on American citizens, yet it began to integrate in the 1960s when it hired temporary Black contract workers to spy on and infiltrate the Black Panther Party globally in order to "neutralize" the organization.[1]

Stokely Carmichael was instrumental in forming the Black Panther *Political* Party after SNCC faded. SNCC, founded as the Student Nonviolent Coordinating Committee in 1960 at the HBCU Shaw College – the alma mater of Ella Baker – was inspired by, and followed, the sit-ins in Jim Crow college towns. Miss Ella Baker would warn students that the movement was about "more than a hamburger" or purchasing power. Some rural people were so poor that they never shopped for food in stores. The right to eat in "all-white" restaurants and establishments sparked the student nonviolent protest. SNCC aligned with community-based organizations: the 1962 Freedom Rides and the 1963 March on Washington. They fought for voting rights, the 1964 Civil Rights Act and the 1965 Voting Rights Act. In 1966, students increasingly protested against the Vietnam War and the draft.[2] Video footage captures Carmichael chanting "Black Power!" after being jailed and beaten during nonviolent protests for civil rights. His cries for "Black Power!" at a June 1966 Greenwood, Mississippi rally were caught on camera as footage also showed a distraught Rev. King (as discussed in Chapter 5). The Black Panther Party for Self-Defense would be formed in Oakland, CA, by Huey

P. Newton and Bobby Seale four months later in October. Carmichael became SNCC chairman in 1967. The Student Nonviolent Coordinating Committee, SNCC, had recruited students as peaceful "shock troops" against violent white nationalists. Yet SNCC leader H. Rap Brown (Jamil Abdullah al-Amin), a political prisoner in Georgia quipped that "violence is as American as cherry pie" and delivered incendiary speeches for Black agency and freedom. The southern SNCC disbanded in the late 1960s, after evolving through rural "Panther" politics taught by sharecroppers and laborers living in impoverished areas.[3] When James Forman and Carmichael moved the all-Black SNCC to California as the Student *National* Coordinating Committee, Angela Davis joined. Forman, Carmichael, and Brown merged their SNCC with the BPP, which lasted for six months and then fell apart. SNCC had become the most influential organization in the southern movement. Yet the Panthers who were all Black and rejected the creed of "nonviolence" were emerging as the "vanguard" in revolutionary struggle.[4]

Huey Newton and the BPP

Huey Newton and Bobby Seale formed the Black Panther Party for Self-Defense in 1966 and later deployed violence to discourage other organizations from using the name "Black Panther Party." Newton and Seale threatened other organizations which Davis had joined, demanding they stop using the "Black Panther" title. In *An Autobiography* Davis recounts being held briefly at gunpoint during a 1967 Black organizing event, in which an aggressor threatens Davis for being in the Black Panther Political Party, hence not the Black Panther Party (for Self-Defense) founded by Newton and Seale. *An Autobiography*'s later paragraphs identify the man as a police agent or agent provocateur who would be expelled by Newton from the BPP. (When the BPP split into the "Newton vs. Cleaver" feud, fomented by the FBI, Oakland leadership organized death squads against east coast or Harlem Panthers who went underground as revolutionaries; Davis remained a staunch ally of Huey Newton and Elaine Brown, who would support her while she was on trial.)

Oakland Panthers carried guns and the US Constitution; their direct aid to poor communities differentiated them from other "Panthers" who largely formed study groups but rarely delivered resources, protections to working class and poor communities. Asserting First Amendment rights to free speech and freedom of assembly, and Second Amendment rights to armed self-defense, Oakland BPP engaged in cultural theatrics and performative politics: boasting of plans to "off the pig" and eat "bacon." Their profane swagger excited some but alienated others;[5] their antagonistic tactics earned them the disapproval of the Alabama Lowndes County Panthers. Harlem Panther veteran Dhoruba bin Wahad claims in a 2013 *Black Power Media* interview that 67 percent of Black people polled stated that they supported the BPP.

That the Panthers believed in armed self-defense to deter police and white nationalist brutality and murders was not the central issue for the FBI. The Alabama Panthers and Birmingham defense units held the same positions, and practiced the same vigilance, that Angela Davis's father and the neighborhood men had used to protect their families and properties. The federal police forces focused on Panther *politics*, which were anti-capitalist and anti-imperialist. Performing "socialism" as communal care for the poor and working classes, publicly patrolling the police, Panthers were not protecting private property or personal families. They were challenging the state and white nationalism and the social order. (US Agricultural Department would appropriate their breakfast program years after the FBI and police destroyed the party.)

Most rank-and-file Panthers lived communally in "Panther pads." Devoted to the "cause," the cadres of young people had quit jobs; dropped out of high school, colleges, universities; severed relationships with families and partners—all to dedicate their lives to "the people." They were imperfect, abusive to each other and to women from whom they wanted sexual favors. Identifying themselves as both "servants of the people" and the "vanguard," Panthers believed that leadership came from "the people": the folks on the corner, in beauty salons, barbershops, pool halls, and churches. They sold their influential newspaper to white college students and lumpenproletariat. They verbally disrespected and, at times, fought police forces that had inflicted so much suffering onto Black communities. The Panthers also surveilled and monitored Black people engaged in crime against the community, for example, drug dealing and prostitution. Eventually, Oakland leadership itself became a criminal organization.

Angela Davis met Huey Newton in 1967 before he was shot and imprisoned. On October 28, 1967, police stopped Newton's car; inside was at least one other Panther. Shots were fired, Newton was critically injured, and two white police officers were shot; one, John Fry, was deceased. Newton was arrested, and although he denied shooting Fry – asserting that he had passed out when he was shot multiple times and did not return fire—he was convicted of manslaughter and sentenced to prison. Davis attended the July 15, 1968, "Free Huey!" rally at the Oakland Auditorium, organized by Kathleen and Eldridge Cleaver. Some 5,000 people attended to hear key speakers: Stokely Carmichael, H. Rap Brown, Bobby Seale, Eldridge Cleaver, and Newton's attorneys Charles Garry and Fay Stender.

In 1968, when the three SNCC leaders—Stokely Carmichael, James Forman, and H. Rap Brown (Jamil Abdullah al-Amin)—were invited to join the BPP executive committee, Davis was not invited. That was not because of her gender. The Central Committee included Kathleen Cleaver, a brilliant militant and operative who had grown up in an international setting when her father worked in the foreign services; attended elite schools and dropped out to organize. Everyone who fought life-and-death battles in the south had survived in war zones where they developed skills in material and physical struggles. As a graduate student, Davis had academic skills but lacked political experience in dangerous environments. The 1968 Alameda County birthday bash for Huey P. Newton was attempting to save him from the death penalty and release. Carmichael/Ture, Brown, and Forman, upon joining the Panther Central Committee, were given designated offices, including Minister of Defense (Brown) and Minister of Foreign Affairs (Forman). But the merger fell apart due to ideological differences. Feeling threatened by Newton and others, Forman, Brown, and Carmichael/Ture left California.

Not all of the Panthers, particularly Oakland Panthers, offered stable leadership. Channeling the fury of radicals and activists traumatized in wars waged by Jim Crow, cops, and prisons, Eldridge Cleaver was nicknamed "Papa Rage."[6] Two days after the April 4, 1968, assassination of Rev. King, as cities burned across the United States, Eldridge Cleaver led an assault against police with seventeen-year-old Panther Bobby Hutton. Hutton had been the first BPP recruit and was the party treasurer. When Hutton laid down his weapons and stripped off his shirt and walked outside to surrender, police shot and killed him. Two police officers had been wounded in the gun exchange. Beaten, arrested, and released on bail, Cleaver fled to Cuba in November 1968. The Cuban government found his presence problematic; months after his arrival, he traveled to Algeria, other Panthers followed, and the split between Newton and Cleaver became public.

Law and Disorder

In the 1969 *Tinker v. Des Moines* decision, the US Supreme Court extended First Amendment speech rights to public schools. *White* elementary, middle, and high school students who wore Black armbands protesting the war in Vietnam were protected. Later, when fourteen University of Wyoming *Black* football players also wore black armbands to protest racism and the war, they were thrown off the team and their scholarships revoked.

The appearance of equality before the law with new Supreme Court rulings proved to be ephemeral. Vigilantes deployed mob violence against social justice activists. Blacks continued to be maimed or murdered in protests for civil and human rights. Law and policing refused to recognize the rights of Black people. The Panthers sought their own security—and although Second Amendment rights applied to all citizens, that right was not protected for Black people. The right to Black self-defense was prohibited—not de jure in the theory of legal rights, but in the de facto denial of them to racially dishonored populations. The mise-en-scène of miscarriage of the law shaped the performance of political struggles against anti-Blackness and war resistance, punctuated by tragedy.

The year 1969 became one of the most striking displays of police violence against Black Panthers. They lived in Black communities and "served the people." On December 4, 1969, FBI COINTELPRO engineered and executed the assassinations of Chicago Black Panthers Fred Hampton and Mark Clark while they slept (likely drugged by the police informant William O'Neal[7]). A week later, on December 11, 1969, the LAPD executed its first Special Weapons and Tactics (SWAT) militarized mission in an attempt to assassinate Panther leader Elmer "Geronimo" Pratt. Pratt was enrolled on the GI bill in political science at UCLA, a student on the campus where Davis taught philosophy. A decorated Purple Heart veteran from the Vietnam War, Pratt allegedly had also been mentored by the Louisiana-based Deacons for Defense and Justice, founded in 1964 to keep civil rights activists from being murdered; there is scant data on how many lives they saved, yet twenty organizations for the protection of nonviolent protesters formed in the south during the civil rights movement of the 1960s. The year 1969 closed as it had begun, with the largely successful police or police agent malfeasance to incarcerate or murder Black Panthers. Most civic-minded American citizens did not bat an eye.

By the end of 1969, the Black Panthers were serving full free breakfasts (milk, bacon, eggs, grits, and toast) to 20,000 school-aged children in nineteen cities daily. The Black Panther Party had created a social service apparatus parallel to the state: one funded not by large nonprofit corporations, universities, or think tanks seeking sites to educate their affluent students in largesse and advocacy democracy, or study-impoverished Blacks. The breakfast program funds, along with sickle cell anemia health activism, clothing drives, etc., came from local communities, neighborhood churches, and local businesses. The community collectively fed and tended children as Panthers coordinated, cooked, and delivered meals, medical attention, and political education. The Panthers provided inspiration for other community-based groups to organize and offer free breakfast programs and self-defense: e.g., the American Indian Movement, Young Lords, Brown Berets, I Wor Kuen, and Young Patriots—reflecting the "Rainbow" and "All Power to the People!" concepts popularized by Fred Hampton in Chicago BPP. Thus, they became high-profile targets for police forces based on their radicalism, efficacy, and popularity. The BPP political education to youths and their families not only critiqued the history of enslavement, labor exploitation, and lynching; it also introduced community members to contemporary revolutionary struggles. The Panthers read and taught Fanon, Mao, Malcolm, Ho Chi Minh, and Guevara. Ideologically, they were the opposition to the Federal Bureau of Investigation and Central Intelligence Agency, US police forces.

FBI Director J. Edgar Hoover's May 1969 memo to all agents read:

The BCP (Breakfast for Children Program) promotes at least tacit support for the Black Panther Party among naïve individuals and, what is more distressing, it provides the BPP with a ready audience composed of highly impressionable youths. Consequently, the BCP represents the best and most influential activity going for the BPP and, as such, is potentially the greatest threat to efforts by authorities to neutralize the BPP and destroy what it stands for.

"The United Front Against Fascism": Panthers, SDS, and White Mother Country Radicals

Angela Davis and Charlene Mitchell were helping the Panthers organize the United Front Against Fascism, a largely white conference that was to create a coalition to contain police violence against radicals.[8] In their April 27, 1969, "Statement by the Central Committee of the Black Panther Party," this sector of the Panther Party, distinct from the underground formations, was explicit about "peaceful co-existence" within their anti-fascist politics:

We will not try to fight fire with fire because all of the people [know] that fire is best put out with water. Therefore, we will not fight racism with racism. But we will fight racism with solidarity. We will not fight capitalism with capitalism (Black capitalism), but with the implementation of socialism and socialist programs for the people. We will not fight U.S. government imperialism with more imperialism because the peoples of the world and other races, especially in America, must fight imperialism with proletarian internationalism. All peoples and revolutionaries must defend themselves with organized guns and force when attacked by the pig power structure.

From July 17 to 21, 1969, the California Panthers set forth the goals for the United Front against Fascism conference in Oakland, for the five thousand attendees.[9] Organizations represented included the CPUSA, SCLC, SDS, Young Lords, and Young Patriots. The multiracial, predominately white gathering analyzed fascism from the perspective of conditions of Blacks in the United States. Yet they used theories from across the globe, including analyses from the Soviet Union.

For Angela Davis, the United States had potential through multiracial voter registration, political inclusion, an organized working class, and strategic reforms, and so was not (proto-)fascist, even as it was important to organize against the emergence of fascism. CPSU foreign policy of forging the "popular front" and "peaceful coexistence" adhered to Soviet mandates and thus shaped Davis's political perspectives, which—given her academic training in philosophy with German Jewish intellectuals, survivors of the Nazi Holocaust—localized fascism as a twentieth-century European phenomenon. According to Spencer, Panthers in 1969 "began to use fascism as a theoretical framework to critique US political economy"; they defined fascism as "the power of finance capital" within "banks, trusts and monopolies" consolidated in "the human property of FINANCE CAPITAL—the avaricious businessman, the demagogic politician, and the racist pig cop."[10]

From the conference, the National Committees to Combat Fascism (NCCF) became "a multiracial nationwide network, to organize for community control of the police." It also became heavily infiltrated by the FBI. NCCF chapters fostered multiracial activism—"a new avenue of involvement in Black Power politics"; however, given its infiltration, the Panthers downsized party membership. By the time the party closed new membership, in April 1970 some eighteen to twenty-two NCCF chapters had been formed, according to the FBI.[11]

"Fascism" in Panther lives stemmed primarily from police threats and in-fighting fostered by police manipulation pitting Black factions and organizations against each other. (The 2021 *Who Killed Malcolm X* Netflix documentary illustrates the tactics used.) *An Autobiography* describes death threats against Davis as mostly coming from white vigilantes and the mentally ill. These threats appeared after her name and image publicized in the press identified her as a communist, anti-war, and Black liberation leader. Those threats could have been orchestrated by police. However, the party she joined in 1968, and would lead until her departure in 1991, was exempt from terrorist police tactics. The CPUSA was not on a neutralization list despite past state persecution; it posed no real threat to US hegemony. An organization of 2000 largely Black working-class youths, on the other hand, was considered an existential threat to empire.

The BPP could not protect their own members from assassination, as the predawn December 4, 1969, Chicago execution of Fred Hampton and Mark Clark proved to the world. The same could not be said for the CPUSA.[12] The United Front against Fascism appeared to be a noble attempt to create a security perimeter to save lives and foster solidarity. But the dying was done disproportionately by Panthers, and the Oakland Panthers had rhetoric, but not a plan; they were not willing to confront armed police or prison guards (unfortunately, that was not clearly relayed to Jonathan Jackson). The ineptitude of a conference that Mitchell and Davis attempted to co-organize with the Oakland BPP indicated the limits of solidarity with, and political imagination within, Panther leadership.

According to *The US Antifascism Reader,* edited by Bill V. Mullen and Christopher Viles,[13] Panthers resurrected CPUSA analyses (those ideas were also tied to the Communist Party of China) from the Popular Front era. Panthers also watered down their "revolutionary" language to create a broad coalition (typical of the popular front). New Left whites found the Oakland Panthers concepts "reformist." The Panthers drifting into the underground and those still working above ground in Harlem and elsewhere were not reformists. Eldridge and Kathleen Cleaver were exiled out of the country, and Newton was imprisoned; so, at the conference, Panther leadership resided in Bobby Seale and David Hilliard. They told the conference that the party was moving away from self-defense or paramilitary tactics—decentralized policing in Black communities which would control police while whites control police in their communities. This would have been difficult in integrating communities, and would allow white nationalist policing to construct a legal perimeter around white neighborhoods. Using the language of "the Man" that Davis rejected, the SDS writers critiqued Seale and Hillard by pointing to *police violence as context*: "Wherever they have organized, the Panthers have been hit hard by the Man: beaten, framed, jailed, held under huge ransoms, murdered." The article states that Panthers understood the necessity of working with whites against American racism and imperialism because they sought a *multiracial* "United Front against Fascism" through an Oakland organizing conference.

Eighty percent of the delegates at the conference – which began on July 19, 1969 – were white. It was, by basic metrics, poorly organized. Seale's opening speech condemned "ideological quibbling." Workshops or discussions were scarce, so collective input/participation was limited; scheduled speeches had unimaginative titles: "Students and Education vs. Fascism," "Workers vs. Fascism," "Doctors vs. Fascism," "Religion vs. Fascism." Men dominated the microphones and were physically aggressive with dissenters. Seale's speech used conventional, polite, "appropriate" language for police. Jettisoning "pigs," he referred to them as "policemen" and "cops". He also sought to link with liberalism and thus capitalism, calling the organizers "progressive forces" rather than "socialists" or "revolutionaries." There was no mention of self-defense or armed struggle. According to Seale, "to defeat fascism," progressive forces had to organize "community control over decentralized police forces."[14] (This language from 1969 is actually the dominant language of academic abolition today.)

By December, the public would recognize that "federal police" (FBI) and "local police"—no matter what you called them—were assassinating Panthers. Fred Hampton and Mark Clark were murdered on December 4, 1969, in Chicago. A week later, on December 11, the LAPD—with assistance from federal police—first deployed SWAT and shot up the Los Angeles Panthers Headquarters in an attempt to assassinate Elmer "Geronimo" Pratt, a purple heart-decorated Vietnam veteran. Police forces failed in their attempt to kill Pratt in the same manner that CPD and FBI killed Hampton and Clark the week prior. The SDS knew what the Oakland Panthers knew: the police were engaged in a neutralization program.

Students for a Democratic Society (SDS) were well-educated and well-organized. They were also militant. They had shed the pacifist civil rights era, as they had witnessed not only Blacks, but also whites murdered by white nationalists and police forces wielding violence against protesters and maroons with immunity. As had the most radical Panthers, they went underground and waged antagonistic war resistance against the state, self-identifying as militant "Mother Country Radicals" by 1969.[15]

They went to the same funerals that SNCC and Panthers attended. With waning patience for "antiquated" CPUSA narratives and "irrelevant" Panther imaginings of liberalization, their news coverage rejected their (grand)parents' communist party and Oakland's turn toward liberalism. The SDS paper dismisses CPUSA historian Herbert Aptheker's speech, "Historical Aspects of the Rising Tide of Fascism Today, at the United Front Against Fascism" conference:

> Aptheker droned on for an hour, irritating many who were worried that Communist Party influence might swing the political line of the United Front to the right. Furthermore, the women's panel, inserted into the program at the last minute and postponed until last on the evening's schedule, was being threatened with extinction by Aptheker's verbosity. As angry women began to stand up in protest, they were forcibly seated by Panther monitors, trying to prevent disruptions.[16]

Roberta Alexander would have been among the women protesters.

SDS reporters note that LA Panther Masai, as a moderator, called protesting women "pigs and provocateurs." Ironically, language not suitable for the police—who were beating, caging, and killing Panthers—was deemed appropriate for women seeking their rights within liberation movement. Despite the verbal abuse and shoving—physical assault—women caucused throughout the conference, and Panther Roberta Alexander gave the keynote on the women's panel addressing male chauvinism within the movement.

The Progressive Labor – Worker Student Alliance (PL-WSA) members were ejected and physically attacked for leafletting against the conference and the Panthers. Most delegates left on Sunday, and did not hear Seale present the United Front program to decentralize police forces with community control—through the right to hire police officers from the community via referendum campaigns, organized by Committees to Combat Fascism, that "initiate petition campaigns to educate and involve people around the police-control demand." Seale told the audience that they would meet in three or four months; his optimism did not reflect reality, as alienated participants were dissatisfied and drifting off. Seale offered upbeat reassurances for the next conference: "we'll be back here 15,000 strong, and we're not going to miss a single worker in the country."[17] The SDS report was more realistic: "Many of the delegates left the conference confused and disappointed" as radicals believed "the Panthers' UF tactic was attempting to enlist liberal support at the expense of revolutionary militancy."[18] SDS stated that it supported self-determination and community control in colonized Black and brown communities, but "not in white communities where racism and white supremacy must be fought." Its post-conference National Interim Committee of SDS statement supported "the demand for community control of decentralized police in the black and brown communities" and pledged to assist in "building support for that demand in white neighborhoods."[19] Then SDS rejected the second part of the proposal using vernacular Oakland Panther leadership had dropped: "we cannot support the demand for 'white community' control and we therefore urge local and regional SDS organizations to work within the National Committees to Combat Fascism to change the wording of the petition … [and] urge that SDS chapters undertake campaigns around pig repression."[20] No future conferences took place; the *Old Mole* asserts that the Panthers' National Committees to Combat Fascism were "essentially branches of the Black Panther Party."

Context for Tragedy and the Making of the (In)Famous Angela Davis

The SDS's analysis on the limitations of Oakland BPP's plan to curb police terror was insightful. However, what neither SDS nor Oakland Panthers could have anticipated was a Black revolutionary teenager—attending a white private high school during the day and serving as Angela Davis's bodyguard after school and on weekends—changing the era of Black revolutionary struggle. He was not a member of the Black Panther Party, but he was on the Soledad Brothers Defense Committee with his mother Georgia Bea Jackson, his sister Penny, and his brother George: George Jackson, the theorist and militarist who, in 1961, had been sentenced to one year to life (an indeterminate sentence) for driving a car used in an armed robbery by teens who stole $71 from a gas station.

George Jackson wrote to Angela Davis from prison. His attorney, Fay Stender, facilitated her entry into co-leading the Soledad Brothers Defense Committee (SBDC). Three Black men were accused, without evidence, of killing a white prison guard and so were facing the death penalty. Davis agreed to assist in their human rights campaign for a fair legal defense. Her standing as a UCLA philosophy professor provided credibility for the SBDC.

Angela Davis met the mother, Georgia Bea Jackson, and her children, who worked on the SBCD to save the lives of George Jackson, Fleeta Drumgo, and John Clutchette. They were accused of the January 16, 1970, killing of prison guard John Vincent Mill following the January 13, 1970, murders of Black prisoners W. L. Nolen, Cleveland Edwards, and Alvin Miller. The three were shot from the guard tower by Vietnam marksman Opie G. Miller, a white guard. All of the slain were leading or supporting a legal petition against the prison administration for permitting prison guards to poison the food of Black prisoners with broken glass and human feces. The prison opened up the yard that had been closed for one year after Aryan nation members attacked and murdered Black prisoners with shanks or homemade knives. Davis was asked to co-lead the Soledad Brothers Defense Committee, around the time that the UC Regents attempted to fire her; the faculty planned to rehire her with independent funds, but her fugitive flight after the August 7, 1970, Marin County Courthouse raid ended that possibility. The de facto head of the SBDF committee was the charismatic leader George Jackson—author of *Soledad Brother* and posthumously *Blood in My Eye*—and his Jewish attorney, Stender – who engineered the *Soledad Brother* book, editing it to make Jackson seem more acceptable to liberals and convincing Jean Genet to write the foreword.

Jackson, the BPP Field Marshall, recruited Panthers from within prison to provide protections to the Black communities once the formerly incarcerated were released. Through the SBDC Angela Davis met the Black men who would change her life. Georgia Bea Jackson's youngest son, Jonathan, became one of her bodyguards. Mrs. Jackson's older son, George, became Davis's lover and "husband." Davis worked to defend Drumgo, Clutchette, and Jackson, who were Black prison abolitionists and militarist revolutionaries. The United Front Against Fascism had offered no strategy for how to stop the violence and death within prisons.

On August 7, 1970, four Black men, ages 17–31, brought Davis into a dangerous spotlight and temporarily transformed her public identity from that of a courageous *communist* academic into a Black revolutionary combatant. High school junior Jonathan Peter Jackson was known by some to be Angela Davis's bodyguard but he was not a BPP member. On August 7, seventeen-year-old Jonathan Jackson used weapons registered in Davis's name in an attempt to free his older brother through a hostage exchange at the Marin County Courthouse. When Jackson and three Black imprisoned men—John McClain, William Christmas, and Ruchell Magee—attempted to flee with the hostages in the van, prison guards in the parking lot fired into the van. Three men died: two Black prisoners and one white judge Harold Haley; the ADA was shot and left partially paralyzed. Prison guards and possibly the assistant district attorney fired shots into or inside the van. Ruchell Magee, assistant District Attorney Gary Thomas, and a white female stenographer/juror were wounded.[21] Jon, a junior in high school, also had Davis's book satchel with several of her books on theory and guerilla warfare, with her name inscribed on the front pages.

In 1970, the California Court of Appeals reversed Huey Newton's involuntary manslaughter conviction in the death of police officer John Frey. Newton was freed on August 5, 1970—two days before Jonathan Jackson led the Marin County Courthouse raid. Newton's eulogy at Jon's funeral described the young man as having committed "revolutionary suicide." Davis was not at the funeral and sent no messages as a fugitive in the CPUSA (not Panther) underground. George Jackson had reportedly told his younger brother that the white prison guards routinely stated that they would soon murder him, as the prison guards believed that George Jackson and the Soledad Brothers—acquitted at trial—had killed John Vincent Mill (the white guard thrown over a tier railing after Opie Miller had shot and killed Black prisoners Nolen, Edwards, and Miller). On trial temporarily with Ruchell Magee as her co-defendant, Davis emerged as an international persona, a persecuted and heroic figure. Ruchell Magee fired no gun and was acquitted in 1973 of all major charges—conspiracy, aggravated kidnapping, murder—by a jury whose verdicts were not entered into the legal record by the presiding judge. The public rarely associates the eighty-four-year-old, released from prison in July 2023, with the context within which Angela Davis became a global figure for the left.

Conclusion

Context and Democracy

Democratic Futures

Angela Davis began to campaign for Democratic Party presidential candidates in 2008 for Barack Obama. Major party candidates were committed to capitalism and US foreign policies detrimental to racialized and exploited nations, as they sought to continue the colonial policies of the past. She began with campaigns for Obama in 2008 and 2012, followed by Hillary Clinton in 2016 and then Joe Biden (and his VP Kamala Harris) in 2020. In 2012, when Davis was campaigning for Obama's second term, Vermont Senator Bernie Sanders, an independent, considered primarying Obama to push him "left" into supporting comprehensive, free medical care, full employment with living wages, and de-escalation of international wars. In a 2014 University of VA interview with SNCC leader Julian Bond, Davis asserted that Barack Obama was a reflection of the "Black Radical Tradition" (the Obama administration allowed the FBI to double the bounty on former Black Panther Assata Shakur; Davis wrote the foreword for the most recent edition of the influential memoir *Assata*). As would be the case with all US presidents, Obama refused to provide clemency for political prisoners; Black Panthers and others, such as Leonard Peltier, remained imprisoned for decades – including those framed by prosecutors or police as part of COINTELPRO. There is little to no public record of Davis publicly critiquing Obama from 2008 to 2016 for failing to review the cases of, or provide clemency for (pardon was unlikely), her former Black comrades or war resisters. Disproportionately, those released during democratic presidencies have been white or Puerto Rican; Black political prisoners served longer sentences. FBI grievances at their losses from violence they initiated (e.g., on the Pine Ridge reservation) led them to block the release of Peltier during the Clinton Administration.

In 2016, when Vermont Independent Senator Sanders primaried Clinton in order to make her embrace more progressive politics, Clinton eventually endorsed parts of his platform: the $15/hour minimum wage; advocacy for reigning in the billionaire class (although Bill and Hillary Clinton, through the Clinton Foundation, were billionaires). Losing the 2016 primary, Sanders endorsed Clinton at the DNC in Philadelphia. As Sanders's opposition—he was the opponent to Clinton/Obama—Davis leveraged the "Black radical" persona. Championing centrist liberalism cemented the alliance between elite radicals and liberals; the convergence elevated radical liberalism by infusing it with the transformative agency of prior decades, yet without the risk-taking rebellions that accompanied 1950s–1970s Black militants. In 2016, Obama's designated successor, Hillary Clinton, led the centrist wing of the Democratic Party. Independent Sanders primaried her as a "democratic socialist" seeking FDR/New Deal concessions from corporate capitalism and the bureaucratic state: universal health care, livable wages, incarceration of predatory police. Clinton surrogates included feminist Gloria Steinem, a Democratic Party insider, who remained an ally of Davis's while maintaining friendships with ultra-conservatives and "war criminals" (in the words of Christopher Hitchens) such as Secretary of State Henry Kissinger, who engineered the carpet bombing in Cambodia during the devastating war in Vietnam, in violation of UN human rights protocols. From heading the Free Angela Davis! fundraising campaign committee to publishing Davis in *Ms. Magazine*, Steinem agreed that the only viable presidential candidates were anti-communists, anti-socialists, and anti-DSA (Democratic Socialists of America, which had leveraged Sanders's campaign). In 2016, Secretary of State Madeleine Albright castigated young women as "traitors" of feminism for leaning left to support Sanders, declaring that there would be a "special place in hell" for them. Steinem shamed socialist, communist, and anti-capitalist women as female groupies seeking potential boyfriends among DSA "Bernie Bros" (the "Bros" were largely a fabrication of pro-capitalist media). Angela Davis took another approach. Leveraging past associations with Black militants, she admonished those who sought to go "left" of the centrist DNC through "virtue signaling"; i.e., the mark of the Black revolutionary became a sign of virtue and, when appended to liberalism, could shield those who wielded it (e.g., politically diverse sectors publicly embrace Martin Luther King, Jr. without mentioning his rejection of capitalism, imperialism and war – stances which made him a revolutionary and a martyr). To a 2016 University of Texas at Austin Black Studies conference's predominantly Black audience, Davis chastised leftists who refused to vote for the centrist-liberal Democratic Party for being "narcissistic."

Return to Brandeis University

Eight years after enrolling in Brandeis, four years after graduating ('65), the UCSD doctoral student hired as a UCLA philosophy professor read 1969 newspaper accounts of seventy Black students, joined by several hundred white students, occupying Brandeis buildings to demand a Black Studies program. When she returned to her alma mater Brandeis in 2020, Davis shared that during the Takeover of Ford Hall she had "felt a little nostalgic about not being there" to offer support, but that she had a good reason not to fly back to the East coast: she was preoccupied with "having been fired" from her first job for being a member of the CPUSA.[1]

In 2020, Angela Davis's alma mater Brandeis University celebrated the fiftieth anniversary of its Black studies program with an interview between two Black women scholars, Davis ('65) and her interlocutor Julieanna Richardson ('76). The highlight of the gathering was Davis's keynote interview. Alumni from over the decades attended and expressed their emotional appreciations for Angela Davis and her contributions as a role model and human and civil rights advocate over five decades. Davis reflected on her statements during the 2016 campaign:

> I was trying to encourage people who were saying that they didn't want to have anything to do with electoral politics because they are revolutionaries, and they wanted to change the world. And I was really attacked in social media when I suggested that people should vote for Hillary Clinton.[2] I said something like "I'm not so narcissistic as to say that I can't bring myself to vote for Hillary Clinton." I mean, that was a practical decision ... we have to find the right candidate.[3]

In her interview, Davis does not mention that her statements at UT Austin foreclosed the possibility of a third-party candidate. Nor does she mention that she herself ran twice on a CPUSA third-party ticket with Gus Hall as his VP candidate. In 1980, Davis and Hall directed progressive voters away from centrist-liberal democrat and incumbent Jimmy Carter. Her archnemesis, Ronald Reagan, as president, would escalate global warfare through attacks on progressives and socialist countries in the "Third World."[4] He would also illegally engage in the Iran-Contra affair, funding the counterrevolutionary Contras in Nicaragua.

Elliot Abrams, working for the Reagan Administration, noted (to the *NYT*) that the Contras had a tendency of kidnapping fourteen-year-old girls as they created anti-socialist death squads throughout Central America, in order to maintain US hegemony. Reagan's military operative, Oliver North, would serve prison time.

In 1988, the CPUSA candidates ran again against both of the major party candidates. This time, US presidential elections pitted the liberal Massachusetts governor Michael Dukakis against George H. W. Bush. Bush had served as Reagan's vice president and as the head of the CIA. Whatever votes Davis-Hall drew could have gone to Dukakis, who suffered through the "Willie Horton" campaign ad by Lee Atwater (and championed by George W. Bush, the future president who worked on his dad's campaign). Using the violent assault on a white family by an incarcerated Black man on work furlough in Massachusetts, whose governor was the democratic presidential candidate, the Bush campaign promoted campaign ads with images of incarcerated (Black) males being furloughed or paroled only to rape (white) women. Bush handily defeated Dukakis.

Gus Hall and Angela Davis saw themselves not as "narcissists," but as principled opponents to capitalism when they ran on third-party CPUSA tickets against Reagan/Carter and Bush/Dukakis. The CPUSA would have been publicly incensed if "narcissist" was applied to communists who had organized, and suffered, for years to advance human rights and the principles of socialist or communist societies. The same happened within sectors of (Black) radicals who refused the "lesser of two evils" mandate within a duopoly democracy when, in 2016, progressives were told to vote for "Her." At UT Austin's conference, Davis didn't name Clinton; she reprised Clinton's campaign slogan – "I'm with HER" – using double negatives when she stated that she was not so narcissistic as to *not* vote for Her. For Davis, pragmatic politics—which the CPUSA would support—defined the DNC. For much of the progressive public, Davis defined Black radicalism. That logically meant that Davis defined Black radicalism as pragmatic politics enmeshed within the DNC. The DNC, though, was hierarchical and facing criticisms because of its cronyism and "Super Delegates" (which included former presidents selecting presidential nominees, withholding funds from disfavored left-leaning candidates such as Sanders). Davis's charge—an off-the-cuff response during Q/A—of "narcissism" was dismissive and an ad hominem attack on the personal character of potential (non)voters or third-party voters. In a rational argument, one would have to provide reasons for voting for the Democratic Party, i.e., assert that DNC centrism/liberalism provides better health and labor protections than FDR's depression-era safety net (unemployment insurance, works projects to upgrade roads and preserve the cultural history of the nation, welfare assistance). The fact is that the DNC is pro-monopoly capitalist and unlike FDR, who wanted to reign in the banks and capital because of the inequities of extreme wealth. Although not FDR-aligned, the Democratic Party does try to protect programs inherited from the New Deal.

Davis's context for delivering voters to the DNC was not based on facts but on fear or "lesser of two evils" hauntings. The Panthers, though confronted their fears and devised a new politics that would follow their liberation agenda. It is strongly possible that if the state had not been so brutishly violent in its opposition to the BPP and the care Panthers provided to people of all races/ethnicities, US society would have more adequate food assistance programs.[5] Police raids of Panther headquarters and houses included officers pouring out milk, setting fire to cereal boxes and, of course, capturing and imprisoning—when not killing—Panthers. With no need for logic, given the high registers of fear within a violent and racially-driven democracy, Davis did not need facts, just psychology. When the persona of Angela Davis became the context, the specificity, complexity, and contradictions of movements or parties (BPP, CPUSA) that had made her (in)famous became secondary. Her iconic status became primary; thus personal narrative overwhelmed political legacies as collective phenomena and legacy of Black militancy. Her memories became "historical objectivity"; her memoir became authoritative text, although many of the individuals that made resistance struggles possible, and the ensuing accommodations probable, are not fully explained or discussed.

The capacity to diagnose reflects the capability to define. The Mayo Clinic defines "narcissism" as a personality trait or disorder in which the overconfident and insecure—with an inflated sense of self-importance—seek attention and admiration while lacking awareness of other people's feelings; "communal narcissists" promote their good deeds. Davis's pejorative use of the term "narcissistic" signifies her capacity to point out, in public, the moral failings that can only be corrected by voting and fidelity to the DNC despite its fidelity to capitalism, militarism, and empire.

The pragmatic mandate to vote for the DNC Obama-Clinton alliance as the "lesser of two evils" was later reprised with the mandate for a Harris-Biden alliance. (Joe Biden, Obama's vice president for two terms, won the democratic primary, outpolling Sanders and Harris.) During a summer 2019 democratic debate, then California Senator Harris (now Vice President) sharply critiqued Biden for opposing desegregation school bussing when he was a Delaware Senator. She noted that in California, she was bussed to schools as a young child, and alluded to Biden's racial bias. The Harris campaign soon printed T-shirts with the phrase "That Little Girl Was Me."[6]

Although more progressive than President Bill Clinton (and Obama), former First Lady and Senator Hillary Clinton promoted the rise of mass incarceration (2 million people are imprisoned in the United States), devastating working class and poor communities. As Secretary of State in the Obama Administration, she championed war hawk policies that led to assassinations and regional destabilizations in the "Third World," including Obama's AFRICOM drone strikes destabilizing Africa.[7] As centrist democrats, Obama and Clinton opposed Sanders's FDR liberalism (universal health care;[8] $15 minimum wage; rigorous taxation of billionaires or the 1 percent). Sanders was influenced by Erica Garner—the NYPD killed her father, Eric Garner, in a chokehold in July 2014 on a Staten Island street. Garner's "It's Not Over" 2016 presidential campaign ad for Sanders includes a clip in which Sanders states that any police officer who kills an unarmed civilian must be prosecuted.[9]

Campaigning for the Democratic Party, Davis added measured critiques about Black politicians Harris and Obama:[10]

> I don't know whether she [Harris] will be the right candidate or not. I'm very cognizant of her history [as a prosecutor] and I don't know whether she is willing to make some efforts to revise her positioning … but politicians are usually opportunistic. … Even someone like Obama, so many people deposited all of their dreams in Barack Obama's lap and what did he do? He didn't even really push to dismantle Guantanamo.[11]

Obama's failure to deliver transformative policies included more than *not* closing Guantanamo. He expanded AFRICOM, funding for predatory police, militarism (destabilized Libya), and enacted draconian laws against government whistleblowers informing the public of corruption. He also expanded deportations and failed to fight for climate protections. He did not mandate the FBI to vigorously pursue and prosecute white nationalists and white militias engaged in terrorism. During the Obama administration, the FBI—which had hunted and killed Black radicals throughout the movement era—doubled the bounty on Assata Shakur, using a Black FBI agent to make the public announcement.

Performance and visuals root within memory more easily than analyses. In 2015, at a memorial for the slain, on international television, President Obama sang *Amazing Grace* and cried at the Emanuel African Methodist Episcopal Church in Charleston, South Carolina, devastated by a white nationalist shooting and killing Black Christians at a prayer circle; when he had entered the church door, parishioners had invited Dylann Roof to join them in prayer. Obama's and other Presidents' records of steering the FBI—to vigorously pursue white supremacist terrorists—remain dismal.

Davis chastises Black citizenry/radicals as naive because they "deposited all of their dreams in Obama's lap." The dismissive register aligns with the descriptor "narcissism" and includes radical (Black) (non)voters who are constantly organizing against police violence and poverty. Davis's lectures steer people to stay disciplined to the party line—in the past, it was set by state-supported or -tolerated communists; today the party line is linked to liberals or radical liberals who view or present themselves as subversive.

Asserting that voters "have to be really sophisticated participants in the arena of electoral politics," she refers only to the Democratic Party as the alternative to a reactionary Trump administration: "[W]e have to make sure that everybody votes. And this will be the first time that many former prisoners will be able to vote."[12] Davis's observation of the rights of *some* of the incarcerated to vote skims over racially driven voter suppression emergent since the 2013 *Shelby County v. Holder*[13] Supreme Court ruling eviscerated the 1965 Voting Rights Act, which was passed after the white nationalist violence in Selma, Alabama. President Lyndon Johnson introduced the legislation eight days after "Bloody Selma;" photos of US white nationalists brutalizing nonviolent Black-led multiracial marchers, and the murder of Viola Liuzzo, made international news. King, Stokely Carmichael, and SNCC marched towards Selma, Alabama, to ensure voting rights for all US citizens. Johnson handed a signing pen to King after the civil rights law was enacted. That appears to be a clear victory, and without context and theory, it would be one. Critical race theorist founder Derrick Bell notes two pillars of US law: "interest convergence" and the "permanence of racism." In the former, the civil rights interests of Blacks advance only when they coincide with the interests of (elite) whites; in the latter, anti-Black violence is systemic and a structural feature of the democracy. Revolutionaries in the movement era understood the structural design that, at times, was overlooked due to police violence. The 1965 Voting Rights Act (VRA) passed not just because Black citizens should have the right to vote; it passed because white politicians (liberal and reactionary) agreed to interest convergence. After VRA protected Black voters who overwhelmingly voted for democratic presidents—Kennedy, Johnson, Carter, Clinton, Obama—voting rights were drastically curtailed by the *Shelby County v. Holder* ruling,[14] in which conservatives argued that a half-century after the passage of the VRA, voting rights protections were unnecessary for "nonwhites." They focused on Sections 4 and 5 of the Voting Rights Act. The conservative leaning Supreme Court 5-4 ruling determined that the voting rights of Blacks, Mexican Americans, Latinx, Native Americans, and Asian Americans no longer needed to be protected by the federal government or the Department of Justice (Eric Holder was attorney general in 2013).

The Democratic Party constitutes, for some, the only "rational choice" amidst rising protofascist politics and the possible reelection of Trump. Davis reflects that the trajectory of history moves forward. Her analytical framework could not anticipate the January 6, 2021 Capitol siege. The Trump administration and its supporters sought to cling to power with claims of a "rigged" presidential election after Trump's losing in the electoral college. The Proud Boys planned to assassinate white, ultra-conservative republican Vice President Mike Pence before he certified the transfer of power to the Biden administration (Speaker of the House democrat Nancy Pelosi was also targeted in attempts to stop the peaceful transition of power).[15]

Davis's writings indicate that she was loyal to Oakland Panther leadership with whom she socialized and at times organized. After decades of leadership in the CPUSA, Davis increasingly focused on prison abolition and feminism, which she views as transformative for liberation. She asserts in her Brandeis talk that the "most recognizable concept associated with feminism" is intersectionality, and that throughout the world, people are familiar with the concept. Because of that familiarity, Davis claims progressive victories: "the work that we've done has made a difference and we have to stop assuming that we're always the underdogs in this … it's true that there can be these problems with the women's March … but there are always people who don't understand the direction of history."

Context is essential for understanding the "direction of history." Alliances also shape comprehension. The historical trajectory is inherently progressive, according to Davis, who suggests that it is only ignorance that allows capitalists, white nationalists, and imperialists to miscomprehend history's inevitable destination for US democracy. Davis uses President Donald Trump as her example, describing him as an aberration from, rather than a concentrated compression of, US white nationalism and imperialism:

> [W]e're dealing with a person who resides at 1600 Pennsylvania Avenue right now who does not recognize the extent to which what he is doing and what he has done militates against the movement of history. And I really think that 50 years from now when people look back, those four years are going to be recognized as a deviation, as a minor deviation.

The Trump administration accelerated racism, capitalism, misogyny, and imperialism; his rhetorical violence denigrated African nations as "sh**hole countries"; his police violence disappeared hundreds to thousands of babies, toddlers, and young children from desperate parents trapped in Immigration Customs Enforcement (ICE) camps. Trump policies promoted the crimes detailed in *We Charge Genocide*. Before and after Trump, Obama and Biden enforced similar policies and acts of disposability without using white nationalist speech. Context provides a lens for analysis so that memories can be compared with the data of material struggles that inform objective history. The "Black Radical Tradition," of which Davis asserts that Barack Obama is a part, is an international Black tradition; she does not mention, as noted above, that Obama increased drone strikes that killed civilian noncombatants, destabilizing Africa;[16] eroded protections for government whistleblowers;[17] failed to enact adequate environmental protections;[18] and refused to mandate oversight laws for billionaire corporations and banks.[19]

During the "peaceful coexistence" of the Cold War, the bloodiest wars were fought in Third World colonies. Davis met the war resisters of the US "internal colonies" in the 1960s and 1970s. She attended the funerals of some of the slain revolutionaries. Her assurances that the future of democracy inevitably will be advancing toward progress and enlightenment are met by the interviewer's brief response: "We hope."[20] Democratic Party politics become the context for Davis sequencing subversive revolutionaries into sensible liberals who must jettison principles, although they acquire few, if any, transactional deliverables from the state and corporations. Feminism is the future, although Davis does not differentiate between different feminist formations:

> First of all, let me say that it is so important that so many women are now in congress, running for office. I'm not too happy about Kamala Harris's history… as a DA and an attorney general in California. Oftentimes, in death penalty struggles and a whole number of campaigns, she was on the other side … this next election is going to be pivotal… we had the wrong candidate the last time around. … I know people many people would be upset when they hear me say this: I voted for Hillary

Clinton and I urged people to vote for Hillary Clinton, but I don't think she was the right candidate. When it comes to electoral politics, we have to make decisions that aren't always principled decisions.

Davis sees the gains garnered through abolition, feminism, and voting as reassurances to future generations that democracy will become more stable, less riddled by inequalities and predatory police/militaries. Her speeches and public memories recontextualize and/or ignore historical radical and revolutionary confrontations. The pragmatic principled opposition to the state—her parents' communist party and your parents' Democratic Party—reconstructs the old revolutionary into the new revolutionary. Yet providing care through marronage and nonviolent war resistance, SNCC's "second civil war" was based in Black-led multiracial cadres who understood that voting advocacy could get you—a conscientious high schooler, university student, sharecropper—imprisoned or killed in direct or indirect advocacy for rights. Following Robert Williams and Lowndes County Panthers, Panthers in cities outside of the south proclaimed their rights to practice armed self-defense; later the BLA underground forces directly countered CIA/FBI/police assassinations. Davis has little public discourse about the warfare that "internal colonies" of the United States fought as war resisters. Around the globe, Panthers such as Chicago Chairman Fred Hampton inspired multiracial resistance formations, which the United States would neutralize through violence or imprisonment; inside the United States, anti-colonial struggles were waged by the Young Lords, American Indian Movement (AIM), White Patriots, I Wor Kuen, and Brown Berets. In a 2023 conversation with this author, Harlem Panther veteran K. Kim Holder observed that one phrase from that era is "never heard anymore": "*All* power to the people!"

In the 1950s and 1960s, amidst the second civil war to resist Black dishonor and death, a fifteen-year-old left her Southern Black family and culture to enroll in a private progressive Manhattan high school. There, she was introduced to and mesmerized by *The Communist Manifesto*. That Black girl memorized Marx and Engels's terse instruction that our endeavor is not to interpret the world but to change it. A decade later, she would converse and align with global iconic revolutionaries and rebel intellectuals. Over five decades of civil and human rights advocacy—working within the contexts of elite academia, Hollywood, celebrity movement culture, publishing, media platforms, politicians—Angela Davis would both interpret and change the world.

Notes

Preface

1   AP, "Black on Death Row in Alabama Granted Retrial" (*The New York Times*, July 3, 1981, https://www.nytimes.com/1981/07/03/us/black-on-death-row-in-alabama-granted-retrial.html).

2   Commission on Integrated Long term Strategy, Discriminate Deterrence (Department of Defense, Washington D.C., 1988).

3   See "World Conference to Review and Appraise the Achievements of the United Nations Decade for Women" (United Nations, Nairobi, July 1985, https://www.un.org/en/conferences/women/nairobi1985).

4   Jacques R. Pauwels, "The Hitler-Stalin Pact of August 23, 1939: Myth and Reality" (*Counterpunch*, August 26, 2019, https://docs.google.com/document/d/1Kq-ZHlHnLzl4OSEq-WRxQwbui-Dw3cS3/edit).

5   Mao Tse-tung, "On the International United Front against Fascism," in *Works of Mao Tse-tung* (Foreign Languages Press Peking, 1967; First Edition 1965; Second Printing 1967, Vol. III, p. 29, http://www.marx2mao.com/Mao/UFAF41.html).

6   Mao Tse-tung, "On the International United Front against Fascism."

7   China and the Soviet Union formed a communist bloc during the Cold War in attempts to survive First World capitalism/imperialism and militarism. Mandating rapid industrialization from agrarian-based economies led to famines in which the West offered no humanitarian aid. China and the USSR developed the concept of peaceful coexistence so that communist states could coexist with capitalist states. It was in direct contrast with theories of mutual antagonistic aggression that supposed the two regimes could not live in peace. The Soviets had a different view of the concept. The People's Republic of China and the USSR engaged in a Sino-Soviet split in the 1950s and 1960s.

8   See Esha Krishnaswamy, host, "The Man, the Myth & Legend of Joseph Stalin with Grover Furr," (*Historic.ly*, April 17, 2020, https://www.historicly.net/p/the-man-the-myth-and-legend-of-joseph#details).

9   Communist-aligned or -linked organizations with which Davis worked closely included the above-mentioned Che-Lumumba Club, 1968 to 1970; the National United Committee to Free Angela Davis (NUCFAD), 1970 to 1972; and the National Alliance against Racist and Political Repression (NAARPR), 1973 to 1986. Organizations such as the Women for Racial and Economic Equality (WREE), founded in 1974, the National Council of Black Lawyers (NCBL), and NAARPR were all interfaced by their connections or allegiance to the CUPSA and, by extension, CPSU.

10 Vivian Gornick, "What Endures of the Romance of American Communism" (*Verso* Blog post, April 28, 2020, https://www.versobooks.com/blogs/4688-what-endures-of-the-romance-of-american-communism).

11 Gornick, "What Endures of the Romance of American Communism." According to Gornick, "unyielding devotion to Soviet Russia" allowed "American Communists to

deceive themselves repeatedly" from the 1930s to 1950s as the Soviet Union became more totalitarian in Eastern Europe, and Communist Party Soviet Union (CPSU) oppression became more obscured.

12   Harvey Klehr and John Earl Haynes, "The Challenges of Espionage and Counterespionage Operations: Running SOLO: FBI's Case of Morris and Jack Childs, 1952–77" (Center for the Study of Intelligence 66, no. 1, March 2022, https://www.cia.gov/resources/csi/studies-in-intelligence/volume-66-no-1-march-2022/running-solo-fbis-case-of-morris-and-jack-childs-1952-77/).

13   See "The CIA's 'Family Jewels.'"

14   Joy James, ed., *Imprisoned Intellectuals: America's Political Prisoners Write on Life, Liberation, and Rebellion* (Lanham: Rowman & Littlefield, 2003), xiii.

15   Lorenzo Komboa Ervin, *Anarchism and the Black Revolution: The Definitive Edition* (London: Pluto Press, 2021).

Introduction

1   Common, "The 100 Most Influential People of 2020: Angela Davis" (*Time Magazine*, September 23, 2020, https://time.com/collection/100-most-influential-people-2020/5888290/angela-davis/). Other influencers included Dr. Anthony Fauci, Director of National Institute of Allergy and Infectious Diseases; Supreme Court Justice John Roberts; entertainer Megan Thee Stallion; and athlete Naomi Osaka.

2   Professor Davis, through politics and personal identity, symbolized the antithesis of the then sitting President.

3   "How to Watch the January 6th Hearings" (*PBS*, June 8, 2022, https://www.pbs.org/newshour/politics/how-to-watch-the-jan-6-hearings).

4   National Women's Hall of Fame, "National Women's Hall of Fame Virtual Induction 2020" (YouTube, December 10, 2020, https://www.youtube.com/watch?v=K4HK6VAYV9w).

5   Joy James & Kalonji Changa, "Slave Rebel or Citizen," *Inquest, May 2 2023*, https://inquest.org/slave-rebel-or-citizen/.

6   Angela Davis, *Angela Davis: An Autobiography*, 3rd edn (1974; repr., Chicago: Haymarket Books, 2021), xiv.

7   Mitchell family, "Charlene Mitchell, Leader of the Campaign to Free Angela Davis" (*Portside: Material of Interest to People on the Left*, December 18, 2022, https://portside.org/2022-12-18/charlene-mitchell-leader-campaign-free-angela-davis); Clay Risen, "Charlene Mitchell, 92, Dies; First Black Woman to Run for President" (*Portside: Material of Interest to People on the Left*, December 23, 2022, https://portside.org/2022-12-23/charlene-mitchell-92-dies-first-black-woman-run-president?utm_source=portside-general&utm_medium=email).

8   See Joy James, *Transcending the Talented Tenth* (New York: Routledge, 1997). The book contains a photograph of Charlene Mitchell, Angela Davis, and Nelson Mandela; the same photo is featured in the family statement on Mitchell's passing. In 1999, *Shadowboxing: Representations of Black Feminist Politics* was published to critique the rise of Black managerial feminism and "neoradicalism" in contemporary progressive politics. See Joy James, *Shadowboxing: Representations of Black Feminist Politics* (New York: Palgrave Macmillan, 1999). See W.E.B. DuBois, *The Souls of Black Folk* (Las Vegas: Millennium Publications, 2014 [1903]).

Chapter 1

1   Elected governor of Alabama in 1962 after campaigning on a racist platform, George Wallace gave a January 1963 inaugural speech in which he shouted, "Segregation now! Segregation tomorrow! Segregation forever!" By June, the Kennedy Administration, having federalized the National Guard, forced him to admit Black students into the University of Alabama.

2   NAACP original founding members included W. E. B. DuBois and the anti-lynching crusader Ida B. Wells, who was marginalized from the NAACP by white philanthropist Mary White Ovington and "talented tenth" scions DuBois and Mary Church Terrill due to her community-based militancy and political radicalism in resistance to anti-Black terrorism.

3   See W. E. B. DuBois, *Black Reconstruction in America: 1860–1880* (New York: Free Press, 1998).

4   Stalin's 1939 Nazi-Soviet Pact led to the dissolution of coalitions formed in the Popular Front. See Mark Naison, *Communists in Harlem during the Depression* (Chicago: University of Illinois Press, 1983); Mark Solomon, *The Cry Was Unity: Communists and African Americans, 1917–1936* (Jackson: University of Mississippi Press, 1998); Salter Daren, "National Negro Congress (1935–1940s)" (*The Black Past: Remembered and Reclaimed*, http://www.Blackpast.org/aah/national-negro-congress).

5   Johnetta Williams, "The Southern Negro Youth Congress (1937–1949)" (*The Black Past: Remembered and Reclaimed*, http://www.blackpast.org/aah/southern-negro-youth-congress-1937-1949).

6   The first international Negro Youth Conference was held in Chicago in 1933. James E. Jackson, Jr., a pharmacy graduate student at Howard, co-planned with other young activists the first SNYC. Henry Winston joined the Young Communist League (YCL) in 1930. The February 13–14, 1937 SNYC inaugural conference was held in Richmond, VA, on the anniversary of Frederick Douglass's birthday; 500 delegates from 13 states participated. The advisory committee included Mary McLeod Bethune and Charles Johnson. With James Jackson's leadership, SNYC organized five thousand members of the Tobacco Stemmers and Laborers Industrial Union with a sit-down strike against the British American Tobacco Company that led to up to a 33 percent increase in wages for workers. SNYC moved its headquarters to Birmingham in 1949, Davis's home town until that same year. See Robin D. G. Kelley, *Hammer and Hoe: Alabama Communists during the Great Depression* (Chapel Hill: The University of North Carolina Press, 2015), 201.

7   Kelley, *Hammer and Hoe*, 197.

8   "The Ways Boston Helped Shape the Life of Martin Luther King, Jr. (GRS'55, Hon.'59)" (*Bostonia: Boston University's Alumni Magazine*).

9   Ninety minutes from Birmingham, Montgomery became the city famous for Rev. Martin Luther King, Jr., and Dexter Avenue Baptist Church—the home of King's mentor Vernon Jones, who antagonized white racists and the Black bourgeoisie with church marquees advertising provocative sermon titles: "It Is Safe to Murder Negroes in Montgomery" and "When the Rapist Is White." Rev. Jones's critique of capitalism and consumerism incensed the Black middle-class years before King alienated the Black bourgeoisie by denouncing imperialism and capitalism. Despite Montgomery being the site of King's church and the Montgomery bus boycott, it was Birmingham that became the epicenter of the civil rights war fought in Alabama.

10   Angela Davis, "Barry Callaghan Interviews Angela Davis in California Prison, 1970,"
      interview by Barry Callaghan (YouTube, August 27, 2010, 4:49, https://www.youtube.
      com/watch?v=8sLIDscuc-M).

11   Davis, "Barry Callaghan Interviews Angela Davis."

12   Viola Liuzzo was a Unitarian from Detroit who marched across Edmund Pettus
      Bridge on Bloody Sunday. Alabama whites justified her murder by charging that she
      had sex with Black men. See "Viola Liuzzo" (National Park Service, last modified July
      13, 2022, www.nps.gov/semo/learn/historyculture/viola-liuzzo.htm).

13   In 1966, civil rights attorney Pauli Murray, who was later co-founder of the National
      Organization for Women (NOW) with Gloria Steinem, wrote the brief for *White
      v. Crook*, which enabled Blacks to vote and join jury rolls. Gardenia White was lead
      plaintiff. See Susan Mallon Ross, "Dialogic Rhetoric: Dorothy Kenyon and Pauli
      Murray's Rhetorical Moves in White v. Crook" (*International Journal of the Diversity*
      6, no. 5 [2007]).

14   Minnie Bruce Pratt, "Lowndes County, Ala.: Roots of Revolution" (*Workers' World/
      Mundo Obrero: Workers and Oppressed Peoples of the World Unite*, April 14, 2016,
      https://www.workers.org/2016/04/14/lowndes-county-ala-roots-of-revolution/). The
      author writes that a "revolutionary movement was born in 1966 in the tiny Alabama
      community of White Hall, Lowndes County—population 831."

15   Charlie Cobb, "From Stokely Carmichael to Kwame Ture" (*Africa News Service*,
      October 21, 2000, http://www.hartford-hwp.com/archives/45a/473.html).

16   Pratt, "Lowndes County."

17   Robin Kelley, "What a Band of 20th-Century Alabama Communists Can Teach Black
      Lives Matter and the Offspring of Occupy," interview by Sarah Jaffe (*The Nation*,
      August 31, 2015, https://www.thenation.com/article/archive/what-a-band-of-20th-
      century-alabama-communists-can-teach-black-lives-matter-and-the-offspring-of-
      occupy/).

18   Marty Roney, "Alabama's Black Belt Helped Form Black Panther Party" (*USA Today*,
      February 1, 2016, https://www.usatoday.com/story/news/nation-now/2016/02/01/
      lowndes-county-black-panther-party-alabama/78943998/).

Chapter 2

1   Max Gordon, reply to Harvey Kehr, "The Communist Party: An Exchange" (*The
      New York Review*, April 14, 1983, https://www.nybooks.com/articles/1983/04/14/the-
      communist-party-an-exchange/).

2   See Nadra Kareem Nittle, "What Is Colorism—Skin Tone Discrimination in
      America" (*Humanities Issues*, March 18, 2017); Shankar Vedantam, *The Hidden Brain*
      (New York: Random House, 2010); Jill Viglione, Lance Hannon, and Robert DeFina,
      "The Impact of Light Skin on Prison Time for Black Female Offenders" (*The Social
      Science Journal* 48, no. 1 [2011]: 250–8). The Montgomery Bus Boycott promoted
      images of valued prisoners based on class, gender, and colorism that reflected the
      white middle classes: "[Rosa] Parks's color and class status made her—rather than
      the younger, poorer, and darker-skinned women (Mary Louise Smith, Aurelia
      Browder, Susan McDonald, and Claudette Colvin) who had been arrested earlier in
      1955 for refusing to give up their seats—the icon around whom the Montgomery Bus
      Boycott was built." Dan Berger, *Captive Nation: Black Prison Organizing in the Civil
      Rights Era* (Chapel Hill: The University of North Carolina Press, 2014), 32.

3   Angela Davis, interview by Julian Bond, *Explorations in Black Leadership* (the
    Institute for Public History at the University of Virginia; co-directors Phyllis Leffler
    and Julian Bond) (Charlottesville, April 15, 2009, https://blackleadership.virginia.
    edu/transcript/davis-angela; video available through C-SPAN at https://www.c-span.
    org/video/?328898-1/angela-davis-oral-history-interview).
4   Kelley, *Hammer and Hoe,* 203.
5   When Sallye Davis joined the SNYC in the 1930s, she met an interracial Chicago
    couple, the Black communist leader Poindexter and his white socialite wife Jane
    Hunzinger. When Angela Davis became an FBI fugitive in 1970 for ten weeks, the
    CPUSA organized her underground. Unlike the BLA (Black Liberation Army) she
    was not targeted by COINTELPRO or police for elimination. Nor did she issue
    communiques of resistance to "the people." Davis's underground was quiet, apolitical,
    and shaped by monied resources, legal connections, and powerful white allies.
    Hunzinger financed her son David Poindexter's and Angela Davis's flight from the FBI
    for two months in 1970. The Poindexter-Hunzinger family was one of several influential
    families that knew Sallye Davis. Hunzinger and a CPUSA network, shaped by Charlene
    Mitchell, safely shepherded her son, David, and Sallye Davis's daughter to trial and
    through acquittals, providing legal talent from Harvard- or Yale-trained attorneys.
6   Decades later, Angela Davis became close friends with their sons, particularly Robert
    Meeropol, and served on the advisory board of the Rosenberg Fund for Children,
    which provides grants to aid children of targeted activists.
7   See Davis, Angela, *Angela Davis: An Autobiography* (New York: Random House, 1974).
8   Davis, *Angela Davis,* 100–1.
9   Davis, *Angela Davis.*
10 Davis, *Angela Davis.*
11 Davis, *Angela Davis.*
12 Davis, *Angela Davis,* 95.
13 Judith Herman, *Trauma and Recovery* (New York: Basic Books, 1997).
14 Davis, *Angela Davis,* 80.
15 Davis, *Angela Davis,* 78–9.
16 Mamie Till Mobley held an open casket funeral in Chicago for the world to witness
    the violence of white supremacy inflicted on her child; historians would later assert
    that those images of the mutilated child, and photographs of pilgrimage mourners
    numbering up to ten thousand, sparked the civil rights movement. The open
    casket turned a funeral into a forum denouncing the United States; photographs
    were shown to the world. King's, Birmingham leaders', and parents' prohibition of
    politicizing assassinations, and scholars' erasure of ensuing riots provide a decorum
    for grief that severs Black suffering from Black rebellion.
17 See Hannah Arendt, "Reflections on Little Rock" (*Dissent* 6, no. 1 [winter 1959]);
    Arendt, "A Reply to Critics" (*Dissent* 6, no. 2 [spring 1959]). Ralph Ellison wrote
    in 1961: "I believe that one of the important clues to the meaning of that [Negro]
    experience lies in the idea, the ideal of sacrifice. Hannah Arendt's failure to grasp the
    importance of this ideal among Southern Negroes caused her to fly way off into left
    field in her—Reflections on Little Rock, in which she charged Negro parents with
    exploiting their children during the struggle to integrate the schools. But she has
    absolutely no conception of what goes on in the minds of Negro parents when they
    send their kids through those lines of hostile people." After her engagement with
    Ellison's critique, Arendt rethought her position. See Ralph Ellison, *Who Speaks for the
    Negro?,* edited by Robert Penn Warren (New York: Random House, 1965), 343.

18 Davis, *Angela Davis.*

19 Davis, *Angela Davis.*

20 *The Black Power Mixtape 1967–1975: A Documentary in 9 Chapters* (directed by Göran Hugo Olsson; produced by Annika Rogell; co-produced by Joslyn Barnes, Danny Glover/Louverture Films, Axel Arnö/Sveriges Television. New York, NY [Orland Park, IL]: Sundance Selects; MPI Media Group [distributor], 2011).

21 Fania Davis, "Restorative Justice: A Justice That Heals" (*Naropa Magazine*, April 2017, http://magazine.naropa.edu/2017-fall/features/restorative-justice.php).

22 F. Davis, "Restorative Justice."

23 Davis, "Barry Callaghan Interviews Angela Davis."

24 On September 9, 1957, President Dwight D. Eisenhower signed the first twentieth-century Civil Rights Act.

25 *The Black Power Mixtape.*

26 Federal Bureau of Investigation, *FBI Memoranda and Reports on Ku Klux Klan May 14 1961*, United States Federal Bureau of Investigation, Alabama Freedom Riders Investigation Files, Collection Number 111, Archives Department (1961), Birmingham Public Library: Digital Collections.

27 Davis, interview by Bond.

28 Sallye Davis's activism spanned from the 1930s to the 1972 acquittal of her daughter, then expanded into 1973 to 1986, through leadership for the National Alliance Against Racist and Political Repression. Sallye Davis attended 1970s USSR and European peace conferences, and 1982 meetings with the Cuban-aligned Marxist Prime Minister of Grenada Maurice Bishop, who was assassinated in an October 19, 1983 coup—the United States, with a Caribbean coalition, invaded Grenada on October 25, defeating Grenadian and Cuban defenses.

29 Angela Davis with Julieanna Richardson, "Keynote by Angela Davis '65 with Julieanna Richardson '76, H'16" (Transcript, Brandeis University, February 8, 2019, https://www.brandeis.edu/now/2019/february/video-transcripts/angela-davis.html).

30 Davis with Richardson, "Keynote by Angela Davis '65 with Julieanna Richardson '76, H'16."

Chapter 3

1 "*Brown v. Board of Education*" (National Archives, https://www.archives.gov/education/lessons/brown-v-board#background).

2 Freeman A. Hrabowski, III, interview by Julian Bond, *Explorations in Black Leadership* (the Institute for Public History at the University of Virginia; co-directors Phyllis Leffler and Julian Bond) (Baltimore, September 19, 2008. https://blackleadership.virginia.edu/transcript/hrabowski-freeman; video available at https://www.youtube.com/watch?v=sGBZpjoW55A&list=PLg8a9eHK4nDV9jlp0rl0QnKDa_KCNsvaE&index=19).

3 The "Little Rock Nine" were Minnijean Brown, Terrance Roberts, Elizabeth Eckford, Ernest Green, Thelma Mothershed, Melba Patillo, Gloria Ray, Jefferson Thomas, and Carlotta Walls. On September 4, 1957, a white mob and the Arkansas National Guard deployed by Governor Orval Faubus prevented the students from entering Central High School in Little Rock, Arkansas. NAACP attorneys, including future Supreme Court justice Thurgood Marshall, obtained a federal district court injunction

banning the state from blocking Black students from entering the high school. International press covered the spectacle of white mobs screaming at dignified Black children seeking an education and enforcement of federal law. Rev. King's September 9 telegram to President Eisenhower cautioned that "the process of integration [would be set] back fifty years" if Eisenhower did not intervene; or the president and federal government could "back up the longings and aspirations of millions of peoples of good will and make law and order a reality." Eisenhower ordered the deployment of the Army 101st Airborne Division to Arkansas to protect the students for the rest of the school year and for the Arkansas National Guard to assist. After Faubus closed Little Rock high schools that summer, the Supreme Court ruled in December 1959 that the Arkansas school board had to reopen and desegregate all city schools. See "Little Rock School Desegregation" (The Martin Luther King, Jr., Research and Education Institute, Stanford University, https://kinginstitute.stanford.edu/encyclopedia/little-rock-school-desegregation).

4   For analyses of *Brown v. Board of Education*'s impact on and significance to Black communities see Frank Kirkland, "The Questionable Legacy of *Brown v. Board of Education*: Du Bois' Iconoclastic Critique" (*Logos Journal*, 2015); and Richard Rothstein, "*Brown v. Board* at 60" (*Economic Policy Institute*, April 17, 2014).

5   Davis, interview by Bond.

6   AFSC adapted the template of the postbellum nineteenth-century white philanthropists in the American Baptist Home Missionary Society, whose president Henry Morehouse coined the term "talented tenth" (popularized in W. E. B. DuBois 1903 *Souls of Black Folk*); white progressive elites created a conduit for their Black counterparts in the south to enroll their children in northern prep schools. The colleges and universities in the AFSC system were also ones that had enrolled Black elites in the previous century: DuBois went to Harvard; Mary Church Terrill and Anna Julia Cooper to Oberlin.

7   "Keynote by Angela Davis '65 with Julieanna Richardson '76, H'16."

8   "Keynote by Angela Davis '65 with Julieanna Richardson '76, H'16."

9   "Keynote by Angela Davis '65 with Julieanna Richardson '76, H'16."

10   Gloria Steinem and Leonard Bebchick, *A Review of Negro Segregation in the United States* (Independent Research Service for Information on the Vienna Youth Festival, 1959), 39.

11   Steinem and Bebchick, *A Review of Negro Segregation*, 48.

12   For an analysis of how the CIA duped NSA students, see Karen M. Paget, *Patriotic Betrayal: The Inside Story of the CIA's Secret Campaign to Enroll American Students in the Crusade Against Communism* (New Haven: Yale University Press, 2015).

13   "March 4, 1877" (Zinn Education Project, https://www.zinnedproject.org/news/tdih/hayes-takes-office).

14   See V. I. Lenin, "Cultural-National Autonomy" (*Critical Remarks on the National Question*, 1913, https://www.marxists.org/archive/lenin/works/1913/crnq/index.htm).

15   See Steinem and Bebchick, *A Review of Negro Segregation*.

16   Steinem would become an icon in her own right, as a feminist and human rights advocate. See Karen Karbo, "How Gloria Steinem Became the 'World's Most Famous Feminist'" (*National Geographic*, May 3, 2021, https://www.nationalgeographic.com/culture/article/how-gloria-steinem-became-worlds-most-famous-feminist).

17   With the Trump administration packing the Supreme Court with arch-conservative justices, and the evisceration of voting rights protections amid the rise of "states'

190

Notes

rights," the 1959 assertion seems implausible: "Now with every step forward the Negro takes, the whole nation moves ahead, for along with segregation many other, more subtle forms of discrimination are being cast out. Every law against segregation, every Supreme Court decision, every municipal ordinance and Interstate Commerce Commission ruling, not only speaks of outlawing prejudice against Negroes but bans discrimination against any person on the ground of race, color, religion, or ethnic origin." Steinem and Bebchick, *A Review of Negro Segregation*, 38.

18   Steinem and Bebchick, *A Review of Negro Segregation*, 47.

19   To select participating Black southern student families and white northern host families, AFSC staff worked with a volunteer committee to "recruit and match families, raise funds, create reading lists, organize all-student gatherings, and address such practical matters as insurance and scheduling trips home twice a year." See "AFSC Southern Student Program" (*American Friends Service Committee*, February 8, 2012, https://www.afsc.org/story/afsc-southern-student-program).

20   See Davis, *Angela Davis*.

21   See Evelyn Brooks Higginbotham, *Righteous Discontent: The Women's Movement in the Black Baptist Church 1880-1920* (Cambridge: Harvard University Press, 1994).

22   See Matthew J. Mancini, *One Dies, Get Another: Convict Leasing in the American South, 1866–1928* (Columbia: University of South Carolina Press, 1996).

23   See Brooks Higginbotham, *Righteous Discontent*.

24   See: W. E. B. DuBois, "Abolition and Communism" (1951; W.E.B. DuBois Papers [MS 312], Special Collections and University Archives, University of Massachusetts Amherst Libraries). A dozen years older than Angela Davis, Martin King differed from Davis's communist family with his highly religious family. Davis's secular family still sent their children to Black Birmingham churches. King became more radical. He engaged in direct action and lived among impoverished Blacks. He and Coretta Scott King moved into a Chicago tenement and stayed for months to comprehend the struggles of poor urban Blacks and dialogue with gang members who sought his counsel. The sentimentality and memory levied upon King after his death was attached to Davis during her lifetime.

25   In contrast to an older Davis—whose politics would lead her to gradually support liberal-centrist candidates—Martin Luther King, Jr. became more alienated from the Democratic Party as he organized with impoverished Black workers and laborers coming together in 1968 for the "Poor People's Campaign," as a direct confrontation with capitalism. Davis, as a teen, had dismissed the Black petit bourgeoisie as inherently counterproductive. Davis and other CPUSA communists became more aligned with the Democratic Party in 2008 during the Obama presidential campaign.

26   Persecuted in the 1940s and 1950s by HUAC and the McCarthy eras, DuBois found that only radical Black trade unionists and activists publicly supported him and hence relinquished any advocacy for the talented tenth.

27   *Du Bois* gave his greetings to the 1963 March on Washington from Ghana, and died shortly after those greetings were delivered on the Washington Mall—from which Rev. Martin Luther King, Jr. delivered the "I Have a Dream" oratory, which was inspired and influenced by a Black woman pastor's sermon the night before and Mahalia Jackson telling Rev. King on stage to tell the masses about "the dream."

28   A New Yorker, Weiss directed her father's Rubin foundation to support progressive causes. She described herself as a "non-communist" and an ally of Angela Davis, the CPUSA's Committee to Defend the Panther 21, as well as Gloria Steinem. Weiss later

helped to create the Gloria Steinem Chair in Media Studies at Rutgers University, first held by Naomi Klein in 2016.

29 See CORA WEISS ORAL HISTORY PROJECT, The Reminiscences of Cora Weiss (Columbia Center for Oral History, Columbia University, 2014).

30 See CORA WEISS ORAL HISTORY PROJECT.

31 See CORA WEISS ORAL HISTORY PROJECT.

32 Forced out of Kenya, the British looted their former colony and mandated that civil servants return to England with the transfer of power to the Africans. Schooling the next generation of leaders was imperiled. In 1961, Mboya flew to Hyannisport to meet Kennedy and requested $100,000 for scholarships and transportation. Kennedy provided the $100,000 from his family foundation, which paid for three charter planes that came in 1961. Wangari Maathai, who was awarded the 2004 Nobel Peace Prize, was on one of the planes funded by Kennedy, as was President Obama's father, Barack Obama, Sr. Mboya, who was himself educated in London, and one of the founders of the Republic of Kenya, was assassinated in 1969. See CORA WEISS ORAL HISTORY PROJECT.

33 Davis, *Angela Davis*, 82–3.

34 See Archie Mafege, "Black Nationalists and White Liberals: Strange Bedfellows" (*Africa Review*, 1993).

35 Ella Baker, "Bigger than a Hamburger" (History Is a Weapon, June 1960, http://www.historyisaweapon.com/defcon1/bakerbigger.html); Ella Baker, "Bigger Than A Hamburger" (Abolition Notes, https://abolitionnotes.org/ella-baker/hamburger).

36 Hrabowski, interview by Bond.

37 See Hrabowski, interview by Bond.

38 Freeman Hrabowski describes schooling in Massachusetts as "great intellectually but … socially very difficult." Davis and Hrabowski might have been in Massachusetts at the same time: she in Waltham, he in Springfield. See Hrabowski, interview by Bond.

39 See Hrabowski, interview by Bond.

40 Hrabowski, interview by Bond.

41 Hrabowski, interview by Bond.

42 Hrabowski, interview by Bond.

43 Hrabowski, interview by Bond. Ralph Ellison would challenge Hannah Arendt's racism in her article in *Commentary*. See: Josh Jones, "How the CIA Funded & Supported Literary Magazines Worldwide While Waging Cultural War Against Communism" (*Open Culture*, October 27, 2017, https://www.openculture.com/2017/10/how-the-cia-funded-supported-literary-magazines-worldwide-while-waging-cultural-war-against-communism.html).

44 Davis, interview by Bond.

45 Hrabowski, interview by Bond.

46 Four years younger than Angela Davis, Rice was Fania Davis's age and shared with Fania Davis the same childhood girlfriends. Her father, Rev. Rice, was Hrabowski's high school counselor. See Hrabowski, interview by Bond.

47 Condoleezza Rice informed the public that George Bush was not racist despite the debacle of "relief" efforts and "shoot-to-kill" edicts for Blacks abandoned after the New Orleans levees broke following Hurricane Katrina in 2005. Asserting that Barack Obama's legacy is part of the "Black radical tradition," Angela Davis deflected analyses of policies from the Obama Administration which promoted

corporate capitalism and globalism, and diminished civil rights through TPP protocols, drone strikes, AFRICOM, and mass deportations of migrants.

48 Hrabowski, interview by Bond.

Chapter 4

1   Davis, *Angela Davis*.
2   Davis, *Angela Davis*, 93–4.
3   Davis, *Angela Davis*.
4   Davis, interview by Bond.
5   E. Franklin Frazier, *Black Bourgeoisie* (New York: Free Press Paperbacks, 1997 [1957]).
6   Davis, *Angela Davis*, 103–4.
7   Melish's belief in Davis's innocence is reflected in his being a trustee of the Angela Davis Legal Defense Fund and his name listed as such on their pamphlet. See Rev. Ralph Abernathy, John J. Abt, Paul E. Miller, with Introduction by Ossie Davis, "On Trial: Angela Davis or America?" published by the Angela Davis Legal Defense Fund. Other trustees include CPUSA Che-Lumumba Club leader Franklin Alexander, Angela Davis's mother Sallye B. Davis, and William Patterson, the leading figure of the (CPUSA) Civil Rights Congress and co-author of the 1951 document for the UN, *We Charge Genocide*. The Defense Fund lists Ossie Davis as chairman and Marvel Cooke as secretary. Melish appears to be the only white member of the Defense Fund. https://digitallibrary.tulane.edu/islandora/object/tulane%3A21146/datastream/PDF/view.
8   See "Rev. W. Howard Melish, 76, Dies; Ousted at Parish in McCarthy Era" (*New York Times*, June 16, 1986).
9   Angela Davis, interview by Terry Rockefeller and Louis Massiah, *Eyes on the Prize II: America at the Racial Crossroads 1965 to 1985* (produced by Blackside, Inc.; executive producer, Henry Hampton; series writer, Steve Fayer; Washington University Libraries Film and Media Archive, Henry Hampton Collection; May 24, 1989, edited for clarity).
10 On September 20, 1958, Izola Curry, a Black woman with paranoid schizophrenia, stabbed Rev. King at a Harlem book signing event. Assisted by multiracial NYPD and doctors, King was rushed into surgery at Harlem Hospital.
11 Davis, *Angela Davis*, 109–10.
12 Davis, *Angela Davis*.
13 Karl Marx and Friedrich Engels, *The Communist Manifesto*, edited by Gareth Stedman Jones (London: Penguin Books, 2002), 258.
14 The Publisher's Note to the 2022 Black Classic Press edition of Rosemari Mealy's *Fidel and Malcolm X: Memories of a Meeting* states that in September 1960, "Muslim leader Malcolm X welcomed Cuban President Fidel Castro" to a midnight meeting at Harlem's Black-owned Hotel Theresa. The Cuban delegation was to attend the UN General Assembly, but their Manhattan hotel had refused to honor their booking and house them. Upon learning of their plight, Malcolm invited the Cuban emissaries to "come uptown" to Harlem, where he claimed they would be greeted "with open arms." Harlemites by the thousands gave Castro a rousing, even magnificent welcome, keeping a round-the-clock vigil—in the pouring rain—outside his balcony window. To Harlem's masses, unfazed by the red-baiting and anti-Cuba

hysteria of the day, Castro was that "bearded revolutionary" who had "told White America to go to hell." Three Black journalists and a photographer from "the Negro press" observed the two leaders speak candidly through interpreters "about self-determination and national liberation." Rosemari Mealy, *Fidel and Malcolm X: Memories of a Meeting* (E-book: Black Classic Press, 2022).

15 Rebecca Onion, "When Malcolm X Met Fidel Castro," *Slate*, August 30, 2016, https://slate.com/news-and-politics/2016/08/the-history-behind-colin-kaepernicks-malcolm-x-meets-fidel-castro-t-shirt.html.

16 United Nationals General Assembly, Fifteenth Session, Official Records, 872nd Plenary Meeting, September 26, 1960. https://documents-dds-ny.un.org/doc/UNDOC/GEN/NL6/007/00/PDF/NL600700.pdf?OpenElement

Chapter 5

1   Hrabowski, interview by Bond.
2   Hrabowski, interview by Bond. Hrabowski has been president of the University of Maryland, Baltimore County since 1992.
3   Hrabowski, interview by Bond.
4   Davis writes: "I was very agitated during those days. Something was happening which could change our lives. But I was too young, so I was told (I was twelve), and a girl at that, to be exposed to the billy clubs and violence of the police." Davis, *Angela Davis*, 102.
5   Hrabowski reflects if, as a parent, he would let his child engage in activism if it meant "trusting your child to be in that jailhouse with white people who don't like you anyway … certainly don't like your children." Hrabowski, interview by Bond.
6   Hrabowski, interview by Bond.
7   Hrabowski, interview by Bond.
8   Hrabowski, interview by Bond.
9   Hrabowski, interview by Bond.
10 Hrabowski, interview by Bond.
11 Hrabowski, interview by Bond.
12 Joy James, "The Womb of Western Theory," *Carceral Notebooks*, 2016; and James, *New Bones Abolition: Captive Maternal Agency and the (After)Life of Erica Garner* (Brooklyn: Common Notions Press, 2023).
13 Hrabowski, interview by Bond.
14 Hrabowski, interview by Bond.
15 In 2008, presidential candidate Barack Obama received the DNC nomination at the Mile High Stadium in Denver, Colorado. Obama's speech invoked the civil rights historic March on Washington in August 1963; Obama referenced the anniversary by speaking of the "preacher"—he did not name Reverend King—and his historic speech. Apparently, the future president of the United States, and the first Black person to be elected POTUS, was not aware that King's speech was delivered on the anniversary of a Black child's torture and murder in Mississippi; hence, so too was Obama's victory linked to Jim Crow terror.
16 For a critique of the March on Washington as a betrayal of poor and working-class Blacks, and an illustration of the government silencing James Baldwin, see Herb Boyd, *Baldwin's Harlem: A Biography of James Baldwin* (New York: Atria Books, 2008).

17   In his 1963 "Letter from a Birmingham Jail," King argued that activists who break
     unjust laws should willingly go to jail. Black radicals countered that the police violated
     constitutional rights and did not go to jail, so why should Black militants who
     were seeking freedom? The concepts and practices of self-defense and community
     defense would be argued throughout the movement. Southern Black pastors such
     as King were persuaded to relinquish weapons used to protect their families. The
     Black Panthers and young radicals outside the south asserted Second Amendment
     rights. Angela Davis's ability to bridge or "transcend" the debate shaped her appeal to
     liberals; she argued the rights her parents enacted: the right to personal and family
     and property protections. She did not argue the rights that Jonathan Jackson and
     Ruchell Magee posited, an echo of Malcolm X: freedom "by any means necessary."
18   See Mao Tse-tung, "Statement Supporting the American Negroes in Their Just
     Struggle against Racial Discrimination by U.S. Imperialism" (*Peking Review*,
     August 8, 1963).
19   Tse-tung, "Statement Supporting the American Negroes."
20   Dr. Martin Luther King Jr., "Eulogy for the Young Victims of the Sixteenth Street
     Baptist Church Bombing," September 18, 1963 (transcript of speech delivered at the
     16th Street Baptist Church, Birmingham, Alabama, https://dailytrust.com/eulogy-
     for-the-young-victims-of-the-sixteenth-street-baptist-church-bombing/).
21   Davis, *Angela Davis*.
22   On November 18, 1977, Chambliss was found guilty of the murder of Carol Denise
     McNair and sentenced to life in prison; he died in 1985 after years of protective
     solitary confinement. In 1995, the FBI unsealed 9,000 pieces of 1960s evidence,
     largely unavailable to Baxley. In 2000, the FBI announced that Blanton, Cash,
     Chambliss, and Cherry bombed 16th Street Baptist Church and arrested Blanton
     and Cherry (Cash died in 1994). In 2002, prosecuting attorney Doug Jones secured
     a conviction of Blanton on four counts of first-degree murder (Blanton was eligible
     for parole from his life sentence in 2021); also in 2002, Cherry was convicted of four
     counts of first-degree murder and given a life (sentence he died in prison of cancer
     two years later). In December 2017, in a special election to replace Jeff Sessions, who
     became attorney general for Donald Trump, Doug Jones secured over 90 percent
     of the vote of African Americans in part because of his prosecution of the bombers
     of the 16th Street Baptist Church; Jones became the first Democratic Senator from
     the state of Alabama in decades.
23   There were three "Bloody Sundays" during 1963–72 while Davis was being
     radicalized into revolutionary struggle: the 1963 Birmingham atrocity, marking
     the repression of civil rights in the United States; the March 1965 Selma March in
     response to the police murder of a nonviolent civil rights dissident; and the Derry,
     Ireland shooting and killings of fourteen Northern Irish protesters in 1972, while
     Angela was on trial.
24   Condoleezza Rice, the future Secretary of State for President George W. Bush,
     collaborated with conservatives to mislead the public into a "twenty-year war" in the
     Middle East. Rice used her official position to spread misinformation campaigns after
     9/11 that Saddam Hussein had weapons of mass destruction in Iraq.
25   Angela Y. Davis, "Remembering Carole, Cynthia, Addie Mae and Denise" (*Essence*
     24, no. 5, February 1993), 92.
26   Davis, "Remembering Carole, Cynthia, Addie Mae and Denise," 92.
27   See Kathy Belew, *Bring the War Home: The White Power Movement and Paramilitary
     America* (Cambridge, MA: Harvard University Press, 2018).
28   Davis, *Angela Davis*.

29 Davis, *Angela Davis*, 92.

30 Davis, *Angela Davis*, 92.

31 Alice Kaplan, *Dreaming in French: The Paris Years of Jacqueline Bouvier Kennedy, Susan Sontag, and Angela Davis* (Chicago: University of Chicago Press, 2012).

32 The Editors of *Encyclopedia Britannica*, "Student Nonviolent Coordinating Committee, SNCC, Student National Coordinating Committee" (*Britannica*, December 17, 2004, https://www.britannica.com/topic/Student-Nonviolent-Coordinating-Committee).

33 H. Rap Brown (Jamil Al-Amin) I currently a political prisoner. https://www.youtube.com/watch?v=8WFFDm-Wyvw

34 The editors of *Encyclopedia Britannica*, "Student Nonviolent Coordinating Committee."

35 Robert Williams's *Negroes with Guns* was published in 1962. When the married couple Robert and Mabel Williams founded a self-defense organization to protect Rev. King and nonviolent civil rights organizers, they were ousted from the NAACP and criminalized and hunted by the FBI and police. Fleeing to Cuba, and later China, Robert Williams convinced Mao Tse-tung – the revolutionary communist leader of China who defeated Japanese and US imperial forces – to issue a statement weeks before the historic August 28, 1963 March on Washington where Rev. King would deliver his "I Have a Dream" speech on civil rights and racial reconciliation.

36 Institute for Humanities Research at Arizona State University, "Who Killed Malcolm X?" (YouTube, April 4, 2022, https://www.youtube.com/watch?v=duGLuly4jDQ).

Chapter 6

1 Mike Davis, *City of Quartz* (London: Verso, 1990).

2 CIA, April 6, 1962. https://www.cia.gov/readingroom/docs/REDCAP_0033.pdf.

3 See Hugh Wilford, *The Mighty Wurlitzer: How the CIA Played America* (Cambridge, MA: Harvard University Press, 2008). Wilford describes journalist Mike Wallace hosting a CBS documentary, *In the Pay of the CIA: An American Dilemma,* which included an interview with Gloria Steinem. Wilford's book notes a letter that Steinem sent to her relatives referencing her activities abroad as an anti-communist employed by the CIA: "(one) can do something toward putting monkey wrenches in the totalitarian works and convincing the uncommitted that it's smarter to stay that way than to trade Western colonialism for Communist imperialism." Wilford, *The Mighty Wurlitzer*, 147.

4 Carol Anne Douglas, "oob investigation" (*Off Our Backs* 5, no. 6 [July 1975], http://www.jstor.org/stable/25772265), 8.

5 See Minna Henrikson and Araba Evelyn Johnston-Arthur, "Festival 1962" (*Radio Helsinki*, December 2015).

6 Davis, *Angela Davis*, 123–4.

7 Davis, *Angela Davis*, 124.

8 "Keynote by Angela Davis '65 with Julieanna Richardson '76, H'16."

9 "Keynote by Angela Davis '65 with Julieanna Richardson '76, H'16."

10 "Keynote by Angela Davis '65 with Julieanna Richardson '76, H'16."

11 "Keynote by Angela Davis '65 with Julieanna Richardson '76, H'16."

12 Jean Genet, incarcerated in a military prison as a deserter, was snubbed by a communist prisoner who refused to be shackled to a "common thief"; Genet began writing while imprisoned.

13 Caroline Moorehead, *A Train in Winter: An Extraordinary Story of Women, Friendship, and Resistance in Occupied France* (New York: Random House, 2012).

14 For Algerians and Martiniqueans, her Americanism, not her coloring, was the anchor. In Cuba, the nation marveled at her coloring and racial ambiguity; in New York City, in 1970 in the Women's House of Detention in Manhattan, an imprisoned Puerto Rican woman asked Davis if she were Puerto Rican.

15 Kaplan, *Dreaming in French*.

16 The GIP (Prison Information Group) organized by Jean Genet and Michel Foucault represented the Black Panther Party, George Jackson, and the 1971 Attica rebellion in New York State with projections, appropriations, and romanticism of Black agency enmeshed in political fetish.

17 Responding to violent atrocities against Black children during the civil rights movement, Simone wrote and recorded *Mississippi Goddamn*. Davis wrote liner notes for Nina Simone's posthumous 2015 album. See Angela Davis, liner notes in *Nina Revisited: A Tribute to Nina Simone* (RCA Records, 2015, compact disc, digital file).

18 Alice Kaplan writes of "the golden age of study abroad that began in the aftermath of the Second World War and continued for three decades, sending thousands of American students into French homes and universities." Usually restricted to whites, that age accommodated Black academic elites: W. E. B. Du Bois studied at the Friedrich Wilhelms-Universität zu Berlin, 1892–1894; and Anna Julia Cooper received her PhD from the Sorbonne in 1924. See Kaplan, *Dreaming in French*.

19 Eric Homberger, "Susan Sontag Obituary" (*The Guardian*, December 29, 2004, https://www.theguardian.com/news/2004/dec/29/guardianobituaries. booksobituaries).

20 See Joy James, "Revolutionary Icons."

21 Kaplan, *Dreaming in French*.

22 See Sara Rzeszutek, *James and Esther Cooper Jackson: Love and Courage in the Black Freedom Movement* (Lexington: The University Press of Kentucky, 2015).

23 Kathleen Belew, interview by Terry Gross (*Fresh Air*, NPR, 2018).

24 Kaplan, *Dreaming in French*.

25 In the summer of 1962, the French repatriated at the rate of 5,000 a day. Thousands of impoverished Algerian workers also came to Paris seeking work. Algerian Muslims were not full French citizens. France's cheap labor from Martinique, Guadeloupe, and French Guiana depressed wages. As an "exotic" American, Davis was less vulnerable to racist violence. *An Autobiography* offers limited discussion of racist violence against Algerian women by police, soldiers, or vigilantes in France; those soldiers and police beat and threw Algerian men into the Seine to drown. See Davis, *Angela Davis*; Kaplan, *Dreaming in French*.

26 Davis, *Angela Davis*.

27 Underreporting of the murder and rape of Black and Indigenous women and girls in the United States includes assaults by the police. The full data of atrocities against Algerian women are unknown. See Janine Jones, "Lively up the Dead Zone: Remembering Democracy's Racist State Crimes (Ashe)" (*Abolition Journal*, December 16, 2016, https://abolitionjournal.org/lively-up-the-dead-zone/). For accounts of Algerian women forced to remove their veils, see Rion Dundon, "These Algerian Women Were Forced to Remove Their Veils to be Photographed in 1960" (*Medium*, December 20, 2016, https:// timeline.com/photos-women-french-algeria-98ee46628854).

28 Davis, *Angela Davis*, 122.

29 Convicted in 2007, James Fowler served a six-month sentence for murder in 2010.

30   "Keynote by Angela Davis '65 with Julieanna Richardson '76, H'16."
31   "Keynote by Angela Davis '65 with Julieanna Richardson '76, H'16."
32   "Keynote by Angela Davis '65 with Julieanna Richardson '76, H'16."
33   "Keynote by Angela Davis '65 with Julieanna Richardson '76, H'16."
34   See Stephen Whitfield, "Refusing Marcuse: 50 Years after One-Dimensional Man"
      (*Dissent*, Fall 2014).

Chapter 7

1   Herbert Marcuse was an intellectual celebrity of activists and the New Left. In 1969,
      Marcuse's *One-Dimensional Man* (1964) sold more than 100,000 copies in the United
      States and was translated into sixteen languages. Marcuse was internationally greeted
      by dignitaries and student activists, celebrated or vilified with tag lines of "Marx,
      Mao and Marcuse" and "unofficial faculty advisor to the New Left." Condemned by
      Catholics and communists, as noted earlier, anti-communist Pope Paul VI attacked
      his books for promoting "disgusting and unbridled" eroticism while communist
      Pravda's Yuri Zhukov condemned him as a "werewolf" and "false prophet." Apartheid
      South Africa banned his books.
2   Nazi Martin Heidegger, dissertation adviser and one-time lover of Hannah Arendt,
      became the rector of the University of Freiburg, where Marcuse received his degree.
      Heidegger used Third Reich decrees to purge all Jewish professors from the faculty.
      Survivors who emerged in academia made ideological choices as loyalty oaths to
      their adopted nations: Marcuse critiqued the United States and advocated socialism
      and social revolution; Arendt aligned with liberalism.
3   The Frankfurt School (Institute for Social Research in Frankfurt, Germany) emerged
      during the Weimar Republic (1918–33); its scholars critiqued capitalism, fascism,
      and communism (Marxist-Leninism).
4   Herbert Marcuse, Sam Keen, and John Raser, "Conversation with Marcuse in
      Psychology Today," in *Philosophy, Psychoanalysis and Emancipation: Collected Papers
      of Herbert Marcuse, Volume 5*, eds. Herbert Marcuse, Douglas Kellner, and Clayton
      Pierce (London: Routledge, 2017), 201–2.
5   Assisted by British and Polish intelligence, the Enemy Objectives Unit located Allied
      bombing targets in Europe, disrupting German oil production; lack of aviation fuel
      and diesel/gasoline helped to ground Hitler's Luftwaffe and render German tanks and
      trucks inoperable.
6   See Franz Neumann, Herbert Marcuse, and Otto Kirchheimer, *Secret Reports on Nazi
      Germany: The Frankfurt School Contribution to the War Effort*, edited by Raffaele
      Laudani (Princeton: Princeton University Press, 2013).
7   Naomi Jaffe joined the Weather Underground, which bombed the Pentagon
      (no injuries to humans) over its war atrocities against Vietnam and US support for
      apartheid in South Africa, and its hiring mercenaries and assassinations of liberation
      movement leaders in the Third World. Mario Savio and Bettina Aptheker were
      leaders in the 1964 Berkeley Free Speech Movement. Anarchist bomber Sam Melville
      was killed in the 1971 National Guard retaking of the Attica Prison in New York.
8   Following the September 1971 suppression of the Attica rebellion, *Ms. Magazine*
      published a letter from Jane Alpert—Swarthmore grad, and Columbia university
      grad student—former partner of Sam Melville, whom she accused of domestic abuse.
      Ms. Magazine editors published Jane Alpert's letter condemning Melville and the

imprisoned men who died in Attica as "chauvinist pigs" who "would not be missed." It is unclear if *Ms.* was outraged not only by patriarchy but also by rebellions against the state waged by the impoverished or imprisoned. In *Ms.*, Albert celebrated the deaths of rebels by prison guards.

> An "open letter" from Miss Alpert, which was published by *Ms.* magazine last year, had urged women to renounce left-wing causes and "work for ourselves." In recounting her own progress from "serious militant leftist" to a radical feminist, she had urged women to break from such "male supremacist" groups as the Weathermen. Melville, Alpert and two others—protesting the war and genocide in Vietnam—had engaged in a serial bombing campaign. They were arrested on November 12, 1969, "after a bomb exploded at the Manhattan Criminal Courts Building at 100 Centre Street—the eighth Government or corporate building to be struck by the group since a wave of bombings began on July 26, 1969."

Albert went underground in May 1970, three months before Angela Davis disappeared into her underground. See Robert Mcg. Thomas Jr., "Jane Alpert Gives up after Four Years" (*New York Times*, November 15, 1974, https://www.nytimes.com/1974/11/15/archives/jane-alpert-gives-up-after-four-years-jane-alpert-surrenders-here.html); Lucinda Franks, "The 4-Year Odyssey of Jane Alpert, From Revolutionary Bomber to Feminist" (*New York Times*, January 14, 1975, https://www.nytimes.com/1975/01/14/archives/the-4year-odyssey-of-jane-alpert-from-revolutionary-bomber-to.html).

9   Judith Moore, "Marxist Professor Herbert Marcuse's Years at UCSD Were Marked by Crisis, Strife, and Controversy: Angel of the Apocalypse" (*San Diego Reader*, September 11, 1986).

10   The Editors of *Encyclopedia Britannica*, "Warsaw Pact" (*Britannica*, updated December 23, 2022, https://www.britannica.com/event/Warsaw-Pact).

11   Marc Olden, *Angela Davis: An Objective Assessment* (New York: Lancer Books, 1973). Manfred Clemenz (1938–) studied American literature at Brandeis as a graduate student. His online bio states that he received a doctorate in sociology and philosophy after studying with Adorno and Horkheimer at the Frankfurt School, specializing in analyses of fascism and racism. He became a professor of sociology and later a psychotherapist. Within Germany, he and other graduate students organized for Davis's defense, 1970–2, finding it absurd that their former classmate had politics similar to those of Black revolutionary militants. See https://www.manfredclemenz.de/.

12   Regina Nadelson, "*Who Is Angela Davis?*" (New York: Peter H. Wyden, 1972).

13   See note 11 on Clemenz, who co-led a German Solidarity Committee for Angela Davis during her trial. Author's papers.

14   Georgia Warnke, "Feminism, the Frankfurt School, and Nancy Fraser" (*Los Angeles Review of Books*, August 4, 2013).

15   Warnke, "Feminism, the Frankfurt School, and Nancy Fraser."

16   Warnke, "Feminism, the Frankfurt School, and Nancy Fraser."

17   Angela Davis, "Explorations in Black Leadership," interview by Julian Bond (*C-Span*, April 15, 2009, https://www.c-span.org/video/?328898-1/angela-davis-oral-history-interview).

18   See Kathleen Belew, *Bring the War Home: The White Power Movement and Paramilitary* (Cambridge, MA: Harvard University Press, 2018).

19   Moore, "Marxist Professor Herbert Marcuse's Years at UCSD."

20   Warnke, "Feminism, the Frankfurt School, and Nancy Fraser."

21 December 2022 conversation, Nicole Yokum and Joy James.

22 Nicole Yokum, written communique to author, December 2022.

23 Moore quoting Marcuse in "Marxist Professor Herbert Marcuse's Years at UCSD."

24 Moore, "Marxist Professor Herbert Marcuse's Years at UCSD."

25 See Angela Davis, "Angela Davis on Protest, 1968, and Her Old Teacher, Herbert Marcuse" (*Literary Hub*, April 3, 2019, https://lithub.com/angela-davis-on-protest-1968-and-her-old-teacher-herbert-marcuse/).

26 Moore, "Marxist Professor Herbert Marcuse's Years at UCSD."

27 Moore, "Marxist Professor Herbert Marcuse's Years at UCSD."

28 Moore, "Marxist Professor Herbert Marcuse's Years at UCSD."

29 Moore, "Marxist Professor Herbert Marcuse's Years at UCSD."

30 Moore, "Marxist Professor Herbert Marcuse's Years at UCSD."

31 Richard McDonough, "Eldridge Cleaver: From Violent Anti-Americanism to Christian Conservativism" (*The Postil Magazine*, February 1, 2021, https://www.thepostil.com/eldridge-cleaver-from-violent-anti-americanism-to-christian-conservativism/).

32 Moore, "Marxist Professor Herbert Marcuse's Years at UCSD." At the age of fifty-nine, Mrs. Inge Werner Neumann Marcuse, wife of Prof. Herbert Marcuse, the political philosopher, died of cancer in La Jolla, Calif. Born in Madgeburg, Germany, she had accompanied her first husband, Prof. Franz Neumann—a professor at Columbia University—to the United States in 1936. He died in 1954. She then married Professor Marcuse and taught French in California. "Mrs. Herbert Marcuse," *New York Times* Obituary (August 2, 1973, https://www.nytimes.com/1973/08/02/archives/mrs-herbert-marcuse.html).

33 Moore, "Marxist Professor Herbert Marcuse's Years at UCSD."

34 See Whitfield, "Refusing Marcuse."

35 Davis, "Angela Davis on Protest."

36 See Davis, "Angela Davis on Protest."

37 Kant quoted in Angela's dissertation prospectus. Author's papers.

38 Kant quoted in Angela Davis's dissertation prospectus, 3. Author's papers.

39 Kant quoted in Davis's dissertation prospectus. Author's papers.

40 Angela Davis's dissertation prospectus, 3. Author's papers.

41 Davis, "Angela Davis on Protest."

42 Davis, "Angela Davis on Protest."

43 Davis, "Angela Davis on Protest."

44 California students were not the only ones in rebellion. Columbia University's radical white students rioted against the Vietnam War and the social order. Some were beaten brutally by police. One jumped out of a window and broke an NYPD officer's back. Black students occupied another building to protest against a proposed segregated gym in Morningside Park that divided the campus from Harlem. During the violent fracas, Black police officers secretly led them down back corridors to off-campus safety. Each segment of students appeared to be organizing in separate silos. University administrations increasingly deployed riot police and the National Guard against student protestors in order to control campuses.

45 Davis, "Angela Davis on Protest."

46 Alongside his wife, whom he does not name, Marcuse acknowledged colleagues who offered helpful critiques for *An Essay on Liberation*. All of the commentators are professors at the most elite US institutions: UC Berkeley's Leo Lowenthal, Princeton's Arno J. Mayer, and Harvard's Barrington Moore, Jr. See "Acknowledgments" in Herbert Marcuse, *An Essay on Liberation* (Boston: Beacon Press, 1971).

47   While Angela Davis was completing her dissertation at Humboldt University and
      touring for her 1974 autobiography, Marcuse referenced her work in his university
      lecture on "Marxism and Feminism": "advanced capitalism gradually created the
      material conditions for translating the ideology of feminine characteristics into
      reality, the objective conditions for turning the weakness that was attached to them
      into strength, turning the sexual object into a subject, and making feminism a
      political force in the struggle against capitalism, against the Performance Principle.
      It is with the view of these prospects that Angela Davis speaks of the revolutionary
      function of the female as antithesis to the Performance Principle [a social norm
      "based on the efficiency and prowess in the fulfilment of competitive economic
      and acquisitive functions," 279], in a paper written in the Palo Alto Jail, "Women
      and Capitalism," December, 1971." See Herbert Marcuse, "Marxism and
      Feminism" (*Women's Studies* 2, 1974: 279–88, http://platypus1917.org/wp-content/
      uploads/archive/rgroups/2006-chicago/marcuse_marxismfeminism.pdf), 284.
48   Marcuse, *An Essay on Liberation*.
49   See Belew, *Bring the War Home*.
50   Davis, "Angela Davis on Protest."
51   Davis, "Angela Davis on Protest."
52   See Marcuse, draft notes for interview with NBC, January 31, 1971 (author's papers).
53   Herbert Marcuse, draft notes.
54   Marcuse, draft notes.
55   Marcuse, draft notes. The *UCSD Alumni Magazine* recognizes its impressive alumna:
      "Marcuse's best-known student, the civil rights activist Angela Davis, M.A. '69."
      In the decades that followed her acquittal, Angela rarely publicly spoke of Marcuse
      until memorials and media following the repatriation of his remains brought him
      back into the spotlight.
56   See Marcuse et al., "Conversation with Marcuse."
57   Quote reprinted in Robert Gooding Williams, "Douglass's Declarations of
      Independence and Practices of Politics."
58   See Marcuse et al. "Conversation with Marcuse."

Chapter 8

1   The government, with the press's tacit approval, understood that future wars
      should not have visuals of casualties and the deceased. Photos of coffins returning
      from Middle Eastern or African wars do not appear on screen. A veil dropped
      over the citizenry's gaze. Later, the *McNeil Hour on PBS* would read the names of
      US personnel that died in the invasion of Iraq (under disinformation campaigns
      from the Bush Administration) and Afghanistan following September 9, 2001 attacks
      on the Pentagon and the World Trade Center. After McNeil retired, the honor roll
      of the dead ended.
2   Bettina Aptheker was key in the National United Committee to Free Angela Davis
      and coedited *If They Come in the Morning*, an anthology of writings by political
      prisoners, including Davis (oddly, Aptheker's name appears missing in recent
      editions of the anthology). Bettina Aptheker, *The Morning Breaks: The Trial of Angela
      Davis* (New York: International Publishers, 1975).
3   See Shelby Grad, "The environmental disaster that changed California and started
      the movement against offshore drilling" (*Los Angeles Times*, April 28, 2017, https://
      www.latimes.com/local/lanow/la-me-santa-barbara-spill-20170428-htmlstory.html).

4   While at Swarthmore College, Fania Davis had been engaged in civil rights protests with Ruth Gilmore (prominent abolitionist and academic) until Gilmore transferred to Yale after her cousin John Huggins, a BPP leader in Los Angeles, was murdered at UCLA.

5   See Garry Wills, *Reagan's America* (New York: Doubleday & Company, 1987).

6   By 1978, CIA disinformation was costing US taxpayers $265 million a year. See Alex Constantine, "Mockingbird: The Subversion of the Free Press by the CIA" (2000, https://archive.org/stream/pdfy-QnKYkrSXDS_UTpW6/Mockingbird+%5BThe+Subversion+Of+The+Free+Press+By+The+CIA%5D_djvu.txt).

7   President Reagan would appoint real-estate mogul William French Smith to the position of the 74th US Attorney General in the Reagan Administration, allowing Smith to continue as a regent after he accepted the post. See Wills, *Reagan's America*.

8   Huey P. Newton, "In Defense of Self-Defense" (June 20, 1967, https://archive.lib.msu.edu/DMC/AmRad/essaysministerdefense.pdf.)

9   Davis, *Angela Davis*.

10   Stokely Carmichael Defines Black Power in a 1965 Interview found on *Youtube* and transcribed here:
     Interviewer: "How did Black Power evolve at that time in Greenwood five years ago?"
     Stokely Carmichael:

> [I]n Mississippi, we had thoughts about using Black Power, but we weren't sure whether or not the people would be ready for it…. [Willie] Ricks was selected to go out ahead of the march and work among the sharecroppers… [to] see how they would react to the term Black Power. And he went about a day's march ahead of the march and… reported to us that he'd been all the way down to Greenwood and everybody was for Black Power. Dr. King was marching with us all the time and… [had to] leave the march…. [W]e got arrested and Ricks got us out of jail and the people were waiting and Dr. King was not there and Black Power came out. …
>
> I just made a speech… showing that it wasn't a question of morality. It wasn't a question of being good or bad. It was simply a question of power and that we Black people had no power and we had to have some power. Only type of power we could have is Black Power. Black power! And since Willie Ricks is a good organizer, the people were well-seasoned. They responded immediately in a healthy manner. Dr. King came back the next day, but it was too late then. Black Power had been established.

11   David Dennis, Jr., "How Dick Gregory Forced the FBI to Find the Bodies of Three Civil Rights Workers Slain in Mississippi," *Still Crew*. August 30, 2017. https://stillcrew.com/how-dick-gregory-forced-the-fbi-to-find-the-bodies-of-goodman-chaney-and-schwerner-fa9790c49ad4. Black militants migrated from the southern movement throughout the country and the globe."

12   David Cooper, ed., *The Dialectics of Liberation (Radical Thinkers)* (London: Verso, 2015).

13   Cooper, *Dialectics*, back cover.

14   Cooper, *Dialectics*, back cover.

15   Davis, *Angela Davis*. At the 1967 London Dialectics conference, Angela Davis met Michael/Malik X (aka Michael de Frietas, Michael Abdul Malik). The poet, author, and criminal ran London's Black House. He was tried in 1972 for the murders of his cousin Joseph Skerritt and white socialite Gale Benson, daughter of conservative British MP Leonard Plugge. Both victims were hacked with cutlasses and buried

alive on a Trinidadian commune, allegedly on the orders of Michael X. The cousin of Malcolm X, Hakim Jamal (Allen Donaldson), cofounder of US Organization with Ron Karenga, brought Benson to the commune (years later he was murdered in Boston). Michael X's literary talents drew the attention and support of prominent intellectuals and death penalty opponents. John Lennon and Angela Davis appealed to the Trinidadian government to commute the death sentence to life in prison. Others who protested the death penalty included attorney William Kunstler; NAACP Roy Wilkins; Dick Gregory; Kate Millet (who signed the NAARPR Call); author William Styron, Alfred Knopf President Robert Gottlieb; PEN International President Heinrich Böll; and Amnesty International. Michael X was hanged in 1975.

16 After the London Conference, Stokely Carmichael traveled in July 1967 to visit Fidel Castro with a SNCC delegation, arguing with Castro about racism and race relations during their chauffeured rides. See Sarah J. Seidman, "Angela Davis in Cuba as Symbol and Subject" (*Radical History Review*, 36 [2020]: 11–35).

17 Davis, *Angela Davis*.

18 Davis, *Angela Davis*.

19 Davis, *Angela Davis*. In the 2021 preface for *An Autobiography*, Angela Davis writes that the greatest error in her thinking during the 1960s–70s was that she did not factor in *gender/heteropatriarchy* and thereby omitted a feminist analysis. In *Abolition. Feminism. Now,* coauthored/edited with Black and white women academics, Davis secures her legacy in feminism, maintaining that the most transformative type of abolition is feminist. See Angela Y. Davis, Gina Dent, Erica R. Meiners, Beth E. Richie, *Abolition. Feminism. Now* (Chicago: Haymarket Books, 2022).

20 Gender essentialism at times overtakes Davis's analyses, which miss the fact that men were caretakers and nurturers in the party, most likely the rank-and-file, and women engaged in violence against other women as well as men—for example, Elaine Brown, while serving as interim "Supreme Commander" for the Oakland BPP, had both women and men who defied authoritarian dictates from the Oakland leadership bull-whipped.

21 Cheryl I. Harris, "Whiteness as Property" (*Harvard Law Review* 106 8.[1993]: 1707–91).

22 Black radicals and revolutionaries have consistently had white allies from before abolitionist John Brown in the 1860s to Black Liberation Army ally Marilyn Buck a century later. For Davis, the "white man" as a reductive term nullifies possible solidarity based on common economic oppression. Yet Black revolutionaries were also communists and socialists: their jargon invoked "the man," but some whites were allies and some whites were "pigs"; others were liberals trying to help (and control) with resources; some tried to remain "neutral." Black Panther supporters included famous whites such as actor Marlon Brandon who bought weapons for the BPP, and infamous ones such as Bo Brown, trans/queer white revolutionary who formed the "George Jackson Brigade" after his 1971 assassination, and did bank robberies and expropriations until they were caught and sent to a women's prison for eight years. See "Support Bo Brown" (Prison Activist Resource Center, November 10, 2018, https://www.prisonactivist.org/alerts/support-bo-brown.); John Dooley, "Rita 'Bo' Brown: The Gentleman Bank Robber" (*Portland Mercury*, June 12, 2003, https://www.portlandmercury.com/news/2003/06/12/29228/rita-bo-brown).

23 Davis, *Angela Davis*.

24 Davis, *Angela Davis*, 150; *Anatomy of Violence*, directed by Deepa Mehta (Hamilton Mehta Productions, 2016). The BBC allegedly destroyed its documentary on the gathering. See Alexander Dunst, "Dialectics of Liberation" (*Hidden Persuaders*, October 25, 2017, http://www.bbk.ac.uk/hiddenpersuaders/blog/dialectics-of-liberation/); Daniel Hahn, "The Dialectics of Liberation: 15-July 30, 1967" (*Roundhouse*, https://50.roundhouse.org.uk/content-items/the-dialectics-of-liberation).

25 Philosopher Nicole Yokum reflects:

> The early Frankfurt School—perhaps most visibly Adorno and Horkheimer—was very critical of the Enlightenment and Enlightenment philosophy as doing violence to difference (on a certain understanding of this). It's interesting how much her project might seem to have been influenced by her studies with Adorno in Frankfurt, although she did not have the relationship with him that she had to Marcuse. (Adorno and Horkheimer's book *Dialectic of Enlightenment* is about enlightened rationality descending into sheer and obvious forms of the brutal violence that is always at its core.)

> December 4, 2022 written communication to author.

26 Angela Davis, interview by Terry Rockefeller and Louis Massiah, *Eyes on the Prize II: America at the Racial Crossroads 1965 to 1985* (produced by Blackside, Inc.; executive producer, Henry Hampton; series writer, Steve Fayer; Washington University Libraries Film and Media Archive, Henry Hampton Collection; recorded on May 24, 1989, edited for clarity).

27 See "Freedom of Information and Privacy Acts Subject: (COINTELPRO BLACK EXTREMIST)" (FBI, https://vault.fbi.gov/cointel-pro/cointel-pro-black-extremists/cointelpro-black-extremists-part-01-of/view).

28 Robert Boyle, "The Criminalization of the Black Panther Party and Rewriting of History" (New York City Jericho Movement, http://www.jerichony.org/bobboyle.html).

29 See MRDAVEYD, "History 101: The Panther 21, Police Repression, the BLA & Cointel-Pro," *DAVEY D's Hip Hop Corner*, December 14, 2015. https://hiphopandpolitics.com/tag/dhoruba-bin-wahad/

30 "The Black Panther Newspaper" (Marxists Internet Archive, https://www.marxists.org/history/usa/pubs/black-panther/index.htm).

31 "The Black Panther Newspaper"—also known as *The Black Panther* Intercommunal News Service, Black Panther Black Community News Service, and Black Community News Service—stopped publication in 1980.

32 *Ramparts'* popularity would increase in 1968 when it published excerpts of *Soul on Ice*, written by Eldridge Cleaver in 1965, while he was imprisoned in Folsom State Prison for raping Black women. Cleaver would become the Minister of Information for the Black Panther Party.

33 See "Ramparts Exposes NSA; Claims Use of CIA Funds" (*The Heights*, Vol. XLVII, No. 15, February 17, 1967).

34 "Work of the CIA with Youths at Festival Is Defended" (*Washington Post*, February 16, 1968), 18.

35 Michael Kazin, "Dancing to the CIA's Tune," review of *The Mighty Wurlitzer: How the CIA Played America*, by Hugh Wilford (*Washington Post Sunday Book Review*, January 27, 2008, http://www.washingtonpost.com/wp-dyn/content/article/2008/01/24/AR2008012402369.html).

36 Boston College (*The Heights* Vol. XLVII, No. 15, February 17, 1967).

37   *Ramparts* magazine ad in the February 14, 1967 issue of *The New York Times*, quoted
     in "Ramparts exposes NSA; claims use of CIA funds" (*The Heights* Vol. XLVII,
     No. 15, February 17, 1967). Boston College students voted to reject the NSA for the
     1963–4 school year, deeming it too politicized.

38   Paul Robeson, Jr.'s father, Paul Robeson, was a legendary supporter and member of
     the CPUSA. The State Department confiscated Paul Robeson Sr.'s passport to limit
     his ability to tour internationally and earn a living as a singer and actor. Eventually
     committed, the senior Robeson became a recluse after suffering from hallucinations
     and psychoses, which some speculate began at an impromptu party where Robeson
     unknowingly drank from a cocktail laced with LSD.

39   Gloria Steinem interviews with the *New York Times* and *Washington Post*. By 1970,
     US colleges and universities were granting 875,000 degrees a year. University and
     college education was the basis for white-collar upward mobility and future business
     and political leaders. Vienna 1959 and 1962 Helsinki International Youth Festivals
     included UC students. The CIA funneled monies through "cut-outs" or dummy
     foundations for the 1959 International Youth festival in Vienna, Austria while Gloria
     Steinem worked with Zbigniew Brzezinski.

40   The 1959 NSA brochure highlights moderate Black leaders from the National Urban
     League and the NAACP and fails to mention the names of progressives SCLC leaders
     Martin Luther King, Jr., Bayard Rustin, and Congress on Racial Equality's (CORE)
     James Farmer—all critics of racism in US domestic and foreign policies. Hugh
     Wilford's *The Mighty Wurlitzer* identifies James Farmer as an anti-communist who
     also worked with the CIA. See Hugh Wilford, *The Mighty Wurlitzer* (Cambridge,
     MA: Harvard Press, 2009). See Karen M. Paget, *Patriotic Betrayal: The Inside Story
     of the CIA's Secret Campaign to Enroll American Students in the Crusade against
     Communism* (New Haven: Yale University Press, 2015), 201.

41   Louis Menand, "A Friend of the Devil: Inside a Famous Cold War Deception" (*The
     New Yorker*, March 16, 2015, https://www.newyorker.com/magazine/2015/03/23/a-
     friend-of-the-devil).

42   Noah Robertson, "Democracy Destroyed: Stories of American Sponsored Coups—
     Iraq" (*Arab America*, October 8, 2020, https://www.arabamerica.com/democracy-
     destroyed-stories-of-american-sponsored-coups-iraq/).

43   Fid Backhouse, "1953 Coup in Iran" (*Britannica*, May 10, 2022, https://www.
     britannica.com/event/1953-coup-in-Iran).

44   See Armando Tinoco, "What Happened in Mexico Today: We Remember the 1968
     Student Massacre" (*Latin Times*, October 2, 2014, https://www.latintimes.com/
     what-happened-mexico-city-today-we-remember-1968-student-massacre-police-
     tlatelolco-square-265915#:~:text=The%20Tlatelolco%20massacre%20is%20one%20
     of%20the%20darkest,opening%20ceremony%20of%20the%201968%20Summer%20
     Olympic%20Games). Also see "'Discriminate Deterrence,' Report of the Commission
     on Integrated Long-Term Strategy" (January 1988, https://findit.library.yale.edu/
     images_layout/view?parentoid=11781573&increment=0).

45   "Four Dead in Ohio" (*Ohio History Connection*, May 17, 2017, https://www.
     ohiohistory.org/four-dead-in-ohio/); HardRainProductions, "Crosby, Stills, Nash,
     and Young 'Ohio'" (YouTube, November 18, 2007, https://www.youtube.com/
     watch?v=JCS-g3HwXdc); The Isley Brothers, "Ohio/Machine Gun" (Neil Young/Jimi
     Hendrix covers), *Live at the Bitter End 1972*—New York, NY, in Andrew O'Brien,
     "'4 Dead in Ohio: 10 Powerful Versions of "Ohio" on the 52nd Anniversary of the

Kent State Massacre (*Live for Live Music*, May 4, 2022, https://liveforlivemusic.com/features/kent-state-neil-young-ohio-50th-anniversary/).

46 Eugene Linden, "Fragging and the United States of Rage," *THEBULWARK*, November 22, 2021.

47 Menand, "A Friend of the Devil."

Chapter 9

1 See Miguel Espinoza, *The Integration of the UCLA School of Law, 1966–1978: Architects of Affirmative Action* (Lanham: Lexington Books, 2017).

2 Davis, *Angela Davis*, 219.

3 President Richard Nixon's 1970 Order No. 4 mandated contractors with the federal government to correct the "underutilization" of minority workers.

4 Angela Davis, ed., *If They Come in the Morning … Voices of Resistance* (New York: Verso, November 2016).

5 Angela Davis, "Philosophical Themes in Black Literature," October 6, 1969, Folder 413, Angela Davis, Ad Hoc Committee Papers, pp. 1–2. Quoted in Casey Shoop, "Angela Davis, the LA Rebellion, and the Undercommons" (*post45org*, February 5, 2019).

6 Angela Davis, "Unfinished Lecture on Liberation—II," in *The Angela Y. Davis Reader*, edited by Joy James (Malden, MA: Blackwell Press, 1998, 53–60).

7 Angela Davis, "Unfinished Lecture on Liberation—II."

8 Heiress Patty Hearst was a member of the Symbionese Liberation Army (SLA) and for a time a follower of Charles Manson who kidnapped and tortured her. See the PBS *American Experience* documentary *Guerrilla: The Taking of Patty Hearst* and "The Rise and Fall of the Symbionese Liberation Army." *Guerrilla: The Taking of Patty Hearst* (directed and produced by Robert Stone; PBS *American Experience*: Robert Stone Productions, 2004). "The Rise and Fall of the Symbionese Liberation Army" (PBS *American Experience*: https://www.pbs.org/wgbh/americanexperience/features/guerrilla-rise-and-fall-symbionese-liberation-army/).

9 "Report of Chancellor Young's Ad Hoc Committee," reprinted as addendum A in *AAUP*, 412. Quoted in Shoop, "Angela Davis, the LA Rebellion."

10 Angela Davis, Public Address, October 24, 1969, UC Berkeley. Quoted in Shoop, "Angela Davis, the LA Rebellion."

11 Quoted in Shoop, "Angela Davis, the LA Rebellion."

12 Angela Davis, Public Address, February 5, 1970, Santa Barbara. Quoted in Shoop, "Angela Davis, the LA Rebellion."

13 Shoop, "Angela Davis, the LA Rebellion."

14 Shoop, "Angela Davis, the LA Rebellion."

15 See Shoop quoting Nash in "Angela Davis, the LA Rebellion."

16 Davis, *Angela Davis*.

17 Davis, *Angela Davis*, 272.

18 The history of affirmative action and job protection is traceable through presidential edicts: John Kennedy's 1961 Executive Order 10925 created the Committee on Equal Employment Opportunity and mandated "affirmative action" for federal hiring to be free of racial bias; Lyndon Johnson's 1965 Executive Order 11246 enforced guidelines

and was amended in 1967 to cover gender; Richard Nixon mandated in 1969 a guarantee for fair hiring.

19   Panthers diminished their chances of deployment to Vietnam by appearing at induction centers in full regalia—Black leather jackets, berets, sunglasses—armed with copies of the *Black Panther Party Paper,* informing military officers that they were eager to go to "Nam" to spread the message of liberation. See Joshua Bloom and Waldo E. Martin Jr., *Black against Empire* (Berkeley: University of California Press, 2013).

20   See Herbert Marcuse, "Reflections on Calley," published in *The New York Times,* May 13, 1971; reprinted in *The New Left and the 1960s: Collected Papers of Herbert Marcuse, Volume* 3, edited by Douglas Kellner (New York: Routledge, 2005).

21   "Crosby, Stills, Nash, and Young 'Ohio'"; The Isley Brothers, "Ohio/Machine Gun."

22   Donna Ladd, "Jackson Tragedy: The RNA Revisited," *Jackson Free Press,* March 5, 2014. https://www.jacksonfreepress.com/news/2014/mar/05/jackson-tragedy-rna-revisited/#:~:text=This%20unassuming%20house%20near%20Jackson,a%20JPD%20officer%2C%20William%20Skinner.

Chapter 10

1   King's younger brother Alfred drowned in a swimming pool in 1969 (the widow said that "the system" killed her husband, who had marched with his older brother and was at the Lorraine Motel when King was shot). Their mother, Alberta Williams King, was shot and killed as she sat at Ebenezer Baptist Church's organ in 1974. The tragedies and mayhem decimating the King family members would be replicated in 1969 through COINTELPRO as federal police or "investigators" began to plan the murders of effective and prominent members of the BPP.

2   Davis, interview by Bond.

3   Davis, interview by Bond.

4   Angela Davis, "Explorations in Black Leadership," interview by Julian Bond (*C-Span,* April 15, 2009, https://www.c-span.org/video/?328898-1/angela-davis-oral-history-interview).

5   CPUSA members left in 1968 when the Soviets invaded Czechoslovakia. The number of infiltrators—FBI agents or informants—is not definitively known. Peter Kihss asserts that 1500 had infiltrated a CPUSA with 8000 members. See Peter Kihss, "1500 Informants for the F.B.I. Reported in Communist Party," *New York Times,* October 18, 1962. By 1988, the CPUSA was supporting the liberal wing of the Democratic Party and had 5-10,000 members. See "Communist Party USA (CPUSA)," Influence Watch. See https://www.influencewatch.org/political-party/communist-party-usa/

6   Kendra Alexander, who chose to stay in the CPUSA when Angela Davis, Charlene Mitchell and about 200 members in leadership left due to the conservatism of the old guard, is a leader who is understudied by students but was one that the federal government took note of given her organizational skills. Kirkland infiltrated SDS and the youth wing of the CPUSA which would have included Che-Lumumba, which was led by Franklin and Kendra Alexander. The Alexanders, according to the Black informant, were encouraging student activists to obtain weapons to defend themselves

and not to back down from violent confrontations. These instructions, according to Kirkland, took place in Chicago and at Camp Webatuck in the Catskills of New York. Kirkland, an anti-communist and anti-Panther, was not a complete anomaly. The Alexanders engaged in arms training violated the instructions from the Central Committee of the CPUSA and the CPSU.

7   See Dorothy Ray Healey, *California Red: A Life in the American Communist Party* (Chicago: University of Illinois Press, 1993).

8   Charlene Mitchell convinced this author to go to the Arturo Schomburg Library in New York City in the 1990s and to study the memoirs of W. E. B. DuBois and his development as a Marxist/communist and his repudiation of Black petit bourgeois elites and the construct of the talented tenth. That research led to the publication by Joy James, *Transcending the Talented Tenth* (New York: Routledge, 1998).

9   The CPUSA had for decades attempted to attract youth and Black and brown Americans. The Progressive Youth Organizing Committee (PYOC) was established in April 1959, which led to the NYC Advance Club, led by Mike Zagarell. Angela, Bettina Aptheker, and likely Angela's biographer, Regina Nadelson, participated in its civil rights activism. In 1961, the W. E. B. DuBois Club was formed in San Francisco from PYOC. Aptheker was a powerful organizer of California students in the DuBois Club in California. In Illinois, the DuBois Club seemed reluctant to have meetings on the South Side of Chicago and in other predominantly Black or brown communities.

10   When Hall died, in 2000, the CPUSA and Angela and other former leaders forced out in 1991 were able to better work with and influence reforms within the reformed party. *Portside*, a CPUSA-linked publication, provides a platform for left readers and popularizes the writings of Angela Davis.

11   See Francis X. Gannon, *Biographical Dictionary of the Left*, Vol. 2 (Boston: Western Islands, 1971), 182.

12   Georges Nzongola-Ntalaja writes in "Patrice Lumumba: The Most Important Assassination of the Twentieth Century" (*The Guardian*, January 17, 2011):

> With the outbreak of the cold war, it was inevitable that the United States and its Western allies would not be prepared to let Africans have effective control over strategic raw materials, lest these fall in the hands of their enemies in the Soviet camp. It is in this regard that Patrice Lumumba's determination to achieve genuine independence and to have full control over Congo's resources in order to utilize them to improve the living conditions of our people was perceived as a threat to Western interests. To fight him, the United States and Belgium used all the tools and resources at their disposal, including the United Nations secretariat, under Dag Hammarskjöld and Ralph Bunche, to buy the support of Lumumba's Congolese rivals, and hired killers.

See Georges Nzongola-Ntalaja, "Patrice Lumumba: The Most Important Assassination of the Twentieth Century," *The Guardian*, January 17, 2011.

13   Peter Kornbluh, "The Death of Che Guevara Declassified" (*The Nation*, October 10, 2017, https://www.thenation.com/article/archive/the-death-of-che-guevara-declassified/).

14   Kornbluh, "The Death of Che Guevara Declassified."

15   Kornbluh, "The Death of Che Guevara Declassified."

16   Angela Davis acknowledges both the BPP's contributions and its limitations. The BPP emerged as a response to the police violence in Black urban communities.

Davis understood Huey Newton and Bobby Seale's decision to patrol neighborhoods with guns and law books as "policing the police" such a brilliant strategy inspired by (inter)national freedom struggles would be limited, according to Davis, because it would remain as symbolic of resistance and overly reliant upon explicit policing strategies to stop police violence.

17   China did not agree with this position, hence the Soviet-Sino split, until its welcoming of President Nixon to Beijing.

18   Charlene Mitchell, interview by Lisa Brock, at Mitchell's home on West 147th Street in Harlem, NY, "No Easy Victories: African Liberation and American Activists over a Half Century, 1950-2000" (July 18, 2004, http://www.noeasyvictories.org/interviews/int04_mitchell.php).

19   Davis, interview by Bond.

20   BPP breakfast program was later adopted by the US Department of Agriculture's Food Breakfast Program to feed children with school breakfasts throughout the United States.

21   Davis, interview by Bond.

22   Davis, *Angela Davis*.

23   Radicals perceived the CPUSA as "staid." Harvard University chapters of SDS and Progressive Labor felt the CPUSA held positions to the "right" of their organizations, yet respected CPUSA members who joined leftist groups as industrious workers. Zagarell is quoted as saying that the CPUSA does not pack meetings as was done in the 1930s, which led activists to distrust and fear that they were "out to take over other Leftist organizations." According to Zagarell, the CPUSA "gains nothing by sponging off the movement." See Stephen D. Lerner, "Political Organization at Harvard" (*The Harvard Crimson*, February 18, 1967).

24   In Committee on Internal Security, "Investigation of Students for a Democratic Society, Part 5 (University of Chicago; Communist Party Efforts with Regard to SDS)" (FBI informer Hearings before the Committee on Internal Security House of Representatives Ninety-First Congress, First Session, August 6–7, 1969).

25   On March 14, 2004, Angela Davis moderated the forum, "Self-Respect, Self-Defense, and Self-Determination," at Oakland's First Congregational Church with Mabel Williams and Kathleen Cleaver speaking about Black women and armed resistance in the civil rights movement. Davis—who did not identify herself as an active member in either the civil rights movement or the Black Panthers—discussed violence and armed self-defense by Black radicals. In a private community setting, off campus, Black women who engaged in armed self-defense were the keynote speakers. See Angela Davis, introducing Mabel Williams and Kathleen Cleaver. "Self Respect, Self Defense & Self Determination." Collision Course Video & The Freedom Archives: March 14, 2004. Video.

Mabel Williams described how she and her husband, North Carolina NAACP leader Robert Williams, coauthored *Negroes with Guns*, advocating in the 1950s for more armed Black patrols to protect civil rights organizers. The NAACP ousted them from the organization. The government framed them for "kidnapping" when they sheltered a white couple in their home during civil unrest. Historians assert that Medgar Evers's missing security detail and NYPD infiltration of Malcolm X's security led to their deaths in, respectively, 1963 and 1965. Williams maintained that armed guards protected civil rights activists, including Reverend King, and reduced the number of Klan murders. Police and FBI forced the family to flee to Cuba, from there they went to China, where Williams advocated Mao to speak out against US racism. In the 1970s, Williams worked as an intermediary to facilitate President Nixon's 1972 visit with Chairman Mao and returned later to the United States; all charges against him were dropped and he was hired to do research at Michigan State.

26   Robert Boyle, "The Criminalization of the Black Panther Party" (New York City Jericho Movement. http://www.jerichony.org/bobboyle.html).

27   Victoria Mercado, a labor organizer highly regarded by Dorothy Ray Healey, worked with the United Farmworkers. She began organizing in 1962, mentored by field/agricultural laborer Cesar Chavez and Dolores Huerta, a middle-class, Mills College-educated activist who became Davis's lifelong friend and ally. Mercado was a close friend of Angela and Fania Davis. She was murdered by a misogynist homophobe in the 1982s.

28   Sarah J. Seidman, "Angela Davis in Cuba as Symbol and Subject" (*Radical History Review* 36 [2020]: 11–35).

29   Quoted in Seidman, "Angela Davis in Cuba."

30   Quoted in Seidman, "Angela Davis in Cuba."

31   Seidman, "Angela Davis in Cuba," 20.

32   Davis, *Angela Davis*.

33   *The Theory and Practice of Communism in 1971* (March 29–30, 1971, U.S. House of Representatives, Committee on Internal Security, Washington, DC, Public Hearings).

34   *Public Affairs*, reprinted in *The Theory and Practice of Communism in 1971*.

35   *The Theory and Practice of Communism in 1971*, Part 1-A (United States House of Representatives, January 18, 1970).

36   *Public Affairs,* reprinted in *The Theory and Practice of Communism in 1971*.

37   *Public Affairs,* exhibit in House Congressional Hearings, January 1970.

38   See Lisa Brock, "Back to the Future: African-Americans and Cuba in the Time(s) of Race" (*Contributions in Black Studies,* Vol. 12 [1994], Art. 3).

39   After the 1959 revolution, led in part by Ernesto Che Guevara and Fidel Castro, Cubans progressed on all fronts in terms of social development. Brock notes that post-revolutionary policies increased Black Cubans' standards of living: "by 1987, employment, infant mortality, and life expectancy rates were better for Blacks in Cuba than for Blacks anywhere in the world - even in the United States." She also notes that "Cubans valued an African heritage and supported African liberation movements unlike other Latin American countries." Brock does not note the continued discontent among Black Cubans concerning racist discrimination or anti-Blackness.

40   See Brock, "Back to the Future."

41   Seidman, "Angela Davis in Cuba."

42   See Brock, "Back to the Future."

43   In addition to being dismissive of Malcolm X's political analyses and postures, Angela Davis described Afropessimism, a school of thought developed by Frank Wilderson III and Jared Sexton, as a form of "narrow nationalism." See Angela Davis and Gayatri Spivak, "Planetary Utopias—Hope, Desire, Imaginaries in a Post-Colonial World" (plenary session at the "Colonial Repercussions" event series at the Akademie der Künste, Berlin, Germany, June 23–24, 2018); and Angela Davis, "Meditations on the Legacy of Malcolm X," in *The Angela Y. Davis Reader*, ed. Joy James (Malden, MA: Blackwell, 1998).

44   After her 1972 visit, Angela delivered privately a report to the CPUSA leadership that
     Castro's "government was increasingly interested in working with African American
     communists after previous encounters with Black activists had soured." Angela
     Davis named Robert F. Williams, author of *Negroes with Guns*, SNCC leader Stokely
     Carmichael, and dissident Panther Eldridge Cleaver as leaders whom Castro felt had
     publicly criticized the leadership of the Cuban Revolution and Cuban socialism for
     their lack of substantive redress to anti-Black racism. Castro confided that the Cuban
     state "felt that they had been in error by establishing such strong relationships with
     them [the Black male militants] at that time." See Seidman, "Angela Davis in Cuba."
45   Seidman, "Angela Davis in Cuba."
46   Both Newton and Cleaver were in Cuba as fugitives fleeing warrants based on assault
     and (attempted) murder charges. See Seidman, "Angela Davis in Cuba."

Chapter 11

1   Roberta Alexander, oral history interview by David P. Cline (Library of Congress,
     2016, https://www.loc.gov/item/2016655433/).
2   Alexander, interview by Cline.
3   Alexander, interview by Cline.
4   The Freedom Riders were an interracial group of civil rights activists who rode
     interstate buses in the segregated South to confront local segregationist laws and
     customs, calling attention to the non-enforcement of US Supreme Court rulings in
     1946 and 1960 that segregated public buses are unconstitutional.
5   The Freedom Riders encountered the worst violence in Mississippi and Alabama.
     On May 14, 1961, stopping outside Anniston, Alabama, white nationalists
     slashed tires, firebombed the Freedom Riders' bus, and brutalized civil rights
     activists; law enforcement was ineffectual, or colluded with the Klan. SNCC
     helped to organize and deploy ten more riders from Nashville to supplement the
     shock troops, helping them complete the ride. The new Freedom Riders were
     arrested just before reaching Birmingham. US Attorney General Robert Kennedy
     instructed integrationist buses to seek protections from the State Highway Patrol.
     Montgomery police were absent or indifferent; white and Black Freedom Riders
     were savagely beaten. Overruling southern governors, the federal government took
     control of the National Guard, who then proceeded to protect the twenty-seven
     riders traveling to Jackson, Mississippi; they were jailed. Freedom Riders achieved
     their goals in September of 1961 when President Kennedy's Interstate Commerce
     Commission banned segregated interstate travel. On May 29, 1961, Attorney
     General Robert F. Kennedy petitioned the Interstate Commerce Commission;
     Blacks no longer had to sit on the back of the bus or use segregated bathrooms and
     cafeterias in bus terminals.
6   Alexander, interview by Cline.
7   Alexander, interview by Cline.
8   Alexander, interview by Cline.
9   Alexander, interview by Cline.
10   Alexander, interview by Cline.
11   Alexander, interview by Cline.

12 Alexander, interview by Cline.

13 Alexander, interview by Cline.

14 Alexander, interview by Cline.

15 DA Edwin L. Miller and Asst. DA Terry J. Knoepp represented the plaintiffs. Defense attorneys were Louis S. Katz, Luther A. Goodwin, and DeAnne E. Fisher of Goodwin and Fisher. Grand jury justices were Gerald Brown, Coughlin, and Whelan. See *People v. Jordan* (Crim. No. 4471, Court of Appeals of California, Fourth Appellate District, Division One August 19, 1971, THE PEOPLE, Plaintiff and Appellant, v. SAMUEL JORDAN et al.).

16 "Red's Sister Jailed on Shooting," *Desert Sun* (43, no. 92, November 19, 1969, https://cdnc.ucr.edu/?a=d&d=DS19691119.2.22&srpos=2&e=-------en--20--1--txt-txIN-Fania+Davis-------).

17 *People v. Jordan*, 1967.

18 Paper Monuments, Trent Smith et al., "Desire Standoff". https://neworleanshistorical.org/items/show/1428

19 San Diego Police Historical Association (http://www.sdpolicemuseum.com/1970s-Riot.html).

20 San Diego Police Historical Association.

21 At a 1991 lecture at Harvard, Angela Davis joked that Fania Davis had such a heated exchange with a police officer or prison guard that she returned home and went into labor eight hours later. All three Davis women—mother, aunt, grandmother—raised the child.

22 Edith Evans Ashbury, "Lawyer for Joan Bird Says She Was 'Worked over' by Police" (*The New York Times*, April 22, 1971, https://www.nytimes.com/1971/04/22/archives/lawyer-for-joan-bird-says-she-was-worked-over-by-police.html).

23 Leslie Oelsner, "Joan Bird Freed in 1,000,000 Bail" (*The New York Times*, July 7, 1970).

24 "The Black Panther Party's Ten-Point Program," UC Press Blog, University of California Press, February 7, 2018, https://www.ucpress.edu/blog/25139/the-black-panther-partys-ten-point-program/.

25 Julian Bond Interview with Angela Davis, "Reflections on Brown," *Explorations in Black Leadership*, University of VA. May 27, 2014. https://blackleadership.virginia.edu/transcript/davis-angela.

Chapter 12

1 Michael Cooper, "When the Photographer Who Shot the Beatles Captured the Moment the Vietnam War Came Home" (*The Guardian*, August 26, 2018, https://www.theguardian.com/us-news/gallery/2018/aug/26/michael-cooper-chicago-68-photographs).

2 Genet's *The Blacks* is a play within a play that attacks racism. It employs thirteen Black actors who play roles of Black and white characters (they played whites in "white-face"). The play revolves around the trial and murder of a white woman within a kangaroo court. The "white" Queen and entourage provide commentary during the trial. *The Blacks* dominated Off-Broadway plays during the 1960s with 1,408 performances and Black theater royalty as its original cast, including James Earl

Jones, Roscoe Lee Browne, Louis Gossett, Cicely Tyson, Godfrey Cambridge, Maya Angelou, and Charles Gordone. Jean Genet, *The Blacks: A Clown Show*, translated by Bernard Frechtman (New York: Grove Press, 1994 [1960]).

3   In 1971, during the Panther 21 trial, Matthews traveled to meet her husband, Michael Tabor, who had gone underground in Algiers and was denounced by Huey P. Newton for the split between Oakland and the Cleavers.

4   Jacqueline Frost, "Jean Genet's May Day Speech, 1970: 'Your Real Life Depends on the Black Panther Party'" (*Social Text*, May 1, 2020).

5   David Hilliard was central in Genet's *Prisoner of Love*; according to his biographer, Edmund White, Genet was in love with Hilliard. See Jean Genet, *Un Captif Amoureux (Prisoner of Love)* (Paris: Gallimard, 1986; in English translation, New York: Picador, 2003); Edmund White, *Genet: A Biography* (New York: Vintage, 1993).

6   Angela Davis's university tour favored elite universities where white students and faculty with resources could contribute more funds for Panther defense.

7   Angela Davis, "Tactfulness of the Heart," Excerpt (unpublished Angela Davis speech, Odeon seminar, Paris, France, organized by Albert Dichy for IMEC, May 25–7, 1991).

8   Angela Davis, speech at the Odeon seminar in Paris, May 25, 26, 27, 1991, http://sisterezili.blogspot.com/2009/01/tactfulness-of-heart-angela-davis-on.html.

9   Davis, "Tactfulness of the Heart."

10   Davis, *Angela Davis*.

11   According to *The New York Times*, Yale President Kingman Brewster Jr. "praised the Panthers and the police in the same breath… in a list that included the cheifs [*sic*] of the New Haven and campus police… [and] Douglas Miranda, captain of the New Haven Panthers." Miranda told protesters and students to go to classes; crowds "responded with cries of 'Right On!' as he condemned 'suicidal' violence in the face of overwhelming police and National Guard force." About 1 a.m., Panthers asked "volunteers" to assemble at their headquarters, broadcasting their message on a local radio station: ""If chairman Bobby gets the chair… then the lights will go out."" See John Darnton, "New Haven Panthers Preached Calm," *The New York Times*, May 4, 1970.

12   Davis, "Tactfulness of the Heart."

13   See Darnton, "New Haven Panthers Preached Calm," quoted in Frost, "Jean Genet's May Day Speech, 1970."

14   Frost writes that Genet's "jacket, shirt, and pair of trousers [were] gifted to him, according to Angela Davis, by a Black shop-owner in Los Angeles who was so moved by Genet's helping the Panthers that he offered him the outfit on the house." Frost, "Jean Genet's May Day Speech, 1970."

15   Quoted from Genet's pamphlet. Reportedly, Genet had links to the Black Panthers in Boston and the International Section established by the Cleavers in Algiers. See Frost, "Jean Genet's May Day Speech, 1970."

16   Hugh Ryan, The Queer History of the Women's House of Detention," *The Activist History Review*, May 31, 2019. https://activisthistory.com/2019/05/31/the-queer-history-of-the-womens-house-of-detention/

17   "Huey P. Newton on Gay, Women's Liberation" (*Workers World*, May 16, 2012, https://www.workers.org/2012/us/huey_p_newton_0524/).

Chapter 13

1   See Seymour M. Hersh, "C.I.A. Reportedly Recruited Blacks for Surveillance of Panther Party" (*The New York Times*, March 17, 1978).
2   The Editors of *Encyclopedia Britannica*, "Student Nonviolent Coordinating Committee, SNCC, Student National Coordinating Committee" (*Britannica*, December 17, 2004, https://www.britannica.com/topic/Student-Nonviolent-Coordinating-Committee).
3   The Editors of *Encyclopedia Britannica*, "Student Nonviolent Coordinating Committee."
4   The Editors of *Encyclopedia Britannica*, "Student Nonviolent Coordinating Committee."
5   Pratt, "Lowndes County."
6   K. Kim Holder received his PhD in 1990 from UMass Amherst, with the dissertation "The History of the Black Panther Party, 1966–1971: A curriculum tool for Afrikan-American studies. The only BPP dissertation to precede Holder's was by Huey P. Newton, who received his doctorate from UC Santa Cruz with a dissertation on COINTELPRO titled "War Against the Panthers: A Study of Repression in America." Huey P. Newton, "War against the Panthers: A Study of Repression in America," PhD diss. (UC Santa Cruz, 1980, https://archive.org/details/WarAgainstThePanthersAStudyOfRepressionInAmerica/mode/2up).
7   See Louis J. Massiah, Thomas Ott, and Terry Kay Rockefeller, *Eyes on the Prize: A Nation of Law? (1968-1971)* (*PBS*, May 9, 2021, https://www.pbs.org/video/eyes-on-the-prize-a-nation-of-law-promo/).
8   "Conference for a United Front against Fascism" (*Bay Area Television Archive*, September 19, 1968, https://diva.sfsu.edu/collections/sfbatv/bundles/207569).
9   In July 1969, the NYPD sent officers to Oakland, California, to monitor the Black Panther Party's nationwide conference calling for community control of police departments. A NYPD memorandum observed that community control "may not be in the interests of the department." For the BPP, the residents in each precinct would elect a Police Councilman who, together with the other fourteen councilmen, would elect a commissioner of police for the division. That commissioner "would define policies within its department." See Boyle, "The Criminalization of the Black Panther Party."
10 Robyn C. Spencer, "The Black Panther Party and Anti-fascism in the United States" (*Duke University Press Blog*, January 26, 2017, https://dukeupress.wordpress.com/2017/01/26/the-black-panther-party-and-black-anti-fascism-in-the-united-states/).
11 Spencer, "The Black Panther Party and Anti-fascism in the United States."
12 During Davis's arrest in October 1970 in New York City, FBI agents did not pull out their weapons. They politely asked if she were "Angela Davis" and requested that she lift her upper lip to view the gap between her teeth. When she confirmed that she was Davis, they arrested her with her companion David Poindexter.
13 "Black Panthers' United Front against Fascism Conference" (*Verso* Blog post, June 3, 2020, https://www.versobooks.com/blogs/4735-black-panthers-united-front-against-fascism-conference).
14 Bill V. Mullen and Christopher Vials, eds. *The US Anti-fascism Reader* (Brooklyn: Verso, 2020).

15   Fred Hampton originally called white rebels the "mother country radicals" and the
     title stuck. See: https://www.buzzfeednews.com/article/alessadominguez/mother-
     country-radicals-zayd-dohrn
16   Mullen and Vials, *The US Anti-fascism Reader.*
17   "Black Panthers' United Front against Fascism conference."
18   "Black Panthers' United Front against Fascism conference."
19   "Black Panthers' United Front against Fascism conference."
20   "Black Panthers' United Front against Fascism conference."
21   Prestigious historical sites and archives such as the Smithsonian originally asserted
     that Jonathan Jackson "stole" Davis's shared weapons held in a communal house for
     Black radicals, but later updated their narrative to indicate that Jackson took the
     weapons. Jonathan had served as Davis's bodyguard at the bequest of his brother
     George Jackson, who headed the SBDC, for which Davis served as its public-facing
     leader.

Conclusion

1   Angela Davis with Julieanna Richardson, "Keynote by Angela Davis '65 with
     Julieanna Richardson '76, H'16" (Transcript, Brandeis University, February 8, 2019,
     https://www.brandeis.edu/now/2019/february/video-transcripts/angela-davis.html).
2   Davis with Richardson, "Keynote by Angela Davis '65 with Julieanna Richardson '76,
     H'16."
3   Davis with Richardson, "Keynote by Angela Davis '65 with Julieanna Richardson '76,
     H'16."
4   Reagan illegally engaged in the Iran-Contra affair with his military operative, Oliver
     North, who would serve prison time. Both North and Reagan assistant secretary
     of state for Latin America Elliot Abrams solicited and delivered funds to counter-
     revolutionary Contras, lied to Congress and engaged in international money
     laundering to fund terrorists. Abrams also noted to the press that the Contras
     had a tendency of kidnapping young girls. North and Abrams violated the Boland
     Amendment (1982, 1984) that prohibited the US government from assisting Contras
     in Nicaragua; the Contras functioned as anti-socialist death squads throughout
     Central America. See David Johnston, "Elliott Abrams Admits His Guilt on 2 Counts
     in Contra Cover-Up," *NYT*, October 8, 1991. https://www.nytimes.com/1991/10/08/
     us/elliott-abrams-admits-his-guilt-on-2-counts-in-contra-cover-up.html
5   According to the Children's Defense Fund report "The State of America's Children
     2021: Child Hunger and Nutrition," before the Covid-19 pandemic, one in seven
     children were food insecure or malnourished. https://www.childrensdefense.org/
     state-of-americas-children-2021/soac-2021-child-hunger/
6   See Christopher Brito, "Kamala Harris' 2020 campaign now selling 'That Little Girl
     Was Me' T-shirts after viral exchange with Joe Biden," *CBS NEWS*, June 28, 2019.
7   In 2016, Hillary Clinton won the popular vote by over 2 million votes but lost the
     electoral college vote. US presidents are not chosen by the popular vote. The electoral
     college determines the executive branch. (Historically shaped by the Three-Fifths
     Clause, the electoral college favored southern slave-owners' bids for the White
     House.)
8   See Bruce Japsen, "Clinton Says Sanders' 'Medicare For All' Would Thwart
     Obamacare" (*Forbes*, February 11, 2016, https://www.forbes.com/sites/

brucejapsen/2016/02/11/in-debate-clinton-stands-ground-against-sanders-single-payer-health-plan/?sh=501907755947).

9   See Joy James, *New Bones Abolition: Captive Maternal Agency and the (After)Life of Erica Garner*, Brooklyn: Common Notions Press, 2023.

10   While serving as the California State prosecutor, Harris's office opposed paying incarcerated firefighters more than $2 a day to battle wild fires (the Thirteenth Amendment legalizes slavery if one is duly convicted of a crime). Harris stepped in to address the issue, but prison slavery is still legal in California. "Slavery abolition" remains lesser known than prison abolition. Years earlier, as San Francisco District Attorney, Harris sought to lower the truancy rates by threatening parents with fines and prosecution if their children did not regularly attend school.

11   Davis with Richardson, "Keynote by Angela Davis '65 with Julieanna Richardson '76, H'16."

12   In 2022, 4.6 million Americans – 2% of the voting population – were ineligible to vote due to a felony conviction. See Christopher Uggen et al., "Locked Out 2022: Estimates of People Denied Voting Rights," *The Sentencing Project*, October 25, 2022. https://www.sentencingproject.org/reports/locked-out-2022-estimates-of-people-denied-voting-rights/

13   Section 5 of the 1965 Voting Rights Act required that states with low Black voter turnout and a history of voter discrimination have their voting laws preapproved by federal oversight or "preclearance" by the Justice Department or a federal court. Section 4b offered a formula to deter discrimination and racial disparities in voting. In the past, Alabama, Alaska, Arizona, Georgia, Louisiana, Mississippi, South Carolina, Texas, and Virginia as well as counties and townships in California, Florida, Michigan, New York, North Carolina, and South Dakota were required to have preclearance to safeguard against voter discrimination based on racial bias. The Supreme Court ruling determined that Section 5 was constitutional, but the US Congress never redesigned "preclearance" to reactivate Section 5 with different requirements. The lack of federal oversight since the 2013 ruling led to evisceration of voting rights: limitations on assistance at polling sites and early voting; closing polling sites; purging voters from state rolls; redrawing districts to dilute votes of Blacks/Latinx, Asians Americans, Native Americans; limiting multilingual ballots; enhancing photo ID restrictions; challenging citizenship status of naturalized citizens; mandating photo IDs with residential addresses for tribal reservations without formal streets. Voter suppression logically would include armed white militia patrolling poll sites used by African/Latinx/Indigenous/Asian American voters.
     See Brian Duignan, "Voter Suppression" (Britannica, September 21, 2020, https:// www.britannica.com/topic/voter-suppression); Elizabeth M. Yang, "Restoring the Voting Rights Act in the Twenty-First Century" (American Bar Association, March 3, 2021, https://www.americanbar.org/groups/crsj/publications/human_ rights_ magazine_home/the-next-four-years/restoring-the-voting-rights-act-in-the-21stcentury/).

14   Twenty-nine states have enacted ninety-four laws to restrict access to voting. See Jasleen Singh and Sara Carter, "States Have Added Nearly 100 Restrictive Laws Since SCOTUS Gutted the Voting Rights Act 10 Years Ago," BRENNAN CENTER FOR JUSTICE, June 23, 2023.

15   Alia Slisco, "Proud Boys Intended to Kill Mike Pence and Nancy Pelosi, FBI Witness Says" (*Newsweek*, January 15, 2021, https://www.newsweek.com/proud-boys-intended-kill-mike-pence-nancy-pelosi-fbi-witness-says-1562062.); Jennifer

Bendery, "Pro-Trump Mob Was 40 Feet from Mike Pence in Capitol Attack, Says Jan. 6 Panel" (*HuffPost*, June 16, 2022, https://www.huffpost.com/entry/mike-pence-capitol-attack-40-feet-jan6_n_62ab86b3e4b0c77098aba8ec).

16 David Chrisinger, "The Surge That No One Is Talking About: The US War in Somalia" (*The War Horse*, June 25, 2020).

17 See Joe Davidson, "Obama's 'Misleading' Comment on Whistleblower Protections" (*Washington Post*, August 12, 2013, https://www.washingtonpost.com/politics/federal_government/obamas-misleading-comment-on-whistleblower-protections/2013/08/12/eb567e3c-037f-11e3-9259-e2aafe5a5f84_story.html); Rashed Mian, "Obama's Legacy: A Historic War against Whistleblowers" (*Long Island Press*, January 14, 2017, https://www.longislandpress.com/2017/01/14/obamas-legacy-historic-war-on-whistleblowers/).

18 Michael Moore's *Fahrenheit 11/9* shows the sense of betrayal in a working class, largely Black community; the stunt of Obama drinking tap water that had poisoned children, adults, and elders and suppressed the vote turnout for Hillary Clinton, according to the documentary. *Fahrenheit 11/9*, directed by Michael Moore (Dog Eat Dog Films, 2018). Clip on YouTube (https://www.youtube.com/watch?v=cvlcI2TmfdI).

19 Forbes Guest Contributor, "Obama's Billionaires" (*Forbes*, July 18, 2012, https://www.forbes.com/forbes/2012/0806/leaderboard-support-obama-billioniares-follow-the-money.html?sh=3a3551ac6966).

20 Davis with Richardson, "Keynote by Angela Davis '65 with Julieanna Richardson '76, H'16."

Bibliography

Afro Marxist. "Black Journal Interview with Angela Davis (1972)." YouTube, 28:16, July 13, 2019. https://www.youtube.com/watch?v=SwD3LGo3a7o.

"AFSC Southern Student Program." *American Friends Service Committee*, February 8, 2012. https://www.afsc.org/story/afsc-southern-student-program.

Alexander, Roberta. Oral history interview by David P. Cline. Library of Congress, 2016. https://www.loc.gov/item/2016655433/.

Anatomy of Violence. Directed by Deepa Mehta. Hamilton Mehta Productions, 2016.

"Angela Davis: Now That Obama Has a Second Term, No More 'Subordination to Presidential Agendas.'" *Democracy Now!*, 2013. https://www.democracynow.org/2013/1/21/angela_davis_now_that_obama_has.

"Angela Davis on Why She's a Communist (1972)." Liberation School, October 5, 2018. https://www.liberationschool.org/angela-davis-on-why-shes-a-communist/.

Arendt, Hannah. "A Reply to Critics." *Dissent* 6, no. 2 (spring 1959), 179–81.

Arendt, Hannah. "Reflections on Little Rock." *Dissent* 6, no. 1 (winter 1959), 45–56.

Ashbury, Edith Evans. "Lawyer for Joan Bird Says She Was 'Worked Over' by Police." *The New York Times*, April 22, 1971. https://www.nytimes.com/1971/04/22/archives/lawyer-for-joan-bird-says-she-was-worked-over-by-police.html.

AUTODIDACT 17. "A Brief History of Black August." *New York Amsterdam News*, August 14, 2014. https://amsterdamnews.com/news/2014/08/14/brief-history-black-august/.

Backhouse, Fid. "1953 coup in Iran." *Britannica*, May 10, 2022. https://www.britannica.com/event/1953-coup-in-Iran.

Baker, Ella. "Bigger than a Hamburger." History Is a Weapon, June 1960. http://www.historyisaweapon.com/defcon1/bakerbigger.html.

Belew, Kathleen, interview by Terry Gross. *Fresh Air*. NPR, 2018.

Belew, Kathy. *Bring the War Home: The White Power Movement and Paramilitary America*. Cambridge, MA: Harvard University Press, 2018.

Bendery, Jennifer. "Pro-Trump Mob Was 40 Feet from Mike Pence in Capitol Attack, Says Jan. 6 Panel." *HuffPost*, June 16, 2022. https://www.huffpost.com/entry/mike-pence-capitol-attack-40-feet-jan6_n_62ab86b3e4b0c77098aba8ec.

Berger, Dan. *Captive Nation: Black Prison Organizing in the Civil Rights Era*. Chapel Hill: The University of North Carolina Press, 2014.

"Black Panthers' United Front against Fascism Conference." *Verso* Blog post, June 3, 2020. https://www.versobooks.com/blogs/4735-black-panthers-united-front-against-fascism-conference.

Bloom, Joshua and Waldo E. Martin Jr. *Black against Empire*. Berkeley: University of California Press, 2013.

Boston College. *The Heights* XLVII, no. 15, February 17, 1967.

Boyd, Herb. *Baldwin's Harlem: A Biography of James Baldwin*. New York: Atria Books, 2008.

Boyle, Robert. "The Criminalization of the Black Panther Party and Rewriting of History." New York City Jericho Movement. http://www.jerichony.org/bobboyle.html.

Brock, Lisa. "Back to the Future: African-Americans and Cuba in the Time(s) of Race." *Contributions in Black Studies* 12 (1994), Art. 3.

Brody, Richard. "'The Rape of Recy Taylor': An Essential, Flawed Documentary at the New York Film Festival." *The New Yorker*, October 3, 2017. https://www.newyorker.com/culture/richard-brody/the-rape-of-recy-taylor-an-essential-flawed-documentary-at-the-new-york-film-festival.

Brooks Higginbotham, Evelyn. *Righteous Discontent: The Women's Movement in the Black Baptist Church 1880–1920*. Cambridge, MA: Harvard University Press, 1994.

"Brown v. Board of Education." National Archives. https://www.archives.gov/education/lessons/brown-v-board#background.

Carmichael, Stokely and Charles Hamilton. *Black Power: The Politics of Liberation in America*. New York: Vintage, 1967.

Center for the Study of Intelligence, Intelligence Community and Policymaker Integration: A Studies in Intelligence Anthology, January 31, 2014, https://www.cia.gov/resources/csi/books-monographs/intelligence-community-and-policymaker-integration/

Channel 4 News. "Angela Davis on Feminism, Communism and Being a Black Panther during the Civil Rights Movement." YouTube, 31:46, May 25, 2018. https://www.youtube.com/watch?v=x3q_qV5mHg0&app=desktop.

Chrisinger, David. "The Surge That No One Is Talking About: The US War in Somalia." *The War Horse*, June 25, 2020.

CIA, April 6, 1982. https://www.cia.gov/readingroom/docs/REDCAP_0033.pdf.

"Claim CIA Responsible for My Lai Massacre." CIA Website, Library. Last modified March 8, 2011. https://www.cia.gov/library/readingroom/docs/CIA-RDP90-01208R000100190053-5.pdf.

Cobb, Charlie. "From Stokely Carmichael to Kwame Ture." *Africa News Service*, October 21, 2000. http://www.hartford-hwp.com/archives/45a/473.html.

Coleman, Angie. "How Does Change Happen: Angela Davis on Movements, Erasure, and the Dangers of Heroic Individualism." *Angie Coleman Blog*. Entry posted January 30, 2017. http://www.angiecoleman.me/music-tech/.

Committee on Internal Security, "Investigation of Students for a Democratic Society, Part 5 (University of Chicago; Communist Party Efforts with Regard to SDS)." FBI informer Hearings before the Committee on Internal Security House of Representatives Ninety-First Congress, First Session, August 6–7, 1969.

Common. "Angela Davis." *Time Magazine*, September 22, 2020. https://time.com/collection/100-most-influential-people-2020/5888290/angela-davis.

"Conference for a United Front against Fascism." *Bay Area Television Archive*, September 19, 1968. https://diva.sfsu.edu/collections/sfbatv/bundles/207569.

Constantine, Alex. "Mockingbird: The Subversion of the Free Press by the CIA." 2000. https://archive.org/stream/pdfy-QnKYkrSXDS_UTpW6/Mockingbird+%5BThe+Subversion+Of+The+Free+Press+By+The+CIA%5D_djvu.txt.

Cooper, David, ed. *The Dialectics of Liberation (Radical Thinkers)*. London: Verso, 2015.

Cooper, Michael. "When the Photographer Who Shot the Beatles Captured the Moment the Vietnam War Came Home." *The Guardian*, August 26, 2018. https://www.theguardian.com/us-news/gallery/2018/aug/26/michael-cooper-chicago-68-photographs.

CORA WEISS ORAL HISTORY PROJECT. The Reminiscences of Cora Weiss. Columbia Center for Oral History Research, Columbia University, 2014.

Daren, Salter. "National Negro Congress (1935–1940s)." *The Black Past: Remembered and Reclaimed*. http://www.Blackpast.org/aah/national-negro-congress.

Darnton, John. "New Haven Panthers Preached Calm." *The New York Times*, May 4, 1970.

Davidson, Joe. "Obama's 'Misleading' Comment on Whistleblower Protections." *Washington Post*, August 12, 2013. https://www.washingtonpost.com/politics/federal_government/obamas-misleading-comment-on-whistleblower-protections/2013/08/12/eb567e3c-037f-11e3-9259-e2aafe5a5f84_story.html.

Davis, Angela. *Angela Davis: An Autobiography*. New York: Random House, 1974.

Davis, Angela. *Angela Davis: An Autobiography*. 3rd ed, Chicago: Haymarket Books, 2021.

Davis, Angela. "Angela Davis and Assata Shakur's Lawyer Denounce FBI's Adding of Exiled Activist to Terrorists List." Interview by Amy Goodman. *Democracy Now!* 2013.

Davis, Angela. "Angela Davis on Protest, 1968, and Her Old Teacher, Herbert Marcuse." *Literary Hub*, April 3, 2019. https://lithub.com/angela-davis-on-protest-1968-and-her-old-teacher-herbert-marcuse/.

Davis, Angela. *Are Prisons Obsolete?* New York: Random House, 2003.

Davis, Angela. "Barry Callaghan Interviews Angela Davis in California Prison, 1970." Interview by Barry Callaghan. YouTube, August 27, 2010, 4:49. https://www.youtube.com/watch?v=8sLIDscuc-M.

Davis, Angela, *If They Come in the Morning … Voices of Resistance.* New York: Verso, November 2016.

Davis, Angela. "How Does Change Happen?" Speech, UC Davis, Freeborn Hall, Davis, CA, October 20, 2006.

Davis, Angela. Interview by Julian Bond. *Explorations in Black Leadership* (the Institute for Public History at the University of Virginia; Codirectors Phyllis Leffler and Julian Bond). Charlottesville, April 15, 2009. https://blackleadership.virginia.edu/transcript/davis-angela. Video available through C-SPAN at https://www.c-span.org/video/?328898-1/angela-davis-oral-history-interview.

Davis, Angela. Interview by Terry Rockefeller and Louis Massiah. *Eyes on the Prize II: America at the Racial Crossroads 1965 to 1985*. Produced by Blackside, Inc.; executive producer, Henry Hampton; series writer, Steve Fayer. Washington University Libraries Film and Media Archive, Henry Hampton Collection. May 24, 1989; edited for clarity.

Davis, Angela. Interview by Tony Brown. *Black Journal*, 67 Interview with Angela Davis, June 17 1972.

Davis, Angela. Liner notes in *Nina Revisited: A Tribute to Nina Simone*. RCA Records, 2015, compact disc. Digital file.

Davis, Angela. "Philosophical Themes in Black Literature." October 6, 1969, Folder 413. Angela Davis, Ad Hoc Committee Papers, 1–2. Quoted in Casey Shoop, "Angela Davis, the LA Rebellion, and the Undercommons." *post45org*, February 5, 2019.

Davis, Angela. Public Address, February 5, 1970, Santa Barbara. Quoted in Casey Shoop, "Angela Davis, the LA Rebellion, and the Undercommons." *post45org*, February 5, 2019.

Davis, Angela, October 24, 1969, UC Berkeley. Quoted in Casey Shoop, "Angela Davis, the LA Rebellion, and the Undercommons." *post45org*, February 5, 2019.

Davis, Angela. "Remembering Carole, Cynthia, Addie Mae and Denise." *Essence* 24, no. 5, February 1993, 92.

Davis, Angela. "Statement of Angela Davis to Jim Jones over Radio Phone-Patch." News release. September 10, 1977. https://jonestown.sdsu.edu/?page_id=19027.

Davis, Angela. "Tactfulness of the Heart." Speech. Odeon seminar, Paris, France, May 1991.

Davis, Angela. *The Angela Y. Davis Reader*. Edited by Joy James. London: Blackwell Press, 1998.

Davis, Angela. "Unfinished Lecture on Liberation—II." In *The Angela Y. Davis Reader*. Edited by Joy James. London: Blackwell Press, 1998. 53–60.

Davis, Angela, and Bettina Aptheker. *If They Come in the Morning: Voices of Resistance*. Chicago: Third Press, 1971.

Davis, Angela, and Eduardo Mendieta. "Politics and Prisons." *Radical Philosophy Review*, vol. 6, no.2, 2003.

Davis, Angela and Gayatri Spivak. "Planetary Utopias—Hope, Desire, Imaginaries in a Post-Colonial World." Plenary session at the "Colonial Repercussions" event series at the Akademie der Künste, Berlin, Germany, June 23–4, 2018.

Davis, Angela, Introducing Mabel Williams and Kathleen Cleaver. "Self Respect, Self Defense & Self Determination." Collision Course Video & The Freedom Archives: March 14, 2004. Video.

Davis, Angela with Julieanna Richardson. "Keynote by Angela Davis '65 with Julieanna Richardson '76, H'16." Transcript. Brandeis University, February 8, 2019. https://www.brandeis.edu/now/2019/february/video-transcripts/angela-davis.html.

Davis, Fania. "Restorative Justice: A Justice That Heals." *Naropa Magazine*, April 2017. http://magazine.naropa.edu/2017-fall/features/restorative-justice.php.

Davis, Fania. "This Country Needs a Truth and Reconciliation Process on Violence against African Americans—Right Now." *Yes! Magazine*, July 8, 2016. http://www.yesmagazine.org/peace-justice/this-country-needs-a-truth-and-reconciliation-process-on-violence-against-african-americans.

Davis, Mike. *City of Quartz*. London: Verso, 1990.

"Red Sister Jailed for Shooting," *Desert Sun* 43, no. 92. November 19, 1969. https://cdnc.ucr.edu/?a=d&d=DS19691119.2.22&e=——-en–20–1–txt-txIN——-1.

Devinatz, Victor G. "Communist Party of the United States of America." *Britannica*, November 22, 2022. https://www.britannica.com/topic/Communist-Party-of-the-United-States-of-America.

"'Discriminate Deterrence' Report of the Commission on Integrated Long-Term Strategy." January 1988. https://findit.library.yale.edu/images_layout/view?parentoid=11781573&increment=0.

Du Bois, W. E. B. (William Edward Burghardt). *Black Reconstruction in America: 1860–1880*. New York: Free Press, 1998.

Du Bois, W. E. B. *The Souls of Black Folk*. Las Vegas: Millennium Publications, 2014 (1903).

Duignan, Brian. "Voter Suppression." *Britannica*, September 21, 2020. https://www.britannica.com/topic/voter-suppression.

Dundon, Rion. "These Algerian Women Were Forced to Remove Their Veils to Be Photographed in 1960." *Medium*, December 20, 2016. https://timeline.com/photos-women-french-algeria-98ee46628854

Dunst, Alexander. "Dialectics of Liberation." *Hidden Persuaders*. October 25, 2017. http://www.bbk.ac.uk/hiddenpersuaders/blog/dialectics-of-liberation/.

Ellison, Ralph. *Who Speaks for the Negro?* Edited by Robert Penn Warren. New York: Random House, 1965.

"Emmett Till Accuser Admits to Giving False Testimony at Murder Trial." *Chicago Tribune*. January 28, 2017. https://www.chicagotribune.com/nation-world/ct-emmett-till-accuser-false-testimony-20170128-story.html.

Espinoza, Miguel. *The Integration of the UCLA School of Law, 1966–1978: Architects of Affirmative Action*. Lanham: Lexington Books, 2017.

Fahrenheit 9/11. Directed by Michael Moore. Dog Eat Dog Films, 2004.

Federal Bureau of Investigation. *FBI Memoranda and Reports on Ku Klux Klan May 14 1961*. United States Federal Bureau of Investigation, Alabama Freedom Riders

Investigation Files, Collection Number 111, Archives Department. N.p., 1961. Birmingham Public Library: Digital Collections.

Fichte, Hubert. "Interview with Hubert Fichte." In Jean Genet's *The Declared Enemy*. Edited by Albert Dichy. Translated by Jeff Fort. Stanford: Stanford University Press, 2004.

Forbes Guest Contributor. "Obama's Billionaires." *Forbes*, July 18, 2012. https://www.forbes.com/forbes/2012/0806/leaderboard-support-obama-billioniares-follow-the-money.html?sh=3a3551ac6966.

"Four Dead in Ohio." *Ohio History Connection*, May 17, 2017. https://www.ohiohistory.org/four-dead-in-ohio/.

Fox, John F. "The Birth of the Federal Bureau of Investigation." FBI, July 2003. https://www.fbi.gov/history/history-publications-reports/the-birth-of-the-federal-bureau-of-investigation.

Franks, Lucinda. "The 4-Year Odyssey of Jane Alpert, From Revolutionary Bomber to Feminist." *New York Times*, January 14, 1975. https://www.nytimes.com/1975/01/14/archives/the-4year-odyssey-of-jane-alpert-from-revolutionary-bomber-to.html.

Frazier, E. Franklin. *Black Bourgeoisie*. New York: Free Press Paperbacks, 1997 (1957).

"Freedom of Information and Privacy Acts Subject: (COINTELPRO BLACK EXTREMIST)." FBI. https://vault.fbi.gov/cointel-pro/cointel-pro-black-extremists/cointelpro-black-extremists-part-01-of/view.

Frost, Jacqueline. "Jean Genet's May Day Speech, 1970: 'Your Real Life Depends on the Black Panther Party.'" *Social Text*, May 1, 2020.

Gannon, Francis X. *Biographical Dictionary of the Left*, Vol. 2. Boston: Western Islands, 1971.

Genet, Jean. *The Blacks: A Clown Show*. Translated by Bernard Frechtman. New York: Grove Press, 1994 (1960).

Genet, Jean. *Un Captif Amoureux (Prisoner of Love)*. Paris: Gallimard, 1986; in English translation, New York: Picador, 2003.

Going Underground on RT. "Angela Davis on Trump vs Biden: We Must Break out of the Corporate Capitalist Two-Party System!" YouTube, June 15, 2020. https://www.youtube.com/watch?v=NoumWoLmeHE.

Gordon, Max, Reply to Harvey Kehr, "The Communist Party: An Exchange." *The New York Review*, April 14, 1983. https://www.nybooks.com/articles/1983/04/14/the-communist-party-an-exchange/.

Gornick, Vivian. "What Endures of the Romance of American Communism." *Verso* Blog post, April 28, 2020. https://www.versobooks.com/blogs/4688-what-endures-of-the-romance-of-american-communism.

Grad, Shelby. "The Environmental Disaster that Changed California and Started the Movement against Offshore Drilling." *Los Angeles Times*, April 28, 2017. https://www.latimes.com/local/lanow/la-me-santa-barbara-spill-20170428-htmlstory.html.

Guerrilla: The Taking of Patty Hearst. Directed and produced by Robert Stone. PBS *American Experience*: Robert Stone Productions, 2004.

"Hagiography." *Merriam-Webster Dictionary*. https://www.merriam-webster.com/dictionary/hagiography.

Hahn, Daniel. "The Dialectics of Liberation: 15–30 July 1967." *Roundhouse*. https://50.roundhouse.org.uk/content-items/the-dialectics-of-liberation.

HardRainProductions. "Crosby, Stills, Nash, and Young 'Ohio.'" YouTube, November 18, 2007. https://www.youtube.com/watch?v=JCS-g3HwXdc.

Harris, Cheryl I. "Whiteness as Property." *Harvard Law Review* 106, no. 8 (1993): 1707–91.

Healey, Dorothy Ray. *California Red: A Life in the American Communist Party*. Chicago: University of Illinois Press, 1993.

Henrikson, Minna and Araba Evelyn Johnston-Arthur. "Festival 1962." *Radio Helsinki*, December 2015.

Henriques, Martha. "Can the Legacy of Trauma Be Passed Down the Generations?" *BBC*, 2019. https://www.bbc.com/future/article/20190326-what-is-epigenetics.

Herman, Judith. *Trauma and Recovery*. New York: Basic Books, 1997.

Hersh, Seymour M. "C.I.A. Reportedly Recruited Blacks for Surveillance of Panther Party." *The New York Times*, March 17, 1978.

Hill, Lance. *The Deacons for Defense: Armed Resistance and the Civil Rights Movement*. Chapel Hill: University of North Carolina Press, 2004.

Homberger, Eric. "Susan Sontag Obituary." *The Guardian*, December 29, 2004. https://www.theguardian.com/news/2004/dec/29/guardianobituaries.booksobituaries.

"How to Watch the January 6th Hearings." PBS, June 8, 2022. https://www.pbs.org/newshour/politics/how-to-watch-the-jan-6-hearings.

Hrabowski III, Freeman A. Interview by Julian Bond. *Explorations in Black Leadership* (the Institute for Public History at the University of Virginia; Codirectors Phyllis Leffler and Julian Bond). Baltimore, September 19, 2008. https://blackleadership.virginia.edu/transcript/hrabowski-freeman. Video available at https://www.youtube.com/watch?v=sGBZpjoW55A&list=PLg8a9eHK4nDV9jlp0rl0QnKDa_KCNsvaE&index=19.

Hrabowski, Julia. Interview by Julian Bond.

"Huey P. Newton on Gay, Women's Liberation." *Workers' World/Mundo Obrero: Workers and Oppressed Peoples of the World Unite*. May 16, 2012. https://www.workers.org/2012/us/huey_p_newton_0524/.

I Am Not Your Negro. Directed by Raoul Peck. Screenplay by James Baldwin. Magnolia Pictures, 2016.

"Icon." *Merriam-Webster Dictionary*. https://www.merriam-webster.com/dictionary/icon.

"I'm Honoring Black Power." *Schomberg Center, New York Public Library*. Last modified 2017. http://pages.email.nypl.org/Blackpowerpledge2017/?utm_source=eNewsletter&utm_medium=email&utm_content=Schomburg_Engagement_20170221_BlackPowerPledge&utm_campaign=BlackPowerPledge.

Institute for Humanities Research at Arizona State University. "Who Killed Malcolm X?" YouTube, April 4, 2022. https://www.youtube.com/watch?v=duGLuly4jDQ.

Institute for Policy Studies. *The Souls of Poor Folk: Auditing America 50 Years after the Poor People's Campaign Challenged Racism, Poverty, the War Economy/Militarism, and Our National Morality*. April 2018.

Intelligence Officer's Bookshelf. *Soledad Brother: The Prison Letters of George Jackson*. New York: Coward-McCann, 1970.

"Interview: Kathleen Cleaver." *Frontline*, Spring 1997. https://www.pbs.org/wgbh/pages/frontline/shows/race/interviews/kcleaver.html.

James, Joy. "Airbrushing Revolution for the Sake of Abolition." *Black Perspectives (AAIHS)*. July 20, 2020.

James, Joy. *Imprisoned Intellectuals: America's Political Prisoners Write on Life, Liberation, and Rebellion*. Lanham: Rowman & Littlefield, 2003.

James, Joy. *In Pursuit of Revolutionary Love*. London: Divided, 2022.

James, Joy. "Introduction." In *The Angela Y. Davis Reader*. Oxford: Blackwell, 1998.

James, Joy. "Introduction: Democracy and Captivity." In *The New Abolitionists: (Neo)Slave Narratives and Contemporary Prison Writings*. New York: SUNY Press, 2005.

James, Joy. *New Bones Abolition: Captive Maternal Agency and the Afterlife of Erica Garner.* Philadelphia: Common Notions Press, 2023.

James, Joy. *Shadowboxing: Representations of Black Feminist Politics.* New York: Palgrave MacMillan, 1999.

James, Joy. "'Sorrow, Tears and Blood': Black Activism, Fractionation and the Talented Tenth." *Viewpoint Magazine*, 2018.

James, Joy. "The Architects of Abolition: George Jackson, Angela Davis and the Deradicalization of Prison." Talk, Brown University, May 6, 2019. https://www.youtube.com/watch?v=z9rvRsWKDx0

James, Joy. "The Womb of Western Theory: Trauma, Time Theft, and the Captive Maternal." *Carceral Notebooks*, 2016.

James, Joy. *Transcending the Talented Tenth.* New York: Routledge, 1996.

Japsen, Bruce. "Clinton Says Sanders' 'Medicare for All' Would Thwart Obamacare." *Forbes*, February 11, 2016. https://www.forbes.com/sites/brucejapsen/2016/02/11/in-debate-clinton-stands-ground-against-sanders-single-payer-health-plan/?sh=501907755947.

Johnson, Gaye Theresa and Alex Lubin. "Angela Davis: An Interview on the Futures of Black Radicalism." *Verso* Blog, October 11, 2017.

Jones, Janine. "Lively up the Dead Zone: Remembering Democracy's Racist State Crimes (Ashe)." *Abolition Journal*, December 16, 2016. https://abolitionjournal.org/lively-up-the-dead-zone/.

Jones, Josh. "How the CIA Funded & Supported Literary Magazines Worldwide While Waging Cultural War against Communism." *Open Culture*, October 27, 2017. https://www.openculture.com/2017/10/how-the-cia-funded-supported-literary-magazines-worldwide-while-waging-cultural-war-against-communism.html

Kant quoted in Angela Davis's dissertation prospectus. Author's papers.

Kaplan, Alice. *Dreaming in French: The Paris Years of Jacqueline Bouvier Kennedy, Susan Sontag and Angela Davis.* Chicago: University of Chicago Press, 2012.

Karbo, Karen. "How Gloria Steinem Became the 'World's Most Famous Feminist.'" *National Geographic*, May 3, 2021. https://www.nationalgeographic.com/culture/article/how-gloria-steinem-became-worlds-most-famous-feminist.

Kazin, Michael. "Dancing to the CIA's Tune." Review of *The Mighty Wurlitzer: How the CIA Played America*, by Hugh Wilford. *Washington Post Sunday Book Review*, January 27, 2008. http://www.washingtonpost.com/wp-dyn/content/article/2008/01/24/AR2008012402369.html.

Kelley, Robin D.G. *Hammer and Hoe: Alabama Communists during the Great Depression.* Chapel Hill: The University of North Carolina Press, 2015.

Kelley, Robin. "What a Band of 20th-Century Alabama Communists Can Teach Black Lives Matter and the Offspring of Occupy." Interview by Sarah Jaffe. *The Nation*, August 31, 2015. https://www.thenation.com/article/archive/what-a-band-of-20th-century-alabama-communists-can-teach-black-lives-matter-and-the-offspring-of-occupy/.

"Keynote by Angela Davis '65 with Julieanna Richardson '76, H'16." Brandeis University, February 8, 2019. https://www.brandeis.edu/now/2019/february/video-transcripts/angela-davis.html.

Kirkland, Frank. "The Questionable Legacy of *Brown v. Board of Education*: DuBois' Iconoclastic Critique." *Logos Journal*, 2015.

King, Martin Luther, Jr. "Eulogy for the Young Victims of the Sixteenth Street Baptist Church Bombing." September 18, 1963. Transcript of speech delivered at the Sixteenth

Street Baptist Church, Birmingham, Alabama. https://dailytrust.com/eulogy-for-the-young-victims-of-the-sixteenth-street-baptist-church-bombing/.

King, Martin Luther, Jr. *Where Do We Go from Here: Chaos or Community*. Boston: Beacon Press, 1967.

Klehr, Harvey and John Earl Haynes. "The Challenges of Espionage and Counterespionage Operations: Running SOLO: FBI's Case of Morris and Jack Childs, 1952–77." Center for the Study of Intelligence 66, no. 1 (March 2022). https://www.cia.gov/resources/csi/studies-in-intelligence/volume-66-no-1-march-2022/running-solo-fbis-case-of-morris-and-jack-childs-1952-77/.

Klehr, Harvey. *The Soviet World of American Communism*. New Haven: Yale University Press, 1998.

Kom'boa Ervin, Lorenzo. *Anarchism and the Black Revolution: The Definitive Edition*. London: Pluto Press, 2021.

Kornbluh, Peter. "The Death of Che Guevara Declassified." *The Nation*, October 10, 2017. https://www.thenation.com/article/archive/the-death-of-che-guevara-declassified/.

Krishnaswamy, Esha, host. "The Man, the Myth & Legend of Joseph Stalin with Grover Furr." *Historic.ly*, 17 April 2020. https://www.historicly.net/p/the-man-the-myth-and-legend-of-joseph#details.

Lenin, V.I. "Cultural-National Autonomy." *Critical Remarks on the National Question*, 1913. https://www.marxists.org/archive/lenin/works/1913/crnq/index.htm.

Lenin, V.I. *What Is to Be Done?* Translated by Tim Delaney. N.p., 1902. Marxists Internet Archive.

Lepre, George. *Fragging: Why U.S. Soldiers Assaulted Their Officers in Vietnam*. Modern Southeast Asia Series. Lubbock: Texas Tech University Press, 2011.

Lerner, Stephen D. "Political Organization at Harvard." *The Harvard Crimson*, February 18, 1967.

Lew-Lee, Lee, Kristin Bell, and Nico Panigutti. *All Power to the People! Black Studies in Video*. New York: Filmmakers Library, 2000.

"Little Rock School Desegregation." The Martin Luther King, Jr. Research and Education Institute, Stanford University. https://kinginstitute.stanford.edu/encyclopedia/little-rock-school-desegregation.

Louis Harris & Associates, *Lou Harris Poll*. New York:, 1969.

MacPhee, Josh. "95: Angela Davis, Part I." *Just Seeds* (blog). Entry posted January 30, 2012.

MacPhee, Josh. "96: Angela Davis, Part II." *Just Seeds* (blog). Entry posted February 6, 2012.

MacPhee, Josh. "97: Angela Davis, Part III." *Just Seeds* (blog). Entry posted February 13, 2012.

Mancini, Matthew J. *One Dies, Get Another: Convict Leasing in the American South, 1866–1928*. Columbia, SC: University of South Carolina Press, 1996.

Mafege, Archie. "Black Nationalists and White Liberals: Strange Bedfellows." *Africa Review*, 1993.

Marable, Manning. "A Life of Reinvention: Manning Marable Chronicles the Life of Malcolm X." Interview by Amy Goodman. *Democracy Now!* 2005.

"March 4, 1877." Zinn Education Project. https://www.zinnedproject.org/news/tdih/hayes-takes-office.

Marcuse, Herbert. "Acknowledgments." In *An Essay on Liberation*. Boston: Beacon Press, 1971.

Marcuse, Herbert. Draft notes for interview with NBC, January 31, 1971. Author's papers.

Marcuse, Herbert. "Marxism and Feminism." *Women's Studies* 2 (1974): 279–88. http://
platypus1917.org/wp-content/uploads/archive/rgroups/2006-chicago/marcuse_
marxismfeminism.pdf.

Marcuse, Herbert. *Marxism, Revolution and Utopia: Collected Papers of Herbert Marcuse*.
New York: Routledge, 2014.

Marcuse, Herbert. "Reflections on Calley." Published in *The New York Times*, May 13,
1971. Reprinted in *The New Left and the 1960s: Collected Papers of Herbert Marcuse,
Volume 3*. Edited by Douglas Kellner. New York: Routledge, 2005.

Marcuse, Herbert. *Soviet Marxism: A Critical Analysis*. New York: Columbia University
Press, 1958.

Marcuse, Herbert, Sam Keen, and John Raser. "Conversation with Marcuse in *Psychology
Today*." In *Philosophy, Psychoanalysis and Emancipation: Collected Papers of Herbert
Marcuse, Volume 5*. Edited by Herbert Marcuse, Douglas Kellner, and Clayton Pierce.
London: Routledge, 2017.

Marks, Ben. "The Iconizing of Angela Davis, From FBI Flyers to Radical Chic Art."
Flashback. Last modified January 14, 2018.

Marshall, Sue. "On Tour for Panthers and Conspiracy." *Los Angeles Free Press*, March 27,
1970.

Marshall, Sue. "The Radical Christian and the American." *Los Angeles Free Press*,
February 26, 1971.

Marx, Karl and Friedrich Engels. *The Communist Manifesto*. Edited by Gareth Stedman
Jones. London: Penguin Books, 2002.

Massiah, Louis J., Thomas Ott, and Terry Kay Rockefeller. *Eyes on the Prize: A Nation of
Law? (1968-1971)*. PBS, May 9, 2021. https://www.pbs.org/video/eyes-on-the-prize-a-
nation-of-law-promo/.

Maudlin, Beth. "Searching for the Revolution in America." *Critique*, July 25, 2008.

McDonough, Richard. "Eldridge Cleaver: From Violent Anti-Americanism to
Christian Conservativism." *The Postil Magazine*, February 1, 2021. https://www.
thepostil.com/eldridge-cleaver-from-violent-anti-americanism-to-christian-
conservativism/.

Mcg. Thomas Jr., Robert. "Jane Alpert Gives up after Four Years." *New York Times*,
November 15, 1974. https://www.nytimes.com/1974/11/15/archives/jane-alpert-gives-
up-after-four-years-jane-alpert-surrenders-here.html.

McGuire, Danielle. *At the Dark End of the Street Black Women, Rape, and Resistance—a
New History of the Civil Rights Movement from Rosa Parks to the Rise of Black Power*.
Toronto: Random House, 2010.

Mealy, Rosemari. *Fidel and Malcolm X: Memories of a Meeting*. E-book: Black Classic
Press, 2022.

Melish, Howard. Interview.

Menand, Louis. "A Friend of the Devil: Inside a Famous Cold War Deception." *The New
Yorker*, March 16, 2015. https://www.newyorker.com/magazine/2015/03/23/a-friend-
of-the-devil.

Mian, Rashed. "Obama's Legacy: A Historic War against Whistleblowers." *Long Island
Press*, January 14, 2017. https://www.longislandpress.com/2017/01/14/obamas-legacy-
historic-war-on-whistleblowers/.

Mitchell, Charlene. Interview by Lisa Brock, at Mitchell's home on West 147th Street in
Harlem, NY. "No Easy Victories: African Liberation and American Activists over a
Half Century, 1950-2000." July 18, 2004. http://www.noeasyvictories.org/interviews/
int04_mitchell.php.

Mitchell family. "Charlene Mitchell, Leader of the Campaign to Free Angela Davis." *Portside: Material of Interest to People on the Left*, December 18, 2022. https://portside. org/2022-12-18/charlene-mitchell-leader-campaign-free-angela-davis.

Monuments, Paper, Trent Smith, and Langston Allston. "Desire Standoff." *New Orleans Historical*. https://neworleanshistorical.org/items/show/1428?tour=91&index=25.

Moore, Judith. "Marxist Professor Herbert Marcuse's Years at UCSD Were Marked by Crisis, Strife, and Controversy: Angel of the Apocalypse." *San Diego Reader*, September 11, 1986.

Moorehead, Caroline. *A Train in Winter: An Extraordinary Story of Women, Friendship, and Resistance in Occupied France*. New York: Random House, 2012.

Morrison, Toni. Review of *Who Is Angela Davis: The Biography of a Revolutionary*, by Regina Nadelson. *The New York Times*, October 29, 1972. https://www.nytimes.com/1972/10/29/ archives/who-is-angela-davis-the-biography-of-a-revolutionary-by-regina.html.

"Mrs. Herbert Marcuse." *New York Times* Obituary, August 2, 1973. https://www.nytimes. com/1973/08/02/archives/mrs-herbert-marcuse.html.

Mullen, Bill V. and Christopher Vials. *The US Anti-fascism Reader*. Brooklyn: Verso, 2020.

Murrell, Gary and Bettina Aptheker. *"The Most Dangerous Communist in the United States": A Biography of Herbert Aptheker*. Boston: University of Massachusetts Press, 2015.

Nadelson, Regina. *Who Is Angela Davis? The Biography of a Revolutionary*. New York: P. H. Wyden, 1972.

Naison, Mark. *Communists in Harlem during the Depression*. Chicago: University of Illinois Press, 1983.

National Women's Hall of Fame. "National Women's Hall of Fame Virtual Induction 2020." YouTube, December 10, 2020. https://www.youtube.com/watch?v=K4HK6VAYV9w.

Negroes with Guns: Rob Williams and Black Power. Directed by Churchill Roberts and Sandra Dickson. PBS: Independent Lens, 2004.

Neumann, Franz, Herbert Marcuse, and Otto Kirchheimer. *Secret Reports on Nazi Germany: The Frankfurt School Contribution to the War Effort*. Edited by Raffaele Laudani. Princeton: Princeton University Press, 2013.

Newton, Huey P. "In Defense of Self-Defense." June 20, 1967. https://archive.lib.msu.edu/ DMC/AmRad/essaysministerdefense.pdf.

Newton, Huey P. "War against the Panthers: A Study of Repression in America." PhD diss. UC Santa Cruz, 1980. https://archive.org/details/ WarAgainstThePanthersAStudyOfRepressionInAmerica/mode/2up.

Nittle, Nadra Kareem. "What Is Colorism—Skin Tone Discrimination in America." *Humanities Issues*, March 18, 2017.

Nzongola-Ntalaja, Georges. "Patrice Lumumba: The Most Important Assassination of the 20th Century." *The Guardian*, January 17, 2011.

Oelsner, Leslie. "Joan Bird Freed in 1,000,000 Bail." *The New York Times*, July 7, 1970.

Olden, Marc. *Angela Davis: An Objective Assessment*. New York: Lancer Books, 1973.

Onion, Rebecca. "When Malcolm X Met Fidel Castro." Slate, August 30, 2016. https://slate. com/news-and-politics/2016/08/the-history-behind-colin-kaepernicks-malcolm-x-meets-fidel-castro-t-shirt.html.

"Organizing the Prisons in the 1960s and 1970s: Part One, Building Movements." *Process: A Blog for American History*. Entry posted September 20, 2016. http://www. processhistory.org/prisoners-rights-1/.

Paget, Karen M. *Patriotic Betrayal: The Inside Story of the CIA's Secret Campaign to Enroll American Students in the Crusade against Communism*. New Haven: Yale University Press, 2015.

Pauwels, Jacques R. "The Hitler-Stalin Pact of August 23, 1939: Myth and Reality." *Counterpunch*, August 26, 2019. https://docs.google.com/document/d/1Kq-ZHlHnLzl4OSEq-WRxQwbui-Dw3cS3/edit.

People v. Jordan, Crim. No. 4471. Court of Appeals of California, Fourth Appellate District, Division One. August 19, 1971.

People v. Samuel Jordan, 19 F. Supp. 3d Cir. August 19, 1971.

Petras, James. "The CIA and the Cultural Cold War Revisited." Review of *Who Paid the Piper: The CIA and the Cultural Cold War*, by Frances Stonor Saunders. *Monthly Review* 51, no. 6 (November 1, 1999).

Petras, James. "The Ford Foundation and the CIA: A Documented Case of Philanthropic Collaboration with the Secret Police." *Rebelión*, December 15, 2001.

Pratt, Minnie Bruce. "Lowndes County, Ala.: Roots of Revolution." *Workers' World/Mundo Obrero: Workers and Oppressed Peoples of the World Unite*. April 14, 2016. https://www.workers.org/2016/04/14/lowndes-county-ala-roots-of-revolution/.

Public Affairs. Exhibit in House Congressional Hearings, January 1970.

"Ramparts Exposes NSA; Claims Use of CIA Funds." *The Heights* XLVII, no. 15. February 17, 1967.

"Report of Chancellor Young's Ad Hoc Committee." Quoted as reprinted as addendum A in *AAUP*, 412, in Casey Shoop, "Angela Davis, the LA Rebellion, and the Undercommons." *post45org*, February 5, 2019.

"Rev. W. Howard Melish, 76, Dies; Ousted at Parish in McCarthy Era." *New York Times*, June 16, 1986.

Risen, Clay. "Charlene Mitchell, 92, Dies; First Black Woman to Run for President." *Portside: Material of Interest to People on the Left*, December 23, 2022. https://portside.org/2022-12-23/charlene-mitchell-92-dies-first-black-woman-run-president?utm_source=portside-general&utm_medium=email.

Robertson, Noah. "Democracy Destroyed: Stories of American Sponsored Coups—Iraq." *Arab America*, October 8, 2020. https://www.arabamerica.com/democracy-destroyed-stories-of-american-sponsored-coups-iraq/.

Rojas, Fabio. Review of *Top Down: The Ford Foundation, Black Power and the Reinvention of Racial Liberalism*, by Karen Ferguson. Reviews in History. Last modified March 2014.

Roney, Marty. "Alabama's Black Belt Helped Form Black Panther Party." *USA Today*, February 1, 2016. https://www.usatoday.com/story/news/nation-now/2016/02/01/lowndes-county-black-panther-party-alabama/78943998/.

Ross, Susan Mallon. "Dialogic Rhetoric: Dorothy Kenyon and Pauli Murray's Rhetorical Moves in White v. Crook." *International Journal of the Diversity* 6, no. 5 (2007), 89–100.

Rothstein, Richard. "*Brown v. Board* at 60." *Economic Policy Institute*, April 17, 2014.

Russell, Kent A. "My Lai Massacre: The Need for an International Investigation." *California Law Review* 58, no. 3 (May 3, 1970), 703–29.

Rzeszutek, Sara. *James and Esther Cooper Jackson: Love and Courage in the Black Freedom Movement*. Lexington: The University Press of Kentucky, 2015.

San Diego Police Historical Association. http://www.sdpolicemuseum.com/1970s-Riot.html.

Sasser, Charles W. "761st Tank Battalion: Patton's Panthers Would Not Quit." The History Reader: Dispatches in History from St. Martin's Press. Last modified July 12, 2011.

Saunders, Frances Stonor. *Who Paid the Piper?: The CIA and the Cultural Cold War.*
    London: Granta Books, 1999.
Seidman, Sarah J. "Angela Davis in Cuba as Symbol and Subject." *Radical History Review*
    36 (2020): 11–35.
SettleforBiden. "She's Settling for Biden. Why Can't You." Instagram, July 22, 2020. https://
    www.instagram.com/p/CC846x1gsGX/?igshid=15ek9n8uxt0pj.
Shoop, Casey. "Angela Davis, the LA Rebellion, and the Undercommons." *post45org,*
    February 5, 2019.
Slisco, Alia. "Proud Boys Intended to Kill Mike Pence and Nancy Pelosi, FBI Witness
    Says." *Newsweek,* January 15, 2021. https://www.newsweek.com/proud-boys-intended-
    kill-mike-pence-nancy-pelosi-fbi-witness-says-1562062.
Snow, Edgar. *Red China Today.* New York: Random House, 1970.
Snyder, Timothy. *On Tyranny: Twenty Lessons from the Twentieth Century.* New York:
    Duggan Books, 2017.
Solomon, Mark. *The Cry Was Unity: Communists and African Americans, 1917–1936.*
    Jackson: University of Mississippi Press, 1998.
Spencer, Robyn C. "The Black Panther Party and Anti-Fascism in the United States." *Duke
    University Press Blog,* January 26, 2017. https://dukeupress.wordpress.com/2017/01/26/
    the-black-panther-party-and-black-anti-fascism-in-the-united-states/.
Street In Harlem, NY. "The Communist Party and the Black Panther Party." Speech, NYU
    Symposium on the Occasion of the James & Esther Jackson Papers Given to Tamiment
    Library, New York, October 28, 2006.
Steinem, Gloria and Leonard Bebchick. *A Review of Negro Segregation in the United
    States.* Independent Research Service for Information on the Vienna Youth Festival,
    1959: 39.
"Support Bo Brown." Prison Activist Resource Center, November 10, 2018. https://www.
    prisonactivist.org/alerts/support-bo-brown.
Taylor, Jeremy. "The X File." Review of *Michael X: A Life in Black and White,* by John
    L. Williams
The Caribbean Review of Books. Last modified February 2009.
Temple, Emily. "7 Writers Who Were Also Editors (and the Books They Edited)." Literary
    Hub. Last modified September 14, 2017. https://lithub.com/7-writers-who-were-also-
    editors-and-the-books-they-edited/.
"The Black Panther Newspaper." Marxists Internet Archive. https://www.marxists.org/
    history/usa/pubs/black-panther/index.htm.
"The Black Panther Party's Ten-Point Program." UC Press Blog, University of California
    Press, February 7, 2018. https://www.ucpress.edu/blog/25139/the-black-panther-
    partys-ten-point-program/
The Black Power Mixtape 1967–1975: A Documentary in 9 Chapters. Directed by Göran
    Hugo Olsson; produced by Annika Rogell; coproduced by Joslyn Barnes, Danny
    Glover/Louverture Films, Axel Arnö/Sveriges Television. New York, NY [Orland Park,
    IL]: Sundance Selects; MPI Media Group [distributor], 2011.
"The CIA's 'Family Jewels.'" National Security Archives. https://nsarchive2.gwu.edu/
    NSAEBB/NSAEBB222/index.htm.
The editors of *Encyclopedia Britannica.* "Student Nonviolent Coordinating Committee,
    SNCC, Student National Coordinating Committee." *Britannica,* December 17, 2004.
    https://www.britannica.com/topic/Student-Nonviolent-Coordinating-Committee.

The editors of *Encyclopedia Britannica*. "Warsaw Pact," *Britannica*, updated December 23, 2022. https://www.britannica.com/event/Warsaw-Pact.

The Isley Brothers, "Ohio/Machine Gun" (Neil Young/Jimi Hendrix covers), *Live at the Bitter End 1972*—New York, NY. In Andrew O'Brien, "'4 Dead In Ohio: 10 Powerful Versions Of "Ohio" On the 52nd Anniversary of the Kent State Massacre. *Live for Live Music*, May 4, 2022. https://liveforlivemusic.com/features/kent-state-neil-young-ohio-50th-anniversary/.

"The Rise and Fall of the Symbionese Liberation Army." PBS *American Experience*: https://www.pbs.org/wgbh/americanexperience/features/guerrilla-rise-and-fall-symbionese-liberation-army/.

The Theory and Practice of Communism in 1971. March 29–30, 1971. U.S. House of Representatives, Committee on Internal Security, Washington, DC: Public Hearings.

"The Ways Boston Helped Shape the Life of Martin Luther King, Jr. (GRS'55, Hon.'59)." *Bostonia: Boston University's Alumni Magazine*.

Tinoco, Armando. "What Happened in Mexico Today: We Remember the 1968 Student Massacre." *Latin Times*, October 2, 2014. https://www.latintimes.com/what-happened-mexico-city-today-we-remember-1968-student-massacre-police-tlatelolco-square-265915#:~:text=The%20Tlatelolco%20massacre%20is%20one%20of%20the%20darkest,opening%20ceremony%20of%20the%201968%20Summer%20Olympic%20Games.

Toffler, Alvin. *Future Shock*. New York: Random House, 1970.

Tse-tung, Mao. "On the International United Front against Fascism." In *Works of Mao Tse-tung*. Foreign Languages Press Peking, 1967; First Edition 1965; Second Printing 1967, Vol. III: 29. http://www.marx2mao.com/Mao/UFAF41.html.

Tse-tung, Mao. "Statement Supporting the American Negroes in Their Just Struggle against Racial Discrimination by U.S. Imperialism." *Peking Review*, August 8, 1963.

Vedantam, Shankar. *The Hidden Brain*. New York: Random House, 2010.

Velázquez, Natasha Gómex. "Tema II: La Critica de Lenin al 'Mx. Legal.'" Teoría e Historia del Marxismo. Class lectura, Universidad de Habana, February 17, 2020.

Viglione, Jill, Lance Hannon, and Robert DeFina. "The Impact of Light Skin on Prison Time for Black Female Offenders." *The Social Science Journal* 48, no. 1 (2011): 250–8.

"Viola Liuzzo." National Park Service, last modified July 13, 2022. www.nps.gov/semo/learn/historyculture/viola-liuzzo.htm.

Warnke, Georgia. "Feminism, the Frankfurt School, and Nancy Fraser." *Los Angeles Review of Books*, August 4, 2013.

"When Wright Broke with the Communists." New Republic, April 19, 2021. https://newrepublic.com/article/162080/richard-wright-broke-communists-man-lived-underground.

White, Edmund. *Genet: A Biography*. New York: Vintage, 1993.

Whitfield, Stephen. "Refusing Marcuse: 50 Years after One-Dimensional Man." *Dissent* (Fall 2014).

Wilderson, Frank, Selamawit Terrefe, and Joy James. "An Ontology of Betrayal." Williams College, November 15, 2022. https://www.youtube.com/watch?v=8p3At6gl0zQ. Transcript January, 2023.

Wilford, Hugh. *The Mighty Wurlitzer*. Cambridge, MA: Harvard Press, 2009.

Wilford, Hugh. *The Mighty Wurlitzer: How the CIA Played America*. Cambridge, MA: Harvard University Press, 2008.

Williams, Johnetta. "The Southern Negro Youth Congress (1937–1949)." *The Black Past: Remembered and Reclaimed*. http://www.blackpast.org/aah/southern-negro-youth-congress-1937-1949.

Williams, Robert F. *Negroes with Guns*. Edited by Marc Schleifer. Eastford: Martino Fine Books, 2013.

Wills, Garry. *Reagan's America*. New York: Doubleday & Company, 1987.

"Work of the CIA with Youths at Festival Is Defended." *Washington Post*, February 16, 1968.

"World Conference to Review and Appraise the Achievements of the United Nations Decade for Women." United Nations, Nairobi, July 1985. https://www.un.org/en/conferences/women/nairobi1985.

Yang, Elizabeth M. "Restoring the Voting Rights Act in the Twenty-First Century." American Bar Association, March 3, 2021. https://www.americanbar.org/groups/crsj/publications/human_rights_magazine_home/the-next-four-years/restoring-the-voting-rights-act-in-the-21st-century/.

Yokum, Nicole. Written communique to author. December 2022.

Yokum, Nicole and Joy James. December 2022 conversation.

Index